LITERARY THEORY AND CRITICISM

The book explores key South Asian writings on cultural theory and literary criticism. It discusses the dynamics of textual contents, rhetorical styles, and socio-political issues through an exploration of seminal South Asian scholarship in the Humanities and Social Sciences. The volume examines concepts and methods of critical studies. It also discusses colonial and postcolonial discourses on art, religion, nationalism, identity, representation, resistance, and gender in the South Asian context. The essays are accompanied by textual questions and intertextual discussions on rhetorical, creative, and critical aspects of the selected texts. The exercise questions invite the reader to explore the mechanics of reading about and writing on discursive pieces in South Asian studies.

Comprehensive and interdisciplinary, this textbook will be indispensable for students and researchers of South Asian studies, cultural theory, literary criticism, postcolonial studies, literary and language studies, women and gender studies, rhetoric and composition, political sociology, and cultural studies.

Arun Gupto is Professor of English at the Institute of Advanced Communication, Education, and Research, Pokhara University, Nepal. He is a former faculty member at the Central Department of English, Tribhuwan University. His areas of research are literary theory, postcolonial studies, and South Asian Studies. A recent book of his is *Goddesses of Kathmandu Valley: Grace, Rage, Knowledge* (Routledge, 2016). He has also written and directed a series of documentaries on South Asian Art and Culture titled *Art of the Lake* (2014), *Four Gray Walls Four Gray Towers* (post-production), and *Anger and the Mahatma* (post-production).

LITERARY THEORY AND CRITICISM

Recent Writings from South Asia

Edited by
Arun Gupto

Routledge
Taylor & Francis Group

LONDON AND NEW YORK

First published 2022
by Routledge
2 Park Square, Milton Park, Abingdon, Oxon OX14 4RN

and by Routledge
605 Third Avenue, New York, NY 10158

Routledge is an imprint of the Taylor & Francis Group, an informa business

© 2022 selection and editorial matter, Arun Gupto; individual chapters, the contributors

The right of Arun Gupto to be identified as the author of the editorial material, and of the authors for their individual chapters, has been asserted in accordance with sections 77 and 78 of the Copyright, Designs and Patents Act 1988.

All rights reserved. No part of this book may be reprinted or reproduced or utilised in any form or by any electronic, mechanical, or other means, now known or hereafter invented, including photocopying and recording, or in any information storage or retrieval system, without permission in writing from the publishers.

Trademark notice: Product or corporate names may be trademarks or registered trademarks, and are used only for identification and explanation without intent to infringe.

British Library Cataloguing-in-Publication Data

A catalogue record for this book is available from the British Library

Library of Congress Cataloging-in-Publication Data
A catalog record has been requested for this book

ISBN: 978-0-367-34832-8 (hbk)
ISBN: 978-1-032-10147-7 (pbk)
ISBN: 978-1-003-21385-7 (ebk)

DOI: 10.4324/9781003213857

Typeset in Sabon
by Deanta Global Publishing Services, Chennai, India

**To my students
and
to my Nieva**

CONTENTS

List of contributors	ix
Foreword	xi
Preface	xiv
Acknowledgements	xviii

Introduction: Theory, criticism, and engaging with the texts   1

PART I
Theory   33

1   DissemiNation: Time, narrative, and the margins of the modern nation   35
HOMI BHABHA

2   Belatedness as possibility: Subaltern histories, once again   69
DIPESH CHAKRABARTY

3   The Blurring of Distinctions: The Artwork and the Religious Icon in
Contemporary India   85
TAPATI GUHA-THAKURTA

4   Women and freedom   115
FIRDOUS AZIM

5   Hyphenated post-colonial: A divergent perspective   131
TARIQ-AMIN KHAN

6   Grassroots texts: Ethnographic ruptures and transnational feminist
imaginaries   150
PIYA CHATTERJEE

VII

CONTENTS

PART II
Criticism 169

7 **Of Mimicry and man: The ambivalence of colonial discourse** 171
HOMI BHABHA

8 **Epilogue: The tantra of contemplative cultural critique** 182
LATA MANI

9 **Post-colonial hybridity:** *Midnight's children* 189
HARISH TRIVEDI

10 **Fragmenting nations and lives:** *Sunlight on a broken column* 203
VRINDA NABAR

11 **Punyakante Wijenaike: Spectral spaces** 223
MINOLI SALGADO

12 **Chokher Bali: The novel of the new age** 243
RADHA CHAKRABORTY

CONTRIBUTORS

Homi K. Bhabha is the Anne F. Rothenberg Professor of the Humanities at Harvard University, USA. He is one of the most important figures in contemporary postcolonial studies and has developed a number of the field's neologisms and key concepts, such as *hybridity, mimicry, difference*, and *ambivalence*. Such terms describe ways in which colonised people have resisted the power of the coloniser, according to Bhabha's theory. In 2012, he received the Padma Bhushan award in the field of literature and education from the Indian government. Some of his works include *Nation and Narration* and *The Location of Culture*, which was reprinted as Routledge Classics.

Dipesh Chakrabarty is the Lawrence A. Kimpton Distinguished Service Professor of History, South Asian Languages and Civilizations, at the University of Chicago, USA. He is the recipient of the 2014 Toynbee Prize that recognises social scientists for significant academic and public contributions to humanity. His key works include *Rethinking Working-Class History: Bengal 1890–1940* (1989), *Provincializing Europe: Postcolonial Thought and Historical Difference* (2000), *The Crises of Civilization: Exploring Global and Planetary Histories* (2018), among many others.

Tapati Guha Thakurta is Director and Professor of History at the Centre for Studies in Social Sciences, Calcutta, and was previously taught at Presidency College, Kolkata. She specialises in cultural history, history of art, and visual studies. Her most notable books include *The Making of a New "Indian" Art: Artists, Aesthetics and Nationalism in Bengal* (2007), *Monuments, Objects, Histories: Institutions of Art in Colonial and Postcolonial India* (2004), and *In the Name of the Goddess: The Durga Pujas of Contemporary Kolkata* (2015).

Firdous Azim is Professor of English at BRAC University in Dhaka, Bangladesh. She is co-editor of *Galpa: Short Stories by Bangladeshi Women* and has published widely on literary, cultural and women's issues, including *The Colonial Rise of the Novel* (1993). She is an active member of Naripokkho, a woman's activist group in Bangladesh.

Tariq Amin-Khan is Associate Professor, Department of Politics and Public Administration, Ryerson University, Toronto, Canada. He is a faculty member of the Yeates School of Graduate Studies, Ryerson University, and honorary member of the Osgoode Hall Graduate Studies in Law, York University, Toronto. His key publications include *The Post-Colonial State in the Era of Capitalist Globalization* (2012) and *Genealogy of the Post-Colonial State in India and Pakistan* (2012).

Piya Chatterjee is Dorothy Cruickshank Backstrand Chair at the Department of Women and Gender Studies and Professor of Feminist, Gender, and Sexuality Studies at Scripps College, Claremont, CA, USA. She is author of *A Time for Tea: Women Labor and Post/Colonial Politics on an Indian Plantation* (2001) and co-editor with Manali Desai and Parama Roy of *States of Trauma: Gender and Violence in South Asia* (2010) and with Sunaina Maira *The Imperial University: Academic Repression and Scholarly Dissent* (2014).

Lata Mani is a feminist historian, cultural critic, contemplative writer, and filmmaker. She has published books and articles on a broad range of issues, from feminism and colonialism, to illness, spiritual philosophy, and contemporary politics. Her key publications include *The Integral Nature of Things: Critical Reflections on the Present* (2013), *Interleaves: Ruminations on Illness and Spiritual Life* (2011), and *Sacred Secular: Contemplative Cultural Critique* (2009), among others.

Harish Trivedi is former Professor of English at the University of Delhi, India, and was Visiting Professor at the University of Chicago, USA and University of London, UK. He is the author of *Colonial Transactions: English Literature and India* (1993; 1995); has co-edited *Literature and Nation: Britain and India 1800–1990* (2000) and Kipling in India (2021); and an edited *Kim* by Rudyard Kipling (2011).

Vrinda Nabar is former Chair of English at the University of Bombay, India and was Visiting Professor at Northwestern University, USA, and the Open University, UK. She published extensively for Indian newspapers and presented programmes for radio and television. Her works include the academic bestseller *Caste as Woman*, *The Bhagavadgita* (Introduction and Translation), *The Endless Female Hungers: A Study of Kamala Das*, and *Snake-Skin and Other Poems of Indira Sant* (translated from the Marathi).

Minoli Salgado is Professor of English literature at the University of Sussex, USA. She has published widely on migrant studies and diasporic literature. She is the author of *Writing Sri Lanka: Literature, Resistance and the Politics of Place* (2007), and has also published poetry, short fiction, and short story criticism internationally.

Radha Chakravarty is Professor of Comparative Literature and Translation Studies, Ambedkar University, Delhi. She has co-edited *The Essential Tagore* (2011) and is the author of *Feminism and Contemporary Women Writers* (2008) and *Novelist Tagore: Gender and Modernity in Selected Texts* (2013). She has translated some of Tagore's important works, as well as the writings of several major Bengali writers from India and Bangladesh. She has also edited and co-edited a number of anthologies of South Asian literature.

FOREWORD

Thank you, Professor Arun Gupto, for inviting me to write this brief foreword to this important and generative volume. I am honoured and grateful. Not only have I enjoyed reading this edited work, but I have also learned a great deal in the process. That such a volume should emanate from Professor Gupto is no surprise at all: If anything, it is inevitable and appropriate. Professor Gupto has been contributing indefatigably, in multiple capacities as writer, critic, editor, theorist, teacher, and institutional intellectual, to the cause of South Asian Studies and its onto-politico-epistemic location in the global picture. Uniquely characteristic of Professor Gupto's sensibility has been his willingness as well as his supreme ability to perform both as a solo researcher as well as an enabler and promoter of collective work in the field. Genres such as edited collections and anthologies have always had a crucial pedagogical and curricular role to play in the judicious dissemination of new knowledges; but alas these genres have often been abused, misused, and travestied in the name of facile opportunism, superficial glitter and glamour, or formulaic expediency. It is not often that a deep and genuine scholar, a true and substantive insider and practitioner of the discourse, takes on the task of compiling and editing a volume that strikes the right balance and succeeds in representing a field of study inclusively, generously, and with strategic selectivity. Such an endeavour calls for a special kind of scholarly magnanimity and a *paramaarthik* rather than a *swaarthik* commitment to the task at hand: No one is better suited to this challenge than Professor Arun Gupto.

As his comprehensive and rigorous introductory essay amply demonstrates, Professor Gupto has a subtle, encyclopedic, historical, and theoretical mastery of the field known as South Asian Studies and its conjunctural and intersectional cohabitation with other adjacent domains such as Postcoloniality, Subaltern Studies, Area Studies, Critical Theory, Postmodernism, and Poststructuralism. I particularly admire the manner in which Professor Gupto attends to the geopolitical as well as historical specificity of the region known as South Asian Studies without in any way negating or preempting a relational understanding of this region within a continuum. The very title of this volume, *Literary Theory and Criticism Writings from South Asia*, reflects symptomatically the rich tension between what Walter Mignolo elegantly has termed, "places where we live" and "places where we think." The title dramatises South Asia literally as a geopolitical and geographical location in the world map, as well as the *locus* of a certain kind of writing; an epistemic location from which emanates a certain kind of thinking and theorising. Adequately bridging the distance and alienating the intimacy that is obtained between "identity politics" and "the politics of representation," the title opens up a *chronotope* that invites transactional readings, cross-hatchings, intersectional collisions and coincidences, and all manner of conjunctural criss-crossings. In this volume South Asia comes alive as both integral and heterogeneous and as a space that resists such easy anthropological characterisations as *emic* and *etic*. Insiders and outsiders aren't what this volume is all about; instead, it is more about the ongoing *pas de deux* between Truth and Method, between rootedness and indigeneity on the one hand and a built-in capacity for meaningful de- and re-territorialisation. The spirit of the volume does justice to that poetic imperative that Ranajit Guha so eloquently invokes in his reading of Rabindranath Tagore: The imperative that "the existential should tangle with the epistemological." It is particularly heart-warming that Nepal pulsates vibrantly in this project.

I will not say much about the selection of essays, mainly because Professor Gupto deals with each one of them insightfully in his introductory essay, except to acknowledge that the configuration of the pieces has been done with much care and sensitivity. The voices represented here constitute a genuinely representative and non-hegemonic bandwidth: The voices are interdisciplinary and each essay addresses South Asia as a theme from the point of view of its own discursive formation. There are established canonical voices as well as younger voices full of stellar promise. The division of the essays into Theory and Criticism makes an important point: That even though the two are not discrete, non-porous modes of operation, it still makes sense to differentiate between interventions that are, text-centric and dedicated to exegesis and close reading, and those that tend to make a pre-text of actual texts in the name of a larger theoretical horizon. As one goes down the Table of Contents, there is a tacit sense of continuity and seamlessness even as one is aware of the relative autonomy of each essay. There is a certain dialogic call and response relationship among the pieces. The conceptual ground covered cumulatively by all the essays is indeed staggering in depth as well as in scope. The range of bibliographical references and erudition honours multiple traditions: Ethnic, regional, national, sub and transnational, vernacular, cosmopolitan, mono-heter-and trans-lingual. What to me is most encouraging and satisfying is that there is no hegemonic aura or presence directing the trajectory of this volume. Professor Gupto's meticulously documented Introduction, subdivided into sections such as *Engaging with the Text*, *Political Commitment*, *Postcolonial Phantom*, *Methods Across Disciplines*, *Sociology*, *Political Science*, *Economics*, *Geography*, and *Literature*, functions superbly both as an overarching survey as well as a close up of the various sites that constitute the domain. Finally, there is the absolutely brilliant and thought-provoking section on *Chapter Selection* and *Exercise Questions*. This is a tour de force: The questions and prompts are creative, imaginative, and full of potential, inviting the student to plunge in, take a deep dive, and emerge with all manner of riches. This section, with its directions, enables the student to make sophisticated connections across the various texts in the volume and their underlying assumptions. What opens up to the student's gaze is an entire field with all its layers, fissures, connectivities, problems, and aporias. The exercises are minimally didactic, and the directives and the questions honour the proactive and meaning-making intelligence of the student and her intellectual autonomy.

FOREWORD

What more can I say, except to commit myself to buying this volume as soon as it appears and to make it the cornerstone of my syllabus in many of my forthcoming courses on Postcoloniality and South Asian Studies.

R. Radhakrishnan
Chancellor's Professor of Humanities
Distinguished Professor of English, Comparative Literature,
and African American Studies
University of California, Irvine, USA

PREFACE

I often wonder what experiences have informed my understanding of literary theory and criticism. In the mid-eighties, I was a curious graduate student in the Central Department of English[1] at Tribhuvan University in Kathmandu. We occasionally read South Asian writers in the classrooms; writings from Rabindranath Tagore, Mulk Raj Anand, R.K. Narayan, and A.K. Ramanujan appeared optionally in the syllabi but reading them gave me a sense of strange provincial closedness. I then became a confident, culturally grounded student. When I began my teaching career in the early nineties, V.S. Naipaul, Chinua Achebe, Wole Soyinka, Derek Walcott, Salman Rushdie, Michael Ondaatje, Maxim Hong Kingston, Jamaica Kincaid, Bharati Mukherjee, and many such writers of non-Western "writing back"[2] generations appeared in the curricula. I was already developing postcolonial critical sensibility. Postcolonial literary critics followed soon. The nineties saw a surge in reading literary theory and consequently, along with frontline literary theorists and critics, Franz Fanon, Edward Said, Gayatri Spivak, Homi Bhabha, R. Radhakrishnan, and the Subaltern collectives appeared everywhere in the university bookshops. In the early nineties, David Lodge's *Modern Criticism and Theory* was the first major textbook for English graduates in Nepal. I started my teaching career by using this book for Literary Theory courses. In those years, except in the South Asian metropolis, in the English departments of many Indian universities, modern theory and criticism was a new genre. In a matter of a decade, Literary Theory became an essential course in English studies. I studied and learned whatever was available on literary theory and criticism coming to the library from England and the United States.

In Nepal, literary theory and criticism was an emphatic area of interest from the early nineties, disliked by the generation of professors on the brink of retirement and encouraged by their immediate junior professors. The older generation was apprehensive about the new genre called Literary Theory because, they thought, interpretations and analyses, were complicated by structuralist, post-structuralist, and postmodernist methods. They did not want to acknowledge that such theories open up the possibilities of interpretations and analyses. Furthermore, using terms of reference from Literary Theory was taken as a fad. But there was no short cut to understanding theory. There was no easy access to quoting where Foucault talks about "discourse" or Derrida talks about "différance" unless you read the bulk of their work. For instance, it was always inadvisable to answer to the students where Nietzsche talks about "the death of god" or Spivak about "the subaltern." Such ideas are spread in their writings and to teach

PREFACE

literary theory and its application, the scholars needed (still need) constant engagement with their texts. When Literary Theory was a new course at the departments in Nepal, students were enthusiastic about theoretical vocabulary; they took wide interest to use theories in fiction and poetry classes. One day, a senior professor turned so furious when a students used a term "sliding signifier," that he smashed the writing chalk on the blackboard. When a colleague who was a well-known teacher of theory presented Roland Barthes's S/Z in a departmental seminar, another senior professor looked stupefied at the blackboard, and complained, "Are we in English department or Mathematics?" But my thanks go to the immediate junior professors[3] who resisted and continued with Barthes and Genettes, Millers and Blooms, Spivkas and Bhabhas.

The pedagogic content of English departments gradually changed in the United States in the sixties when Literary Theory appeared as a genre. The seventies and the eighties were the hey days of Literary Theory from Yale, Columbia to the leading universities of the United States.[4] The change in interpretative mechanism, due to the advent of literary theory, was expanded from textual interpretive and analytical tradition of literary texts as propounded by new criticism to addressing wide socio-cultural issues, almost everything under the sun and the moon, from race, gender, identity, ecology, to capitalism. We were late in its reception in Nepal because F.R. Leavis, I.A. Richards, and T.S. Eliot were the favourites of the senior professors and anything beyond those new critics were not at all welcomed. The Western educated professor would proudly claim that "he is a trained Leavisian" and cannot accept discourses beyond the "great tradition" of literature. From the early nineties, the English academia in Nepal transformed the nature of English pedagogy in the country. The Central Department of English – a decisive pedagogic body of Tribhuvan University – introduced modern theory and criticism, which had hitherto not ventured to the critical arenas that came after New Criticism. Formalist criticism, Reader Response Theory, Structuralism, Poststructuralism, Psychoanalysis, Postcolonialism, and Feminist Criticism opened up the areas of literary interpretations and analyses in the classrooms. Students and teachers could discuss, for instance, Shakespeare's colonial mindset in *The Tempest*, the ideology behind Keats's famous declaration about autumn as the "Season of mists and mellow fruitfulness,"[5] and closeted homosexuals in the Victorian literature.

More changes could be seen in English academia. From the eighties onwards, South Asian writers were visible and discoursed regularly from North America, the United Kingdom, to South Asia; there were few university English programmes without South Asianists (the terms is provisionally used) like Naipaul, Rushdie, Spivak, Bhabha, and Radhakrishnan. There are hundreds of such English writers outside the native English canon who fare as South Asian writers by origin or by cultural connectivities. They have significant presence not only in English departments but in the Humanities and Social Sciences at large. English department course contents in Nepal not only included South Asian writers but gradually introduced Nepali writers writing in English. Thus, my interest in South Asian writings in English grew.

The phrase South Asia is a contested term. Locating such writers and identifying them within the South Asian fold may not have any proven standard, but they can function well within the fold by cultural locations, cultural traces, and subject matters. One does not have any sound logic to include them in the regional category of South Asia[6] or exclude them from the fold. But connectivity is also a perspective by

xv

themes and contexts. Furthermore, locating such writers and categorising them in the tradition of South Asian literary theory and criticism may still be a contested effort for multiple reasons. There is no disciplinary given to bringing South Asian writers into the English departmental "literary theory and criticism" fold as there is no normative disciplinary regulation to include sociological and political essays in "literary criticism and theory" anthologies published in England and North America. From linguistics to politics, multiple issues are included in the genre. The tradition of theory and criticism courses has a significant trait of being cross-disciplinary and by this very heuristic pedagogic nature this anthology is multidisciplinary in content. For instance, the essays raise issues like home, nation, nationalism, identities, feminism, ethnicities, partition, religion, and art.

Writing this book and accompanying each chapter with critical and analytical exercises, I want to propose to students and teachers that there can hardly ever be a classroom discussion without theory. Freud is never gone but critiqued and questioned, deconstruction is never outdated, high theory is never doomed, and postcolonialism has never not been significant in the syllabi. Such claims are made more by teachers and less by students. The foundations of knowledge whether relevant or politically incorrect are always readable and discursive to position oneself in the tradition of thought. Kristeva and Butler presupposes reading Freud, de Saussure is always a relevant background to comprehend Lacan, feminism, queer theory, and Spivak. Classroom atmosphere is a back-and-forth interaction; it is a commitment to the tradition of scholarship. Personal likes and dislikes come late, very late.

Thus, there is a further academic responsibility which scholars may have to take into consideration. The responsibility is to be able to speak on a subject first and then only claim the authority to pass judgements (if passing judgement is necessary at all). We hear debaters in popular media, for instance, that homosexuality is a disease or climate change is a hoax. Before passing such judgements, a scholar must be able to speak on the subject conceptually. The responsibility which the classroom teaches us is to realise that one must be able to speak and explain about the concept for a considerable amount of time before passing any judgement. I may pronounce that I do not like Nietzsche or Bhabha because I am not interested in what they say. Personal interests certainly determine in choosing courses and reading particular writers and schools, and pursuing research. But passing judgements or critically analysing an issue is a different exercise altogether: It demands some knowledge about the issue. This very "responsibility of knowing and then passing judgement" helps answering and discoursing questions in the exercise sections of the book because the writer has to engage in developing thesis statements and then elaborating, exemplifying, and analysing the issue. Answering the questions demands such responsibility.

Notes

1 All the "central" departments of the university are the decisive bodies for introducing national syllabi, evaluation procedures, and conducting doctoral studies. Since Tribhuvan University (TU) is the largest institution in the country with hundreds of constituent and affiliated colleges, its programs have wider influence. Only recently have new universities been opened but TU is still the primary educational centre in terms of its huge size.

PREFACE

2 The popular term writing back refers to postcolonial resistance and answering back to Western ideologies.

3 Some of the frontline academics whom I referred to as junior professors of that phase are the ones who are instrumental in revising the courses in the early nineties. I was trained under Prof. Shreedhar Lohani and Prof. Abhi Subedi. My colleagues who shared this new academic atmosphere were Sanjeev Uprety and Sajag Rana (to name a few) who took academic responsibilities as years passed by.

4 We would know about the scholarly news from the copies of *The Chronical of Higher Education* and the books like Vincent B. Leitch's *American Literary Criticism from the 30s to the 80s* (1998 ed.) and Joseph Gibaldi's *Introduction to Scholarship in Modern Languages and Literatures* (1992 ed.) which were available to Nepali English academia.

5 See Geoffrey H. Hartman: "Poem and Ideology: Keats's 'To Autumn' in Kroeber, Karl & Gene W. Ruoff. (Eds.). (1993). *Romantic Poetry: Recent Revisionary Criticism*. New Brunswick: Rutgers UP.

6 Gayatri Spivak talks about the double bind of treating *Guide* as an Indian novel. She writes, "Harish Trivedi . . . complained that I don't treat Guide as an 'Indian' novel. I don't know how to?" See Gayatri Chakravorty Spivak (2012) *An Aesthetic Education in the Era of Globalization*. Cambridge: Harvard University Press (X).

ACKNOWLEDGEMENTS

Students have always been my source of inspiration. They are so many that they are the invisible faces constantly in dialogue with me.

I thank Prof. Shreedhar Lohani for his exceptional scholarship, a teacher who is constantly with me to tell me about the nuances of theory and criticism, about art and philosophy, and many other things about interdisciplinary scholarship. A companionship with exceptional academics like Professors Manzoorul Islam, Abhi Subedi, Kaiser Haq, and Fakrul Alam is always inspirational. Friends like Sajag Rana, Prof. Sanjeev Upreti, Prof. Sangita Rayamajhi and students like Pushpa Acharya are instrumental in building up an aura of profound scholarship with whom I taught and learned over the years in the Central Department of English at Tribhuvan University.

Our workshop sessions at the Institute of Advanced Communication, Education, and Research (IACER) for almost four years with Prof. Gayatri Spivak in Kathmandu on Rethinking South Asian Studies research were cutting edge discursive sessions to think and rethink about cultural studies, feminist discourses, deconstruction, and subaltern studies, and many other issues within the Humanities. I have also learned through email exchanges with her for more than a decade. I sometimes think that her one-liners, anecdotes, comments, dissatisfactions, and rare appreciations could be a book by itself.

In the recent years, I have been working with brilliant researchers in Nepal, India, and Bangladesh, the USA, and Canada on Comparative South Asian Studies. Dr. Pushpa Damai, Dr. Shreyoshi Chettri, Dr. Subhasree Ghosh, Dr. Diksha Dhar, Pushpa Acharya, Bibhushana Paudel, and Salil Subedi always gave me very profound valuable suggestions. I would not have been able to work comfortably without the help and inspiration of Sedunath Dhakal, Khagendra Nepal, Sadat Khan, Shankar Paudel, Renuka Khatiwada, Menuka Gurung, and Meghraj Adhikari who are in the research team of Nepal-Bangladesh memory studies.

I cannot just thank Dr. Pallabi Gupta, my daughter with her husband Dr. Bibek Adhikari, for constant academic sessions in Nepal, the USA, and online discussions: Pallabi has gone through the manuscript meticulously. Her editorial hard work has helped me shape the manners and matters of the anthology. A Victorianist by academic training and a postcolonial by family legacy, the questions she asked and ideas she suggested have helped me shape the contents of the book. Soma Gupta, my wife, has creative insights which have always been discursively included in the exercise sections of the book. She read me out Tagore's novels in Bengali whenever I found difficulty in comprehending the contents. She talked to me about Indian and Bengali theatre, feminist consciousness, and liberalism and many other ideas which helped me a lot to devise my propositions in general.

I thank my students and colleagues of IACER where I teach and of the Central Department of English, Tribhuvan University where I spent decades of teaching. I thank Krishna Niroula, Phatik Poudel, Tara Adhikari, Kumar Adhikari, Baldev Adhikari, Ujjwal Prasai, Rohit Dhungel, my colleagues at IACER, for their constant support to build up an atmosphere to give continuity to research. Whenever possible, I have discussions and dialogues with academics like Dr. Ishwory Pandey, Dr. Laura Gonzales, Dr. Dhurba Karki, Dr. Anirudra Thapa, Dr. Tika Lamsal, Dr. Santosh Poudel, and Dr. Shiva Rijal.

My special thanks to the authors and Routledge who have given me permission to use their chapters from the anthologies published in Routledge. They are 1. Homi Bhabha (1990) "DissemiNation: Time, Narrative, and the Margins of the Modern Nation" in Homi Bhabha. Eds. *Nation and Narration*. London: Routledge. 2. Dipesh Chakrabarty (2011) "Belatedness as Possibility: Subaltern Histories, Once Again" in Elleke Boehmer and Rosinka Chaudhuri. Eds. *The Indian Postcolonial: A Critical Reader*. London: Routledge. 3. Tapati Guha Thakurta (2011) "The Blurring of Distinctions: The Artwork and Religious Icons in Contemporary India" Elleke Boehmer and Rosinka Chaudhuri. Eds. *The Indian Postcolonial: A Critical Reader*. London: Routledge. 4. Firdous Azim (2007) "Woman and Freedom" in Kuan-Hsing Chen and Chua Beng Huat. Eds. *The Inter-Asia Cultural Studies Reader*. London: Routledge. 5. Tariq Amin-Khan (2013) "Introduction" *The Post-Colonial State in the Era of Capitalist Globalization*. London: Routledge. 6. Piya Chatterjee (2013) "Grassroots Texts: Ethnographic Ruptures and Transnational Feminist Imaginaries" in Gita Rajan and Jigna Desai. Eds. *Transnational Feminism and Global Advocacy in South Asia*. London: Routledge. 7. Homi Bhabha (1994) "Of Mimicry and Man: The Ambivalence of Colonial Discourse" in Homi Bhabha. Ed. *Location of Culture*. London: New York. 8. Lata Mani (2009) "Epilogue: The Tantra of Contemplative Cultural Critique" in *SacredSecular: Contemplative Cultural Critique*. London: Routledge. 9. Harish Trivedi (2000) "Postcolonial Hybridity: *Midnight's Children*" in Richard Allen and Harish Trivedi. Eds. *Literature and Nation: Britain and India 1800–1990*. London: Routledge. 10. Vrinda Nabar. "Fragmenting Nations and Lives: *Sunlight on a Broken Column*" in Richard Allen and Harish Trivedi. Eds. *Literature and Nation: Britain and India 1800–1990*. London: Routledge. 11. Minoli Salgado (2007) "Puyakante Wijenaike: Spectral Spaces" *Writing Sri Lanka: Literature, Resistance and the Politics of Place*. London: Routledge. 12. Radha Chakrabarty. (2016) "Chokher Bali: The Novel of the New Age" *Novelist Tagore: Gender and Modernity in Selected Texts*. London: Routledge.

INTRODUCTION

Theory, criticism, and engaging with the texts

This book aims to introduce students to the manners and matters of academic engagement by reading and analysing a selection of essays from various disciplines within the – Humanities and Social Sciences. There are twelve essays that are divided into two categories, "Theory" and "Criticism." The anthology invites discourses on the dynamics of textual contents, rhetorical styles, and socio-political issues of the essays. To engage the readers with the mechanics of reading and writing, each essay is followed by a systematically developed set of exercise questions. These questions appear in several categories: Textual, rhetorical, discussion, intertextual, creative, and critical. The exercises help the readers comprehend the subject matters ensuring them a discursive experience.

What binds the issues raised in these essays can be placed under three discursive areas around these key terms: Nation/nationalism, identities, and feminism. The chapters cover a range of subject matters: Ambivalence of nationalism and its colonial and postcolonial discourses of identity, women's identity as resistance and empowerment, the relationship between art, literature, religion, home and nation, and so on. Since these subject matters find their roots in multiple disciplines, by reading them, students develop strong analytical, critical, and writing skills.

The introduction begins by offering a critical review of the terms "Theory" and "Criticism" used in the Anglo-American English departments that have provided pedagogic guidelines across the departments of English globally. I also discuss theory in relation to humanistic considerations. The selected chapters, as one can see, have political undertones in them and consequently, I discuss the conceptual relations of the texts with the political. Since many of the chapters in the volume, in one way or another, address colonial and postcolonial issues, I talk about the term "postcolonial" in allegorical modes.

As rhetorical consideration is one of the focuses in the exercises that follow the essays, a brief survey of rhetoric in relation to the chapters is offered to help students understand the nuances of rhetoric practised and used in English departments. I then explore popular research methods used in the Humanities and Social Sciences (Sociology, Political Science, Economics, Geography, and Literature). These disciplines, more or less, provide methods to deal with the subject matters of the Humanities and Social Sciences. Furthermore, these chapters deal with multidisciplinary methods and methodologies that equip readers with diverse research skills. As the chapters strive to encourage readers to find their own meanings and distinct interpretations by reading

DOI: 10.4324/9781003213857-101

and answering the exercise questions that follow, annotating the essays in this section would be counterproductive. Therefore, I refrain from prefacing the essays so that my summaries don't influence the readers' experience of critically engaging with them.

The selection in this volume is based on the writers who have South Asian connectivities.[1]

Travelling theories

The advent of literary theory in England and North America changed the nature of literary criticism when theories travelled from other disciplines and were welcomed in English departments. Disciplines and departments have their theories, and they travel. For instance, linguistic theory of structuralism methodologically directed anthropology when Claude Levi-Strauss was looking for the tools to analyse the kinship relationships among Bororo Indians of South America; similarly, structuralism travelled to English literature departments as a technique of literary interpretations. Likewise, English departments – I would like to pause and explain that I do not use the term "English Departments" lightly – and its associated departments like Cultural Studies, Interdisciplinary American Studies, Rhetoric and Composition, Women's and Gender Studies in the Anglo-American universities use Marxism and feminism as tools of interpretation. Literary Theory as an area of study became popular in North American English departments from the sixties onwards (Culler, 1992: 203). Traditionally, in literature departments, literary theory encompasses theoretical discourse from any discipline – particularly from the Humanities and Social Sciences. Culler writes,

> Theory in this sense is not a set of methods for literary study but an unbounded corpus of writings about everything under the sun, from the most technical problems of academic philosophy to the body in its relations to medical and ethical discourses.
>
> (p. 203)

The very approach to discourse almost everything from culture to nature, Plato to Heidegger, Erasmus to Rorty in English departments makes theory a domain of "unbounded corpus." Typically, Plato's writings are discoursed in literary theory anthologies as they are discoursed within political theory or sociological theory anthologies and courses. Theories of Plato travel in Religious Studies departments, Cultural Studies programmes, and Rhetoric and Composition. Theories travel and crisscross from disciplines of linguistics to anthropology, political science to literature, film studies to media and communication, and cultural studies to international relations programmes. For the last five to six decades, Literary Theory as a genre has transformed the interpretative and analytical outlook of Literary criticism. If we observe the history of departments and particularly those that have welcomed interdisciplinary modality, we see that theories have evolved – more so in the recent times – from their purist locations and travelled across disciplinary boundaries. By the idea "purist," I mean, how departmentally, pedagogy had, not long ago, tried to associate concepts of

INTRODUCTION

Anthropocene with environmental studies, notions of tragedy with literature, and the theory of falsification with Economics only.

We know in English department academic practices that "Literary theory" has multiple origins and hence the traditional concept of criticism has also changed its analysing and interpreting features from what it was before. As theories came from various disciplines in the Anglo-American English departments, the nature and role of criticism also changed by moving beyond the heydays of literary criticism of F.R. Leavis, T.S. Eliot, and Northrop Frye, to name a few.[2]

Almost two decades ago, Martha Nussbaum looked at the range of issues, topics, and writers that literary theory covered (and has covered more in its expansionist mode): The questions about realism, relativism, subjectivism, about scepticism and justification, about nature of language as common grounds between literary theory and philosophy (1989, p. 59). She writes:

> And in pursuit of these questions literary theory discusses and teaches not only the work of philosophers who write directly about literary matters (such as Nietzsche, Heidegger, Hans George Gadamer…) but also the ideas of many… who do not…Indeed with several prominent contemporary figures – above all Jacques Derrida and Richard Rorty – there is no clear answer to the question, to which profession do they belong.
>
> (1989, p. 59)

Literary theory has evolved out of its disciplinary travels. The signs of travelling can be seen in the contents of the edited anthologies published almost forty or fifty years ago to present ones. We can observe that cross-disciplinarity is pervasive in Hazard Adams's *Critical Theory since Plato* (1971), David Lodge's *Modern Criticism and Theory* (1888), Raman Selden's *The Theory of Criticism from Plato to the Present: A Reader* (1988), Vincent B. Leitch's *The Norton Anthology of Theory and Criticism* (2001), to Richard J. Lane's *Global Literary Theory: An Anthology* (2013). The travels are evident from Aristotle's *Poetics* to Liu Kang's "The Internet in China: Emergent Cultural Formation and Contradictions." In my academic lifetime from being a student to teacher, the rules of anthologised games have covered "catharsis" to "digital humanities." There are students and probably teachers in the English departments who have not heard, let alone read, G. Wilson Knight's *The Wheel of Fire*, still, a radical democratic teacher introduces Knight's book or extracts from the book in a "Literary Theory and Criticism" course along with Slavoj Žižek's *The Courage of Hopelessness: A Year of Acting Dangerously*. Literary theory and criticism thus cover almost everything under the sun.

The word "theory" is always a contested term of reference, particularly in English academia in relation to the courses titled "Literary Theory," "Theory and Criticism," and "Critical Theory," to list a few. Referring to Gilles Deleuze's statement on theory,[3] Spivak writes, "the production of theory is also a practice; the opposition between abstract 'pure' theory and 'concrete' applied practice is too quick and easy" (*Critique*,1999, p. 256). The entire debate about theory is based on the problematic assumptions like elitism and purism which are devoid of practical approaches to

3

literary works. Aijaz Ahmad without pretention puts forwards an explanation about theory:

> Facts require explanations, and all explanations, even bad ones, presume a configuration of concepts, we provisionally call "theory". In other words, theory is not simply a desirable but a necessary relation between facts and their explanations.
>
> (2000 p. 34)

The problem arises when explanation, analysis, and interpretation are taken as representing the meaning of the text as pure over concrete practice.[4] A theoretician does not try to control the meaning of a text but pluralize by cutting across the so called pure meaning. Furthermore, there are academics in almost every English department who consider theory as an alien imposition on literary texts by decoupling theory with practice. Anti-theory is not a school of thought but a tendency to take an anti-theoretical stand. "Theory or not theory" is not a Hamletian dilemma. Theory presupposes application or practice. Is there nothing "nobler in the mind to suffer / the slings and arrows of outrageous" theory "or to take arms against a sea of troubles, /And, by opposing, end" theory? "Theory" as a troublemaker has always been contested among the teachers of English academia from the other side of the aisle. Every interpretation is both theorising and applying on literary texts or any text for that matter. Theory does not destroy the beauty of interpretation but opens up windows of interpretation. A non-theoretical stand is a futile war cry. Gerald Graff is suggestively critical of non-theorists:

> For any teacher of literature is unavoidably a literary theorist. Whatever a teacher says about a literary work, or leaves unsaid, presupposes a theory.... There is not such a thing as "just reading" a text, transparently, in a non contextual vacuum, for there is no reading that does not bring to bear a certain context, interpret from a certain angle or set of interests, and thus throw one set of question into relief while leaving others unasked.
>
> (p. 250)

Evidently, an indulgence to literary work or any work for that matter cannot be reduced to conclusions drawn from first impressions or hurried judgements by a teacher or student if the classroom is considered as a location of serious discourse. Such indulgence limits classroom discussions. Graff does not believe that theory is of an optional interest (1989, p. 251).[5]

The other problem is about the identity of literary theory in English departments. There are claims from some academic quarters that the heyday of literary theory in English departments is a thing of past. There is a strange academic desire to witness the heydays of literary theory in terms of its rise and fall. If you look at the entire range of courses offered in English departments at the universities across the world, theory is always essential as a course as fiction and poetry are. But there certainly have been changes in regard to approaching the contents of theory. They are methodological transformations from a (high) theory phase of the seventies and eighties to theory becoming part and parcel of interpreting and analysing vocabulary. Literary theory has travelled as

INTRODUCTION

additions to literary vocabulary; it has bombarded with vocabularies from structuralism to deconstruction, Marxism to feminism, new historicism to postcolonialism. The claim regarding the fall of theory can be written back in Shelleyan mode,

> I silently laugh at my own cenotaph
> And out of the caverns of rain,
> Like a child from the womb, like a ghost from the tomb,
> I arise and unbuild it again.

("The Cloud")

Literary theory changes but cannot die. Striking death blows to ideas are not the norms of scholarship. Sigmund Freud may not be favoured but to understand Julia Kristeva, one needs to understand Freudian theories.

There are a range of courses offered related to Literary Theory and Criticism in English departments under titles such as, "A Seminar on Literary Criticism," "Practical Criticism," "Critical Approaches," and "Critical Theory and Practice." The teachers assume that students learn the techniques of reading, interpreting, and analysing. At times, essays, for instance, from David Lodge or Hazard Adams anthologies are minimally applied on literary texts or not applied at all except for some background readings on contents raised in such volumes. Courses focusing on the foundational essays selected from Lodge and Adams, for instance, concentrate on reading and discussing theories. The ultimate goal, however, is to educate students about the interpretive mechanism of any text from poems and novels to any genre for that matter.

Engaging with the text is a matter of functional significance. Jeremy Hawthorn in *Unlocking the Text: Fundamental Issues in Literary Theory* introduces students with multiple terms associated with criticism: He differentiates Critical method, Critical technique, and Critical approach[6] in subtle ways. He explains what response, appreciation, evaluation, exegesis, scholarship, and explication are.[7] He sheds light on the difference between interpretation and analysis which can always be useful in classroom interactions.

Hawthorn writes that interpretation is "the most problematic and disputed term in literary-theoretical debate," he further explains:

> we can make a broad distinction between interpretation as a process of getting at, revealing, or communicating a pre-existing meaning, and interpretation as a process of creating something new and personal to the interpreter as an extension of a pre-existing text. In brief – the interpreter as elucidator/translator and the interpreter as a creative performer or producer; the interpreter as midwife and the interpreter as parent.

(1987, p. 24)

Analysis is a matter of

> relating of textual details to its effects in a manner not normally compatible with ordinary reading. It is also a clear break with conventional reading habits. It can contribute importantly to interpretative investigation.

(1987, p. 28)

Along with interpretation and analysis, discussion is an important term in the context of this book. Hawthorn observes that William Empson in "Honest to Othello" discusses Iago's use of the words "honest" and "honesty.". It may also be understood as comparison as F.R. Leavis does in *Revaluation* while comparing Shelley's "To a Skylark" and Keats's "Ode to a Nightingale" (1987, p. 29–30). Discussion can be understood as reasoning: Drawing conclusion based on a set of premises. The reasoning can be valid deductive if the conclusion is drawn from the premises with certainty where all the premises and conclusions have truth value. If any one of the propositions in the premises and conclusions have false value, the reasoning is deductive but invalid. Furthermore, if the conclusion is drawn from the premises with probability, the argument is inductive. Based on the truth and false values, an inductive argument is strong or weak.

Furthermore, how one discusses is a matter of how methods and techniques are used to argue with explanations. In brief, criticism gives significance to such activities from reading to argumentation. A student of literature and any other discipline who is interested in close reading of a text (a poem or any text, for that matter) may find such terms of reference and their understanding useful.

Literary criticism traditionally focuses on such wider modes of interacting with the text with the terms of reference I discussed above. The techniques of interpretation and analysis should not be the modes of close reading practised in literature departments only. Close reading is a disciplined act of keen observation of the material provided. The material can be a novel, a painting, or even a case of political corruption in South Asia. Traditionally, disciplines of social sciences work on empirical methods for their research whereas literature depends on close textual analysis. If literature is predominantly less concerned about empirical approaches, social sciences too do not practice the techniques of close reading in their research. Spivak has raised this very disjunction in *Death of a Discipline*. The disciplines of social science, which foreground an empirical approach to textualities, cannot be ignorant about close reading.[8] The disconnections among disciplines using methods of research can find some solution in the very notion of theories travelling from one discipline to another. I will discuss the methods across some disciplines I have selected in the later part of this Introduction but the solutions to how it can be done need elaborate exploration and discussions, which for now is not my focus.

Theory and humanistic commitment

The genre literary theory or the term theory can be conceptualised in terms of humanistic consideration. Theory performs a significant role; it functions with humanistic responsibilities. Let me begin with an anecdote regarding subaltern studies in relation to the subaltern collectives, the writers who propounded the methods of subaltern historiography. Subaltern history is not merely a mode of rewriting Indian history from the point of view of the contributions of the subaltern in India's struggle for freedom. There are multiple issues which are raised in the process of this particular historiography. While writing about the roles of the subaltern, the historiographers simultaneously discoursed about religion and ethnic relations, nationalism, agrarian communities, ecology, folk culture, status of women, exploitation and violence, and

INTRODUCTION

many such socio-political issues. The painstaking research from libraries to the empirical domain would not have been possible without a sense of humility towards the objects of study. In a graduate class in Kathmandu, a student has asked how can we liberate Nepal dalits. The desire to liberate the dalits of Nepal by graduate research papers or theses was both ridiculous and arrogant. The attempt to study the margin is not the effort to represent them, it rather is the sense of how to understand them, their ideas. The humility of research makes us think that primarily the subaltern is a location of knowledge. The subaltern collective writers make it possible to talk about the subaltern with this very sense of humility, almost un-baggaging the university erudite location, and inculcating the humility of unlearning oneself, the preparedness of knowing the object of knowledge.

The insensitiveness of using theory has another example. Spivak recollects an encounter with a Sudanese scholar. *In Other Worlds: Essays in Cultural Politics*, Spivak explains her reservation when the scholar tells Spivak that she has "written a structuralist functionalist dissertation on female circumcision in the Sudan." Spivak admits that she "was ready to forgive the sexist term," but her "disinterested stance" (1989, p. 134) of theoretical application was not easy to be forgiven. The structuralist functionalist stand was neutral to women's misery and pain. The "disinterested stance" is evident while writing a book on "Chaupadi"[9] practice from a stylistic point of view. If a Nepali researcher like the Sudanese scholar analyses declarative and imperative verbs used among family members while scolding the menstruating girl for not following forbidden norms, such a stance is gross scholarly coldness towards such a painful incident. Such an attempt to research and writing is a violence to the issue.

Application of theory to a subject matter is not merely a matter of technical appropriateness. Understanding theory invites insightfulness; insights about theory leads to academic responsibilities. What Spivak thought about the Sudanese scholar is suggestively similar to what Homi Bhabha expresses:

> the function of theory within the political process…makes us aware that our political referents and priorities – the people, the community, class struggle, anti-racism, gender difference, the assertion of an anti-imperialist, black or third perspective – are not there in some primordial, naturalistic sense.
>
> (*Location*, 1994, p. 38)

Bhabha's concern about the application of theory is about awareness towards injustices. What Bhabha expresses about the function of theory is what Jacques Derrida understands by the function of university:

> everything that concerns the question and the history of truth, in its relation to the question of man, of what is proper to man, of human rights, of crimes against humanity, and so forth, all of this must in principle find its space of discussion without condition and without presupposition, its legitimate space of research and reelaboration, *in* the University and, within the University, above all *in* the Humanities.
>
> (2001, p. 25)

The very intellectual activity is democratic in approach in the spaces of university. The activity is both a painstaking task and an act of interpretive joy. Humanistic consideration is a very subtle act when theory takes intellectual responsibility as political commitment as Bhabha explains or scholarly responsibility as Derrida conceives.

Roland Barthes is particular about intellectual activity while explaining what structuralism is as an act of intelligibility. Though he talks about structuralist criticism, his implication regarding the subtleness of interpretive act is suggestive of a grave responsibility of unlocking a text, not humanistic responsibility literally but the insightfulness which theory shapes the critic into with a sense of proportion, which is not merely a technical act. The very act of criticism as intellectual activity comes from the insight of application of theory. He proposes that criticism makes the reader understand about the practice of taking texts into multiple signs or pieces and summoning them into intelligibility. Roland Barthes explains what structuralist activity is: It is an intellectual activity. The explanation is appropriate to understand the objective of criticism:

> The goal of structuralist activity, whether reflexive or poetic, is to reconstruct an "object" in such a way as to manifest thereby the rules of functioning (the "functions") of this object. Structure is therefore actually a simulacrum of the object, but a directed *interested* simulacrum, since the imitated object makes something appear which remained invisible, or if one prefers, unintelligible in the natural object.
>
> ("The Structuralist Activity" 1992, p. 1128)[10]

Any object or text has the possibility of interpretation (all objects have); the interpretive possibility considers the object invisible by delving into the underlying structures, codes, or rules of functioning. This very structuralist mechanism of making the invisible visible is not merely the structuralist agenda that Barthes explains, but is the very act of criticism at large. All interpretation is in a sense structuralist activity. A very intellectual activity of opening-up the text. Barthes explains the act of interpretation in terms of structuralist methodology. Barthes does not evoke any humanistic commitment while explaining what structuralist criticism is but what is discursive in his explanation is that he takes interpretation with the intensity of responsibility.

Political commitment

The humanistic consideration of theoretical enterprise is political in nature. Theoretical enterprises underpinned with political commitments[11] are the academic marks of writers and critics who are collectively known as, for example, postcolonialists, subaltern historians, Marxist theorists, and feminist critics. Theoretical enterprise is always political, and criticism is never un-politically textual. All theories that aim to educate are political: Even aesthetic theories aim to educate the reader about the pleasures of the text. The aesthetics of reading is about pleasure derived from the texts. Aesthetic is political when it is aimed to "educate" the reader from the point of view of the materiality of art and literature. It may be difficult to posit discourses as non-political.

INTRODUCTION

From Homi Bhabha to Radha Chakrabarty in the volume, the essays are political. In "Mimicry and Man" Bhabha discourses on mimicry and critiques the relationship of colonial and postcolonial identities. Dipesh Chakrabarty in "Belatedness as Possibility" critiques Western ideology of prescribing what contemporary art is. In "The Blurring of Distinctions: The Artwork and the Religious Icon in Contemporary India" Tapati Guha Thakurta explains the politics of religion to reject and accept what is sacred and secular. Minoli Salgado in "Punyakante Wijenaike: Spectral Spaces" argues about how home is an indeterminate space for the marginalised.

Politics is an overarching theme in cultural discourses. Ashis Nandy while talking about the health of gods and goddesses in South Asia reads the political permissibility of who performs religious themes.[12] Gayatri Spivak's[13] discourse in "Can the Subaltern Speak?" on the subaltern is about the political failure of the completion of the speech act and hence the subaltern cannot speak. R. Radhakrishnan[14] reads in *Theory in an Uneven World*, how postcolonial perspectives both permit and reject postmodernism as a guilt of European modernism. Sara Suleri exposes the imperial politics of the sublime.[15]

There is no respite from politics: All texts are extra-textual and hence are political and contextual in a broader sense of the term. Furthermore, for academic orientations in the Humanities and English classrooms, politics has methodological significance. Politics is not merely a subject matter but a perspective that can be used to interpret and analyse literature in general. The presence of political discourse can be found from entertainment discourses to environmental studies. The Anglo-imperial cricket subtly illustrated its modes of test matches as the game of superior Victorian culture to the Caribbean and Indian cultures; soccer played on the dusty and muddy fields was the game of British soldiers and colonised locals. Cricket as the game of the British elites was gradually taken over by the natives. Like the story of English, the spectacle of cricket is not devoid of politics. Discourses on English language and cricket are political. Scientific texts arguably have not escaped politics: Textbooks of gynaecology reflecting patriarchal ideology is recently understood in the labs that "Egg traps the sperm" and they "wiggle ineffectually side to side" (Emily Martin, 1999, p.184) unlike sperm being active and consequently men being dynamic and energetic.

What then is non-political? To look for discourses beyond politics may be as much an emphatic possibility as much as claiming everything is everything. Associating politics with every kind of discourse provides scopes to the readers to delve into the dynamism of texts with the exercise questions related to cultural issues at large. We find multiple avenues to discuss theory and criticism in South Asia if politics is acknowledged as the key notable of textualities; texts are textualities (plural, multiple, interdisciplinary in content) and hence they are always already political.

One of the most discoursed political enterprises is postcolonial debate in various disciplines of the Humanities and Social Sciences. Social and economic conditions have determined the presence of colonial (neo-colonial to be particular) conditions and postcolonial academic counter arguments to examine both the past and the present of colonial conditions. In the following section, my objective is not to present an elaborate critical summary of postcolonialism, but rather to narrate and interpret anecdotal renderings of colonialism and postcolonialism.

Post-colonial phantom

The term "South Asia" is both a colonial cartographic construct and a scholarly term of agreement. One may assume a regional commonality to read a trend in theory and criticism within this construct and acceptance. South Asia/an Studies is a functional nomenclature. The region also has a scholarly compactability due to its contribution in postcolonial writings, subaltern studies, and feminist discourses, and myriad sociological and cultural discourses. The anthology *Theory and Criticism: Recent Writings from South Asia* speaks about and from a geopolitical location which is constructed and yet accepted.

Is there anything exclusive about recent South Asian writing in English? Is there anything called South Asian writing and/or Pakistani, Indian, Bangladeshi, and Nepali writings in English? Indian English is an accepted register though agreeing to a linguistic homogeneity of vast regions like India or South Asia is always a forcible connectivity. A collection of twelve essays looking at the nature, role, and function of language and ideas will never be sufficient to claim the characteristics of South Asian writing in English, even volumes cannot. It still may be necessary to theorise on recent South Asian writings in English to address the areas of theory and criticism, at least propositionally. The volume presupposes that there is South Asian writing despite the fact that periodising and categorising is dangerous. To borrow Dipesh Chakravarty's idea from *Provincializing Europe*, categories are "resources" ("Introduction" 2000, p. 6) and hence I assume that such a compilation tries to find a collective knowledge production to initiate looking at the features of recent theory and criticism in South Asia.

South Asian writings in English are not merely colonial and postcolonial in relation to the ideas of representation and resistance though a history of four hundred years of overwhelming Western presence is inherent in various disciplines of knowledge, in everydayistic expression and behaviour. The overwhelmingness is dominant, hegemonic, internalised, resisted, and appropriated: Disavowal can be epistemically dangerous. Even the use of the term "civilisation" is a colonial gift, explains Dipesh Chakrabarty.[16] The overriding term "Hinduism" has the similar history of Western prescription and South Asian acceptance of an otherwise vast fluid tradition[17] which never could have imagined Hinduism as singularity. The colonial is hegemonic, pervasive, epistemologically imposing, technologically liberating, administratively functional.

The term postcolonial is loaded with history and South Asian writing has been metonymically postcolonial for many hundreds of years, that means, they are related but they cannot be substituted metaphorically. The relationship also means that the former colonial as well as neo-colonial subject is constantly interpellated by Western ideology; postcolonial "national consciousness" (to borrow Franz Fanon's term) is burdened by Western capitalist and democratic ideas, Spivak's "native informant" is always well placed in Europe or the West in general; and the orientalised orient is never no-go. South Asia cannot do away with such Western notables associated with South Asian discourses. Even a renowned Nepali literary intellectual Laxmi Prasad Devkota is called a "romantic" poet as a canonical literary personality. Bal Krishna Sama is Shakespeare of Nepal. The measuring scales are frequently colonial touchstones.

Yet colonial history cannot be obviously seen as the pervasive hegemonic feature of recent South Asian writings, and yet we realise the double bind of South Asian

INTRODUCTION

writings as both postcolonial and purely indigenous in subject matters. Though "post-ality" in postcolonialism saves South Asian literatures and pervasive discourses from being colonial, the prefix "post" both accepts coloniality and disavows it, the prefix's very presence may be interesting to many scholars when colonialism is like the phantom on the shoulder of legendary king Vikramaditya. Vikramaditya and Betala, a phantom[18] are two main characters in the popular Indian tale titled *Betalpachisi* or *Vetala Panchavimsiti*. *Betalpachisi* is a book of twenty-five tales said to be written by Betalbhatta, one of nine geniuses in the court of legendary King Vikram.[19] As the story goes, the king is requested by a tantric yogi to bring a corpse hanging on a tree to his ritual place. When the king goes to the forest and carries the corpse on his shoulder, the phantom inside the corpse puts forth a condition before going with him. It tells a story with a riddle. The phantom warns: if he speaks, he will return and if the king does not intentionally solve the riddle, the king's head will roll down. The intelligent king always solves the riddle and the phantom returns to the tree and the king goes again to bring the corpse to the tantric. The phantom will again tell a story and the king will solve the riddle and the phantom will go back on the branch. It went on for twenty-four times. The phantom tells twenty-four stories; the twenty-fifth episode is the end of the series where the phantom alerts the king of the evil intention of the yogi. The king kills the yogi who had intended to sacrifice him on the altar of the goddess of the temple to give completion to his black magic.

King Vikram never leaves the phantom; he never wants to be free from the phantom of the forest, he speaks to answer the riddle and carries the phantom on his back. The stories the phantom tells the king burdens our scholarly shoulders as a colonial phantom on our back. As soon as we speak to it, it leaves us, we go back to carry it again, we cannot reject it, disown it. The phantom leaves only when he wishes. The phantom does not wish to leave, and the king too does not wish to return without the corpse.

Lee Falk's famous masked Phantom[20] has to perform his heroism in the jungles of imaginary country Bangalla in Africa. The skull cave, the Bandar tribe, the wolf called Devil, the horse called Hero, and the pigmies are his associates. This Phantom is the twenty-first hero in line. He carries the bloodline of Christopher Columbus from his material side. He is the superman who saves the natives from the evil doers, the Western hero with the gift of civilisation with "white man's burden" to rescue the non-Western natives.

Betalpachisi's phantom is the native's choice of bearing it, as he returns to take it back every time it leaves him, every time it escapes, Vikram goes back to fetch it. The linguistic imperialism, English language is a load on the native's shoulder which puts him in an ambivalent situation of leaving him (her) if he speaks and at the same time not allowing him to be silent. The phantom inside the corpse finally leaves with a boon that the stories that he told to Vikram will be remembered forever. The master story-teller has left but the narrative is remembered. It is like the load of English is left as narrative long after the colonial master is gone. The load of English is neither domination, nor hegemony, rather it is now the native's complete choice to remember its narrative full of plots, riddles, and the charms of the language. The power of the narratives, of the language is with him even after the phantom is gone.

Falk's hero is imposed upon us like our saviour. The popular culture in stories and cartoon strips remind us that supermen and women are in fact the white people saving

11

people of color from the evils. We are not free from the phantom-mime (I am reminded of Bhabha's notion of mimicry). The king ought to take the phantom to a sorcerer to give him a ritual ending but every time the king solves the riddle of its stories, the phantom gets back on to the tree. Postcolonial phantom-mime is almost no-go, it never leaves even after the imperial author, the phantom is gone.

Despite the valid claims that South Asian literary writing, theory, and criticism have indigenous traditions from Sanskrit and vernacular traditions of poetics, the modern twentieth century onwards critical tradition has always been the centre of debate regarding colonial and/vs indigenous traditions, hence my participation in such discourse cannot be innovative and contributory.[21]

Use of rhetoric in the selected essays

One of the goals of this anthology is to participate in discoursing the rhetorical features of the selected writings in the volume. Rhetorical aspects in recent South Asian English writings have not been discoursed elaborately. I attempt to let the readers trace some aspects of rhetoric in the exercise sections of each chapter. Observing rhetoric in recent South Asian writing is propositional in nature in the context of the book, which provides avenues of reading both simple and complex writings. Tracing patterns of arguments, discourses, descriptions, explanations, and interpretations in such writing facilitates understanding for academic purpose. In the essays selected there are uses of analogy to put forward contents to show agreements, disagreements, disputes, and contestations. At times, the texts are exploratory, they use data, and use aphorism. Using topics of testimony, precedence, historical or authorial evidence, strengthens their propositions. Some writers are fond of proposing concepts and analyse their propositions. Furthermore, many of these writers use definitions of the key terms to clarify their arguments, and at the same time use lucid language to keep the reader engaged. There are many instances in the selected essays when the writers use hypothesis and prove them deductively and inductively in subsequent paragraphs. There are writers in the compilation who depend on personal experiences to elaborate their claims and propositions. I provide a few examples of rhetorical styles in the following paragraphs. I will engage the readers with more rhetorical styles in each exercise section of the chapters in the volume. These selected examples of rhetoric will help the readers, students in particular, engage with rhetorical questions. I have selected some writers only to prepare a platform for the students about the nuances of rhetoric.

Homi Bhabha's essay "DissemiNation: Time, Narrative, and the Margins of the Modern Nation" is methodological in nature which comes from a deconstructive tradition of writing, a significant line of communication evolved all the way from Socratic tradition, many times evident in Gayatri Spivak's writings via Derridian writing techniques. By Derridian style I mean the writing styles of recognising double binds, the using of paradox and oxymoron, and at the same time avoiding linear writings, and conceiving binary opposites. By giving methodological significance to concepts, Bhabha's writing avoids rigid claims; his writings rather place the reader in slippages, double binds, and hence constantly opens up dialogues. He does not give truth value to ideas but takes them as strategies which is due to the tendency of providing methodological weight to concepts. Ideas are tools or methods for him rather than being denotative. This is what the nature of language is in the domain of the humanities: Open ended, provisional, propositional, and hence deconstructive. His language exemplifies the very deconstructive double bind: "language bears within itself the necessity of its own critique" (Derrida, "Structure," 1967, p. 358). The very modality of Bhabha is evident when he engages in discoursing nation:

> The discourse of nationalism is not my main concern. In some ways it is the historical certainty and settled nature of that term against which I am attempting to write of the western nation as an obscure and ubiquitous form of living the *locality* of culture.

Bhabha soon provides constant slippages of what nation is: "a form of living that is more around temporality than about historicity: a form of living that is more complex than 'community'; more symbolic that 'society'; more connotative than 'country'." He continues in the same vein of in-determining what nation is (1990, p. 292).

Obscurity in Homi Bhabha's writings is a matter of classroom debates with both fun and seriousness. Bhabha's writings do not allow the reader easy access to comprehensibility until the reader persists. The persistent readings unfold the meanings once one realises the fact that the seriousness of subject matters needs serious language and not to reduce writing as the job of the writer to simplify ideas whereas the reader sits idly to receive the blessing of understanding from one paragraph to another and with a final stroke of comprehension in a concluding paragraph. Bhabha is difficult when readers choose a comfort zone of comprehension. Similarly, Spivakian writings too demand readers to come out of "his"[22] comfort zone. Derrida writes:

> A text is not a text unless it hides from the first comer, from the first glance, the law of its composition and the rules of the game. A text remains, moreover, forever imperceptible. Its law and its rules are not, however, harbored in the inaccessibility of a secret; it is simply that they can never be booked, in the present, into anything that could rigorously be called a perception.
>
> (*Dissemination*, 1981, p. 69)

Since there is no pure act of perception (Stanley Fish, 1980, p. 168), the interpretive game of hide and seek both disturbs and engages the reader.

Dipesh Chakraborty's essay in the selection focuses on key terms: Belatedness, newness, repetition, generality, displacement, disguise, and possibility. The entire writing is structured to expose the problem of contemporaneity as merely the characteristics of Western modernism. The reader has to connect the terms with the cluster of circularities to grasp his thesis of "belatedness as possibility." Each thematic circle leads to one final concluding circle "belatedness as possibility." The smaller circles are those eight terms (there are more thematic circle-clusters in the essay, and it depends on the reader how those clusters can be noticed) connected with another. The rhetoric of cluster of circles leading to a bigger circle, his thesis, can only be understood if the themes are spread systematically in the reader's mind. A tree diagram may not be as useful to see the entirety of his argument because all those key terms are linked with one another and are not separate, hence circularity is his rhetorical strategy (readers are free to notice other strategic modes). To understand how meanings are constructed, his choice of words, what he wants to accomplish, and how effective his communication is, are playfully understood by the circle-clusters. Such an approach works with other writings too, but Chakraborty's rhetoric is visualised through how he weaves arguments by connecting the key terms to put forward his point.

It is one of the finest samples of structured writing. For instance, the problem of "belatedness" raised in relation to the catalogue the writer refers to is exemplified in the context of "subaltern studies" as both belated and with possibility; the argument further moves to defining and understanding the problem of "repetition" and "recognition;" the circle moves forwards to discourse what "newness" is. "Repetition" is further contrasted with "generality." Then with the example of a subaltern studies project, the writer discusses how subaltern writings are both an addition to Marxist ideas and yet are different and new through the devices like "disguise" and "displacement." Conceiving of these terms of reference as circles is to observe how the essay is tunefully connected. As I mention, a rhetoric of a tree diagram may also be conceived to structure the essay, but the rhetoric of circularity is a matter of observing interconnectedness: It is not about one argument leading to another but about seeing how arguments are interconnected.

Firdous Azim's essay "Women and Freedom" displays communicative relationship with the reader. "The paper will look at," "I would like to," "I will be looking," "Let us…," and many such phrases mark an interesting feature of her writing, not exclusively South Asian or Bengali but discernibly reader oriented; she constantly engages with the addressee. The shift from one topic to another is almost regularly featured by the vocative articulation, an eloquence with sincerity towards readership in mind. The commitment to the reader is a conative aspect of her language to put forwards her arguments. Readers may find it easy to go along with what she wants to put forwards by frequently clarifying her position to the readers. Such a technique is not aimed at providing a comfort zone to the reader but is aimed at constant engagement with the issues by being aware of readership. Azim's essay is explanatory and argumentative. The mannerism is striking when we compare Azim with Tapati Guha Thakurta's "The Blurring of Distinctions: The Artwork and Religious Icons in Contemporary India." Thakurta is *subtly* confrontational by the very contextual demand of exposing the wrong of the claims of Hindutva tradition. Azim targets the readers directly as if "I am talking to you" in contrast with Thakurta's "I am talking about them." The reader will find more differential strategic nuances.

Lata Mani reflectively engages with the reader. She also is aware of her conceptual position. One of the major aspects of Lata Mani's "Epilogue: Tantra of Contemplative Cultural Critique" is that the concept Tantra is given methodological significance. The concept is used to map and analyse culture traits of contemporary times. The purpose is achieved through, she writes in "Introduction" of the book *SacredSecular*, "personal and analytical" journey (p. 1). Derrida's poetic rendering on the nature of text may speak of Mani's reflective writing:

The text occupies the place before "me": it regards me, invests me, announces me to myself, keeps watch over the complicity of I entertain with my most

secret present, surveys my heart's core – which is precisely a city, and a labyrinthine one – as if from the top of a watchtower planted inside me like that
"transparent column" which having no inside of its own, is driven, being a
pure outside, into that which tries to close upon itself. The column puts space
into time and divides what is compact. Its transparence is also reflective.

(Dissemination, 1981, p. 374)

The nature of language is not merely a matter of what is present on the pages, as we
read the text, the past informs the present, the pre-text, the context, the knowledge in
the text at large and the knowledge of the reader at large work in simultaneity.

I propose readers, particularly students, to take many such strategies into consideration. Textual discussions (in the exercises) will provide ample opportunities to mark
rhetorical movements of the writings. The underlying purpose of rhetorical questions
is to create interest in readers to engage in the joys of reading.

Methods across disciplines

The essays are selected from various disciplines and their key methodological discussion can be useful to deal with the exercises as well as being helpful to understanding
how these disciplines use larger perspectives or methodologies and how they use tools
or methods. Methodologies are larger strategic disciplinary lenses that researchers
become familiar with, within the working of the disciplines. Traditionally, literature
differs in its methodological orientation to anthropology or political science from art
history though there are no exclusive methodological domains in interdisciplinary orientations. There, however, are methodologies across disciplines of knowledge. The
exercise questions address issues of multiple disciplines, the methodologies of social
sciences can help understand the nature of questions and their answers and discussions.

The purpose of this section is to compare and analyse methodologies used in
Sociology, Political Science, Economics, Geography, and Literature. First, I discuss the
ideas of comparativism put forward by Émile Durkheim and Max Weber in view with
how they are used by Sociologists and Political Scientists. I trace the ideas of comparative method, radical plurality, and multi-paradigmatic methods used in these disciplines. The next methodological focus is to read the relationship between concept and
theory understood in Geography (logical positivism and post-positivism), Economics
(apriorism and falsification), and Literature (tropes and concepts).

Sociology

A significant area of sociological inquiry is comparativism. Émile Durkheim explains
the comparative method thus:

We have only one way of demonstrating that one phenomenon is the cause
of another. This is to compare the cases where they are both simultaneously
present or absent, so as to discover whether the variations they display in these
different combinations of circumstances provide evidence that one depends
upon the other. When the phenomena can be artificially produced at will by

the observer, the method is that of experimentation proper. When, on the other hand, the production of facts is something beyond our power to command, and we can only bring them together as they have been spontaneously produced, the method used is one of indirect experimentation, or the comparative method.

We have seen that sociological explanation consists exclusively in establishing relationships of causality, that a phenomenon must be joined to its cause, or, on the contrary, a cause to its useful effects. Moreover, since social phenomena clearly rule out any control by the experimenter, the comparative method is the sole one suitable for sociology.

(1982, *Rules*, p. 147)

He further writes:

To illustrate an idea is not to prove it. What must be done is not to compare isolated variations, but series of variations, systematically constituted, whose terms are correlated with each other in as continuous gradation as possible and which moreover cover an adequate range.

(1982, *Rules*, p. 155)[23]

Max Weber's writings too exemplify a lot of comparative allusions.[24] Weber's idea of comparativism primarily focuses on individual characteristics. A particular historical context in time and space has its own features which have to be taken into account in compartivist approaches. From the individual, the particular, or the historical given to reaching out to see universal connectivity is what Weber proposes: The connectivity of 1618 Defenstration of Prague with the rise of capitalism, is the example of particularism connected to bigger narrative. Such connectivity is possible when one can first comprehend the uniqueness of an event.

This is a necessary result of the nature of historical concepts which attempt for their methodological purposes not to grasp historical reality in abstract general formulæ, but in concrete genetic sets of relations which are inevitably of a specifically unique and individual character.

(Weber, *Protestant*, 2005, p.14)

Leading sociologists like Herbert Spencer, Émile Durkheim, and Max Weber were comparativists. A. Beteille explains:

The comparative method developed and employed by Durkheim and his successors was designed to free the investigation from the investigator's own biases and preconceptions. The first step was the detailed and careful observation of facts; Durkheim specified the conditions for such observation, and the development of intensive fieldwork on the one hand and of survey research on the other greatly extended the depths and range of observation. Not that ideas, beliefs and values were to be excluded from observation; but they were to be treated as facts existing independently of the moral and political preferences of the observer. Once the techniques of observation had been perfected, one would need only patience and care, and it would not matter who made the observation.

(1998, p. 142)

Spivak proposes a similar search of exclusivities in many of her books and essays. Her particularism is evident in her Birbhoom works.[25] She suggests something similar when she writes: "I would like to distinguish my position from the pan-Asianism that we have known from the nineteenth century in figures such as Shinpei Goto, Sun Yat Sen, and Rabindranath Tagore (2008, *Other Asias*, p. 2). Spivak's position is about finding the uniqueness in the local instead of establishing similarities and thus universalising the local issues in grand narrative scale.

Along with comparativism, the classificatory method also is one of the important sociological approaches to research. Both Durkheim and Radcliffe-Brown have discoursed classification (Beteille, 1998, p. 144). Classification led to the division of areas and regions by the social theorists. "Durkheim's classification of societies is of special interest, firstly, because it was consciously linked to his comparative method, and, secondly, because it was made in accordance with a set of rules" (1998, p. 144). Weber's theory of classification was different because he focused on multiple standpoints "that could be compared and contrasted across both time and space" (1998, p.146).

Weber made wide and extensive comparisons among human societies in different places at different times, but those comparisons did not presuppose in either principle or practice any single scheme of classification covering all human societies. His principle strategy of comparison and contrast was through the construction of ideal types, which enabled the selection and use of facts to establish significant similarities and differences. The construction of ideal types, (unlike Durkheim's social types or social species) is not necessarily linked to the comparative method as such, but Weber harnessed the device for making the most extensive historical and sociological comparisons and contrasts.

(1998, p.146)

One may try to use and appropriate Distant comparativism in reference to Derrida and Spivak (see Spivak's *Death of a Discipline*) and also in relation to how Weber talks about differences at the cost of similarities. Comparativism and Distant comparativism are not merely the research methods for crossing areas of study from one place to another or from one temporality to another, but also crisscrossing the disciplines like close textual reading with literary training and using sociological approaches of comparativism like Durkheim's "isolated variation" and Weber's study of particularity and its global scope.

Furthermore, there may be a possibility to conceptualise the Aristotelian phronetic approach mentioned by Bent Flyvbjerg (see the section "Political Science" below). All such studies also lead to encompassing "multi-paradigmatic" methods and "radical plurality" used by contemporary research in political science.

Political science

On suggesting research in comparative politics Pennings et al. write,

> We contend that the comparative approach and its methodological applica-
> tion must be conducted by means of theory-driven research questions. This
> is to say: a research question must be formulated as a point of departure of
> comparative investigation, which enables the student to reflect on what, when
> and how to compare and for what purpose. If not, the comparison becomes a
> recording instrument only. This, however, is not our goal, nor is it in our view
> scientific. Scientific activities always imply the quest for explanations, which
> are not only empirically based and yield systematic results, but also lead to
> results which are plausible. It is vital to realize that throughout this book we
> shall contend that empirical-analytical analysis is an instrument to develop
> social and political knowledge that is both scientifically valid and plausible
> for a wider audience.
>
> (2006, p. 6)

Along with comparativism, the research in political science talks about being scientific
in methodology. Such researches, however, have recently focused on more connectivities with other disciplinary methods. The methodological debate in general in the
Western social sciences up to the end of the nineteenth century was about natural sciences versus human sciences. America followed a naturalistic model without much of
a hitch up to the mid-twentieth century. That is why behaviourism in political science
was the dominant influential mode of scientific methodology. It now has given way to
"radical plurality"[26] which mixes methods as appropriate in ways that appreciate that
all social phenomena, including politics, are human practices mediated through language that require both interpretation and explanation. (Sanford F. Schram & Brian
Caterino, 2006, p. 3–4). They inform:

> With time, the decline of behaviorism in political science by the end of the
> twentieth century opened the way for a variety of what today are often called
> "interpretive" approaches, such as critical theory, hermeneutics, post-struc-
> turalism, and feminism, that arose in the wake of these earlier influences.
>
> (2006, p. 5)

Thus, post-pragmatic political methods which may be understood as multi-paradigmatic methods and radical plurality have been the significant methodological positions
in the recent decades. This is one of the most essential approaches the contemporary
research adopts in the Humanities and Social Sciences. Radical plurality, dialogics, or
multiple adaptation provides scopes for "freedom to contradict" (Spivak, "Imperative
to Re-imagine the Plural" in *Aesthetic*: p. 335).

Bent Flyvbjerg's *Making Social Science Matter* can provide some methodological
inputs in the context of interpretive approach. His contribution in methodological
discourse is significantly appropriated by contemporary political scientists. He writes:

INTRODUCTION

In this book, I will present a way out of the Wars by developing a conception of social science based on a contemporary interpretation of the Aristotelian concept of *phronesis*, variously translated as prudence or practical wisdom. In Aristotle's words *phronesis* is a "true state, reasoned, and capable of action with regard to things that are good or bad for man." *Phronesis* goes beyond both analytical, scientific knowledge (*episteme*) and technical knowledge or know-how (*techne*) and involves judgments and decisions made in the manner of a virtuoso social and political actor. I will argue that *phronesis* is commonly involved in social practice, and that therefore attempts to reduce social science and theory either to *episteme* or *techne*, or to comprehend them in those terms, are misguided.

(2001, p. 2)

The Aristotelian idea of *episteme* and *techne* are different from *phronesis*. Context-oriented practicality and value, thus, for Flyvbjerg, should determine research in social science which is how social sciences can encompass humanistic attitudes and beliefs.

Regardless of the lack of a term for *phronesis* in our modern vocabulary, the principal objective for social science with a phronetic approach is to carry out analyses and interpretations of the status of values and interests in society aimed at social commentary and social action, i.e. praxis.

(2001, p. 60)

Aristotle writes about prudence or phronesis as an action which is akin to social science rigour of empirical work, but such field of action must have the honesty of working with the idiom of the local; thus, living and knowing them is action. This is how the particulars can be comprehended.

And prudence is not concerned with the universals alone but must also be acquainted with the particulars: it is bound up with action, and action concerns the particulars. Hence even some who are without knowledge – those who have experience, among others – are more skilled in acting than are others who do have knowledge.

(Aristotle, 2011, p. 124)

Social science field works explain the Aristotelian idea of prudence, more visibly in Spivakian West Bengal schoolwork and subaltern collective research in general. What is significant in terms with prudence for a researcher is to focus on the exclusivities of the local as particularities.

Economics

Adam Smith's *An Inquiry into the Nature and Cause of the Wealth of Nations* is as relevant as David Richardo or John Maynard Keynes are.

19

The "interest" claim (in the citation below) of the author may be questionable when it comes to any discipline of knowledge, but what the writer puts forward regarding the theories or "revolutions" in economics is relevant for our purpose to look for theories and methods from across the disciplines and across historical development of ideas.

> When the natural scientist has come to the frontier of knowledge, and is ready for new exploration, he is unlikely to have much to gain from a contemplation of the path by which his predecessors have come to the place where he now stands. Old ideas are worked out; old controversies are dead and buried. The Ptolemaic system may live on in literature, or it may form the framework of a mathematical exercise; it has no direct *interest* (my emphasis) to the modern astronomer.
>
> Our position in economics is different; we cannot escape in the same way from our own past. We may pretend to escape; but the past crowds in on us all the same. To "neoclassical" succeeds "neomercantilist"; Keynes and his contemporaries echo Ricardo and Malthus; Marx and Marshall are still alive. Some of us are inclined to be ashamed of this traditionalism, but when it is properly understood it is no cause for embarrassment; it is a consequence of what we are doing, or trying to do.
>
> (John Hicks, 1980, p. 207)

Consequently, some of the traditional methods have their research significance from one discipline to another. Discoursed in the domain of Economics, for instance, Apriorism and Falsification methods have very useful interdisciplinary implications.

Apriorism is an apriori true mode of an assumption of rationality and it is a necessary requirement of research introduced in economics in the early nineteenth century by Nassau Senior and popularised by Robbins and von Mises.[27] Falsificationism is a hypothesis or a theory that can be proved as false. Science is falsifiable or can be testable, and the unfalsifiable is unscientific. Falsifiability keeps scientific work moving.

> *Falsificationism* contrasts sharply with apriorism. Its purpose is to expose maximally theories to the logical possibility of empirical counter-examples. The criterion of goodness of a theory is a function of its falsifiability together with its success in withstanding attempts to falsify it. If, other things being equal, theory *A* is more falsifiable than theory *B* and has survived non-trivial efforts to falsify it, then theory *A* is better than theory *B*.
>
> (Sapiro J Latsis "Research," 1980, p. 7)

M. Blaugh explains:

> A hasty reading of *The Logic of Scientific Discovery* suggests the view that a single refutation is sufficient to overthrow a scientific theory; in other words, it convicts Popper of what Lakatos has called "naive falsificationism". But a moment's reflection reminds us that many physical and virtually all social phenomena are stochastic in nature, in which case an adverse result implies the

INTRODUCTION

improbability of the hypothesis being true, not the certainty that it is false. To discard a theory after a single failure to pass a statistical test would, therefore, amount to intellectual nihilism. Patently, nothing less than a whole series of refutations is likely to discourage the adherents of a probabilistic theory.

("Kuhn," 1980, p. 151)

The comparativism here is conceptually driven which may help comprehend what and how theories work in various disciplines. For instance, a researcher's initial plan is to use apriorism which are "ultimate unanalyzable categories" (Latsis, 1980, p. 4). It is about the general principles which hold truth by definition: Relations are essential and necessary human ideas. The theories of conflict then move to contradict the principal of relations. The theories of international relation in strict binarism, idealism versus realism, can be the foundations of his preliminary research with the examples from India and China. The third theory which he may use is constructivism, the middle ground between the two. He extends his ideas by bringing in Daoism and Confucianism as modes of idealism. His area of research is conflict and international relations. The researcher's proposition still is under consideration which needs more clarity.

Geography

What can be the inputs from methods of geographical research for students studying issues related to, for instance, the Silk Road, the spread of Buddhism, and the travel accounts of Buddha? More particularly: How do Buddha images travel from South Asia to Central Asia, China, and Japan? In this context, the methods of geography support the works within the fields of art, religion, and history. The geographer's question[28] is about the organisation of spaces and their arrangements. Taking into account the system of arrangements, the researcher can inquire how Buddha's imagistic identity is formed in various spaces from South to Central Asia, throughout the ancient Silk Road. How do territorial spaces in terms of plains, deserts steeps, and mountains shape the images of Buddha from Nepal and India to Central Asia in sculptures and paintings? A similar identity question can be traced in terms of travelling Bodhisattas images and rituals, for instance from Nepal to Tibet, from China to Japan.

There can be two major areas of research informed by the methodology of Geography, especially for some researchers who are engaged in field work with the background of literary research experiences. Theory and observation and their interaction are significant research purposes of a geographer (Rhoades and Wilson, 2010, p. 28).

Presuppositions about the world influence observation and one of the major perspectives about presupposition is logical positivism, which is an inductive, empirical mode of inquiry. It was later criticised. A priori or the theory-laden approach is independent of experience and is deductive which is to conceive a general theory and move towards testing the theory (Rhodes and Wilson, 2010, p. 28). There are, however, post-positivist arguments.

Differences between these perspectives depend on the degree to which observation is viewed as "theory-dependent." If observation is highly dependent on theory, especially a theory under test, information derived from the observation may be biased and unhelpful in evaluating the theory. Thus, whenever theory-dependent observations are used to evaluate theory, the research process can be said to be somewhat circular. This view laid the ground for relativistic conceptions of science which maintain that the relative value of theoretical ideas must be judged on the basis of social criteria since observation, which is biased by theory, cannot be used to adjudicate among different ideas. A corollary of *relativism* is that objectivity no longer is preserved in any absolute sense; all ideas fall or stand based on their relative merits as defined within a social context.

(2010: p. 28)

Understanding the relative value of theory and the social criteria means theories must have contextual merits. Spivak raises the problems of failing in rescuing women in the Arab world due to this very use of a preconceived concept without considering the contextual merits (Spivak, *Aesthetic*, 2013, p.124). Close reading is not about reading a book, it is emphasising how many strands with which social empirical data is made (Spivak's well-known assumption). In this context one important proposition can be that without theory data cannot be gathered to observe or to see the phenomena. That is why, in Spivak's language, strands are the base of close reading. There still is a scope for using "senses" as a researcher's tool. A researcher enters a field of observation prompted by the old method of observation of logical positivism in its strict orthodox sense. Regarding nature conservation study and research, the researcher uses senses to observe along with the performing languages in the local, as an extension of the "senses" so as to develop his or her theory being aware of the contextual merits.

The other end of post-postitivism is Realism:

Realism, in fact, argues that the theory-ladenness of observation is *necessary* for objectivity: only by viewing the world through the lens of theory can we hope to discern what the world is really like. In other words, science without concepts is blind and the notion of building knowledge from theory-neutral observations, even if such observations could be obtained, is fundamentally misguided. This necessitates that both background knowledge and observational information serve as forms of evidence in the testing of a theory; empirical data are not ignored, but neither are they viewed as the absolute arbiter when a theory is evaluated. Viewed in this light, theory-dependence does not threaten objectivity, but instead provides the basis for collection of appropriate observations for theory testing (Rhoads and Thorn 1996).

(Rhoads and Wilson, 2010, p. 29)

Within such observational modalities, one of the important things the natural scientists and physical geographers propose is observation as a method of data collection:

observation is viewed not as information obtained directly through the senses (vision, hearing), as the logical positivists maintained, but as data gathered using elaborate theory-dependent processes that often involve instrumentation

INTRODUCTION

(consider the images gathered by recording or real-time sensing devices mounted on aircraft or satellites, that have no intimate contact with the objects they are observing). To this extent, most scientific observations now consist of a causal chain that links a human observer to natural phenomena via the technology they employ for data collection, management and analysis (Rhoads and Thorn 1996), and that draws on background knowledge about how specific technologies can generate data on the phenomenon. This view emphasizes that there is distinction between "data" and "phenomena" that complements the difference between "observation" and "theory" (Rhoads and Thorn 1996). Science then can be construed as a search for phenomena through the acquisition of data that relies on theory-dependent technology and techniques.

(Rhodes and Wilson, 2010, p. 29)

Thus, the study can be based on collecting data on the phenomena based on theory-dependent techniques and technology. How do we view a researcher's position? How does a researcher use performance as technique and technologies based on their theory?

Working with concepts draws influences from both the humanities and social sciences.[29] Literature produces narratives and figures (hence both fictions and fact) to comprehend the world. That is how concepts about the world are built. Literature works with tropes to mis/represent the world. Furthermore, concepts and tropes are deconstructive in nature because they are expressed in language which carries within it the necessity of its own inquiry (to recall Derrida in "Structure, Sign, and Play").[30]

Before exploring what concept is and how it works in literature, my purpose is to read what social science research takes concepts and theories to mean. Concepts are "mental abstractions" (Ruane, 2005, p. 47) and they work through words. Concepts work with the help of theory which in turn are about-ness and how-ness of a process or the world we live in. Theories are building blocks of concepts. A researcher has to work empirically to test how theory works or how theory is appropriate or inappropriate, valid or invalid, probable or improbable. But for all such research modality concepts are always necessary for our study.

In relation to theory, Karl Popper is very particular about genuine scientific method or research in comparison with non-empirical method. He proposes a problem:

The problem which troubled me at the time was neither, "When is a theory true?" nor, "When is a theory acceptable?" My problem was different. I *wished to distinguish between science and pseudo-science*; knowing very well that science often errs, and that pseudo-science may happen to stumble on the truth.

(1962, p. 32)

Popper further emphasises upon true empirical method:

I knew, of course, the most widely accepted answer to my problem: that science is distinguished from pseudoscience – or from "metaphysics" – by its *empirical method*, which is essentially *inductive*, proceeding from observation

LITERARY THEORY AND CRITICISM

or experiment. But this did not satisfy me. On the contrary, I often formulated my problem as one of distinguishing between a genuinely empirical method and a non-empirical or even a pseudo-empirical method – that is to say, a method which, although it appeals to observation and experiment, nevertheless does not come up to scientific standards. The latter method may be exemplified by astrology, with its stupendous mass of empirical evidence based on observation – on horoscopes and on biographies.

(1962, p. 32–3)

Social Science methodology and Popper can be read along with how concepts are taken in the domain of literature. Popper's focus, however, was science and non-science:

Popper's principal problem in *The Logic of Scientific Discovery* was to find a purely logical demarcation rule for distinguishing science from nonscience. He repudiated the Vienna Circle's principle of verifiability and replaced it by the principle of falsifiability as the universal, *a priori* test of a genuinely scientific hypothesis. The shift of emphasis from verification to falsification is not as innocent as appears at first glance, involving as it does a fundamental asymmetry between proof and disproof. From this modest starting point, Popper has gradually evolved over the years a powerful anti-inductionist view of science as an endless dialectical sequence of "conjectures and refutations".8

(M. Blaug, 1980, p. 151)

Theories and concepts have their special roles to play in the domain of literary research. I move forwards to conceptualise how they work in the domain of literature.

Literature

I take up the question of how a researcher works in the field of literature. She tries to respond, evaluate, appreciate, explicate, interpret, and/or analyse with critical methods, techniques, and approaches.[31] One of the most visible aspects which a researcher looks into with a piece of literature is what both new critics and deconstructionists use in terms of interpretation and analysis.

Appropriate references from new critic sympathisers Wellek and Warren's *Theory of Literature* and post-structuralist Paul de Man's *Aesthetic Ideology* and *Resistance Theory* will help researchers to find some avenues to mark out and use the methodologies. One way to read a poem or a novel is to explore how concepts in literature are found through the study of tropes or figures, or "knot" (Paul de Man, *Aesthetic Ideology*, 1996, p. 44) to plot (narrative). Concepts can be understood through representationality. Mimesis is a trope: "Mimesis becomes one trope among others, language choosing to imitate a nonverbal entity" (Paul de Man, *Resistance to Theory*, 2006, p.10). Furthermore, Wellek and Warren write about literary language in terms of tropes and techniques:

It abounds in ambiguities; it is, like every other historical language, full of homonyms, arbitrary or irrational categories such as grammatical gender; it is

24

INTRODUCTION

permeated with historical accidents, memories, and associations. In a word, it is highly "connotative." Moreover, literary language is far from merely referential. It has its expressive side; it conveys the tone and attitude of the speaker or writer. And it does not merely state and express what it says; it also wants to influence the attitude of the reader, persuade him, and ultimately change him. There is a further important distinction between literary and scientific language: in the former, the sign itself, the sound symbolism of the word, is stressed. All kinds of techniques have been invented to draw attention to it, such as meter, alliteration, and patterns of sound.

(1987, p. 13)

Similarly, de Man focuses on the nature of language:

Neither is there any doubt about what it is in language that thus renders it nebulous and obfuscating: it is, in a very general sense, the figurative power of language. This power includes the possibility of using language seductively and misleadingly in discourses of persuasion as well as in such intertextual tropes as allusion, in which a complex play of substitutions and repetitions takes place between texts.

("The Epistemology of Metaphor," 1996, p. 35–40)

Such "ambiguities" to "patterns of sound," "tropes" are the researcher's domain of working with the concepts. "Concepts are tropes" writes De Man.[32] There is no essentialist need to bring in a similar tradition of Indian poetics, but they may be useful for the researchers interested in Sanskrit poetics.[33]

With such a training on reading literature within the domain of tropes and techniques, a researcher may read political and economic documents with what is called close textual reading of either texts or develop a reading (and hence observing, interpreting, and analysing) habit of such a scholarship. The rigour of reading should accompany empirical research (one of the major ideas of Spivak in *Death of a Discipline*).[34] Let me elaborate.

Empirical research can take issues as narratives. In postcolonial writings where one of the major inquiries are historically embedded narratives, narrative analysis can be a significant approach drawn from the methods used by narratologists like Vladimir Propp, Mikhail Bakhtin, and Roland Barthes. The use of annals which use dates and events and chronicles which is plot-like structure may be studied with narrative analysis.[35] My proposed ongoing research "Rethinking South Asia through a Study on Nepal's Encounter with the British Empire" provides ample scope to use narrative analysis and interpret colonial and postcolonial narratives like annals and chronicles. Additionally, the narratives provide scopes to read figurativeness (as explained by Wellek and Warren and de Man) to analyse texts within postcolonial discursivity.

The researchers need to open up to various methodologies from the disciplines of the Humanities and Social Sciences. Along with choosing themes for their research, it may be relevant for them to use various disciplinary methods when appropriate.

25

Spivak writes: "learn comparativism not only from texts or disciplinary method but reach-out techniques in material studied" (*Aesthetic*, 2013, p. 467). Understanding "techniques" in the texts or comprehending ideas as methods prompts a research to approach to comparativism. Instead of giving truth value to an idea the researcher gives methodological significance to the idea (as Derrida implies in "Structure, Sign, and Play in the Discourse of the Human Sciences"). Comparativism is methodological orientation.

Since the essays in the collection belong to various disciplines, methodological issues are important to understand while reading and answering questions. Disciplines work within their own terms of reference and methodological orientations. Interdisciplinary is not merely about borrowing ideas of a particular discipline but also knowing how one particular discipline functions.

Chapter selection and exercise questions

The chapters reflect the subject matters of the Humanities and Social Sciences. This compilation has twelve writers of South Asian connectivities which are categorised in Theory and Criticism. The selection under Theory raises multiple social issues and the essays under Criticism primarily focus on social issues in relation to literature. The anthology prepares the reader to engage in three distinct features of South Asian writings: Textual, rhetorical, and contextual. The purpose of the anthology with the help of exercises is to develop an interdisciplinary discourse with the help of the essays selected. Each selection is followed by interactive exercises. The essays represent the concepts and methods of literary studies, cultural studies, postcolonialism, feminism, historiography, art, and religion related to South Asia.

After each essay, there are sets of "Textual Questions," "Rhetorical Questions," "Discussion Questions," "Intertextual Discussions," and "Critical and Creative Thinking Questions." "Textual Questions" provide close readings of the essays whereas "Rhetorical Questions" help readers comprehend stylistic and compositional skills. "Intertextual Discussions" generate discourses and help practice writing in the broader context of the issue raised in the essays. Finally, "Critical and Creative Questions" allow students to observe, analyse, reason, and also generate and express new ideas; this particular exercise section is not introduced to just answer questions but to initiate ideas about critical thinking and consequently the questions and information are not always related to the contents of the essays. I rather seek to connect some key ideas related to the essays.

The anthology has wider academic significance because essays related with literary theory, literary criticism, cultural studies, gender studies, and postcolonial theory are the core course contents of the departments in the Humanities and Social Sciences in general and English departments in particular. Furthermore, such selections are followed by innovative and interactive close reading exercises and rhetorical questions which generally are used in Writing and Composition departments only. There are almost no anthologies focusing on South Asian writings of theory and criticism with exercises and a multiplicity of reading possibilities. Finally, the writers selected have wider epistemic influence whose writings need both political and stylistic understanding.

INTRODUCTION

Notes

1 Such connectivities can be understood on various levels, ranging from the issues related to South Asia, authors' cultural associations with the region, and a range of postcolonial discourses.

2 I cited these names only because they are well-known names in South Asian English departments.

3 See page 256 in Spivak, Gayatri Chakravorty (1999). *Critique of Postcolonial Reason: Towards a History of Vanishing Present*. Cambridge: Harvard University Press.

4 In reference to Gilles Deleuze's notion of theory, Spivak writes, "An important point is being made here: the production of theory is also a practice; the opposition between abstract 'pure' theory and concrete 'applied' practice is too quick and easy" (*Critique*: 1999, 256). See Spivak, Gayatri Chakravorty. (1999). *A Critique of Postcolonial Reason: Towards a History of Vanishing Present*. Cambridge: Harvard UP.

5 The essay by Graff (1989) holds a sound logic about what we mean by theory and reading practices in the classroom.

6 See Hawthorn, Jeremy. (1987). *Unlocking the Text: Fundamental Issues in Literary Theory*. London: Edward Arnold. He writes: *Critical method* is about a critic's attempt to understand or explicate a work in terms of its generic nature, or in terms of its relationship with its genesis, or in terms of the wider human problems with which it is concerned. *Critical Technique* is basically about comparison and analysis as Eliot would say in his essays on criticism. Furthermore, Critical Approach is less precise than method, but it covers both a critic's implicit or explicit theoretical assumptions and also his or her methods and techniques. Very often schools or types of criticism are referred to as "approaches," like the Marxist approach.

7 Ibid. *Response* is less favorable term that is in use these days but important to consider as what happens to us as a result of reading a work. It is also about immediate and unmediated reaction to the text. *Appreciation* is also a similar term but is old fashioned now. It privileges the authority of the text. *Evaluation* is a term that is more related to judicial mode but is ambivalently used in critical vocabulary. *Exegesis* comes from the tradition of biblical study and nowadays is used to understand the production of annotated scholarly editions of texts. Other critical activities are the following. *Scholarship* is the establishment of facts rather than interpretation, but the term is not detached to interpretation. *Explication* is uncovering the literary work's primary meaning or elucidation of textual cruces, baffling words in or in a section of literary works which seem not to make sense. Scholarship, explication, and interpretation are very closely related words.

8 Gayatri Chakravorty Spivak (2003) elaborates on the border crossing regarding the modes of research in Comparative Literature and Area Studies in *Death of a Discipline*. New York: Columbia University Press.

9 Women during menstruation are expelled and isolated in a distant hut, animal shed, etc. in miserable conditions. The practice is still prevalent in some countryside of Nepal despite the Supreme Court's verdict in 2005 against the practice.

10 See Adams, Hazard. (Ed.). (1992). *Critical Theory Since Plato*. Fort Worth, Harcourt Brace Jovanovich. (1128–30).

11 See p. 33 for the terms "theoretical enterprise" and "political" used in Bhabha, Homi. (2009). *The Location of Culture*. London: Routledge.

12 See (2002) "A Report on the Present State of Health of the Gods and Goddesses in South Asia" in *Time Warps*. Delhi: permanent black. The essay does not feature in the anthology.

13 Gayatri Spivak's text is not used in this anthology though her ideas and issues are used in various exercises when appropriate.

14 R Radhakrishnan's text too does not feature in this anthology.

15 See Suleri, Sara (1992). "Edmund Burke and the Indian Sublime" in *The Rhetoric of English India*. Chicago: The University of Chicago Press (24–48). Suleri's work too does not appear in the anthology.

16 See https://www.youtube.com/watch?v=9ABmMC6zC8I.

LITERARY THEORY AND CRITICISM

17 See Viswanathan, Gauri: "Colonialism and the Construction of Hinduism" and Smith, David "Orientalism and Hinduism" in Flood, Gavin (2003). *The Blackwell Companion to Hinduism*. Oxford: Blackwell.

18 The phantom in Sanskrit is *Phishacha*.

19 *Betalpachisi* is a popular short story written in Hindi.

20 Kit Walker is the name of the twenty-first Phantom who is the hero of the comic strip *The Phantom* by Lee Falk. He lives in Bangalla, an imaginary country in Africa. In the early episodes the location of Phantom's heroism was somewhere near India, only later the place was replaced by African region. His abode is in a modified cave in a deep forest. The cave is a treasure room of chronicles and rare mythical and historical objects like the snake that killed Egyptian queen Cleopatra, legendary Kind Arthurs's sword, Excalibur, and Shakespearean play, *Hamlet*'s original script. The comic strip was very popular up till the late twentieth century.

21 See Xie, Shaobo (1997). "Rethinking the Problem of Postcolonialism" in *New Literary History* 28.1 (7–19), Mishra, Vijaya & Bob Hodge (2005): "What was Postcolonialism" in New Literary History. 36.3 (375–402), and Huggan, Graham (2013). "Introduction" in *The Oxford Handbook of Postcolonial Studies*. New Delhi: OUP.

22 I deliberately use "him" to contextualize an event. From 2011 to 2016, Gayatri Spivak almost regularly visited the Institute of Advanced Communication, Education, and Research (IACER) in Kathmandu to work with the researchers to develop methodologies regarding Rethinking South Asian Studies. A local journalist praised her global scholarly contribution but also wrote that she is a difficult writer. It is kind of patriarchal racism, she told me looking at the Himalayan mountains.

23 See chapter "Debate on Explanation on History and Sociology" in Durkhheim, Emile. *The Rules of Sociological Method*. Ed. Steven Lukes. (1982). Trans. W.D. Halls. New York: The Free Press.

24 See for example pages 169–71 when he talks about types and stratum in "Introduction" in Weber, Max. *Complete Writing on Academic and Political Vocations*. Ed. John Dreijmanis. (2008). Trans. Gordon C. Wells. New York: Algora.

25 Birbhum is a district in West Bengal, India. Prof. Spivak is a teacher at a remote village school there. She divides her time between Columbia University and the Birbhum school.

26 For the history of social science methodology see Schram, Sanford F., & Brian Caterino. (Eds.). (2006). *Making Political Science Matter: Debating Knowledge, Research, and Method*. New York: New York UP.

27 For apriorism and falsificationism in economics see Sapiro J. Latsis. (1980). "A Research Programme in Economics" in Sapiro, J. Latsis. Ed. *Methods and Appraisal in Economics*. London: Cambridge UP. Mises writes: "The fact that man does not have the creative power to imagine categories at variance with the fundamental logical relations and with the principles of causality and teleology enjoins upon us what may be called *methodological apriorism*" (35); also see pages 38ff, and 64 in the sections "The A Priory and Reality" and "The Procedure of Economics" in Mises, Ludwig, von (1963) *Human Action: A Treatise on Economics*. 4th revised ed. San Francisco: Fox & Wilkes. For further reference see Robbins, Lionel. C. (1945). *An Essay on the Nature and Significance of Economic Science*. 2nd ed. London: Macmillan.

28 The two the methodological orientations in geography are the following: How spaces are set up and organised and what the relationship between and among such arrangements are. In the context of such arrangements how do we address human identity, territorial identity like nation and state, and many other issues ranging from environment to technology? A geographical paradigm as a body of literature that forms assumptions about how a thing is and how should we critique it (see "Introduction" by John Paul Jones III and Basil Gomez and "Theorizing our World" by Ian Graham Ronald Shaw et al. in Basil Gomez Gomez, Basil, & John Paul Jones III. (Eds.). (2010). *Research Methods in Geography: A Critical Introduction*. Singapore: Wiley-Blackwell.) The basic question from the point of view of post-structuralist paradigm of geography (Shaw et al., 2010, 19) may be to inquire how the colonial institutions constructed the spaces of the colonized. The Post-structuralist geographical paradigm

INTRODUCTION

is about how space is socially constructed. Consequently, expanded questions may be how space is transformed into parts, regions, and continents, conceived as real and imaginative, as climatic and political regions, as ideal and sinful, as virtual and physical, separated into men's and women's, into power-spaces? The other significant methodology is about Discrete Causality (causality of *a* causing *b* or *a* causing *b*, and *b* also affecting *a*) and Embedded Causality (instead of *a* causing *b*, the method talks about multiple phenomena involved in complicated and multiple causality (Shaw et al., 2010, 14).

29 Learning by concepts have different considerations in mathematics which uses symbols (natural science uses % for percentage), and social science uses by words to express concepts (Ruane: 2005, p. 47). Ruane writes: "Concepts are not part of the empirical world. Concepts are *mental abstractions* and as such they are the antithesis of concrete empiricism." . . . "Concepts work their way into research via theory. At some point in your college education, you've no doubt been introduced to social theory. Theories are sets of logically related or linked ideas (abstractions) about how the world or some process works. The fundamental building blocks of theory are concepts. In other words, theories consist of a series of statements (propositions) about relationships between concepts" (48). "If theory offers *ideas* (concepts) about how the world works, research is about empirically documenting (showing) whether or not those ideas are correct. Consequently, research can be seen as either an effort to (a) test established theory or (b) generate new theory. (Research conducted to test established theory is called *deductive research*; research that starts in the empirical realm and tries to generate theory is called *inductive research*.) In either scenario, research must encounter concepts. Good research either begins with or ends in the realm of concepts and theory" (49). Social science aims at field research and observation. He writes: "After all, field research is essentially about people-watching. It entails spending time observing the normal or natural flow of social life in some specific social/cultural setting. Field research involves an extremely systematic and rigorous study of everyday life. Field researchers are committed to long-term observation" (164). Ruane, Janet M. (2005) *Essentials of Research Methods: A Guide to Social Science Research*. Oxford: Blackwell.

30 see Derrida, Jacques in Bibliography.

31 See Bibliography for Jeremy Hawthorn "Introductory" *Unlocking the Text: Fundamental Issues in Literary Theory*.

32 "It is entirely legitimate to conclude that when Condillac uses the term "abstraction," it can be "translated" as metaphor or, if one agrees with the point that was made with reference to Locke about the self-totalising transformation of all tropes, as trope. As soon as one is willing to be made aware of their epistemological implications, concepts are tropes and tropes concepts . . . no discourse would be conceivable that does not make use of abstractions: "[abstractions] are certainly absolutely necessary" (*AI*, 1996, 43). He further writes that allegory which is "sequential and narrative" ("Pascal's Allegory of Persuasion" *AI*,51). "Allegory is the purveyor of demanding truths. . . (*AI, 51*). All such motifs are the methods of literature since literature is woven around figurativeness, narratives, and allegories. One more thing: literature works with concepts and concepts are not figures like de Man says, "irony is not a concept" (*AI*, 164). De Man engages in an elaborate discussion on Irony as a concept or not in *Resistance to Theory*. Also see Cleanth Brooks' *The Well Wrought Urn* as a parallel reading with De Man.

33 In the Indic literary critical tradition, Yaksa's concept of *Upama* in his text *Nirukta*, Bhamaha and Dandin of *alankara* tradition and subsequent tradition of poetics have elaborate discourses on tropes and figurativeness. Kashmiri critics Udbhata and Vamana, and Rudrata later continued alankara criticism. Dhanamjaya and Kuntaka are two other major names. Kuntaka's "vakroti" as evasive language or the language of metaphor and suggestiveness in *Vakrotijivita* emphasises the very nature of language which shapes literature. "Poetry is that word and sense together enshrined in a style revealing the artistic creativity of the poet on the one hand and giving delight to the man of taste on the other.... That 'meaning' is what is signified, and 'word' is that which signifies, is so well known that it needs no elaboration" (Kuntaka "Language of Poetry and Metaphor" in G. N. Devy. (Ed.). (2007). *Indian Literary Criticism: Theory and Interpretation*. Hyderabad: Orient Longman, 47).

North Indian Mahima, Bhoja, Rudrabhatta, and Mammata, Ruyyaka, Southeast Indian Vidyadhara, Vidyanatha, and Visvanatha, and AppayyaDiksita are some of the significant names. I have not included the dramaturgists.

34 See Bibliography.

35 For a detail study see White, Hayden. (1987). *The Content of the Form: Narrative Discourse and Historical Representation*. Baltimore: The Johns Hopkins University Press.

Bibliography

Adams, Hazard (Ed.). (1992). *Critical Theory Since Plato*. Fort Worth, Harcourt Brace Jovanovich. pp. 1128–30.

Ahmad, Aijaz. (2000). *In Theory: Classes, Nations, Literatures*. London: Verso.

Aristotle. (2011). *Nicomachean Ethics*. Trans. Robert C. Bartlett and Susan D. Collins. Chicago: University of Chicago Press.

Barthes, Roland (1992). "Structuralist Activity" in Hazard Adams (Ed.). *Critical Theory Since Plato*. Fort Worth, Harcourt Brace Jovanovich. (1128–30).

Beteille, A. (1998). "The Comparative Method and the Standpoint of the Investigator" in *Sociological Bulletin*, Vol. 47, No. 2, pp. 137–154.

Bhabha, Homi. (1992). (Ed.). "DissemiNation: Time, Narrative, and the Margins of the Modern Nation" in *Nation and Narration*. New York: Routledge (291–322).

Bhabha, Homi. (1994). *The Location of Culture*. New York: Routledge.

Blaug, M. (1980). "Kuhn vs Lakatos or Paradigms vs Research Programmes in the History of Economics" in *Methods and Appraisal in Economics*. Ed. Sapiro J. Latsis. London: Cambridge University Press (149–180).

Brooks, Cleanth. (1970). *The Well Wrought Urn: Studies in the Structure of Poetry*. Florida: Harcourt Brace.

Chakrabarty, Dipesh. (2000). "Introduction: in *Provincializing Europe: Postcolonial Thought and Historical Difference*. Princeton: Princeton University Press. (p 6).

Culler, Jonathan. (1992). "Literary Interpretation" in *Introduction to Scholarship in Modern Languages and Literatures*, Ed. Joseph Gibaldi. 2nd ed. New York: MLA.

De Man, Paul. (1996). "The Epistemology of Metaphor" in *Aesthetic Ideology (Theory and History of Literature. Vol. 65)*. Minneapolis: U of Minnesota P. 34–50

———. (2006). *The Resistance to Theory: Theory and History of Literature*. Vol. 33. 6th ed. Minneapolis: U of Minnesota P.

Derrida, Jacques. (1967). "Structure, Sign, and Play in the Discourses of the Human Sciences" in *Writing and Difference*. Trans. Alan Bass. London: Routledge (351–70).

———. (1981). *Dissemination*. Trans. Barbara Johnson. New York: University of Chicago.

———. (2001). "The Future of the Profession or the University Without Condition (Thanks to the "Humanities," What *Could Take Place Tomorrow*)" in *Jacques Derrida and the Humanities: A Critical Reader*. Ed. Tom Cohen. Cambridge: CUP (24–57).

Dreijmanis, J. (Ed.). (2008). "Introduction" in Max Weber's Complete Writings on Academic and Political Vocations. Trans. Gordon C. Wells. New York: Algora (1–23).

Durkheim, Emile. (1982). *The Rules of Sociological Method*. Ed. Steven Lukes. Trans. W.D. Halls. New York: Free Press.

Flyvbjerg, Bent. (2001). *Making Social Science Matter: Why Social Science Fails and How It Can Succeed Again*. Trans. Steven Sampson. Cambridge: CUP.

Fish, Stanley. (1980). *Is There a Text in This Class? The Authority of Interpretive Communities*. Cambridge. Harvard University Press.

Graff, Gerald. (1989). "The Future of Theory in the Teaching of literature." in *The Future of Literary Theory*. Ed. Ralph Cohen. New York: Routledge (250–67).

INTRODUCTION

Hawthorn, Jermey. (1987). "Introductory" in *Unlocking the Text: Fundamental Issues in Literary Theory*. London: Hodder Arnold (3–33).

Hicks, Sir John. (1980). "'Revolutions' in Economics" in *Methods and Appraisal in Economics*. Ed. Sapiro J. Latsis. London: Cambridge University Press (207–218).

Huggan, Graham (2013). "Introduction" in *The Oxford Handbook of Postcolonial Studies*. New Delhi: OUP.

Jones III, John Paul. (2010). ""Introduction" and "Theorizing our World"" in *Research Methods in Geography: A Critical Introduction*. Ed. Basil Gomez and John Paul Jones III. Singapore: Wiley-Blackwell (1–25).

Kuntaka. (2007). "Language of Poetry and Metaphor" in *Indian Literary Criticism: Theory and Interpretation*. Ed. G.N. Devy. Hyderabad: Orient Longman (46–60).

Latsis, Sapiro J. (1980). "A Research Programme in Economics" in *Methods and Appraisal in Economics*. Ed. Sapiro J Latsis. London: Cambridge University Press (1–41).

Ludwig von, Mises. (1963). "The Procedure of Economics" in *Human Action: A Treatise on Economics*. 4th revised ed. San Francisco: Fox & Wilkes. (64–68).

Mani, Lata. (2016). "Introduction" in *SacredSecular*. London: Routledge. (1–4).

Martin, Emily. (1999). "The Egg and the Sperm: How Science has Constructed a Romance Based on Stereotypical Male-Female Roles" in Janet Price & Margrit Shildrick. (eds). *Feminist Theory and Body: A Reader*. New York: Routlege.

Mishra, Vijaya & Bob Hodge (2005): "What was Postcolonialism" in *New Literary History*. 36.3 (375–402).

Nussbaum, Martha. (1989). "Perceptive Equilibrium: Literary Theory and Ethical Theory" in *The Future of Literary Theory*. Ed. Ralph Cohen. New York: Routledge (58–85).

Pennings, Paul, Hans Keman, & Jan Kleinnijenhuis. (eds). (2006). *Doing Research in Political Science: An Introduction to Comparative Methods and Statistics*. 2nd ed. London: SAGE.

Popper, Karl R. (1962). *Conjectures and Refutations: The Growth of Scientific Knowledge*. New York: Basic Books.

Robbins, Lionel C. (1945). *An Essay on the Nature and Significance of Economic Science*. 2nd ed. London: Macmillan.

Rhoads, Bruce L. and David Wilson. (2010). "Observing Our World" in *Research Methods in Geography: A Critical Introduction*. Ed. Basil Gomez and John Paul Jones III. Singapore: Wiley-Blackwell (26–40).

Ruane, Janet M. (2005). *Essentials of Research Methods: A Guide to Social Science Research*. Oxford: Blackwell.

Said, Edward W. (2008). *Music at the Limits: Three Decades of Essays and Articles on Music*. London: Bloomsbury.

Sapiro, J. Latsis. (1980). "A Research Programme in Economics" in *Methods and Appraisal in Economics*. Ed. J. Latsis Sapiro. London: Cambridge University Press (1–43).

Schram, Sanford F. and Brian Caterino (eds). (2006). *Making Political ScienceMmatter: Debating Knowledge, Research, and Method*. New York: New York UP.

Shaw, Ian Graham Ronald. (2010). "Theorizing our World" in *Research Methods in Geography: A Critical Introduction*. Ed. Basil Gomez and John Paul Jones III. Singapore: Wiley-Blackwell (9–25).

Spivak, Gayatri Chakravorty. (1989). *In Other Worlds: Essays in Cultural Politics*. New York: Metheun.

Spivak, Gayatri Chakravorty. (1999). "Literature" in *A Critique of Postcolonial Reason: Toward a History of the Vanishing Present*. Cambridge: Harvard UP (112–197).

———. (2003). *Death of a Discipline*. Calcutta: Seagull.

———. (2008). *Other Asias*. Malden: Blackwell.

———. (2013). "Culture: Situating Feminism" in *Aesthetic Education in the Era of Globalization*. London: Harvard UP (119–136).

Suleri, Sara (1992). "Edmund Burke and the Indian Sublime" in *The Rhetoric of English India*. Chicago: The University of Chicago Press (24–48).

Viswanathan, Gauri.(2003). "Colonialism and the Construction of Hinduism" in *The Blackwell Companion to Hinduism*. Ed. Flood, Gavin. Oxford: Blackwell.

Shelley, P. B. (1970). "The Cloud" in *The Norton Anthology of Poetry*. Margaret Ferguson et al. *Shorter Fourth Edition*. New York: W. W. Norton & Company.

Smith, David. (2003). "Orientalism and Hinduism" in *The Blackwell Companion to Hinduism*. Ed. Flood, Gavin. Oxford: Blackwell.

Weber, Max. (2005). *The Protestant Spirit and the Spirit of Capitalism*. London: Routledge-E-library.

Wellek, Rene and Austin, Warren. (1987). *Theory of Literature*. Revised ed. New York: Harcourt Brace, 1984.

White, Hayden. (1987). *The Content of the Form: Narrative Discourse and Historical Representation*. Baltimore: Johns Hopkins University Press.

Xie, Shaobo (1997). "Rethinking the Problem of Postcolonialism" in *New Literary History* 28.1 (7–19).

Part I

THEORY

1

DISSEMINATION

Time, narrative, and the margins of the modern nation[1]

Homi Bhabha

(In memory of Paul Moritz Strimpel (1914–87):

Pforzheim – Paris – Zurich – Ahmedabad – Bombay – Milan – Lugano.)

The time of the nation

1   The title of my essay – DissemiNation – owes something to the wit and wisdom of Jacques Derrida, but something more to my own experience of migration. I have lived that moment of the scattering of the people that in other times and other places, in the nations of others, becomes a time of gathering. Gatherings of exiles and emigrés and refugees, gathering on the edge of 'foreign' cultures; gathering at the frontiers; gatherings in the ghettos or cafés of city centres; gathering in the half-life, half-light of foreign tongues, or in the uncanny fluency of another's language; gathering the signs of approval and acceptance, degrees, discourses, disciplines; gathering the memories of underdevelopment, of other worlds lived retroactively; gathering the past in a ritual of revival; gathering the present. Also the gathering of the people in the diaspora: indentured, migrant, interned; the gathering of incriminatory statistics, educational performance, legal statutes, immigration status – the genealogy of that lonely figure that John Berger named the seventh man. The gathering of clouds from which the Palestinian poet Mahmoud Darwish asks 'where should the birds fly after the last sky?'

2   In the midst of these lonely gatherings of the scattered people, their myths and fantasies and experiences, there emerges a historical fact of singular importance. More deliberately than any other general historian, Eric Hobsbawm[2] writes the history of the modern western nation from the perspective of the nation's margin and the migrants' exile. The emergence of the later phase of the modern nation, from the midnineteenth century, is also one of the most sustained periods of mass migration within the west, and colonial expansion in the east. The nation fills the void left in the uprooting of communities and kin, and turns that loss into the language of metaphor. Metaphor, as the etymology of the word suggests, transfers the meaning of home and belonging, across the 'middle passage', or the central European steppes, across those distances, and cultural differences, that span the imagined community of the nation-people.

DOI: 10.4324/9781003213857-1

35

LITERARY THEORY AND CRITICISM

3   The discourse of national*ism* is not my main concern. In some ways it is the historical certainty and settled nature of that term against which I am attempting to write of
the western nation as an obscure and ubiquitous form of living the *locality* of culture.
This locality is more *around* temporality than *about* historicity: a form of living that
is more complex than 'community'; more symbolic than 'society'; more connotative
than 'country'; less patriotic than *patrie*; more rhetorical than the reason of state; more
mythological than ideology; less homogeneous than hegemony; less centred than the
citizen; more collective than 'the subject'; more psychic than civility; more hybrid in
the articulation of cultural differences and identifications – gender, race or class – than
can be represented in any hierarchical or binary structuring of social antagonism.

4   In proposing this cultural construction of nationness as a form of social and textual
affiliation, I do not wish to deny these categories their specific historicities and particular meanings within different political languages. What I am attempting to formulate
in this essay are the complex strategies of cultural identification and discursive address
that function in the name of 'the people' or 'the nation' and make them the immanent
subjects and objects of a range of social and literary narratives. My emphasis on the
temporal dimension in the inscription of these political entities – that are also potent
symbolic and affective sources of cultural identity – serves to displace the historicism
that has dominated discussions of the nation as a cultural force. The focus on temporality resists the transparent linear equivalence of event and idea that historicism proposes; it provides a perspective on the disjunctive forms of representation that signify
a people, a nation, or a national culture. It is neither the sociological solidity of these
terms, nor their holistic history that gives them the narrative and psychological force
that they have brought to bear on cultural production and projections. It is the mark
of the ambivalence of the nation as a narrative strategy – and an apparatus of power
– that it produces a continual slippage into analogous, even metonymic, categories,
like the people, minorities, or 'cultural difference' that continually overlap in the act
of writing the nation. What is displayed in this displacement and repetition of terms is
the nation as the measure of the liminality of cultural modernity.

5   Edward Said aspires to such secular interpretation in his concept of 'wordliness'
where 'sensuous particularity as well as historical contingency...exist *at the same level
of surface particularity* as the textual object itself' (my emphasis).[3] Fredric Jameson
invokes something similar in his notion of 'situational consciousness' or national allegory, 'where the telling of the individual story and the individual experience cannot
but ultimately involve the whole laborious telling of the collectivity itself'.[4] And Julia
Kristeva speaks perhaps too hastily of the pleasures of exile – 'How can one avoid
sinking into the mire of common sense, if not by becoming a stranger to one's own
country, language, sex and identity?'[5] – without realizing how fully the shadow of the
nation falls on the condition of exile – which may partly explain her own later, labile
identifications with the images of *other* nations: 'China', 'America'. The nation as metaphor: *Amor Patria*; *Fatherland*; *Pig Earth*; *Mothertongue*; *Matigari*; *Middlemarch*;
Midnight's Children; *One Hundred Years of Solitude*; *War and Peace*; *I Promessi
Sposi*; *Kanthapura*; *Moby Dick*; *The Magic Mountain*; *Things Fall Apart*.

6   There must also be a tribe of interpreters of such metaphors – the translators of
the dissemination of texts and discourses across cultures – who can perform what
Said describes as the act of secular interpretation. 'To take account of this horizontal,

36

secular space of the crowded spectacle of the modern nation...implies that no single explanation sending one back immediately to a single origin is adequate. And just as there are no simple dynastic answers, there are no simple discrete formations or social processes'.[6] If, in our travelling theory, we are alive to the *metaphoricity* of the peoples of imagined communities – migrant or metropolitan –then we shall find that the space of the modern nation-people is never simply horizontal. Their metaphoric movement requires a kind of 'doubleness' in writing; a temporality of representation that moves between cultural formations and social processes without a 'centred' causal logic. And such cultural movements disperse the homogeneous, visual time of the horizontal society because 'the present is no longer a mother-form [read mother-tongue or mother-land] around which are gathered and differentiated the future (present) and the past (present)...[as] a present of which the past and the future would be but modifications'.[7] The secular language of interpretation then needs to go beyond the presence of the 'look', that Said recommends, if we are to give 'the nonsequential energy of lived historical memory and subjectivity its appropriate narrative authority. We need another time of *writing* that will be able to inscribe the ambivalent and chiasmatic intersections of time and place that constitute the problematic 'modern' experience of the western nation.

7   How does one write the nation's modernity as the event of the everyday and the advent of the epochal? The language of national belonging comes laden with atavistic apologues, which has led Benedict Anderson to ask: 'But why do nations celebrate their hoariness, not their astonishing youth?'[8] The nation's claim to modernity, as an autonomous or sovereign form of political rationality, is particularly questionable if, with Partha Chatterjee, we adopt the post-colonial perspective:

> Nationalism...seeks to represent itself in the image of the Enlightenment and fails to do so. For Enlightenment itself, to assert its sovereignty as the universal ideal, needs its Other; if it could ever actualise itself in the real world as the truly universal, it would in fact destroy itself.[9]

Such ideological ambivalence nicely supports Gellner's paradoxical point that the historical necessity of the idea of the nation conflicts with the contingent and arbitrary signs and symbols that signify the affective life of the national culture. The nation may exemplify modern social cohesion but

> Nationalism is not what it seems, and above all not what it seems to itself... The cultural shreds and patches used by nationalism are often arbitrary historical inventions. Any old shred would have served as well. But in no way does it follow that the principle of nationalism...is itself in the least contingent and accidental.[10]

The problematic boundaries of modernity are enacted in these ambivalent temporalities of the nation-space. The language of culture and community is poised on the fissures of the present becoming the rhetorical figures of a national past. Historians transfixed on the event and origins of the nation never ask, and political theorists possessed of the 'modern' totalities of the nation – 'Homogeneity, literacy and anonymity are the key traits'[11] – never pose, the awkward question of the disjunctive representation of the social, in this double-time of the nation. It is indeed only in the disjunctive time of the nation's modernity – as a knowledge disjunct between political rationality and its impasse, between the shreds and patches of cultural signification and the certainties of a nationalist pedagogy – that questions of nation as narration come to be posed. How do we plot the narrative of the nation that must mediate between the teleology of progress tipping over into the 'timeless' discourse of irrationality? How do we understand that 'homogeneity' of modernity – the people – which, if pushed too far, may assume something resembling the archaic body of the despotic or totalitarian mass? In the midst of progress and modernity, the language of ambivalence reveals a politics 'without duration', as Althusser once provocatively wrote: 'Space without places, time without duration.'[12] To write the story of the nation demands that we articulate that archaic ambivalence that informs modernity. We may begin by questioning that progressive metaphor of modern social cohesion – *the many as one* –shared by organic theories of the holism of culture and community, and by theorists who treat gender, class, or race as radically 'expressive' social totalities.

8   *Out of many one*: nowhere has this founding dictum of the political society of the modern nation – its spatial expression of a unitary people – found a more intriguing *image* of itself than in those diverse languages of literary criticism that seek to portray the great power of the idea of the nation in the disclosures of its everyday life; in the telling details that emerge as metaphors for national life. I am reminded of Bakhtin's wonderful description of a 'national' *vision of emergence* in Goethe's *Italian Journey*, which represents the triumph of the realistic component over the Romantic. Goethe's realist narrative produces a national-historical time that makes visible a specifically Italian day in the detail of its passing time, 'The bells ring, the rosary is said, the maid enters the room with a lighted lamp and says: *Felicissima notte! ...*If one were to force a German clockhand on them, they would be at a loss.'[13] For Bakhtin it is Goethe's vision of the microscopic, elementary, perhaps random tolling of everyday life in Italy that reveals the profound history of its locality (*Lokalität*), the spatialization of historical time, 'a creative humanization of this locality, which transforms a part of terrestrial space into a place of historical life for people'.[14]

9   The recurrent metaphor of landscape as the inscape of national identity emphasizes the quality of light, the question of social visibility, the power of the eye to naturalize the rhetoric of national affiliation and its forms of collective expression. There is, however, always the distracting presence of another temporality that disturbs the contemporaneity of the national present, as we saw in the national discourses with which I began. Despite Bakhtin's emphasis on the realist vision in the emergence of the nation in Goethe's work, he acknowledges that the origin of the nation's visual *presence* is the effect of a narrative struggle. From the beginning, Bakhtin writes, the realist and Romantic conceptions of time co-exist in Goethe's work, but the ghostly (*Gespenstermässiges*), the terrifying (*Unerfreuliches*), and the unaccountable (*Unzuberechnendes*) are consistently 'surmounted' by the structural aspects of the visualization of time: 'the necessity of the past and the necessity of its place in a line of continuous development...finally the aspect of the past being linked to a necessary future'.[15] National time becomes concrete and visible in the chronotope of the local, particular, graphic, from beginning to end. The narrative

structure of this *historical* surmounting of the 'ghostly' or the 'double' is seen in the intensification of narrative synchrony as a graphically visible position in space: 'to grasp the most elusive course of pure historical time and fix it through unmediated contemplation'.[16] But what kind of 'present' is this if it is a consistent process of surmounting the ghostly time of repetition? Can this national time-space be as fixed or as immediately visible as Bakhtin claims?

10 If in Bakhtin's 'surmounting' we hear the echo of another use of that word by Freud in his essay on *The Uncanny*, then we begin to get a sense of the complex time of the national narrative. Freud associates *surmounting* with the repressions of a 'cultural' unconscious; a liminal, uncertain state of cultural belief when the archaic emerges in the midst or margins of modernity as a result of some psychic ambivalence or intellectual uncertainty. The 'double' is the figure most frequently associated with this uncanny process of 'the doubling, dividing and interchanging of the self'.[17] Such 'double-time' cannot be so simply represented as visible or flexible in 'unmediated contemplation'; nor can we accept Bakhtin's repeated attempt to read the national space as achieved only in the *fullness of time*. Such an apprehension of the 'double and split' time of national representation, as I am proposing, leads us to question the homogeneous and horizontal view familiarly associated with it. We are led to ask, provocatively, whether the *emergence* of a national perspective – of an élite or subaltern nature – within a culture of social contestation, can ever articulate its 'representative' authority in that fullness of narrative time, and that visual synchrony of the sign that Bakhtin proposes.

11 Two brilliant accounts of the emergence of national narratives seem to support my suggestion. They represent the diametrically opposed world views of master and slave which between them account for the major historical and philosophical dialectic of modern times. I am thinking of John Barrell's[18] splendid analysis of the rhetorical and perspectival status of the 'English gentleman' within the social diversity of the eighteenth-century novel; and of Huston Baker's innovative reading of the 'new *national* modes of sounding, interpreting and speaking the Negro in the Harlem Renaissance'.[19] In his concluding essay Barrell surveys the positions open to 'an equal, wide survey' and demonstrates how the demand for a holistic, representative vision of society could only be represented in a discourse that was *at the same time* obsessively fixed upon, and uncertain of, the boundaries of society, and the margins of the text. For instance, the hypostatized 'common language' which was the language of the gentleman whether he be Observer, Spectator, Rambler, 'Common to all by virtue of the fact that it manifested the peculiarities of none'[20] – was primarily defined through a process of negation – of regionalism, occupation, faculty – so that this centred vision of 'the gentleman' is so to speak 'a condition of empty potential, one who is imagined as being able to comprehend everything, and yet who may give no evidence of having comprehended anything'.[21] A different note of liminality is struck in Baker's description of the 'radical maroonage' that structured the emergence of an insurgent Afro-American expressive culture in its expansive, 'national' phase. Baker's sense that the 'discursive project' of the Harlem Renaissance is modernist is based less on a strictly literary understanding of the term, and more appropriately on the agonistic enunciative conditions within which the Harlem Renaissance shaped its cultural practice. The transgressive, invasive structure of the black 'national' text, which thrives on rhetorical strategies of hybridity,

deformation, masking, and inversion, is developed through an extended analogy with the guerilla warfare that became a way of life for the maroon communities of runaway slaves and fugitives who lived dangerously, and insubordinately, 'on the frontiers or margins of *all* American promise, profit and modes of production'. From this liminal, minority position where, as Foucault would say, the relations of discourse are of the nature of warfare, emerges the force of the people of an Afro-American nation, as Baker 'signifies upon' the extended metaphor of maroonage. For warriors read writers or even 'signs':

> these highly adaptable and mobile warriors took maximum advantage of local environments, striking and withdrawing with great rapidity, making extensive use of bushes to catch their adversaries in cross-fire, fighting only when and where they chose, depending on reliable intelligence networks among non-maroons (both slave and white settlers) and often communicating by horns.[22]

Both gentleman and slave, with different cultural means and to very different historical ends, demonstrate that forces of social authority and subalternality may emerge in displaced, even decentred, strategies of signification. This does not prevent them from being representative in a political sense, although it does suggest that positions of authority are themselves part of a process of ambivalent identification. Indeed the exercise of power may be both more politically effective and psychically *affective* because their discursive liminality may provide greater scope for strategic manoeuvre and negotiation. It is precisely in reading between these borderlines of the nation-space that we can see how the 'people' come to be constructed within a range of discourses as a double narrative movement. The people are not simply historical events or parts of a patriotic body politic. They are also a complex rhetorical strategy of social reference where the claim to be representative provokes a crisis within the process of signification and discursive address. We then have a contested cultural territory where the people must be thought in a double-time; the people are the historical 'objects' of a nationalist pedagogy, giving the discourse an authority that is based on the pregiven or constituted historical origin or event; the people are also the 'subjects' of a process of signification that must erase any prior or originary presence of the nation-people to demonstrate the prodigious, living principle of the people as that continual process by which the national life is redeemed and signified as a repeating and reproductive process. The scraps, patches, and rags of daily life must be repeatedly turned into the signs of a national culture, while the very act of the narrative performance interpellates a growing circle of national subjects. In the production of the nation as narration there is a split between the continuist, accumulative temporality of the pedagogical, and the repetitious, recursive strategy of the performative. It is through this process of splitting that the conceptual ambivalence of modern society becomes the site of *writing the nation*.

The space of the people

12 The tension between the pedagogical and the performative that I have identified in the narrative address of the nation, turns the reference to a 'people' – from whatever political or cultural position it is made – into a problem of knowledge that haunts the

symbolic formation of social authority. The people are neither the beginning or the end of the national narrative; they represent the cutting edge between the totalizing powers of the social and the forces that signify the more specific address to contentious, unequal interests and identities within the population. The ambivalent signifying system of the nation-space participates in a more general genesis of ideology in modern societies that Claude Lefort has described so suggestively. For him too it is 'the enigma of language', at once internal and external to the speaking subject, that provides the most apt analogue for imagining the structure of ambivalence that constitutes modern social authority. I shall quote him at length, because his rich ability to represent the *movement of* political power *beyond* the blindness of Ideology or the insight of the Idea, brings him to that liminality of modern society from which I have attempted to derive the narrative of the nation and its people.

> In Ideology the representation of the rule is split off from the effective operation of it...The rule is thus extracted from experience of language; it is circumscribed, made fully visible and assumed to govern the conditions of possibility of this experience...The enigma of language – namely that it is both internal and external to the speaking subject, that there is an articulation of the self with others which marks the emergence of the self and which the self does not control – is concealed by the representation of a place 'outside' – language from which it could be generated...We encounter the ambiguity of the representation as soon as the rule is stated; for its very exhibition undermines the power that the rule claims to introduce into practice. *This exorbitant power must, in fact, be shown, and at the same time it must owe nothing to the movement which makes it appear ...To be true to its image, the rule must be abstracted from any question concerning its origin; thus it goes beyond the operations that it controls.... Only the authority of the master allows the contradiction to be concealed, but he is himself an object of representation; presented as possessor of the knowledge of the rule, he allows the contradiction to appear through himself.*
>
> The ideological discourse that we are examining has no safety catch; it is rendered vulnerable by its attempt to make visible the place from which the social relation would be conceivable (both thinkable and creatable) by its inability to define this place without letting its contingency appear, without condemning itself to slide from one position to another, without hereby making apparent the instability of an order that it is intended to raise to the status of essence.... [The ideological] task of the implicit generalisation of knowledge and the implicit homogenization of experience could fall apart in the face of the unbearable ordeal of the collapse of certainty, of the vacillation of representations of discourse and as a result of the splitting of the subject.[23]

How do we conceive of the 'splitting' of the national subject? How do we articulate cultural differences within this vacillation of ideology in which the national discourse also participates, sliding ambivalently from one enunciatory position to another? What comes to be represented in that unruly 'time' of national culture, which Bakhtin surmounts in his reading of Goethe, Gellner associates with the rags and patches of everyday life, Said describes as 'the nonsequential energy of lived historical memory and subjectivity' and Lefort re-presents again as the inexorable *movement of signification* that both constitutes the exorbitant image of power and deprives it of the certainty and stability of centre or closure? What might be the cultural and political effects of the liminality of the nation, the margins of modernity, which cannot be signified without the narrative temporalities of splitting, ambivalence, and vacillation?

13 Deprived of the unmediated visibility of historicism 'looking to the legitimacy of past generations as supplying cultural autonomy'[24] – the nation turns from being the symbol of modernity into becoming the symptom of an ethnography of the 'contemporary' within culture. Such a shift in perspective emerges from an acknowledgement of the nation's interrupted address, articulated in the tension signifying the people as an *a priori* historical presence, a pedagogical object; and the people constructed in the performance of narrative, its enunciatory 'present' marked in the repetition and pulsation of the national sign. The pedagogical founds its narrative authority in a tradition of the people, described by Poulantzas[25] as a moment of becoming designated by *itself*, encapsulated in a succession of historical moments that represents an eternity produced by self-generation. The performative intervenes in the sovereignty of the nation's *self-generation* by casting a shadow between the people as 'image' and its signification as a differentiating sign of Self, distinct from the Other or the Outside. In place of the polarity of a prefigurative self-generating nation itself and extrinsic Other nations, the performative introduces a temporality of the 'in-between' through the 'gap' or 'emptiness' of the signifier that punctuates linguistic difference. The boundary that marks the nation's selfhood interrupts the self-generating time of national production with a space of representation that threatens binary division with its difference. The barred Nation *It/Self*, alienated from its eternal self-generation, becomes a liminal form of social representation, a space that is *internally* marked by cultural difference and the heterogeneous histories of contending peoples, antagonistic authorities, and tense cultural locations.

14 This double-writing or dissemi-*nation*, is not simply a theoretical exercise in the internal contradictions of the modern liberal nation. The structure of cultural liminality – *within the nation* – that I have been trying to elaborate would be an essential precondition for a concept such as Raymond Williams' crucial distinction between residual and emergent practices in oppositional cultures which require, he insists, a 'nonmetaphysical, non-subjectivist' mode of explanation. Such a space of cultural signification as I have attempted to open up through the intervention of the performative, would meet this important precondition. The liminal figure of the nation-space would ensure that no political ideologies could claim transcendent or metaphysical authority for themselves. This is because the subject of cultural discourse – the agency of a people – is split in the discursive ambivalence that emerges in the contestation of narrative authority between the pedagogical and the performative. This disjunctive temporality of the nation would provide the appropriate time-frame for representing those residual and emergent meanings and practices that Williams locates in the margins of the contemporary experience of society. Their designation depends upon a kind of social ellipsis; their transformational power depends upon their being historically displaced:

DISSEMINATION

> But in certain areas, there will be in certain periods, practices and meanings
> which are not reached for. There will be areas of practice and meaning which,
> almost by definition from its own limited character, or in its profound defor-
> mation, the dominant culture is unable in any real terms to recognize.[26]

When Edward Said suggests that the question of the nation should be put on the contemporary critical agenda as a hermeneutic of 'worldliness', he is fully aware that such a demand can only now be made from the liminal and ambivalent boundaries that articulate the signs of national culture, as 'zones of control *or* of abandonment, of recollection *and* of forgetting, of force *or* of dependence, of exclusiveness *or* of sharing' (my emphasis).[27]

15   Counter-narratives of the nation that continually evoke and erase its totalizing boundaries – both actual and conceptual – disturb those ideological manoeuvres through which 'imagined communities' are given essentialist identities. For the political unity of the nation consists in a continual displacement of its irredeemably plural modern space, bounded by different, even hostile nations, into a signifying space that is archaic and mythical, paradoxically representing the nation's modern territoriality, in the patriotic, atavistic temporality of Traditionalism. Quite simply, the difference of space returns as the Sameness of time, turning Territory into Tradition, turning the People into One. The liminal point of this ideological displacement is the turning of the differentiated spatial boundary, the 'outside', into the unified temporal territory of Tradition. Freud's concept of the 'narcissism of minor differences'[28] – reinterpreted for our purposes – provides a way of understanding how easily that boundary that secures the cohesive limits of the western nation may imperceptibly turn into a contentious *internal* liminality that provides a place from which to speak both of, and as, the minority, the exilic, the marginal, and the emergent.

16   Freud uses the analogy of feuds that prevail between communities with adjoining territories – the Spanish and the Portuguese, for instance – to illustrate the ambivalent identification of love and hate that binds a community together: 'it is always possible to bind together a considerable number of people in love, so long as there are other people left to receive the manifestation of their aggressiveness'.[29] The problem is, of course, that the ambivalent identifications of love and hate occupy the same psychic space; and paranoid projections 'outwards' return to haunt and split the place from which they are made. So long as a firm boundary is maintained between the territories, and the narcissistic wounded is contained, the aggressivity will be projected onto the Other or the Outside. But what if, as I have argued, the people are the articulation of a doubling of the national address, an ambivalent *movement* between the discourses of pedagogy and the performative? What if, as Lefort argues, the subject of modern ideology is split between the iconic image of authority and the movement of the signifier that produces the image, so that the 'sign' of the social is condemned to slide ceaselessly from one position to another? It is in this space of liminality, in the 'unbearable ordeal of the collapse of certainty' that we encounter once again the narcissistic neuroses of the national discourse with which I began. The nation is no longer the sign of modernity under which cultural differences are homogenized in the 'horizontal' view of society. The nation reveals, in its ambivalent and vacillating representation,

LITERARY THEORY AND CRITICISM

the ethnography of its own historicity and opens up the possibility of other narratives of the people and their difference.

17   The people turn *pagan* in that disseminatory act of social narrative that Lyotard defines, against the Platonic tradition, as the privileged pole of the *narrated*, 'where the one doing the speaking speaks from the place of the referent. As narrator she is narrated as well. And in a way she is already told, and what she herself is *telling* will not undo that somewhere else she is *told*'.[30] This narrative inversion or circulation – which is in the spirit of my splitting of the people – makes untenable any supremacist, or nationalist claims to cultural mastery, for the position of narrative control is neither monocular or monologic. The subject is graspable only in the passage between telling/told, between 'here' and 'somewhere else', and in this double scene the very condition of cultural knowledge is the alienation of the subject. The significance of this narrative splitting of the subject of identification is borne out in Lévi-Strauss' description of the ethnographic act.[31] The ethnographic demands that the observer himself is a part of his observation and this requires that the field of knowledge – the total social fact – must be appropriated from the outside like a thing, but like a thing which comprises within itself the subjective understanding of the indigenous. The transposition of this process into the language of the outsider's grasp – this entry into the area of the symbolic of representation/signification – then makes the social fact 'three dimensional'. For ethnography demands that the subject has to split itself into object and subject in the process of identifying its field of knowledge; the ethnographic object is constituted 'by dint of the subject's capacity for indefinite selfobjectification (without ever quite abolishing itself as subject) for projecting outside itself ever-diminishing fragments of itself'.

18   Once the liminality of the nation-space is established, and its 'difference' is turned from the boundary 'outside' to its finitude 'within', the threat of cultural difference is no longer a problem of 'other' people. It becomes a question of the otherness of the people-as-one. The national subject splits in the ethnographic perspective of culture's contemporaneity and provides both a theoretical position and a narrative authority for marginal voices or minority discourse. They no longer need to address their strategies of opposition to a horizon of 'hegemony' that is envisaged as horizontal and homogeneous. The great contribution of Foucault's last published work is to suggest that people emerge in the modern state as a perpetual movement of 'the marginal integration of individuals'. 'What are we to-day?'[32] Foucault poses this most pertinent ethnographic question to the west itself to reveal the alterity of its political rationality. He suggests that the 'reason of state' in the modern nation must be derived from the heterogeneous and differentiated limits of its territory. The nation cannot be conceived in a state of *equilibrium* between several elements co-ordinated, and maintained by a 'good' law.

> Each state is in permanent competition with other countries, other nations... so that each state has nothing before it other than an indefinite future of struggles. Politics has now to deal with an irreducible multiplicity of states struggling and competing in a limited history...the State is its own finality.[33]

What is politically significant is the effect of this finality of the state on the liminality of the representation of the people. The people will no longer be contained in that national discourse of the teleology of progress; the anonymity of individuals; the spatial horizontality of community; the homogeneous time of social narratives; the historicist visibility of modernity, where 'the present of each level [of the social] coincides with the present of all the others, so that the present is an *essential* section which makes the essence *visible*'.[34] The finitude of the nation emphasizes the impossibility of such an expressive totality with its alliance between an immanent, plenitudinous present and the eternal visibility of a past. The liminality of the people – their double inscription as pedagogical objects and performative subjects – demands a 'time' of narrative that is disavowed in the discourse of historicism where narrative is only the agency of the event, or the medium of a naturalistic continuity of Community or Tradition. In describing the marginalistic integration of the individual in the social totality, Foucault provides a useful description of the rationality of the modern nation. Its main characteristic, he writes,

> is neither the constitution of the state, the coldest of cold monsters, nor the rise of bourgeois individualism. I won't even say it is the constant effort to integrate individuals into the political totality. I think that the main characteristic of our political rationality is the fact that this integration of the individuals in a community or in a totality results from a constant correlation between an increasing individualisation and the reinforcement of this totality. From this point of view we can understand why modern political rationality is permitted by the antinomy between law and order.[35]

From *Discipline and Punish* we have learned that the most individuated are those subjects who are placed on the margins of the social, so that the tension between law and order may produce the disciplinary or pastoral society. Having placed the people on the limits of the nation's narrative, I now want to explore forms of cultural identity and political solidarity that emerge from the disjunctive temporalities of the national culture. This is a lesson of history to be learnt from those peoples whose histories of marginality have been most profoundly enmeshed in the antinomies of law and order – the colonized and women.

Of margins and minorities

19   The difficulty of writing the history of the people as the insurmountable agonism of the living, the incommensurable experiences of struggle and survival in the construction of a national culture, is nowhere better seen than in Frantz Fanon's essay *On National Culture*.[36] I start with it because it is a warning against the intellectual appropriation of the culture of the people (whatever they may be) within a representationalist discourse that may be fixed and reified in the annals of History. Fanon writes against that form of historicism that assumes that there is a moment when the differential temporalities of cultural histories coalesce in an immediately readable present. For my purposes, he focuses on the time of cultural representation, instead of immediately historicizing the event. He explores the space of the nation without immediately identifying it with the historical institution of the state. As my concern here is not with the history of

nationalist movements, but only with certain traditions of writing that have attempted to construct narratives of the imaginary of the nation-people, I am indebted to Fanon for liberating a certain, uncertain time of the people. The knowledge of the people depends on the discovery, Fanon says, 'of a much more fundamental substance which itself is continually being renewed', a structure of repetition that is not visible in the translucidity of the people's customs or the obvious objectivities which seem to characterize the people. 'Culture abhors simplification', Fanon writes, as he tries to locate the people in a performative time: 'the fluctuating movement that the people are *just* giving shape to'. The present of the people's history, then, is a practice that destroys the constant principles of the national culture that attempt to hark back to a 'true' national past, which is often represented in the reified forms of realism and stereotype. Such pedagogical knowledges and continuist national narratives miss the 'zone of occult instability where the people dwell' (Fanon's phrase). It is from this *instability* of cultural signification that the national culture comes to be articulated as a dialectic of various temporalities – modern, colonial, postcolonial, 'native' – that cannot be a knowledge that is stabilized in its enunciation: 'it is always contemporaneous with the act of recitation. It is the present act that on each of its occurrences marshalls in the ephemeral temporality inhabiting the space between the "I have heard" and "you will hear"'.[37]

20   I have heard this narrative movement of the post-colonial people, in their attempts to create a national culture. Its implicit critique of the fixed and stable forms of the nationalist narrative makes it imperative to question those western theories of the horizontal, homogeneous empty time of the nation's narrative. Does the language of culture's 'occult instability' have a relevance outside the situation of anti-colonial struggle? Does the incommensurable act of living – so often dismissed as ethical or empirical – have its own ambivalent narrative, its own history of theory? Can it change the way we identify the symbolic structure of the western nation?

21   A similar exploration of political time has a salutary feminist history in *Women's Time*.[38] It has rarely been acknowledged that Kristeva's celebrated essay of that title has its conjunctural, cultural history, not simply in psychoanalysis and semiotics, but in a powerful critique and redefinition of the nation as a space for the emergence of feminist political and psychic identifications. The nation as a symbolic denominator is, according to Kristeva, a powerful repository of cultural knowledge that erases the rationalist and progressivist logics of the 'canonical' nation. This symbolic history of the national culture is inscribed in the strange temporality of the future perfect, the effects of which are not dissimilar to Fanon's occult instability. In such a historical time, the deeply repressed past initiates a strategy of repetition that disturbs the sociological totalities within which we recognize the modernity of the national culture – a little too forcibly for, or against, the reason of state, or the unreason of ideological misrecognition.

22   The borders of the nation are, Kristeva claims, constantly faced with a double temporality: the process of identity constituted by historical sedimentation (the pedagogical); and the loss of identity in the signifying process of cultural identification (the performative). The time and space of Kristeva's construction of the nation's finitude is analogous to my argument that it is from the liminality of the national culture that

the figure of the people emerges in the narrative ambivalence of disjunctive times and meanings. The concurrent circulation of linear, cursive, and monumental time, in the same cultural space, constitutes a new historical temporality that Kristeva identifies with psychoanalytically informed, feminist strategies of political identification. What is remarkable is her insistence that the gendered sign can hold such exorbitant historical times together.

23   The political effects of Kristeva's multiple, and splitting, women's time leads to what she calls the 'demassification of difference'. The cultural moment of Fanon's 'occult instability' signifies the people in a fluctuating movement *which they are just giving shape to*, so that postcolonial time questions the teleological traditions of past and present, and the polarized historicist *sensibility* of the archaic and the modern. These are not simply attempts to invert the balance of power within an unchanged order of discourse. Fanon and Kristeva seek to redefine the symbolic process through which the social imaginary – nation, culture, or community – become subjects of discourse, and objects of psychic identification. In attempting to shift, through these differential temporalities, the alignment of subject and object in the culture of community, they force us to rethink the relation between the time of meaning and the sign of history *within* those languages, political or literary, which designate the people 'as one'. They challenge us to think the question of community and communication *without* the moment of transcendence; their excessive cultural temporalities are in contention but their difference cannot be negated or sublated. How do we understand such forms of social contradiction?

24   Cultural identification is then poised on the brink of what Kristeva calls the 'loss of identity' or Fanon describes as a profound cultural 'undecidability'. The people as a form of address emerge from the abyss of enunciation where the subject splits, the signifier 'fades', the pedagogical and the performative are agonistically articulated. The language of national collectivity and cohesiveness is now at stake. Neither can cultural homogeneity, or the nation's horizontal space be authoritatively represented within the familiar territory of the *public sphere*: social causality cannot be adequately understood as a deterministic or overdetermined effect of a 'statist' centre; nor can the rationality of political choice be divided between the polar realms of the private and the public. The narrative of national cohesion can no longer be signified, in Anderson's words, as a 'sociological solidity'[39] fixed in a 'succession of *plurals*' – hospitals, prisons, remote villages – where the social space is clearly bounded by such repeated objects that represent a naturalistic, national horizon.

25   Such a pluralism of the national sign, where difference returns as the same, is contested by the signifier's 'loss of identity' that inscribes the narrative of the people in the ambivalent, 'double' writing of the performative and the pedagogical. The iterative temporality that marks the movement of meaning *between* the masterful image of the people and the movement of its sign interrupts the succession of plurals that produce the sociological solidity of the national narrative. The nation's totality is confronted with, and crossed by, a supplementary movement of writing. The heterogeneous structure of Derridean supplementarity in *writing* closely follows the agonistic, ambivalent movement between the pedagogical and performative that informs the nation's narrative address. A supplement, according to one meaning, 'cumulates and accumulates

LITERARY THEORY AND CRITICISM

presence. It is thus that art, *techne*, image, representation, convention, etc. come as supplements to nature and are rich with this entire cumulating function' (pedagogical).[40] The *double entendre* of the supplement suggests, however, that 'It intervenes or insinuates itself *in-the-place-of* .... If it represents and makes an image it is by the *anterior* default of a presence...the supplement is an adjunct, a subaltern instance.... As substitute, it is not simply added to the positivity of a presence, it produces no relief.... Somewhere, something can be filled up *of itself*...only by allowing itself to be filled through sign and proxy' (performative).[41] It is in this supplementary space of doubling – *not plurality* – where the image is presence and proxy, where the sign supplements and empties nature, that the exorbitant, disjunctive times of Fanon and Kristeva can be turned into the discourses of emergent cultural identities, within a nonpluralistic politics of difference.

26   This supplementary space of cultural signification that opens up – and holds together – the performative and the pedagogical, provides a narrative structure characteristic of modern political rationality: the marginal integration of individuals in a repetitious movement between the antinomies of law and order. It is from the liminal movement of the culture of the nation – at once opened up and held together – that minority discourse emerges. Its strategy of intervention is similar to what parliamentary procedure recognizes as a supplementary question. It is a question that is supplementary to what is put down on the order paper, but by being 'after' the original, or in 'addition to' it, gives it the advantage of introducing a sense of 'secondariness' or belatedness into the structure of the original. The supplementary strategy suggests that adding 'to' need not 'add up' but may disturb the calculation. As Gasché has succinctly suggested, 'supplements...are pluses that compensate for a minus in the origin'.[42] The supplementary strategy interrupts the successive seriality of the narrative of plurals and pluralism by radically changing their mode of articulation. In the metaphor of the national community as the 'many as one', the *one* is now both the tendency to totalize the social in a homogenous empty time, and the repetition of that minus in the origin, the less-than-one that intervenes with a metonymic, iterative temporality. One cultural effect of such a metonymic interruption in the representation of the people, is apparent in Julia Kristeva's political writings. If we elide her concepts of women's time and female exile, then she seems to argue that the 'singularity' of woman – her representation as fragmentation and drive – produces a dissidence, and a distanciation, within the symbolic bond itself which demystifies 'the *community* of language as a universal and unifying tool, one which totalises and equalises'.[43] The minority does not simply confront the pedagogical, or powerful master-discourse with a contradictory or negating referent. It does not turn contradiction into a dialectical process. It interrogates its object by initially withholding its objective. Insinuating itself into the terms of reference of the dominant discourse, the supplementary antagonizes the implicit power to generalize, to produce the sociological solidity. The questioning of the supplement is not a repetitive rhetoric of the 'end' of society but a meditation on the disposition of space and time from which the narrative of the nation must *begin*. The power of supplementarity is not the negation of the preconstituted social contradictions of the past or present; its force lies – as we shall see in the discussion of *Handsworth Songs* that follows – in the renegotiation of those times, terms, and traditions through which we turn our uncertain, passing contemporaneity into the signs of history.

DISSEMINATION

27   *Handsworth Songs*,[44] is a film made by the Black Audio Collective during the uprisings of 1985, in the Handsworth district of Birmingham, England. Shot in the midst of the uprising, it is haunted by two moments: the arrival of the migrant population in the 1950s, and the emergence of a black British peoples in the diaspora. And the film itself is part of the emergence of a black British cultural politics. Between the moments of arrival and emergence is the incommensurable movement of the present; the filmic time of a continual displacement of narrative; the time of oppression and resistance; the time of the performance of the riots, cut across by the pedagogical knowledges of state institutions, the racism of statistics and documents and newspapers, and then the perplexed living of Handsworth songs, and memories that flash up in a moment of danger.

28   Two memories repeat incessantly to translate the living perplexity of history, into the time of migration: the arrival of the ship laden with immigrants from the ex-colonies, just stepping off the boat, always just emerging – as in the phantasmatic scenario of Freud's family romance – into the land where the streets are paved with gold. Another image is of the perplexity and power of an emergent peoples, caught in the shot of a dreadlocked rastaman cutting a swathe through a posse of policemen. It is a memory that flashes incessantly through the film: a dangerous repetition in the present of the cinematic frame; the edge of human life that translates what will come next and what has gone before in the writing of History. Listen to the repetition of the time and space of the peoples that I have been trying to create:

> In time we will demand the impossible in order to wrestle, from it that which is possible, In time the streets will claim me without apology, In time I will be right to say that there are no stories…in the riots only the ghosts of other stories.

The symbolic demand of cultural difference constitutes a history in the midst of the uprising. From the desire of the possible in the impossible, in the historic present of the riots, emerge the ghostly repetition of other stories, other uprisings: Broadwater Farm, Southall, St. Paul's, Bristol. In the ghostly repetition of the black woman of Lozells Rd, Handsworth, who sees the future in the past: There are no stories in the riots, only the ghosts of other stories, she told a local journalist: 'You can see Enoch Powell in 1969, Michael X in 1965'. And from that gathering repetition she builds a history.

29   From across the film listen to another woman who speaks another historical language. From the archaic world of metaphor, caught in the movement of the people she translates the time of change into the ebb and flow of language's unmastering rhythm: the successive time of instaneity, battening against the straight horizons and the flow of water and words:

> I walk with my back to the sea, horizons straight ahead
> Wave the sea away and back it comes,
> Step and I slip on it.
> Crawling in my journey's footsteps
> When I stand it fills my bones.

The perplexity of the living must not be understood as some existential, ethical anguish of the empiricism of everyday life in 'the eternal living present', that gives liberal discourse a rich social reference in moral and cultural relativism. Nor must it be too hastily associated with the spontaneous and primordial *presence* of the people in the liberatory discourses of populist ressentiment. In the construction of this discourse of 'living perplexity' that I am attempting to produce we must remember that the space of human life is pushed to its incommensurable extreme; the judgement of living is perplexed; the topos of the narrative is neither the transcendental, pedagogical Idea of history nor the institution of the state, but a strange temporality of the repetition of the one in the other – an oscillating movement in the governing *present* of cultural authority.

30   Minority discourse sets the act of emergence in the antagonistic *in-between* of image and sign, the accumulative and the adjunct, presence and proxy. It contests genealogies of 'origin' that lead to claims for cultural supremacy and historical priority. Minority discourse acknowledges the status of national culture – and the people – as a contentious, performative space of the perplexity of the living in the midst of the pedagogical representations of the fullness of life. Now there is no reason to believe that such marks of difference – the incommensurable time of the subject of culture – cannot inscribe a 'history' of the people or become the gathering points of political solidarity. They will not, however, celebrate the monumentality of historicist memory, the sociological solidity or totality of society, or the homogeneity of cultural experience. The discourse of the minority reveals the insurmountable ambivalence that structures the *equivocal* movement of historical time. How does one encounter the past as an anteriority that continually introduces an otherness or alterity within the present? How does one then narrate the present as a form of contemporaneity that is always belated? In what historical time do such configurations of cultural difference assume forms of cultural and political authority?

Social anonymity and cultural anomie

31   The narrative of the modern nation can only begin, Benedict Anderson suggests in *Imagined Communities*, once the notion of the 'arbitrariness of the sign' fissures the sacral ontology of the medieval world and its overwhelming visual and aural imaginary. By 'separating language from reality' (Anderson's formulation), the arbitrary signifier enables a national temporality of the 'meanwhile', a form of 'homogenous empty time'; the time of cultural modernity that supersedes the prophetic notion of simultaneity-along-time. The narrative of the 'meanwhile' permits 'transverse, cross-time, marked not by prefiguring and fulfilment, but by temporal coincidence, and measured by clock and calendar'.[45] Such a form of temporality produces a symbolic structure of the nation as 'imagined community' which, in keeping with the scale and diversity of the modern nation, works like the plot of a realist novel. The steady onward clocking of calendrical time, in Anderson's words, gives the imagined world of the nation a sociological solidity; it links together diverse acts and actors on the national stage who are entirely unaware of each other, except as a function of this synchronicity of time which is not prefigurative but a form of civil contemporaneity realized in the *fullness* of time.

DISSEMINATION

32   Anderson historicizes the emergence of the arbitrary sign of language – and here he is talking of the process of signification rather than the progress of narrative – as that which had to come before the narrative of the modern nation could begin. In decentring the prophetic visibility and simultaneity of medieval systems of dynastic representation, the homogeneous and horizontal community of modern society can emerge. The people-nation, however divided and split, can still assume, in the function of the social imaginary, a form of democratic 'anonymity'. However there is a profound ascesis in the sign of the anonymity of the modern community and the time – *meanwhile* – of its narrative consciousness, as Anderson explains it. It must be stressed that the narrative of the imagined community is constructed from two incommensurable temporalities of meaning that threaten its coherence. The space of the arbitrary sign, its separation of language and reality, enables Anderson to stress the imaginary or mythical nature of the society of the nation. However, the differential time of the arbitrary sign is neither synchronous nor serial. In the separation of language and reality – in the *process* of signification – there is no epistemological equivalence of subject and object, no possibility of the mimesis of meaning. The sign temporalizes the iterative difference that circulates within language, of which meaning is made, but cannot be represented thematically within narrative as a homogeneous empty time. Such a temporality is antithetical to the alterity of the sign which, in keeping with my account of the supplementary nature of cultural signification, singularizes and alienates the holism of the imagined community. From that place of the 'meanwhile', where cultural homogeneity and democratic anonymity make their claims on the national community, there emerges a more instantaneous and subaltern voice of the people, a minority discourse that speaks betwixt and between times and places.

33   Having initially located the imagined community of the nation in the homogeneous time of realist narrative, towards the end of his essay Anderson abandons the 'meanwhile' – his pedagogical temporality of the people. In order to represent the collective voice of the people as a performative discourse of public identification, a process he calls unisonance, Anderson resorts to another time of narrative. Unisonance is 'that special kind of contemporaneous community which language alone suggests',[46] and this patriotic speech-act is not written in the synchronic, novelistic 'meanwhile', but inscribed in a sudden primordiality of meaning that 'looms up *imperceptibly* out of a horizonless past' (my emphasis).[47] This movement of the sign cannot simply be historicized in the emergence of the realist narrative of the novel. It is at this point in the narrative of national time that the unisonant discourse produces its collective identification of the people, not as some transcendent national identity, but in a language of incommensurable doubleness that arises from the ambivalent splitting of the pedagogical and the performative. The people emerge in an uncanny simulacral moment of their 'present' history as 'a ghostly intimation of simultanaeity across homogeneous empty time'. The weight of the words of the national discourse comes from an '*as it were* – Ancestral Englishness'.[48] It is precisely this repetitive *time* of the alienating anterior – rather than origin – that Lévi-Strauss writes of, when, in explaining the 'unconscious unity' of signification, he suggests that 'language can only have arisen all at once. Things cannot have begun to *signify* gradually'.[49] In that sudden timelessness of 'all at once', there is not synchrony but a break, not simultaneity but a spatial disjunction.

51

LITERARY THEORY AND CRITICISM

34   The 'meanwhile' is the barred sign of the processual and performative, not a simple present continuous, but the present as succession without synchrony – the iteration of the arbitrary sign of the modern nation-space. In embedding the *meanwhile* of the national narrative, where the people live their plural and autonomous lives within homogeneous empty time, Anderson misses the alienating and iterative time of the sign. He naturalizes the momentary 'suddenness' of the arbitrary sign, its pulsation, by making it part of the historical emergence of the novel, a narrative of synchrony. But the suddenness of the signifier is incessant, instantaneous rather than simultaneous. It introduces a signifying space of repetition rather than a progressive or linear seriality. The 'meanwhile' turns into quite another time, or ambivalent sign, of the national people. If it is the time of the people's anonymity it is also the space of the nation's anomie.

35   How are we to understand this anteriority of signification as a position of social and cultural knowledge, this time of the 'before' of signification, which will not issue harmoniously into the present like the continuity of tradition – invented or otherwise? It has its own national history in Renan's 'Qu'est ce qu'une nation?' which has been the starting point for a number of the most influential accounts of the modern emergence of the nation – Kamenka, Gellner, Benedict Anderson, Tzvetan Todorov. It is the way in which the pedagogical presence of modernity – the Will to be a nation – introduces into the enunciative present of the nation a differential and iterative time of reinscription that interests me. Renan argues that the non-naturalist principle of the modern nation is represented in the *will* to nationhood – not in the identities of race, language, or territory. It is the will that unifies historical memory and secures present-day consent. The will is, indeed, the articulation of the nation-people:

> A nation's existence is, if you will pardon the metaphor, a daily plebiscite, just as an individual's existence is a perpetual affirmation of life.... The wish of nations, is all in all, the sole legitimate criteria, the one to which one must always return.[50]

Does the will to nationhood circulate in the same temporality as the desire of the daily plebiscite? Could it be that the iterative plebiscite decentres the totalizing pedagogy of the will? Renan's will is itself the site of a strange forgetting of the history of the nation's past: the violence involved in establishing the nation's writ. It is this forgetting – a minus in the origin – that constitutes the *beginning* of the nation's narrative. It is the syntactical and rhetorical arrangement of this argument that is more illuminating than any frankly historical or ideological reading. Listen to the complexity of this form of forgetting which is the moment in which the national will is articulated: 'yet every French citizen has to have forgotten *[is obliged to have forgotten]* Saint Bartholomew's Night's Massacre, or the massacres that took place in the Midi in the thirteenth century.'[51]

36   It is through this syntax of forgetting – or being obliged to forget – that the problematic identification of a national people becomes visible. The national subject is produced in that place where the daily plebiscite – the unitary number – circulates in the grand narrative of the will. However, the equivalence of will and plebiscite, the identity of part and whole, past and present, is cut across by the 'obligation to forget',

or forgetting to remember. This is again the moment of anteriority of the nation's sign that entirely changes our understanding of the pastness of the past, and the unified present of the will to nationhood. We are in a discursive space similar to that moment of unisonance in Anderson's argument when the homogenous empty time of the nation's 'meanwhile' is cut across by the ghostly simultaneity of a temporality of doubling and repetition. To be obliged to forget – in the construction of the national present – is not a question of historical memory; it is the construction of a discourse on society that *performs* the problematic totalization of the national will. That strange time – forgetting to remember – is a place of 'partial identification' inscribed in the daily plebiscite which represents the performative discourse of the people. Renan's pedagogical return to the will to nationhood is both constituted and confronted by the circulation of numbers in the plebiscite which break down the identity of the will – it is an instance of the supplementary that 'adds to' without 'adding up'. May I remind you of Lefort's suggestive description of the ideological impact of suffrage in the nineteenth century, where the danger of numbers was considered almost more threatening than the mob: 'the idea of number as such is opposed to the idea of the substance of society. Number breaks down unity, destroys identity.'[52] It is the repetition of the national sign as numerical succession rather than synchrony that reveals that strange temporality of disavowal implicit in the national memory. Being obliged to forget becomes the basis for remembering the nation, peopling it anew, imagining the possibility of other contending and liberating forms of cultural identification.

37   Anderson fails to locate the alienating time of the arbitrary sign in his naturalized, nationalized space of the imagined community. Although he borrows his notion of the homogeneous empty time of the nation's modern narrative from Walter Benjamin, he fails to read that profound ambivalence that Benjamin places deep within the utterance of the narrative of modernity. Here, as the pedagogies of life and will contest the perplexed histories of the living people, their cultures of survival and resistance, Benjamin introduces a non-synchronous, incommensurable gap in the midst of storytelling. From this split in the utterance, from the unbeguiled, belated novelist there emerges an ambivalence in the narration of modern society that repeats, uncounselled and unconsolable, in the midst of plenitude:

> The novelist has isolated himself. The birthplace of the novel is the solitary individual, who is no longer able to express himself by giving examples of his most important concerns, is himself uncounselled and cannot counsel others. To write a novel means to carry the incommensurable to extremes in the representation of human life. In the midst of life's fullness, and through the representation of this fullness, the novel gives evidence of the profound perplexity of the living.[53]

It is from this incommensurability in the midst of the everyday that the nation speaks its disjunctive narrative. It begins, if that's the word, from that anterior space within the arbitrary sign which disturbs the homogenizing myth of cultural anonymity. From the margins of modernity, at the insurmountable extremes of storytelling, we encounter the question of cultural difference as the perplexity of living, and writing, the nation.

Cultural difference

38 Despite my use of the term 'cultural difference', I am not attempting to unify a body of theory, nor to suggest the mastery of a sovereign form of 'difference'. I am attempting some speculative fieldnotes on that intermittent time, and intersticial space, that emerges as a structure of undecidability at the frontiers of cultural hybridity. My interest lies only in that movement of meaning that occurs in the writing of cultures articulated in difference. I am attempting to discover the uncanny moment of cultural difference that emerges in the process of enunciation:

> Perhaps it is like the over-familiar that constantly eludes one; those familiar transparencies, which, although they conceal nothing in their density, are nevertheless not entirely clear. The enunciative level emerges in its very proximity.[54]

Cultural difference must not be understood as the free play of polarities and pluralities in the homogeneous empty time of the national community. It addresses the jarring of meanings and values generated in-between the variety and diversity associated with cultural plenitude; it represents the process of cultural interpretation formed in the perplexity of living, in the disjunctive, liminal space of national society that I have tried to trace. Cultural difference, as a form of intervention, participates in a supplementary logic of secondariness similar to the strategies of minority discourse. The question of cultural difference faces us with a disposition of knowledges or a distribution of practices that exist beside each other, *Abseits*, in a form of juxtaposition or contradiction that resists the teleology of dialectical sublation. In erasing the harmonious totalities of Culture, cultural difference articulates the difference between representations of social life without surmounting the space of incommensurable meanings and judgements that are produced within the process of trans-cultural negotiation.

39 The effect of such secondariness is not merely to change the 'object' of analysis – to focus, for instance, on race rather than gender or native knowledges rather than metropolitan myths; nor to invert the axis of political discrimination by installing the excluded term at the centre. The analytic of cultural difference intervenes to transform the scenario of articulation – not simply to disturb the rationale of discrimination. It changes the position of enunciation and the relations of address within it; not only what is said but from where it is said; not simply the logic of articulation but the *topos* of enunciation. The aim of cultural difference is to re-articulate the sum of knowledge from the perspective of the signifying *singularity* of the 'other' that resists totalization – the repetition that will not return as the same, the minus-in-origin that results in political and discursive strategies where adding-*to* does not add-up but serves to disturb the calculation of power and knowledge, producing other spaces of subaltern signification. The identity of cultural difference cannot, therefore, exist autonomously in relation to an object or a practice 'in-itself', for the identification of the subject of cultural discourse is dialogical or transferential in the style of psychoanalysis. It is constituted through the *locus* of the Other which suggests both that the object of identification is ambivalent, and, more significantly, that the agency of identification is never pure or holistic but always constituted in a process of substitution, displacement or projection.

40 Cultural difference does not simply represent the contention between oppositional contents or antagonistic traditions of cultural value. Cultural difference introduces into the process of cultural judgement and interpretation that sudden shock of the successive, nonsynchronic time of signification, or the interruption of the supplementary question that I elaborated above. The very possibility of cultural contestation, the ability to shift the ground of knowledges, or to engage in the 'war of position', depends not only on the refutation or substitution of concepts. The analytic of cultural difference attempts to engage with the 'anterior' space of the sign that structures the symbolic language of alternative, antagonistic cultural practices. To the extent to which all forms of cultural discourse are subject to the rule of signification, there can be no question of a simple negation or sublation of the contradictory or oppositional instance. Cultural difference marks the establishment of new forms of meaning, and strategies of identification, through processes of negotiation where no discursive authority can be established without revealing the difference of itself. The signs of cultural difference cannot then be unitary or individual forms of identity because their continual implication in other symbolic systems always leaves them 'incomplete' or open to cultural translation. What I am suggesting as the *uncanny* structure of cultural difference is close to Lévi-Strauss' understanding of 'the unconscious as providing the common and specific character of social facts...not because it harbours our most secret selves but because...it enables us to coincide with forms of activity which are both *at once ours and other*'.[55]

41 Cultural difference is to be found where the 'loss' of meaning enters, as a cutting edge, into the representation of the fullness of the demands of culture. It is not adequate simply to become aware of the semiotic systems that produce the signs of culture and their dissemination. Much more significantly we are faced with the challenge of reading, into the present of a specific cultural performance, the traces of all those diverse disciplinary discourses and institutions of knowledge that constitute the condition and contexts of culture. I use the word 'traces' to suggest a particular kind of discursive transformation that the analytic of cultural difference demands. To enter into the interdisciplinarity of cultural texts – through the anteriority of the arbitrary sign – means that we cannot contextualize the emergent cultural form by explaining it in terms of some pre-given discursive causality or origin. We must always keep open a supplementary space for the articulation of cultural knowledges that are adjacent and adjunct but not necessarily accumulative, teleological, or dialectical. The 'difference' of cultural knowledge that 'adds to' but does not 'add up' is the enemy of the *implicit* generalization of knowledge or the implicit homogenization of experience, to borrow Lefort's phrase.

42 Interdisciplinarity, as the discursive practice of cultural difference, elaborates a logic of intervention and interpretation that is similar to the supplementary question that I posed above. In keeping with its subaltern, substitutive – rather than synchronic – temporality, the subject of cultural difference is neither pluralistic nor relativistic. The frontiers of cultural difference are always belated or secondary in the sense that their hybridity is never simply a question of the admixture of pre-given identities or essences. Hybridity is the perplexity of the living as it interrupts the representation of the fullness of life; it is an instance of iteration, in the minority discourse, of the time of the arbitrary sign – 'the minus in the origin' – through which all forms of cultural meaning

are open to translation because their enunciation resists totalization. Interdisciplinarity is the acknowledgement of the emergent moment of culture produced in the ambivalent movement between the pedagogical and performative address, so that it is never simply the harmonious addition of contents or contexts that augment the positivity of a pre-given disciplinary or symbolic *presence*. In the restless drive for cultural translation, hybrid sites of meaning open up a cleavage in the language of culture which suggests that the similitude of the *symbol* as it plays across cultural sites must not obscure the fact that repetition of the *sign* is, in each specific social practice, both different and differential. It is in this sense that the enunciation of cultural difference emerges *in its proximity*; to traduce Foucault, we must not seek it in the 'visibility' of difference for it will elude us in that enigmatic transparency of writing that conceals nothing in its density but is nevertheless not clear.

43   Cultural difference emerges from the borderline moment of translation that Benjamin describes as the 'foreignness of languages'.[56] Translation represents only an extreme instance of the figurative fate of writing that repeatedly generates a movement of equivalence between representation and reference, but never gets beyond the equivocation of the sign. The 'foreignness' of language is the nucleus of the untranslatable that goes beyond the transparency of subject matter. The transfer of meaning can never be total between differential systems of meaning, or within them, for 'the language of translation envelops its content like a royal robe with ample folds...[it] signifies a more exalted language than its own and thus remains unsuited to its content, overpowering and alien'.[57] It is too often the slippage of signification that is celebrated, at the expense of this disturbing alienation, or overpowering of content. The erasure of content in the invisible but insistent structure of linguistic difference does not lead us to some general, formal acknowledgement of the function of the sign. The ill fitting robe of language alienates content in the sense that it deprives it of an immediate access to a stable or holistic reference 'outside' itself – in society. It suggests that social conditions are themselves being reinscribed or reconstituted in the very act of enunciation, revealing the instability of any division of meaning into an inside and outside. Content becomes the alien *mise en scene* that reveals the signifying structure of linguistic difference which is never seen for itself, but only glimpsed in the gap or the gaping of the garment. Benjamin's argument can be elaborated for a theory of cultural difference. It is only by engaging with what he calls the 'purer linguistic air' – the anteriority of the sign – that the reality-effect of content can be overpowered which then makes all cultural languages 'foreign' to themselves. And it is from this foreign perspective that it becomes possible to inscribe the specific locality of cultural systems – their incommensurable differences – and through that apprehension of difference, to perform the act of cultural translation. In the act of translation the 'given' content becomes alien and estranged; and that, in its turn, leaves the language of translation *Aufgabe*, always confronted by its double, the untranslatable – alien and foreign.

The foreignness of languages

44   At this point I must give way to the *vox populi*: to a relatively unspoken tradition of the people of the pagus – colonials, postcolonials, migrants, minorities – wandering peoples who will not be contained within the *Heim* of the national culture and its

unisonant discourse, but are themselves the marks of a shifting boundary that alienates the frontiers of the modern nation. They are Marx's reserve army of migrant labour who by speaking the foreignness of language split the patriotic voice of unisonance and become Nietzsche's mobile army of metaphors, metonyms, and anthropomorphisms. They articulate the death-in-life of the idea of the 'imagined community' of the nation; the worn-out metaphors of the resplendent national life now circulate in another narrative of entry permits and passports and work permits that at once preserve and proliferate, bind and breach the human rights of the nation. Across the accumulation of the history of the west there are those people who speak the encrypted discourse of the melancholic and the migrant. Theirs is a voice that opens up a void in some ways similar to what Abraham and Torok describe as a radical *antimetaphoric*: 'the destruction in fantasy, of the very act that makes metaphor possible – the act of putting the original oral void into words, the act of introjection'.[58] The lost object – the national *Heim* – is repeated in the void that at once prefigures and pre-empts the 'unisonant', which makes it *unheimlich*; analogous to the incorporation that becomes the daemonic double of introjection and identification. The object of loss is written across the bodies of the people, as it repeats in the silence that speaks the foreignness of language. A Turkish worker in Germany: in the words of John Berger:

> His migration is like an event in a dream dreamt by another. The migrant's intentionality is permeated by historical necessities of which neither he nor anybody he meets is aware. That is why it is as if his life were dreamt by another.... Abandon the metaphor.... They watch the gestures made and learn to imitate them...the repetition by which gesture is laid upon gesture, precisely but inexorably, the pile of gestures being stacked minute by minute, hour by hour is exhausting. The rate of work allows no time to prepare for the gesture. The body loses its mind in the gesture. How opaque the disguise of words.... He treated the sounds of the unknown language as if they were silence. To break through his silence. He learnt twenty words of the new language. But to his amazement at first, their meaning changed as he spoke them. He asked for coffee. What the words signified to the barman was that he was asking for coffee in a bar where he should not be asking for coffee. He learnt girl. What the word meant when he used it, was that he was a randy dog. Is it possible to see through the opaqueness of the words?[59]

Through the opaqueness of words we confront the historical memory of the western nation which is 'obliged to forget'. Having begun this essay with the nation's need for metaphor, I want to turn now to the desolate silences of the wandering people; to that 'oral void' that emerges when the Turk abandons the metaphor of a *heimlich* national culture: for the Turkish immigrant the final return is mythic, we are told, 'It is the stuff of longing and prayers...as imagined it never happens. There is no final return'.[60]

45   In the repetition of gesture after gesture, the dream dreamt by another, the mythical return, it is not simply the figure of repetition that is *unheimlich*, but the Turk's desire to survive, to name, to fix – which is unnamed by the gesture itself. The gesture continually overlaps and accumulates, without adding up to a knowledge of work or labour. Without the language that bridges knowledge and act, without the objectification of

the social process, the Turk leads the life of the double, the automaton. It is not the struggle of master and slave, but in the mechanical reproduction of gestures a mere imitation of life and labour. The opacity of language fails to translate or break through his silence and 'the body loses its mind in the gesture'. The gesture repeats and the body returns now, shrouded not in silence but eerily untranslated in the racist site of its enunciation: to say the word 'girl' is to be a randy dog, to ask for coffee is to encounter the colour bar.

46   The image of the body returns where there should only be its trace, as sign or letter. The Turk as dog is neither simply hallucination or phobia; it is a more complex form of social fantasy. Its ambivalence cannot be read as some simple racist/sexist projection where the white man's guilt is projected on the black man; his anxiety contained in the body of the white woman whose body screens (in both senses of the word) the racist fantasy. What such a reading leaves out is precisely the axis of identification – the desire of a man (white) for a man (black) – that underwrites that utterance and produces the paranoid 'delusion of reference', the man-dog that confronts the racist language with its own alterity, its foreignness.

47   The silent Other of gesture and failed speech becomes what Freud calls that 'haphazard member of the herd',[61] the Stranger, whose languageless presence evokes an archaic anxiety and aggressivity by impeding the search for narcissistic love-objects in which the subject can rediscover himself, and upon which the group's *amour propre* is based. If the immigrants' desire to 'imitate' language produces one void in the articulation of the social space – making present the opacity of language, its untranslatable residue – then the racist fantasy, which disavows the ambivalence of its desire, opens up another void in the present. The migrant's silence elicits those racist fantasies of purity and persecution that must always return from the Outside, to estrange the present of the life of the metropolis; to make it strangely familiar. In the process by which the paranoid position finally voids the place from where it speaks, we begin to see another history of the German language.

48   If the experience of the Turkish *Gastarbeiter* represents the radical incommensurability of translation, Salman Rushdie's *The Satanic Verses* attempts to redefine the boundaries of the western nation, so that the 'foreignness of languages' becomes the inescapable cultural condition for the enunciation of the mother-tongue. In the 'Rosa Diamond' section of *The Satanic Verses* Rushdie seems to suggest that it is only through the process of dissemi*Nation* – of meaning, time, peoples, cultural boundaries and historical traditions – that the radical alterity of the national culture will create new forms of living and writing: 'The trouble with the English is that their history happened overseas, so they don't know what it means'.[62]

49   S.S. Sisodia the soak – known also as Whisky Sisodia – stutters these words as part of his litany of 'what's wrong with the English'. The spirit of his words fleshes out the argument of this essay. I have suggested that the atavistic national past and its language of archaic belonging marginalizes the present of the 'modernity' of the national culture, rather like suggesting that history happens 'outside' the centre and core. More specifically I have argued that appeals to the national past must also be seen as the anterior space of signification that 'singularizes' the nation's cultural totality. It introduces a form of alterity of address that Rushdie embodies in the double narrative figures of Gibreel Farishta/Saladin Chamcha, or Gibreel Farishta/Sir Henry

DISSEMINATION

Diamond, which suggests that the national narrative is the site of an ambivalent identification; a margin of the uncertainty of cultural meaning that may become the space for an agonistic minority position. In the midst of life's fullness, and through the representation of this fullness, the novel gives evidence of the profound perplexity of the living. Gifted with phantom sight, Rosa Diamond, for whom repetition had become a comfort in her antiquity, represents the English *Heim* or homeland. The pageant of a 900 year-old history passes through her frail translucent body and inscribes itself, in a strange splitting of her language, 'the well-worn phrases, *unfinished business, grandstand view*, made her feel solid, unchanging, sempiternal, instead of the creature of cracks and absences she knew herself to be'.[63] Constructed from the well-worn pedagogies and pedigrees of national unity – her vision of the Battle of Hastings is the anchor of her being – and, at the same time, patched and fractured in the incommensurable perplexity of the nation's living, Rosa Diamond's green and pleasant garden is the spot where Gibreel Farishta lands when he falls out from the belly of the Boeing over sodden, southern England.

50   Gibreel masquerades in the clothes of Rosa's dead husband, Sir Henry Diamond, ex-colonial landowner, and through this post-colonial mimicry, exacerbates the discursive split between the image of a continuist national history and the 'cracks and absences' that she knew herself to be. What emerges, at one level, is a popular tale of secret, adulterous Argentinian amours, passion in the pampas with Martín de la Cruz. What is more significant and in tension with the exoticism, is the emergence of a hybrid national narrative that turns the nostalgic past into the disruptive 'anterior' and displaces the historical present – opens it up to other histories and incommensurable narrative subjects. The cut or split in enunciation – underlining all acts of utterance – emerges with its iterative temporality to reinscribe the figure of Rosa Diamond in a new and terrifying avatar. Gibreel, the migrant hybrid in masquerade, as Sir Henry Diamond, mimics the collaborative colonial ideologies of patriotism and patriarchy, depriving those narratives of their imperial authority. Gibreel's returning gaze crosses out the synchronous history of England, the essentialist memories of William the Conqueror and the Battle of Hastings. In the middle of an account of her punctual domestic routine with Sir Henry – sherry always at six – Rosa Diamond is overtaken by another time and memory of narration and through the 'grandstand view' of imperial history you can hear its cracks and absences speak with another voice:

> Then she began without bothering with once upon atime and whether it was all true or false he could see the fierce energy that was going into the telling... this memory jumbled rag-bag of material was in fact the very heart of her, her self-portrait.... So that it was not possible to distinguish memories from wishes, guilty reconstructions from confessional truths, because even on her deathbed Rosa Diamond did not know how to look her history in the eye.[64]

And what of Gibreel Farishta? Well he is the mote in the eye of history, its blind spot that will not let the nationalist gaze settle centrally. His mimicry of colonial masculinity and mimesis allows the absences of national history to speak in the ambivalent, ragbag narrative. But it is precisely this 'narrative sorcery' that established Gibreel's own re-entry into contemporary England. As the belated post-colonial he marginalizes and

59

LITERARY THEORY AND CRITICISM

singularizes the totality of national culture. He is the history that happened elsewhere, overseas; his postcolonial, migrant presence does not evoke a harmonious patchwork of cultures, but articulates the narrative of cultural difference which can never let the national history look at itself narcissistically in the eye. For the liminality of the western nation is the shadow of its own finitude: the colonial space played out in the imaginative geography of the metropolitan space; the repetition or return of the margin of the postcolonial migrant to alienate the holism of history. The postcolonial space is now 'supplementary' to the metropolitan centre; it stands in a subaltern, adjunct relation that doesn't aggrandise the *presence* of the west but redraws its frontiers in the menacing, agonistic boundary of cultural difference that never quite adds up, always less than one nation and double.

51   From this splitting of time and narrative emerges a strange, empowering knowledge for the migrant that is at once schizoid and subversive. In his guise as the Archangel Gibreel he sees the bleak history of the metropolis: 'the angry present of masks and parodies, stifled and twisted by the insupportable, unrejected burden of its past, staring into the bleakness of its impoverished future'.[65] From Rosa Diamond's decentred narrative 'without bothering with once upon atime' Gibreel becomes – however insanely – the principle of avenging repetition: 'These powerless English! – Did they not think that their history would return to haunt them? – "The native is an oppressed person whose permanent dream is to become the persecutor" (Fanon)...He would make this land anew. He was the Archangel, Gibreel – *And I'm back'*.[66]

52   If the lesson of Rosa's narrative is that the national memory is always the site of the hybridity of histories and the displacement of narratives, then through Gibreel, the avenging migrant, we learn the ambivalence of cultural difference: it is the articulation *through* incommensurability that structures all narratives of identification, and all acts of cultural translation.

> He was joined to the adversary, their arms locked around one another's bodies, mouth to mouth, head to tail...No more of these England induced ambiguities: those Biblical-satanic confusions...Quran 18:50 there it was as plain as the day...How much more practical, down to earth comprehensible...Iblis/ Shaitan standing for darkness; Gibreel for the light...O most devilish and slippery of cities...Well then the trouble with the English was their, Their – In a word Gibreel solemnly pronounces, that most naturalised sign of cultural difference...The trouble with the English was their...in a word...their weather.[67]

The English weather

53   To end with the English weather is to invoke, at once, the most changeable and immanent signs of national difference. It encourages memories of the 'deep' nation crafted in chalk and limestone; the quilted downs; the moors menaced by the wind; the quiet cathedral towns; that corner of a foreign field that is forever England. The English weather also revives memories of its daemonic double: the heat and dust of India; the dark emptiness of Africa; the tropical chaos that was deemed despotic and ungovernable and therefore worthy of the civilizing mission. These imaginative geographies that spanned countries and empires are changing; those imagined communities that played

DISSEMINATION

on the unisonant boundaries of the nation are singing with different voices. If I began with the scattering of the people across countries, I want to end with their gathering in the city. The return of the diasporic; the postcolonial.

54 *Handsworth Songs*; Fanon's manichean colonial Algiers; Rushdie's tropicalized London, grotesquely renamed *Ellowen Deeowen* in the migrant's mimicry: it is to the city that the migrants, the minorities, the diasporic come to change the history of the nation. If I have suggested that the people emerge in the finitude of the nation, marking the liminality of cultural identity, producing the double-edged discourse of social territories and temporalities, then in the west, and increasingly elsewhere, it is the city which provides the space in which emergent identifications and new social movements of the people are played out. It is there that, in our time, the perplexity of the living is most acutely experienced.

55 In the narrative graftings of my essay I have attempted no general theory, only a certain productive tension of the perplexity of language in various locations of living. I have taken the measure of Fanon's occult instability and Kristeva's parallel times into the 'incommensurable narrative' of Benjamin's modern storyteller to suggest no salvation, but a strange cultural survival of the people. For it is by living on the borderline of history and language, on the limits of race and gender, that we are in a position to translate the differences between them into a kind of solidarity. I want to end with a much translated fragment from Walter Benjamin's essay, *The Task of the Translator*. I hope it will now be read from the nation's edge, through the sense of the city, from the periphery of the people, in culture's transnational dissemination:

> Fragments of a vessel in order to be articulated together must follow one another in the smallest details although they need not be *like* one another. In the same way a translation, instead of making itself similar to the meaning of the original, it must lovingly and in detail, form itself according to the manner of meaning of the original, to make them *both* recognisable as the broken fragments of the greater language, just as fragments are the broken parts of a vessel.[68]

Textual and rhetorical questions

Textual

1. Homi Bhaba writes against the "settled nature of the term" "national*ism*," and what he wants to formulate in this essay "are the complex strategies of cultural identification and discursive address that function in the name of 'the people' or 'the nation' and make them the immanent subjects and objects of a range of social and literary narratives." Consequently, he displaces transparent and linear understanding of the terms like nation and nationalism. By proposing "temporality," "complex," "symbolic," "connotative," "patric," "rhetorical," "mythological," and "hegemonic" to understand national*ism*, does he privilege the terms or is he aware of such privileging? Explain (paragraphs 3 and 4).

2. Bhabha finds problems in connecting European modernity with the idea of nation. Why does he allude to "atavistic apologues" and "hoariness" (Benedict

LITERARY THEORY AND CRITICISM

Anderson's terms)? Furthermore, why does he write that nation is tamed by "the teleology of progress" called Enlightenment or modernity and what is the problem with such a control? He also explains nation as narration in these paragraphs. Elaborate (paragraphs 7 and 8).

3. Bhabha questions the "homogeneous and horizontal view familiarly associated with" representation of the national. Explain what he proposes while discussing Goethe's *Italian journey*. Does he answer the question? Read paragraphs 8, 9 and 10 to locate Bhabha's answer.

4. In paragraphs 8 and 9, Bhabha compares Bakhtin's commentary on Goethe by alluding to Freud. Bhabha writes that Bakhtin

> acknowledges that the origin of the nation's visual presence is the effect of a narrative struggle. "From the beginning, Bakhtin writes, the realist and Romantic conceptions of the time co-exist in Goethe's work, but the ghostly (*Gespenstermässiges*), the terrifying (*Unerfreuliches*), and the unaccountable (*Unzuberechnendes*) are constantly "surmounted" by the structural aspects of the visualization of the time."

> For Freud, Bhabha writes, "surmounting is the repression of the cultural unconscious, a liminal uncertain state of cultural belief." By alluding to Bakhtin and Freud, does Bhabha critique "national spaces achieved only in the *fullness of time*?"

5. Bhabha writes in the section "The foreignness of languages," "Having begun this essay with the nation's need for metaphor, I want to turn now to the desolated silences of the wandering people." What does he propose in this penultimate section? Paraphrase in three paragraphs.

Rhetorical

1. Deconstructive strategy of writing recognises the nature of language as undecidable, indeterminate, and methodological. Deconstructive interpretation accepts that there are some residues always left to decode the meanings perpetually. Bhabha's writing is always aware of this "wit and wisdom" of Derridian writings. How can you trace such strategic use of language (or language is already always strategic) when he seemingly privileges terms like "temporality," "complex," "symbolic," "connotative," "patric," "rhetorical," "mythological," and "hegemonic?" The double bind is manifest in his selection of the terms. Reason after reading paragraph 3 (you may refer to Textual Question 1).

2. Bhabha uses Said and Jameson to support his argument about "nation as the measure of the liminality of cultural modernity." He brings Kristeva to resist his position. How do the three writers help Bhabha put forwards the idea of nation? (paragraph 5).

3. Paraphrase the following passage to show how Bhabha problematises the failures of the historians and political theorists to ask some pertinent questions about nation and narration.

DISSEMINATION

Historians transfixed on the event and origins of the nation never ask, and political theorists possessed of the "modern" totalities of the nation – "Homogeneity, literary and anonymity are the key traits" – never pose, the awkward question of the disjunctive representation of the social, in this double-time of the nation. It is indeed only in the disjunctive time of the nation's modernity – as a knowledge disjunct between political rationality and its impasse, between the shreds and patches of cultural signification and the certainties of nationalist pedagogy – that questions of nation as narration come to be posed.

(Paragraph 7)

4. "Time" is the key word in Bhabha's essay. How does "the time of the nation" fare metaphorically when he uses the following phrases in this section of the chapter? The phrases are "the moment of the scattering of the people," "gathering," "exile," "mass migration," "temporal dimensions," "advent of the epochal." Weave an argument to justify the title "The time of the nation."
5. In the section "Of Margins and Minorities," Bhabha brings in Fanon and Kristeva to put forwards his argument. How does he treat the two authors? Trace the premises he employs to use the authors as references.

Discussion questions

1. Bhabha's essay can be relevant to critiquing the homogenous and linear version of nation in the Hindutva account of Indian nation like *Aryabarta* and *Bharatbarsha*. Where then do nations and nation-spaces like Bangladesh, Nepal, Pakistan, Afghanistan, and Sri-Lanka posit themselves?
2. Rabindranath Tagore asks: What is the Nation? In *Nationalism*,[69] he exposes the dangers of nationalism:

It is the aspect of a whole people as an organized power. This organization incessantly keeps up the insistence of the population on becoming strong and efficient. But this strenuous effort after strength and efficiency drains man's energy from his higher nature where he is self-sacrificing and creative. For thereby man's power of sacrifice is diverted from his ultimate object, which is moral, to the maintenance of this organization, which is mechanical. Yet in this he feels all the satisfaction of moral exaltation and therefore becomes supremely dangerous to humanity....
Nationalism is a great menace. It is the particular thing which for years has been at the bottom of India's troubles.

(2009, 74)

What do you think about the serge of nationalism in recent times in the United States, Europe, and South Asia? Can a unifying idea like nationalism be dangerous? How can homogeneity be menacing? Discuss.

LITERARY THEORY AND CRITICISM

Inter-textual discussions

1. Partha Chatterjee in *Nationalist Thought and the Colonial World: A Derivative Discourse*[70] informs, "three modular forms were available to the third world nationalism in the 20th century."[71] He further writes, "Third world nationalism in the 20th century thus came to acquire a modular character." ... "Above all, the very idea of nation is now nestled firmly in virtually all print languages, and nation-ness is virtually inseparable from political consciousness" (20–21). This very idea of nationalism as western gift has no foundation, or at least a feeble one, in the surge of historical Hindi language television serials related to King Puru and the Maurayan Empire, and many such other narratives. Argue for or against this assertion. C.A. Bayly's explanation may help you devise some of your arguments. He writes about the connectivity between western vs. vernacular forms of nationalism:

    > Modern Indian nationalism which solidified in the context of western institutions and international capitalism was evidently of a different order from earlier forms of regional and community patriotism. Nevertheless, these political forms did have some features and locations in common. Old patriotism created conceptual realms, clusters of institutions and popular sentiments which facilitated the rooting of later nationalism. This challenges the view that Indian nationalism was in every respect a recent phenomenon and one entirely derived from, or at least subordinated to, "modern" European forms. For, while televised soap operas throughout Asia and a few ultra-nationalist publicists trace the roots of Asian nationalisms back to the beginnings of time, most historians of Asia continue to see nationalisms entirely as the product of modernity, and embarrassingly for them, this is a very recent and almost wholly colonial modernity.
    >
    > (2001, 2)[72]

2. Franz Fanon is one of the strongest critics of nationalism that evolved after decolonisation of the former colonies. In *The Wretched of the Earth*,[73] he is critical of nationalism as "tragic mishap," and national consciousness as "empty shell" and "the result of the intellectual laziness of the national middle class." Read "The Pitfalls of National Consciousness" from the book and analyse his views in the context of decolonised South Asian nations. Here are some paragraphs from the book mentioned.

    > History teaches us clearly that the battle against colonialism does not run straight away along the lines of nationalism. For a very long time the native devotes his energies to ending certain definite abuses: forced labor, corporal punishment, inequality of salaries, limitation of political rights, etc. This fight for democracy against the oppression of mankind will slowly leave the confusion of neo-liberal universalism to emerge, sometimes laboriously, as a claim to nationhood. It so happens that the unpreparedness of the educated classes, the lack of practical links between them and the mass of

64

DISSEMINATION

the people, their laziness, and, let it be said, their cowardice at the decisive moment of the struggle will give rise to tragic mishaps.

(148)

National consciousness, instead of being the all-embracing crystallization of the innermost hopes of the whole people, instead of being the immediate and most obvious result of the mobilization of the people, will be in any case only an empty shell, a crude and fragile travesty of what it might have been. The faults that we find in it are quite sufficient explanation of the facility with which, when dealing with young and independent nations, the nation is passed over for the race, and the tribe is preferred to the state (148). These are the cracks in the edifice which show the process of retrogression, that is so harmful and prejudicial to national effort and national unity.

(149)

This traditional weakness, which is almost congenital to the national consciousness of underdeveloped countries, is not solely the result of the mutilation of the colonized people by the colonial regime. It is also the result of the intellectual laziness of the national middle class, of its spiritual penury, and of the profoundly cosmopolitan mold that its mind is set in.

(149)

Critical and creative thinking

1. "An Irish Airman Foresees his Death"[74] by W.B. Yeats refers to heroism and patriotism.
   Find similar writings about how fighting for a nation with patriotic zeal is a futile heroism.
2. Sun Ge, a Chinese researcher, writes in "How Does Asia Mean?":[75]

   In the context of Japanese intellectual history, the question of Asia is often associated with following "accepted observation": after the *Meiji Ishin* (Resistance), there are two lines of thinking among intellectuals in Japan regarding the question of Asia: one is represented by Fukuzawa Yukuchi's (1960) idea of "Disassociating from Asia and integrating with Europe" (*Datsu-A rou*), and the other is represented by Okakura Tenshin's advocation of "Asia is one". The former upholds that Japan should forsake the "unmanageable allies" in Asia so as quickly to join the ranks of the European and American powers. The latter stresses the commonality of Asia civilizations in the embodiment of the value of "love" and "beauty" which cannot be offered and superseded by the European civilizations.

   (2007,11)

   Nation, with such an idea of disassociation with a vast region like Asia, speaks about the modernity of western progress at large by ignoring the immediate cultural connectivities. The Asia is "the other" for Yukuchi. Does he want to see the liberation of Japan by associating with European modernity and its continuity? By the same token, whom should Islam associate or disassociate with? – with Europe because it is an Asian religion or with Europe because it is closer to the Christianity of the Western metaphysics?

3. After discussing Partha Chatterjee's "The Thematic and the Problematic" in *Nationalist Thought in the Colonial World: A Derivative Discourse*, R. Radhakrishnan in "Nationalism, Gender, and the Narrative of Identity" in *Diasporic Mediation: Between Home and Location* argues: "If in Western nationalism the thematic and the problematic are reciprocally and organically grounded, in the case of postcolonial nationalism the thematic and the problematic remain disjunct from each other" (196). Both Chatterjee and Radhakrishnan find a double bind in postcolonial nationalism. You may like to read Chatterjee's "Chapter 2" and Radhakrishnan's "Chapter 9" to find how arguments are always already deconstructive in nature.[76]

Notes

1 In memory of Paul Moritz Strimpel (1914–87): Pforzheim – Paris – Zurich – Ahmedabad – Bombay – Milan – Lugano.

2 I am thinking of Eric Hosbawm's great history of the 'long nineteenth century', especially *The Age of Capital 1848–1875* (London: Weidenfeld & Nicolson, 1975) and *The Age of Empire 1875–1914* (London: Weidenfeld & Nicolson, 1987). See especially some of the suggestive ideas on the nation and migration in the latter volume, ch. 6.

3 E. Said, *The World, The Text and The Critic* (Cambridge, Mass.: Harvard University Press, 1983), p. 39.

4 F. Jameson, 'Third World literature in the era of multinational capitalism', *Social Text*, (Fall 1986).

5 J. Kristeva, 'A new type of intellectual: the dissident', in Toril Moi (ed.), *The Kristeva Reader* (Oxford: Blackwell, 1986), p. 298.

6 E. Said, 'Opponents, audiences, constituencies and community', in Hal Foster (ed.), *Postmodern Culture* (London: Pluto, 1983), p. 145.

7 J. Derrida, *Dissemination*, trans. Barbara Johnson (Chicago: Chicago University Press, 1981), p. 210.

8 B. Anderson, 'Narrating the nation', *The Times Literary Supplement*.

9 P. Chatterjee, *Nationalist Thought and the Colonial World: A Derivative Discourse* (London: Zed, 1986).

10 E. Gellner, *Nations and Nationalism* (Oxford: Basil Blackwell, 1983), p. 56.

11 ibid., p. 38.

12 L. Althusser, *Montesquieu, Rousseau, Marx* (London: Verso, 1972), p. 78.

13 M. Bakhtin, *Speech Genres and Other Late Essays*, ed. C. Emerson and M. Holquist, trans. V. W. McGee (Austin, Texas: University of Texas Press, 1986) p. 31.

14 ibid., p. 34.

15 ibid., p. 36 and *passim*.

16 ibid., pp. 47–9.

17 S. Freud, 'The Uncanny', in *The Standard Edition of the Complete Psychological Works of Sigmund Freud*, ed. J. Strachey (London: Hogarth, 1955), p. 234. See also pp. 236, 247.

18 John Barrell, *English Literature in History, 1730–80* (London: Hutchinson 1983).

19 Houston A. Baker Jr, *Modernism and the Harlem Renaissance* (Chicago: Chicago University Press, 1987), esp. chs. 8–9.

20 Barrell, op. cit., p. 78.

DISSEMINATION

21 ibid., p. 203.

22 Richard Price, *Maroon Societies* quoted in Baker op. cit., p. 77.

23 Claude Lefort, *The Political Forms of Modern Society* (Cambridge: Polity, 1986), pp. 212–14, my emphasis.

24 A. Giddens, *The Nation State and Violence* (Cambridge: Polity, 1985), p. 216.

25 N. Poulantzas, *State, Power, Socialism* (London: Verso, 1980), p. 113.

26 R. Williams, *Problems in Materialism and Culture* (London: Verso, 1980), p. 43. I must thank Prof. David Lloyd of the University of California, Berkeley, for reminding me of Williams' important concept.

27 E. Said, 'Representing the colonized', *Critical Inquiry*, vol. 15, no. 2 (Winter 1989).

28 S. Freud, *Civilisation and Its Discontents*, Standard Edition (London: Hogarth, 1961), p. 114.

29 Freud, op. cit., p. 114.

30 J.-F. Lyotard and J.-L. Thebaud, *Just Gaming*, trans. Wlad Godzich (Manchester: Manchester University Press, 1985), p. 41.

31 C. Lévi-Strauss, *Introduction to the Work of Marcel Mauss*, trans. Felicity Baker (London: Routledge, 1987). Mark Cousins pointed me in the direction of this remarkable text. See his review in *New Formations*, no. 7 (Spring 1989). What follows is an account of Lévi-Strauss' argument to be found in Section 11 of the essay, pp. 21–44.

32 M. Foucault, *Technologies of the Self*, ed. H. Gutman *et al.* (London: Tavistock, 1988).

33 ibid., pp. 151–4. I have abbreviated the argument for my convenience.

34 L. Althusser, *Reading Capital* (London: New Left Books, 1972), pp. 122–32. I have, for convenience, produced a composite quotation from Althusser's various descriptions of the ideological effects of historicism.

35 Foucault, op.cit., pp. 162–3.

36 F. Fanon, *The Wretched of the Earth* (Harmondsworth: Penguin, 1969). My quotations and references come from pp. 174–90.

37 J.-F. Lyotard, *The Postmodern Condition*, trans. Geoff Bennington and Brian Massumi (Manchester: Manchester University Press, 1984), p. 22.

38 Moi, op.cit., pp. 187–213. This passage was written in response to the insistent questioning of Nandini and Praminda in Prof. Tshome Gabriel's seminar on 'syncretic cultures' at the University of California, Los Angeles.

39 Anderson, op.cit., p. 35.

40 J. Derrida, *Of Grammatology*, trans. G. C. Spivak (Baltimore, Md: Johns Hopkins University Press, 1976), pp. 144–5. Quoted in R. Gasché, *The Tain of the Mirror* (Cambridge, Mass.: Harvard University Press, 1986), p. 208.

41 ibid., p. 145.

42 Gasché, op.cit., p. 211.

43 Moi, op.cit., p. 210. I have also referred here to an argument to be found on p. 296.

44 All quotations are from the shooting script of *Handsworth Songs*, generously provided by the Black Audio and Film Collective.

45 Anderson, op. cit., p. 30.

46 ibid., 132.

47 ibid.

48 ibid.

49 Lévi-Strauss, op.cit., p. 58.

50 This collection, ch. 2, pp. 19–20.

51 ibid., p. 11.

52 Lefort, op.cit., p. 303.

53 W. Benjamin, 'The storyteller', in *Illuminations*. trans. Harry Zohn (London: Cape, 1970), p. 87.

54 M. Foucault, *The Archaeology of Knowledge*, trans. A. M. Sheridan Smith (London: Tavistock, 1972), p. 111.

55 C. Lévi-Strauss, op.cit., p. 35.

56 Benjamin, op.cit. p. 75.

57 W. Benjamin 'The Task of the Translator', *Illuminations* (London: Cape, 1970), p. 75.

58 N. Abraham and M. Torok, 'Introjection – Incorporation', in S. Lebovici and D. Widlocher (eds), *Psychoanalysis in France* (London: International Universities Press, 1980), p. 10.

59 J. Berger, *A Seventh Man* (Harmondsworth: Penguin, 1975). I have composed this passage from quotations that are scattered through the text.

60 Berger, op.cit., p. 216.

61 S. Freud, *Group Psychology and the Ego*, Standard Edition vol. XVIII (London: Hogarth, 1961), p. 119.

62 S. Rushdie, *The Satanic Verses* (New York: Viking, 1988), p. 337.

63 ibid., p. 130.

64 ibid., p. 145.

65 ibid., p. 320.

66 ibid., p. 353.

67 ibid., p. 354. I have slightly altered the presentation of this passage to fit in with the sequence of my argument.

68 Timothy Bahti and Andrew Benjamin have translated this much-discussed passage for me. What I want to emphasize is a form of the articulation of cultural difference that Paul de Man clarifies in his reading of Walter Benjamin's complex image of amphora.
[Benjamin] is not saying that the fragments constitute a totality, he says that fragments are fragments, and that they remain essentially fragmentary. They follow each other metonymically, and they never constitute a totality.
Paul de Man, *The Resistance to Theory*(Manchester: Manchester University Press, 1986), p. 91

69 Tagore, Rabindranath (reprint 2009). "Nationalism in India" in *Nationalism*. Delhi: Penguin (64–87).

70 See Partha Chatterjee. (1986). *Nationalist Thought and the Colonial World: A Derivate Discourse*. London: Zed.

71 See Chapter 1 of Partha Chatterjee's *Nationalist Thought and the Colonial World: A Derivate Discourse* for Creol nationalism, linguistic nationalism, and official nationalism.

72 See C.A. Bayly (2001). "Patriotism and Political Ethics in Indian History" in *Origins of Nationality in South Asia: Patriotism and Ethical Government in the Making of Modern India*. Delhi: OUP. (1–35).

73 See Franz Fanon. (1963). "The Pitfalls of National Consciousness" in *The Wretched of the Earth*. Trans. Constance Farrington. New York: Grove Weidenfeld. (148–149).

74 Check www.poetryfoundation.org/poems/57311/an-irish-airman-foresees-his-death or Ferguson, Margaret et al. (Eds.). (2004). *The Norton Anthology of Poetry*. 5th ed. New York: W. W. Norton.

75 See Sun Ge. "How does Asia mean?" (Trans. Hui Shiu-Lun & Lau Kinchi) in Chen Kuan-Hsing & Chua Beng Huat. (Eds.). (2007). *The Inter-Asia Cultural Studies Reader*. London: Routledge.

76 See Partha Chatterjee. (1986). "The Thematic and the Problematic" in *Nationalist Thought in the Colonial World: A Derivative Discourse*. London: Zed Books. See R. Radhakrishnan (1996) "Nationalism, Gender, and the Narrative of Identity" in *Diasporic Mediation: Between Home and Location*. Minneapolis: University of Minnesota Press.

2

BELATEDNESS AS POSSIBILITY

Subaltern histories, once again

Dipesh Chakrabarty

1 Even though I will be discussing historiography, not art, in the main body of this chapter, I have to acknowledge that the chapter owes its title to the accident of an invitation I received recently from the noted historian of visual culture in South Asia, Professor Christopher Pinney, to speak at a conference on art history he had organized at the Northwestern University in Chicago in May 2008. The topic of belatedness was being discussed at the conference, and the invitation made me remember that my most recent encounter with the theme of belatedness was at an exhibition of Indian art held in Chicago in 2007.

2 A marvellous exhibition of 'contemporary art from India' was held at the Chicago Cultural Center that year. The art works of Gulammohammed Sheikh, Nalini Malani, Subodh Gupta, Vivan Sundaram and others were impressive and brilliant in their own right. But the catalogue of the exhibition, *New Narratives: Contemporary Art from India* made it clear what the sense of time was that underwrote words like 'new' or 'contemporary'.

3 Indian art could be 'contemporary' because, as the curator, Betty Seid,[1] put it in her introduction to the volume, it 'reflect[ed] her [India's] world recognition as a major player in the new millennium'. American museums had avoided purchasing or exhibiting contemporary Indian art until it became truly contemporary, something that had moved from being 'stuck in an ethnographic mode of self-comparison' to a state where 'contemporary artists from India *of the world* happen to be living and working in India'.[2] So 'Western curators of contemporary art' are now 'beginning to catch on about India' but it is easy to see why: they are catching on because Indian artists are, at long last, catching up!

4 Has the curse of belatedness ever been lifted from India, I wondered? The same catalogue goes on to speak of the history of modernism and feminist art in India thus: 'Like Modernism, feminist art came to India later than to the West'.[3] Indian art does not become 'global' or of 'the world' until it arrives at the point that is recognized in the West as 'contemporary' – a point at which the West presumably has always been, at least long before Indian art got there. 'The communication capabilities of our electronic age have provided global cognition of the art-making world that was unavailable to many mid-twentieth century artists of India', the catalogue essay explains, and continues:

DOI: 10.4324/9781003213857-2

> Before independence in 1947, Western modern art was virtually unknown in India. Indian artists had not been exposed to the gradual evolution of modern art history. Rather, they were bombarded with the entirety of it, with exhibitions in India and with newly available opportunities to study and travel abroad.[4]

I felt honoured by Professor Pinney's invitation but, for me, it spoke to the issue of belatedness in ways both formal and personal. I was, first of all, a belated choice for the conference. Their second keynote speaker absented himself at the last moment and I was parachuted into the conference to fill the gap. I felt that I was in a situation somewhat similar to what the All India Radio once used to describe as being 'in the place of the scheduled artiste'. I was invited most cordially but belatedly – not anybody's fault; but that was how it worked out. Besides, some of the themes adumbrated in the conference statement Professor Pinney had circulated also spoke to the idea of belatedness. The conference, the statement said, was meant to be a window into 'the logic of a certain sort of historiographic practice'. Certain modes of art production are disqualified from the canons of art history by being seen as 'belated' – modernism in India would be an example, I presumed. 'Is there a single temporality at stake?' the statement asked. In fact, it was issued in a spirit of rebellion against any such judgement: 'Is the putatively universalizing space of the white cube itself only a Euro-American fantasy … ? Would a global practice dictate a heterogeneity which eschewed the possibility of the "global"? … Can territories be abandoned in favor of "flows"?' And it also met the question of judgement head on: 'How can the attributions of value occur in unfamiliar aesthetic worlds? … Are such attributions … necessary to a World Art?'[5]

5   So in agreeing to speak belatedly about belatedness, I was reminded of a joke in my hometown of Calcutta. Bengali senior citizens are often addressed by adding a respectful 'da' at the end of their names: thus Ashisda for Ashis Nandy, or Ranajitda for Ranajit Guha. When Derrida visited the city a few years ago to inaugurate and speak at a book fair, people ignorant of foreign ways assumed that he was probably an older Bengali man whose real name was 'Deri', a word that in Bangla quite appropriately means 'delay', and that it was as a mark of respect that he was called 'Deri-da'. So when it was clear that I could be at the conference only in somebody else's place, the chain of association to the noted philosopher led me to one of the thoughts that I will be elaborating in this chapter – the relationship between belatedness and displacement, for I do think that it is through that connection that belatedness becomes an opportunity, or a 'possibility', an association I gesture towards in the title of this chapter.

6   The questions raised by Professor Pinney in his conference statement reverberate in the halls of subaltern histories that I frequent in the course of my work as a historian. The theme of belatedness and a certain spirit of rebellion against it were written all over *Subaltern Studies*. That discussion was a critical part of the process through which *Subaltern Studies*, a series that we could once think of only ever as an *Indian* project, became a part of global or world history. So while Professor Pinney's conference bracketed the word 'world' in the expression '(World) Art', let me speak of the world as it is constituted when we convert belatedness into possibilities. You will see that the same problem of judgement that occurs in art history when the trope of

BELATEDNESS AS POSSIBILITY

belatedness is used occurs in political historiography as well: how do we evaluate developments in subaltern history as that history becomes part of an emergent global formation?

II

7 Right from the moment of its birth, *Subaltern Studies* was greeted by several commentators as a 'belated' project, carrying out in the subcontinent what British 'history from below' had accomplished a long time ago. Arif Dirlik was one of the better known of these critics. Belatedness in history was not a new problem as such. Alexander Gerschenkron, the reputed Harvard historian who wrote a book in the early 1960s, *Economic Backwardness in Historical Perspective*, saw the problem of Russian modernization through the prism of belatedness and the politics of having to 'catch up' with the more 'modern' nations.[6] The Indian Prime Minister Nehru would often say after independence that India had to accomplish in decades what the Americans had achieved over a few hundred years. 'Belatedness', as I tried to argue in *Provincializing Europe*, was an integral part of a certain kind of historicist outlook that was born in the nineteenth century. As my quotations from the catalogue volume of last year's exhibition in Chicago will have shown, the outlook still informs discussions of art history in the public realm.

8 The problem of belatedness speaks to a problem of repetition and recognition in history. If something happens that resembles something else within a field that is conceptually structured by before–after relationships, then that which comes later is seen as belated. This in turn raises a question that Homi Bhabha once asked, using Rushdie's words with some sense of urgency: How does newness enter the world?[7] How do we know what is new in what seems like repetition?

9 I want to submit to you two propositions that may seem a little paradoxical. My first proposition is that newness enters the world through acts of displacement. My second proposition is that newness confounds judgement because judgement tends to see the new as repetition and therefore deficient. Newness is hard to distinguish from a simulacrum, a fake that is neither a copy nor original. To be open to the new is to engage in a Heideggerian struggle: to hear that which I do not already understand. Judgement, and in my case I mean political judgement, makes this a very difficult task. In the rest of this chapter I will elaborate and explain my propositions by using *Subaltern Studies* as an example.

10 Before I do so, however, it may be helpful to take a page out of Gilles Deleuze, surely someone who has in our times thought more than most about some of these questions. Deleuze makes a primary distinction between 'repetition' and 'generality' in order to make a further distinction between 'repetition' and 'resemblance'. 'Repetition is not generality', he says and adds: 'repetition and resemblances are different in kind – extremely so'. Generality, according to Deleuze, 'presents two major orders: the qualitative order of resemblances and the quantitative order or equivalences. Cycles and equalities are their respective symbols'. Repetition, on the other hand, refers to 'non-exchangeable and non-substitutable singularities'. To repeat 'is to behave in a certain manner, but in relation to something unique or singular that has no equal or equivalent'.[8]

71

If exchange is the criterion of generality, theft and gift are those of repetition. ... This is the apparent paradox of festivals: they repeat an 'unrepeatable'. They do not add a second or third time to the first, but carry the first time to the 'nth' power ... [I]t is not the Federation Day which commemorates or represents the fall of the Bastille, but the fall of the Bastille which celebrates and repeats in advance all the Federation Days; or Monet's first water lily which repeats all the others. Generality, as generality of the particular, thus stands opposed to repetition as universality of the singular. The repetition of a work of art is like singularity without a concept, and it is not by chance that a poem must be learned by heart.[9]

The distinction hinted at in this passage between law and poetry, history and memory, is what gives repetition its power to transgress. 'The theatre of repetition is opposed to the theatre of representation, just as movement is opposed to the concept and to representation which refers it back to the concept'.[10] Deleuze makes it clear that repetition is how newness enters the world but it does so in disguise and through displacement – 'disguise no less than displacement forms part of repetition' – for repetition (this is Deleuze's reading of Kierkegaard and Nietzsche) is 'the double condemnation of habit and memory' both of which, as we shall see, underlie political judgement.[11] Repetition thus constitutes a crisis of political judgement.

III

11 Now I want to elaborate the themes of displacement and disguise, the two aspects of Deleuzian repetition, through the example of *Subaltern Studies*. First, let me document the theme of displacement and then I will turn to the more difficult question of disguise.

12 *Subaltern Studies*, the series with which I have been associated since 1982, was an instance of politically motivated historiography. Political judgement was central to this project. It came out of a Marxist tradition of history writing in South Asia and was markedly indebted to Mao and Gramsci in the initial formulations that guided the series. The tradition of history writing on the Left in India was deeply, though perhaps unsurprisingly, influenced by English Marxist or socialist historiography, the so-called 'history from below' tradition pioneered by the likes of Edward P. Thompson, Eric Hobsbawm, Christopher Hill, George Rudé, and others. Thompson's work on English popular history was predicated on the question: what contributions did the lower orders of society make to the history of English democracy? Historians in the *Subaltern Studies* series begin by asking a similar question: What contributions did the subaltern classes make on their own to the politics of nationalism in India, and hence to Indian democracy as well?[12] But here the similarity ended. English Marxist narratives of popular histories were moulded on a developmental idea of time: the peasant, in that story, either became extinct or was superseded to give rise to the worker who, through machine breaking, Chartism, and other struggles for rights, one day metamorphosed into the figure of the citizen or the revolutionary proletariat. The peasant or tribal of the third world who – as if through a process of telescoping of the

centuries – suddenly had the colonial state and its modern bureaucratic and repressive apparatus thrust in his face, was, in this mode of thinking, a 'pre-political' person. He or she was someone who did not understand, as it were, the operative languages of modern, governing institutions while having to deal with them. In terms of the English 'history from below' propositions, it was only over time, and by undergoing a process of intellectual development, that the subaltern classes could mature into a modern political force.

13   *Subaltern Studies* began by repudiating this developmental idea of 'becoming political'. The peasant or the subaltern, it was claimed, was *political* from the very instant they rose up in rebellion against the institutions of the Raj.[13] Their actions were political in the sense that they responded to and impacted on the institutional bases of colonial governance: the Raj, the moneylender, and the landlord. We did not then think much about the implications of our claim that the subaltern could be political without undergoing a process of 'political development'. Yet the implications of that claim were writ large on our historiography.

14   I should explain that the legacies of both imperialism and anti-colonialism speak to each other in this implicit debate about whether the subaltern became political over time (through some kind of pedagogic practice) or whether the figure of the subaltern was constitutionally political. Developmental time, or the sense of time underlying a stadial view of history, was indeed a legacy bequeathed by imperial rule in India. This is the time of the 'not yet' as I called it in *Provincializing Europe*. European political thinkers such as Mill (or even Marx) employed this temporal structure in the way they thought history. Nationalists and anti-colonialists, on the other hand, repudiated this imagination of time in the twentieth century in asking for self-rule to be granted right away, without a period of waiting or preparation, without delay, 'now'. What replaced the structure of the 'not yet' in their imagination was the horizon of the 'now'.[14]

15   The British argued against giving self-rule to educated Indians in the nineteenth century by saying that they were not representative of the larger masses of the Indian 'people'. The answer came from Gandhi who, following his entry into Indian politics during the First World War, made the main nationalist party, the Indian National Congress, into a 'mass' organization. He did so by enlisting peasants as ordinary, so-called 'fouranna' members with voting rights within the party. The 'mass base' of the Congress enabled its leaders to claim the status of being 'representative' of the nation even if the poor and the non-literate formally did not have any electoral power under the Raj. The educational gap that separated the peasant from the educated leaders was never considered a problem in this idea of representation. The peasant, it was assumed, was fully capable of making citizenly choices that colonial rule withheld from him or her. From the very beginning of the 1920s, Gandhi spoke in favour of universal adult franchise in a future, independent India. The peasant would thus be made a citizen overnight (at least with respect to voting) without having to live out the developmental time of formal or informal education – that was the 'now' the nationalists demanded. In the constitutional debates that took place in the Constituent Assembly right after independence, the philosopher, and later statesman, Radhakrishnan argued for a republican form of government by claiming that thousands of years of civilization had – even if formal education was absent – already prepared the peasant for such a state.[15]

16   What underwrote this anti-colonial but populist faith in the modern-political capacity of the masses was another European inheritance, a certain kind of poetics of history: romanticism. It is, of course, true that the middle-class leaders of anti-colonial movements involving peasants and workers never quite abandoned the idea of developmental time and a pedagogical project of educating the peasant. Gandhi's writings and those of other nationalist leaders often express a fear of the lawless mob and see education as a solution to the problem.[16] But this fear was qualified by its opposite, a political faith in the masses. In the 1920s and the 30s, this romanticism marked Indian nationalism generally – many nationalists who were not Communist or of the Left, for instance, would express this faith. Francesca Orsini, who works on Hindi literature, recently excavated a body of evidence documenting this tendency. To take but stray examples from her selection, here is Ganesh Shankar Vidyarthi (1890–1931), the editor of the Hindi paper *Pratap*, editorializing on 31 May 1915:

> The much-despised peasants are our true bread-givers [*annadata*], not those who consider themselves special and look down upon the people who must live in toil and poverty as lowly beings.[17]

Or Vidyarthi again on 11 January 1915:

> Now the time has come for our political ideology and our movement not [to] be restricted to the English-educated and to spread among the common people [*samanya janta*], and for Indian public opinion [*lokmat*] to be not the opinion of those few educated individuals but to mirror the thoughts of all the classes of the country ... democratic rule is actually the rule of public opinion.[18]

One should note that this romantic-political faith in the masses was populist as well in a classical sense of the term. Like Russian populism of the late nineteenth century, this mode of thought not only sought a 'good' political quality in the peasant, but also, by that step, worked to convert the so-called 'backwardness' of the peasant into an historical advantage. The peasant, 'uncorrupted' by the self-tending individualism of the bourgeois and oriented to the needs of his or her community, was imagined as already endowed with the capacity to usher in a modernity different and more communitarian than what was prevalent in the West.[19] The contradiction entailed in the very restricted nature of franchise under colonial rule and the simultaneous induction of the peasant and the urban poor into the nationalist movement had one important consequence. The very restrictions put on constitutional politics then meant that the field, the factory, the bazaar, the fair and the street became major arenas for the struggle for independence and self-rule. And it is in these arenas that subaltern subjects with their characteristic modes of collective mobilization (that included practices of public violence) entered public life.

17   The inauguration of the age of mass-politics in India was thus enabled by ideologies that displayed some of the key global characteristics of populist thought. There was, firstly, the tendency to see a certain political goodness in the peasant or in the masses. In addition, there was the tendency also to see historical advantage where, by colonial

judgement, there was only backwardness and disadvantage. To see 'advantage' in 'backwardness' – that is, to see belatedness as an opportunity – was also to challenge the time that was assumed by stadial views about history, it was to twist the time of the colonial 'not yet' into the structure of the democratic and anti-colonial 'now'.

18   I give this potted history of the romantic-populist origins of Indian democratic thought – though not of Indian democracy as such and the distinction is important – to suggest a point fundamental to my exposition. The insistence, in the early volumes of *Subaltern Studies* (first published in 1982) and in Ranajit Guha's *Elementary Aspects of Peasant Insurgency in Colonial India* (1983), that the peasant or the subaltern was always-already political – and not 'pre-political' in any developmentalist sense – was in some ways a recapitulation of a populist premise that was implicit in any case in the anti-colonial mass movements in British India.[20] But there was, in my sense, a displacement as well, of this term. The populism in *Subaltern Studies* was more intense and explicit. There was, first of all, no 'fear of the masses' in *Subaltern Studies* analysis. Absent also – and this went against the grain of classically Marxist or Leninist analysis – was any discussion of the need for organization or a party. Guha and his colleagues drew inspiration from Mao (particularly his 1927 report on the peasant movement in the Hunan district) and Gramsci (mainly his *Prison Notebooks*). But their use of Mao and Gramsci speaks of the times when *Subaltern Studies* was born. This was, after all, the seventies: a period of global Maoism that Althusser and others had made respectable. Excerpts from Gramsci's notebooks had come out in English in 1971. Both Gramsci and Mao were celebrated as a way out of Stalinist or Soviet Marxism after Czechoslovakia of 1968. Many of the historians in *Subaltern Studies* were participants in or sympathizers of the Maoist movement that shook parts of India between 1969 and 1971.[21]

19   Yet, significantly, neither Mao's references to the need for 'leadership of the Party' nor Gramsci's strictures against 'spontaneity' featured with any degree of prominence in what we wrote. Guha's focus in his *Elementary Aspects of Peasant Insurgency* remained firmly on understanding how rebellious peasants mobilized themselves in nineteenth-century British India, that is to say, before the age of Gandhian 'mass nationalism'. Guha sought to comprehend the peasant as a collective author of these uprisings by doing a structuralist analysis of the space- and time-creating practices of mobilization, communication, and public violence that constituted rebellion (and thus, for Guha, a subaltern domain of politics). There were limitations, from Guha's socialist point of view, to what the peasants could achieve on their own but these limitations did not call for the mediation of a party. A cult of rebellion marked the early efforts of *Subaltern Studies*, reminiscent of one of Mao's sayings that was popular during the Cultural Revolution: 'to rebel is justified'. Rebellion was not a technique for achieving something; it was its own end. Indeed, from a global perspective, one might say that *Subaltern Studies* was the last – or the latest – instance of a long global history of the Left: the romantic-popular search for a non-industrial revolutionary subject that was initiated in Russia, among other places, in the nineteenth century. This romantic populism shaped much of Maoism in the twentieth century, and left its imprint on the antinomies and ambiguities of Antonio Gramsci's thoughts on the Party as the Modern Prince.

LITERARY THEORY AND CRITICISM

20   The once-global and inherently romantic search for a revolutionary subject outside of the industrialized West has thus had a long history, travelling from Russia in the late nineteenth century to the colonial and semi-colonial (to use a Maoist expression) 'third' world in the twentieth century. The political potential of this romanticism is exhausted today. But looking back one can see what plagued this history of a search for a revolutionary subject in the relatively non-industrialized countries of the world. Such a subject by definition could not be the proletariat. Yet it was difficult to define a world-historical subject that would take the place of the industrial working classes that did not exist, not in great numbers anyway, in the peasant-based economies drawn into the gravitational pull of the capitalist world. Would the revolution, as Trotsky said, be an act of substitutionism? Would the Party stand in for the working classes? Could the peasantry, under the guidance of the party, be the revolutionary class? Would it be the category 'subaltern' or Fanon's 'the wretched of the earth'?

21   When the young, left-Hegelian Marx thought up the category of the proletariat as the new revolutionary subject of history that would replace the bourgeoisie – and he did this before Engels wrote his book on the Manchester working class in 1844 – there was a philosophical precision to the category. It also seemed to find a sociological correlate in working classes born of the industrial revolution. But names like 'peasants' (Mao), 'subaltern' (Gramsci), 'the wretched of the earth' (Fanon), 'the party as the subject' (Lenin/Lukács) have neither philosophical nor sociological precision. It was as if the search for a revolutionary subject that was *not-the-proletariat* (in the absence of a large working class) was an exercise in a series of displacements of the original term, the proletariat. A telling case in point is Fanon himself. The expression 'the wretched of the earth', as Fanon's biographer David Macey has pointed out, alluded to words of the Communist Internationale, in the song – '"Debout, les damnés de la terre"/ Arise, ye wretched of the earth' – where it clearly referred to the proletariat. Yet Fanon used it to mean something else, something other than the proletariat. This other subject he could not quite define but he was clear that in the colony it could not be the proletariat. One only has to recall how, quite early on in his book, he cautioned: 'Marxist analysis should always be slightly stretched every time we have to deal with the colonial problem'.[22]

22   A collective subject with no proper name, a subject who can be named only through a series of displacements of the original European term 'the proletariat' – this is a condition both of failure and of a new beginning. The failure is easy to see. It lies in the lack of specificity or definition. Where is the beginning? First of all, the very imprecision is a pointer to the inadequacy of Eurocentric thought in the context of a global striving for a socialist transformation of the world. Outside of the industrialized countries, the revolutionary subject was even theoretically undefined. The history of this imprecision amounts to the acknowledgment that if we want to understand the nature of popular political practices globally with names of subjects invented in Europe, we can only resort to a series of stand-ins (never mind the fact that original may have been a simulacrum as well). Why? Because we are working at and on the limits of European political thought even as we admit an affiliation to nineteenth-century European revolutionary romanticism. Recognizing the stand-in nature of categories like 'the masses', 'the subaltern' or 'the peasant' is, I suggest, the first step towards writing histories of

BELATEDNESS AS POSSIBILITY

democracies that have emerged through the mass-politics of anti colonial nationalism. There is a mass-subject here, no doubt. But it can only be apprehended by consciously working through the limits of European thought. A straightforward search for a revolutionary world-historical subject only leads to stand-ins. The global and theoretical failure to find a proper name for the revolutionary subject that is not-the-proletariat thus inaugurates the need for new thought and research outside the West, resulting in a series of displacements of the once-European category, the proletariat.

IV

23 To sum up, then, much socialist political thought has been made possible outside of the West by a continual process of working through European categories in order to displace them from the locus of their original signification. So much for the theme of displacement that, as Deleuze reminded us, was a critical part of the transgressive power of repetition. But what about the theme of disguise?

24 The theme of disguise pertains to our capacity to name and recognize the new. It is here that the tension (to speak with Deleuze) between generality and repetition, between law and poetry, between history/sociology and memory, reveals itself at its most intense and demonstrates how political judgement seeks to tame the new.

25 Consider once again the foundational text of *Subaltern Studies*, Ranajit Guha's *Elementary Aspects of Peasant Insurgency in Colonial India*. What is the status of the category 'political' in Guha's (and our) polemic with Hobsbawm that the peasants and the tribals were not 'pre-political', that they were in fact as political as the British or the middle classes?[23] The status is ambiguous: the peasants were political in the already-understood sense of the terms – in that they dealt with the institutions of colonial rule – but they were also 'political' in some other sense about which we were not clear at all. The political claim that nineteenth-century peasant rebellions were political could only be made on the assumption – and this remains an assumption – that we already knew completely what 'being political' meant. What was new about peasant resistance in nineteenth-century India could only be expressed in the guise of the old category: 'politics'.

26 Something very similar happens – to cite a distant example that will show that the problem is more than historiographical or merely Indian – in the Australian historian Henry Reynold's path-breaking work on Aboriginal resistance to White occupation in nineteenth-century Australia. Take his book, *Fate of a Free People*, analysing Aboriginal resistance in nineteenth-century Tasmania. Reynolds is aware of the European roots of the modern idea of the political. He writes how some European settlers were astonished to find among Aboriginals 'ideas of their natural rights' which Reynolds regards, rightly, as European attempts at interpreting 'in European terms' the world-making they encountered among the Aboriginals. Yet, in resisting histories written by earlier White historians and chroniclers, Reynolds, much like Guha, insists on the applicability of the category 'political' in describing Aboriginal resistance. He challenges 'the clear assumption that the Tasmanians were incapable of taking political action' and deliberately describes the nineteenth-century Aboriginal leader, Walter Arthur, as 'the first Aboriginal nationalist', tearing the idea of 'nationalism' from all its

LITERARY THEORY AND CRITICISM

anchorage in the history of modern institutions.[24] Clearly, 'politics' and 'nationalism' are under-determined, part-sociological and part-rhetorical categories here, not completely open to the demand for clarification. And it is in their rhetorical imprecision that the disguising of the new happens.

27   Or take Partha Chatterjee's category of 'the governed' – again, a term in the series of displacements of the revolutionary subject that I have already traced before. Having documented the struggle for survival (including the stealing of electricity) – within which lessons are indeed learned by subaltern and other groups – that goes on every day in the city of Calcutta, he suddenly, towards the end of his lectures on the theme, makes 'the governed' the creators of something that even Aristotle might recognize: democracy. 'What I have tried to show', he writes, 'is that alongside the abstract promise of popular sovereignty, people in most of the world are devising new ways in which they can choose how they should be governed'. He recognizes that 'many of the forms of the political society' and their unlawful activities that he describes perhaps would not have met with 'Aristotle's approval'. Yet he believes that the 'wise Greek', if he could see Chatterjee's evidence, might actually recognize an 'ethical justification' for democracy in popular action that he might otherwise have disapproved of.[25] My point is, again, the ambiguity of this move, the claim that while popular action in everyday Calcutta does not always look democratic, it still heralds a democracy to come. It is, of course, entirely possible that everyday life in Calcutta looks forwards to a future for which we just do not have a category yet. But in Chatterjee's prose, it is, once again, in the ambiguity of old and new uses of the word 'democracy' that the actual 'newness' of what goes on in Calcutta both shows and hides itself. Now we see it, now we don't.

28   My last example of disguise of the new is Hardt and Negri's well-known category of the 'multitude', once again a candidate for inclusion in my list of terms that displace the original revolutionary subject of Europe. The disguise is ironical for a book that, in its first half, struggles – in a Deleuzian vein – to capture that which is about domination in the world: Empire. Yet their revolutionary agency 'the multitude', while conceived of as immanent in a Spinozist way, has to acquire an 'adequate consciousness' (resonances of Hegel–Marx here) in order to be political. 'How can the actions of the multitude become political?' they ask. Their answer: 'The only response we can give ... is that the action of the multitude becomes primarily political when it begins to confront directly and with *an adequate consciousness* the central repressive operations of Empire'.[26]

29   I am then left to ask my final question: why does displacement combine with disguise to create the very structure of repetition? It goes back, I think, to a problem that Marx referred to a long time ago. Newness enters the world as a challenge to judgement and law. That is why Deleuze refers to it through the figure of poetry. Political judgement is tied to the old. It is salutary to remember that even Homi Bhabha, whose generative mediations on the postcolonial condition would not have much to say about the conditions for the struggle for socialism (as conventionally understood), began his journey as a postcolonial theorist with a gesture towards connecting with socialist politics as it was known in Britain in the 1980s.[27] I think Marx, in a moment of reflection on the problem of repetition and resemblance in history – and thus on the figure of the belated – put his finger on the necessary disguise of the new. The lines are very well known indeed but may bear repetition in the context of this discussion. Let me give Marx the final word with one minor qualification:

BELATEDNESS AS POSSIBILITY

> Men make their own history, but they do not make it just as they please. ... The tradition of all the dead generations weighs like a nightmare on the brain of the living. And just when they seem ... engaged in creating something that has never yet existed ... they anxiously conjure up the spirits of the past to their service and borrow from them names, battle cries and costumes in order to present the new scene of world history in this time-honoured disguise and this borrowed language.

Marx expects this process to have a happy Hegelian ending. He, as you know, compares this process to a person's experience of learning a new language:

> a beginner who has learnt a new language always translates it back into his mother tongue, but he has assimilated the spirit of the new language and can freely express himself in it only when he finds his way in it without recalling the old and forgets his native tongue in the use of the new.[28]

We are rightly suspicious of such happy endings. We remain interested in remainders and failures of translation that always come back to haunt and trouble what translation achieves. This is indeed where we may have to part with Marx and his progenies in contemplating the problem of repetition and belatedness in our time.

Textual and rhetorical questions

Textual

1. The problem is only when the West recognises a Pakistani literary work or an Indian painting does it become global and contemporary. That is, for the West, Indian art is "catching up" and getting out of "belatedness." This is what the catalogue of the exhibition declared. Dipesh Chakrabarty interferes and sees possibility in "belatedness." What is the possibility that arises out of "arriving late"? Identify the examples of "belatedness as possibility" in the essay (50–60 words).
2. Chakrabarty brings in Homi Bhabha who asks, "How does newness enter the world? How do we know what is new in what seems like repetition?" Chakrabarty answers Bhabha's question by proposing that newness enters "through acts of displacement" and it "confounds judgment." Furthermore, by bringing in Deleuze, Chakrabarty argues that "repetition has the power to transgress." Read how Deleuze distinguishes repetition and generality and then conclude by writing about how Chakrabarty answers Bhabha in detail. Focus on the key terms "disguise" and "displacement" while also discussing newness. Read paragraphs 8, 9, 10, and 11 (200 words).
3. After discussing the origin of *Subaltern Studies*, the essayist elaborates the theme of "disguise" and "displacement" through the example of Subaltern Studies. He accepts that there is a similarity between Subaltern Studies and Thompson's "history from below" historiography but the former was *belated* and this is where the possibility of newness arose: "Similarity ended" he writes. Explain how "similarity ended" according to Chakrabarty. Focus on paragraph 12 (50 words).

LITERARY THEORY AND CRITICISM

4. Chakrabarty writes that peasants are "already endowed with the capacity to usher in a modernity," and their "collective mobilization." Whereas colonial judgement about the peasants was about their "'backwardness'." This is where the essayist sees advantage in backwardsness or belatedness as opportunity. Analyse after reading paragraph 16 and 17 (50 words).

5. By citing Ranagit Guha, Chakrabarty talks about the romantic search of *Subaltern Studies*. What is that romantic search? Do you think that the search is related to the "displacement" of the original term "proletariat?" Do you think the term "subaltern" is used for the Romantic quest? (100 words).

Rhetorical

1. The essay is a model of structured writing. Write a paragraph of six to seven sentences connecting the terms belatedness, newness, repetition, generality, displacement, and disguise. Your paragraph will be a summary of Chakrabarty's thesis.

2. Frantz Fanon "cautioned" in *The Wretched of the Earth*, "Marxist analysis should always be slightly stretched every time we have to deal with the colonial problem" (paragraph 21). Explain why and how Fanon's quote can be read as the conclusion of the premise propositions in the paragraph. What are the premises the essayist provides to conclude, with the help of Fanon? Do you think the terms "precision" and "displacement" will be helpful to answer the question?

3. The essayist cites Henry Reynold, Partha Chatterjee, and Hardt and Negri (in paragraph 26, 27, and 28). What is his reason for alluding to their works?

Discussion questions

1. Dipesh Chakrabarty writes, "the academic discourse of history – that is, 'history' as a discourse produced at the institutional site of the university – is concerned, Europe remains the sovereign theoretical subject of all histories, including the ones we call 'Indian,' 'Chinese,' 'Kenyan,' and so on." ("Postcoloniality and the Artifice of History," 340).[29] Similarly, Stuart Hall writes about "ethnographic museums, in other words institutions whose representational strategies feature the ethnographic objects or artefacts of 'other cultures'" and he asks us to think, "How the West classifies, categorizes and represents other cultures is emerging as a topic of some debate"(153).[30]

   Both Chakrabarty and Hall question the modes of Western representation of Asia or Africa. Do you think the idea of "not yet" and "belatedness" is the consequence of colonial representation of the others as Europe's museum items and hence museumising is about not considering "the other" as modern in a Western sense of the term? Discuss Western ideology of representation with examples (700 words).

2. Subaltern Studies is not merely a "history from below" but a location of knowledge which addresses multiple issues like representation, identity, resistance,

historiography, ethnicity, margin, agrarian consciousness, and so on. The project does not merely locate Indian peasants in nationalist struggle but initiates discussion on spontaneity, consciousness, organisation, violence, discipline, nationalism, capitalism, caste, and feminism. Write an essay after reading selected essays from the list below (2000 words):

From *Subaltern Studies* Volumes:

- Ranajit Guha: "On Some Aspects of the Historiography" and "The Prose of Counter-Insurgency"
- Gyan Pandey: "Peasant Revolt and Indian Nationalism"
- Partha Chatterjee: "Caste and Subaltern Consciousness" and "The Nation and Its Women"
- Gyanendra Pandey: "The Prose of Otherness"
- Veena Das: "Subaltern as Perspective"

From Ludden, David. (Ed.). *Reading Subaltern Studies: Critical History, Contested Meaning, and the Globalisation of South Asia.* Delhi: permanent black, 2002:

- Javeed Alam: "Peasantry, Politics, and Historiography: Critique of New Trend in Relation to Marxism"
- Sangeeta Singh et al: "Subaltern Studies II: A Review Article"

Inter-textual discussions

1. Dipesh Chakrabarty's *Habitations of Modernity* is an elaborate discourse on the problem of the Eurocentric model of modernity. Such ideology claims "the belated is out" as we have read in the essay above. Textual Question 3 can be understood in detail in relation to his book which sees a problem in the singularity of modernity. Similarly, Fredric Jameson and Masao Miyoshi in *The Cultures of Globalization*[31] propose a thesis:

   > The centrality of Europe as world system is not the sole fruit of an internal superiority accumulated during the European Middle Ages over against other cultures. Instead, it is also the fundamental effect of the simple fact of the discovery, conquest, colonization, and integration (subsumption) of Amerindia. The simple fact will give Europe the determining *comparative advantage* over the Ottoman-Muslim world, India, China. Modernity is the fruit of these events, not their cause.
   >
   > (1998, 4–5)

   Critique globalisation and modernity as Western prescriptions, domination, and hegemony (500 words).

2. What is late in the West is what is exotic. Exotic is accepted as the movie *Slumdog Millionaire* being accepted as shown by the Oscars it won. The exotic as "the other" is approved and consumed in Western art and literature. What is your viewpoint on this? (300 words).

LITERARY THEORY AND CRITICISM

Critical and creative thinking

1. What do you think about the ideas contained in the following two passages?

> Representation starts from the principle that the sign and the real are equivalent (even if this equivalence is Utopian, it is a fundamental axiom). Conversely, simulation starts from the Utopia of this principal of equivalence, from the radical negation of the sign as value, from the sign as reversion and death sentence of every reference. Whereas representation tries to absorb simulation by interpreting it as false representation, simulation envelops the whole edifice of representation as itself a simulacrum.
> (Jean Baudrillard, "Simulacra and Simulation" 404–05)[32]

and

> Disneyland is a perfect model of all the entangled orders of simulation. To begin with it is a play of illusions and phantasms: Pirates, the Frontier, Future World, etc. This imaginary world is supposed to be what makes the operation successful. But what draws the crowds is undoubtedly much more the social microcosm, the miniaturized and religious reveling in real America, in its delights and drawbacks. You park outside, queue up inside, and are totally abandoned at the exit.
> ("Simulacra and Simulation" 405)

2. Read the difference between Parody and Pastiche in Fredric Jameson's "Postmodernism, or The Cultural Logic of Late Capitalism."[33] Explain postcolonialism in terms of Mimicry (see Homi Bhabha: "Of Mimicry and Man: The Ambivalence of Colonial Discourse").[34] Do you think parody, pastiche, and mimicry can be studied as the postmodern and postcolonial theories of representation?
3. The philosophical idea of old and new, past and renewed are paradoxical. For a change, let us take the concept of "new" philosophically. Friedrich Nietzsche in *Thus Spoke Zarathustra*[35] collapses the sequence of time. There is nothing new: Zarathustra proclaims,

> "And this slow spider that creeps along in the moonlight, and this moonlight itself, and I and you at this gateway whispering together, whispering of eternal things – must we not all have been here before?"
> ("Third Part: On the Vision and the Riddle" 126)

> The animals add, "Everything goes, everything comes back, the wheel of being rolls eternally. Everything dies, everything blossoms again; the year of being runs eternally."... "Everything breaks, everything is joined anew, the same house of being builds itself eternally. Everything parts, everything greets itself again; the ring of being remains loyal to itself eternally."
> (175)

Notes

Thanks are due to the editors of this volume for their editorial suggestions.

Notes

1 Betty Seid, *New Narratives: Contemporary Art from India* (Ahmedabad and Ocean Township, NJ: Mapin, Grantha, 2007).
2 *New Narratives*, p. 13.
3 *New Narratives*, p. 15.
4 *New Narratives*, p. 19.
5 Conference statement, '(World) Art: Art History and Global Practice', Northwestern University, 23–24 May 2008.
6 Alexander Gerschenkron, *Economic Backwardness in Historical Perspective – A Book of Essays* (Cambridge, MA: Belknap Harvard, 1962).
7 Homi Bhabha, 'How Newness Enters the World: Postmodern Space, Postcolonial Times and the Trials of Cultural Translation' in his *The Location of Culture* (London: Routledge, 1994).
8 Gilles Deleuze, *Difference and Repetition*, trans. Paul Patton (New York: Columbia University Press, 1994), p. 1.
9 Deleuze, *Difference*, pp. 1–2.
10 Deleuze, *Difference*, p. 10.
11 Deleuze, *Difference*, pp. xvi, 7.
12 See E. P. Thompson, *Whigs and Hunters* (Harmondsworth: Penguin Books, 1977).
13 I discuss this in some detail in my essay 'A Small History of *Subaltern Studies*' in my *Habitations of Modernity: Essays in the Wake of Subaltern Studies* (Chicago: The University of Chicago Press, 2002), Ch. 1.
14 See the discussion in the Introduction to my book *Provincializing Europe: Postcolonial Thought and Historical Difference* (Princeton, New Jersey: Princeton University Press, 2000).
15 See *Provinicializing Europe*, 'Introduction' for details.
16 See Gyanendra Pandey's essay on the topic in Ranajit Guha and Gayatri Chakravorty Spivak (eds), *Selected Subaltern Studies* (New York: Oxford University Press, 1988).
17 Francesca Orsini, 'The Hindi Public Sphere and Political Discourse in the Twentieth Century', unpublished paper presented at a conference on 'The Sites of the Political in South Asia', Berlin, October 2003.
18 Ibid.
19 For an excellent discussion of this point, see Andrzej Walicki, *The Controversy over Capitalism: Studies in the Social Philosophy of the Russian Populists* (Notre Dame, Indiana: University of Notre Dame Press, 1989), Chapters 1 and 2, in particular the section of 'The Privilege of Backwardness'.
20 Ranajit Guha, *Elementary Aspects of Peasant Insurgency in Colonial India* (Delhi: Oxford University Press, 1983), Chapter 1.
21 Shahid Amin, 'De-Ghettoising the Histories of the non-West'; Gyan Prakash, 'The Location of Scholarship'; in my 'Globalization, Democracy, and the Evacuation of History?' in Jackie Assayag and Veronique Benei (eds), *At Home in Diaspora: South Asian Scholars and the West* (Bloomington, Indiana: Indiana University Press, 2003).
22 Frantz Fanon, *The Wretched of the Earth*, trans., Constance Farrington (New York: Grove Press, 1963), p. 40.
23 Ranajit Guha, *Elementary Aspects of Peasant Insurgency in Colonial India* (Delhi: Oxford University Press, 1983), Chapter 1.
24 Henry Reynolds, *Fate of a Free People* (Ringwood, Victoria: Penguin, 1995), pp. 11, 23, 69.
25 Partha Chatterjee, *The Politics of the Governed: Reflections on Popular Politics in Most of the World* (New York: Columbia University Press, 2004), pp. 77–8.

26 Michael Hardt and Antonio Negri, *Empire* (Cambridge, MA: Harvard University Press, 2000), p. 399.
27 Bhabha, 'The Commitment to Theory'.
28 Karl Marx, 'The Eighteenth Brumaire of Louis Bonaparte', in Karl Marx and Frederick Engels, *Selected Works*, vol. 1 (Moscow: Progress Publishers, 1969), p. 398.
29 See Ashcroft, Bill et al. (2009). *The Post-Colonial Studies Reader*. 2nd ed. London: Routledge.
30 Hall, Stuart. (2003 Reprint). *Representations: Cultural Representations and Signifying Practices*. London: Sage.
31 Jameson, Fredric & Masao Miyoshi (Eds.). (1998). *The Cultures of Globalization*. Durham: Duke University Press.
32 Lodge, David. (1988). *Modern Criticism and Theory: A Reader*. 2nd ed. Delhi: Pearson. 404–12).
33 Fredric Jameson. (1993). from "Postmodernism, or The Cultural Logic of Late Capitalism" in Joseph Natoli & Linda Hutcheon. *A Postmodern Reader*. Albany: State University of New York Press.
34 See in section II.
35 Friedrich Nietzsche. (Reprint 2006). *Thus Spoke Zarathustra: A Book for All and None*. Trans. Adrian del Caro. Adrian del Caro & Robert B. Pippin. (Eds.). Cambridge: Cambridge University Press.

3

THE BLURRING OF DISTINCTIONS
The Artwork and the Religious Icon in Contemporary India[1]

Tapati Guha-Thakurta

Posing the Problem

1 This chapter explores a set of contentions and paradoxes that have arisen from the repeated blurring of distinctions between the 'artistic' and the 'religious' object across different institutional and public sites in contemporary India. This is the central, recurrent problem that I track across two divergent sites of art production and reception. In the first case, I revisit the unabated Hindu right-wing campaign against India's veteran modern artist, Maqbool Fida Husain, that began to snowball from 1996 around Husain's 'offence' of painting Hindu divinities in the nude (Figure 3.1). Notwithstanding two definitive rulings of the Delhi High Court and Supreme Court of India (in May and September 2008) that have acquitted the artist of the many 'criminal' charges that were levelled against him,[2] the campaign has refused to let go of its target, forcing the artist into a life of self-imposed exile in Dubai.[3] If the 'Husain affair' has come over time to exemplify the siege of culture by the Hindu Right and the beleaguered state of the 'secular' in contemporary India, it also throws into the open a deep instability in the status of the nation's 'artistic' and 'religious' imagery, in the representational licences they enjoy and in the public fields of their circulation.

2 While the first part of the chapter maps this shrinking space of artistic autonomy and authority, the second part turns to a set of other tropes of conflations between the 'sacred' and 'secular' designation of objects, as they move in and out of a vortex of overlapping identities in new public fields of display and spectatorship. From the worlds of art, it enters a separate domain of a public festival in the city of Calcutta: one organized each autumn around the worship of goddess Durga. I take up here a recent trend of the striking reconfiguration of Durga icons as 'works of art' in the streets of Calcutta during this annual event (Figure 3.2) that comes out of a longer history of the growing secularization of this domain of festivity and visual productions. What is involved here is less a situation of contention and conflict, more one of porous boundaries that allow the 'artistic' and the 'religious' the liberty to trespass into and inhabit each other's domains.

3 While the qualities of 'iconicity' and 'sacredness' can be seen to belong as much to the 'artwork' as to the 'religious object', modern history (not just in the West but equally in India) produced a series of crucial distinctions that set apart these different orders of iconicity, the practices that support them and the discursive spheres they

DOI: 10.4324/9781003213857-3

85

Figure 3.1 M.F. Husain, 'Saraswati' (Pen and Ink on Paper, c. 1970). Reproduced Courtesy of the Artist.

Figure 3.2 Durga Pantheon in a North Bengal Folk Art Style – Behala Tapoban Club Puja, 2004. Reproduced Courtesy of the Visual Archive of the Centre for Studies in Social Sciences, Calcutta (CSSSC).

inhabit. These distinctions, introduced and fine-tuned by modernity, are both ontological and institutional, and the relative weight of these differentiating criteria has
been a subject of continuing debate in aesthetic and sociological theories of art.[4] In
India, as elsewhere, the very identity of 'art' in the modern era has been grounded on
this separation of domains between the 'secular' and the 'religious', on the elaborate
distilling of the new 'secular' worlds in which both the art of the ancient and medieval
past as well as the modern art of the nation came to be positioned. Together, the evolv-
ing discipline of art history and modern art practices served to render art into one of
the most powerful secular-ritual objects of national life. The modern epistemology of
'art', we find, could accommodate as effectively the religious productions and iconographies of the nation's past as the new repertoire of divine and mythological imagery
in the art of the present. If the Indian art tradition came to be invested with a uniquely
'spiritual' and 'transcendental' character, the 'spiritual' served here as a markedly secular designation, one that would give a body of the religious objects of the past a new
sacral stature of 'art'.[5]

4   We need to remind ourselves of this well-established history to guard against a lin-
gering trend of Orientalist and nationalist projections that emphasize the quintessen-
tially 'religious' nature of India's artistic traditions as against the secularization of art
in the West. Of longstanding prestige is a distinctly separate domain that we denomi-
nate as 'art' in India, and treat apart from the fields of both organized religion and
popular faith. And it is only through recognizing this categorical distinction that we
can grapple with the spectre of violation and threat, or with the conflation of identities that the current collapsing of this boundary presents to visual objects and subjects
across this divide. As we shall see, the allegations against the paintings of Maqbool
Fida Husain have forced us to rethink how we draw the line, not just between 'art' and
'obscenity', but also between the 'artistic' and 'religious' image – a line that may never
have existed in earlier tradition, but fell powerfully in place in modern Indian history,
and now needs to be redrawn and policed with great urgency. Using the case of new
kinds of ritual art productions for the Durga Puja festival in contemporary Calcutta, I
will also show how this line between the 'artistic' and the 'religious' keeps strategically
shifting and disappearing in other public contexts, to enable a new order of modern
practices to permeate the existing field of the 'religious'.

5   It is important that we do not confuse the current collapsing of 'religious' and
'artistic' identities of images as a clash between 'traditional' and 'modern' dispensa-
tions. For, as we know, what is countering the secular entity of contemporary art is not
its religious other, but a political and communal entity of 'Hindus', who share many
of the same markers of contemporaneity as the artists they detest. The modernity of
the new regimes of religious identities and productions will repeatedly reappear, in
the escalating attacks on M. F. Husain and in the spectacles produced around Durga
Puja in different urban locations in Calcutta. In the case of the anti-Husain campaign,
notions of the 'religious' can be seen to surface within a wholly modern political register of rights and claims, with its vocabulary of offence and outrage, and its claims to
objects and iconographies. In the case of the Durga creations in the city of Calcutta,
the 'religious' will be shown to take on a new set of modern vanities of 'art', its hanker-
ing for a spiritual aesthetic, and often its distinctly modernist nostalgia for the retrieval
of disappearing rural and folk art practices. The claims of artistic production and

LITERARY THEORY AND CRITICISM

the markings of the 'secular' labour are to leave their imprints in a festival field that remains constitutively grounded in the performance of the ritual event. The result is a continuous re-inscription of devotional affect – surrounding the homecoming of the goddess – within the body of the urban spectacle. An ongoing concern of the article will be with the vexed interface of the 'artistic' and the 'religious' across these domains, with the public fields of locations of these varied bodies of art practice, and the kinds of iconographic transgressions that these enable or foreclose.

The nudes that offend: More notes on the 'Husain affair'[6]

The offence and the allegations

6   In September 1996, a line drawing of the goddess Saraswati by M. F. Husain, one of the artist's large repertoire of stylized female nudes done in the 1970s (Figure 3.1) became the object of sudden moral outrage among local activists of the Vishva Hindu Parishad (VHP), a right-wing political group allied to the Bharatiya Janata Party (BJP). It produced a spiralling curve of violence against the artist's works and property that moved over time from Indore and Bhopal to Ahmedabad, Mumbai, New Delhi and, more recently, to London. What came to be dragged into the centre of the country's fanatical *Hindutva* politics as a result was the hallowed world of modern Indian art, and its most cherished object of representation: the female nude. Why was M. F. Husain targeted, and what were the particular political circumstances that propelled this 'pogrom' against him and his art? What made Husain's nude goddesses any the less defensible from those that we encounter in traditional Indian painting and sculpture, or in the works of several other modern Indian artists? Continuously raised and debated, these questions have remained dangerously unresolved.

7   M. F. Husain (born in 1915) has been the most flamboyant and effervescent artistic personality of post-Independence India: one of the last surviving figures of the modernist era of progressive art movements in Calcutta, Bombay and Madras that coincided with India's independence.[7] His biographers highlight the way in which this Muslim artist, born in the small western Indian town of Pandharpur, emerged from his early working-class background and worlds of practising faith to reinvent himself as a secular and modernist artistic persona. It is in this capacity that he then proceeded to draw freely on Hindu religious and mythic iconographies as a source of inspiration for his art. That he could visualize the Hindu pantheon with such empathy and candour became the surest mark of his secular identity. Over the years, this lanky, bearded, barefoot artist, once a painter of cinema hoardings, acquired an iconic stature, no less than his signatorial array of horses, his images of Mother Teresa and Indira Gandhi, or his pageant of playful divine heroines (Figure 3.3). It was precisely his celebrity stature, public visibility and showmanship, compounded by the accident of his religion, that made Husain most vulnerable to the cultural bigotry of the country's Hindu right-wing during the mid and late 1990s. Through the attack on Husain, it was the whole privileged world of modern art and the privileged stature of the artist as 'super-citizen' that were being called into question within a new politicized public domain that staked its own control over artistic representation.[8]

88

Figure 3.3 M. F. Husain, Goddess Durga Astride a Tiger (Acrylic on Canvas, c. 1980). Reproduced Courtesy of the Artist.

8   These attacks on Husain, as has been widely commented upon, were triggered by external factors that had nothing to do with either art or religion. In 1996, there was a series of specific animosities brewing between Husain and the BJP government of Madhya Pradesh, led by Sunderlal Patwa, over the running of a major art institution in the state (Bhopal's Bharat Bhavan) and the allocation of land for Husain's art gallery at Indore, that directly motivated the first protesters and the first wave of attacks.[9] These hostilities were then quickly transmitted on to the local units of the Shiv Sena in Mumbai and the Bajrang Dal in Ahmedabad who turned their ire on Husain's flat in Mumbai and on his art gallery at Ahmedabad (the Husain-Doshi Gufa). It became all too clear that what was at work against Husain was a Hindu right-wing political vendetta, of the most violent kind, riding on trumped-up concerns about licence and morality in art and the norms of Hindu iconography. Yet, the sheer virulence with which these 'extra-artistic' factors have come to repeatedly disrupt the secure practices of modern art forces one to take stock of the flow of charges against these artistic representations and the construction of the 'crimes' of the artist. What the allegations did

expose was the wide rift that existed between the nude as a symbol of high art and the nude as a target of popular, public disapproval, straining the thin boundary that marks out the 'artistic' from the 'obscene', testifying to the perennially contentious status of the unclothed body (especially the naked female body) in the public domain.[10]

Nudity has been held out as Husain's cardinal and most pernicious offence. His audacity, it was alleged, lay not only in the public depiction of nude female bodies but also in labelling these figures with names of Hindu goddesses like Saraswati, Lakshmi or Parvati. This act of disrobing the goddesses was seen not just as a gross misrepresentation of Hindu mythology (so he would paint a near-naked Draupadi even where legend protected her from being fully disrobed) but also as sign of outright disrespect (Figure 3.4). Worse still (we are told) is Husain's predilection for depicting goddesses in sexual union with the animals that carry them. Cast into the stereotypical image of the Muslim sexual predator, nudity in his hands came to be construed as acts of sexual violation: acts tantamount to the 'rape of Hindu goddesses'. And the root cause for such mischief was shown to reside in 'the nature of the religion and culture which Husain embraces'.[11] The entire campaign revolved around the naming of Husain as a Muslim artist, producing a terrifying equation between the painter's religion, his immoral passion for nude female figures and his urge to disrespect Hindu sentiments.

In the years that have followed, the target of attack moved from Husain's paintings of Draupadis and Sitas to his figuration of 'Bharat-Mata' ('Mother India'), where a hot-red nude female body is morphed on to the map of India, flanked by the topography of the Himalayas and the oceans, and inscribed with the names of cities and the official national symbol of the Buddhist wheel (Figure 3.5). The offence to Hindu religion is seen to expand here into an even graver insult and abuse of the nation. To prove that he uses nudity as an instrument of deliberate humiliation, there are websites that lay out pairs of Husain's paintings, where he is shown to paint his mother,

Figure 3.4 M. F. Husain, 'Draupadi in the Game of Dice' (lithograph, 1983), *Mahabharata* Series. Reproduced Courtesy of the Peabody Art Museum, Salem.

Figure 3.5 M. F. Husain, 'Bharat-Mata' (Acrylic on canvas, 2005). Reproduced Courtesy of the Artist and Apparao Galleries, Chennai.

his daughter, the Prophet's daughter Fatima and all Muslim ladies (i.e. all women he respects) fully clothed while stripping all his Hindu goddesses and his figure of Bharat-Mata.[12] From the local and national, the campaign against Husain moved on to a global arena. In 2006, an exhibition of his paintings of Hindu divinities at the Asia House was stalled by a Hindu human rights group. An even more crucial marker of the 'global' is cyber-space, which now serves as the main site for the proliferation and circulation of anti-Husain propaganda – an endlessly expansive space from where a new global political community of Hindus is being mobilized in moral defence of the nation and its iconographies.

11   Right from the start of the campaign, the protestors have been vocal in their assertion of Husain's 'crime'. While there is no clear legal definition of what constitutes 'obscenity' in art, the legal proscriptions work around the purported offence and disorder that a work deemed to be obscene can cause in the public domain. The contestation of what constitutes the public spaces of viewing and circulation of art has remained at the heart of the debates. A number of clauses from the Indian Penal Code – relating to the 'Indecent Representation of Women', 'Offences Relating to Religion' and 'Offences against Public Tranquillity' – were invoked to frame the charges. The last of these was

the most insidious, where the concrete evidence for offended religious sentiments was seen to lie in the public disorder that this injury incited. The burning of the artist's effigy, the destruction of his painting, the ransacking of his gallery and apartment – all became 'proof' of the public outrage that Husain's paintings were causing, providing a ready reason for their removal from the public scene. The legal defenders of the artist have been arguing, all along, that if this was at all an 'art-crime', it was less a crime *by* art, far more a crime *against* art.[13] It has been argued, for instance, that the prime offender in the Husain case should have been the person who, in the first instance, searched out and dragged into the public domain and published in the local periodical of Bhopal, *Vichar Mimansa*, the so-called 'offensive' painting of the nude Saraswati. The charges of criminal offence need to be turned on those who have instigated and perpetrated the attacks on Husain's paintings and property, prevented the exhibition and sale of his paintings, banned the screening of his film, *Gaja-Gamini*, in theatres in Mumbai and Ahmedabad, and threatened the artist with murderous assault.

The defence and the apology

12   Coming in the wake of the *fatwa* against Salman Rushdie and India's banning of *The Satanic Verses*, these attacks on Husain raised the spectre of a global siege of artistic freedom. Armed with a battery of counter-arguments, the artistic and intellectual community in India mobilized itself in a huge show of solidarity around Husain.[14] What is instructive, though, is the way that this defence has had to constantly shift its grounds from what was most directly at stake – the 'freedom of artistic expression' – to justify instead the Indian authenticity and legitimacy of Husain's nudes. The nature of the charges made it imperative that scholars corrected the falsified notions of tradition that were being used against Husain, to explain that there was nothing about his imagery that transgressed the bounds of either 'art' or Indian religious iconography. The crux of this art historical defence lay in looking back to India's long artistic tradition of the female nude, highlighting the ritual validity of nudity in Indian sculptural iconography, pointing to the innumerable instances of unclothed female figures (divine and semi-divine) in Indian sculpture and temple architecture. In his interviews of 1996–7, the artist himself participated actively in this mode of self-legitimization, projecting his art as an integral 'part of India's five-thousand-year-old culture', going to lengths to show how heavily his vocabulary was informed by the past traditions of Indian sculpture, and how as 'a quintessential Indian' he had internalized the spirit of Hindu myths and icons.[15]

13   These counter-stances, however, did little to change public perceptions or stem the tide of the assaults. The celebration of the sexual feminine imagery of ancient Indian art, especially the erotic temple sculptures of a site like Khajuraho, could go hand in hand with the continued polemics against Husain's nudes in another public sphere, allowing the elaborate construction of the artistic legitimacy of the one versus the perceived illegitimacy of the other (Figures 3.6a and 3.6b).[16] The female nude, it has been argued, stands 'not only at the centre of the definition of art, but also on the dangerous edge of the category, brushing against obscenity. The female nude is the border, the *parergon* as Derrida calls it, between art and obscenity'.[17] What the shifting art historical fortunes of the temple maidens of Khajuraho and the nude goddesses of Husain

Figure 3.6 a Dancing Surasundari (Celestial Maiden) Putting on an Anklet, Parsvanatha Temple, Khajuraho (Sandstone, Tenth Century). Photograph, Courtesy, American Institute of Indian Studies, New Delhi. *b* M. F. Husain, Untitled (Lithograph, 1974). Reproduced Courtesy of the Artist.

point to are the tenuousness of such borders – and the highly contingent and motivated nature of the charge of the 'obscene' in the way it accretes around a certain body of imagery in a particular time and place, and absolves others. Such contingencies are what enabled Khajuraho's gradual passage from the 'shame and stigma' to the pride of its erotic sculptures in the art history of post-Independence India. They have also allowed for a range of far bolder and eroticized representations of the mythic female form to thrive in the work of several other modern Indian artists, while suddenly placing under censure Husain's fairly innocuous, taut and bony line drawing of Saraswati.

14   The moot issue lay in determining which body of imagery could seek the immunities and licences of modern art, and remain in this insulated sphere, and which others were to be inappositely thrust into an unprotected public domain. The autonomy of the sphere of modern art practices is what came most severely under threat in the campaign against Husain. Its freedoms and authority faced the greatest checks. From a secure, fortified shield, the 'modern' would become a slippery and unstable ground for Husain. This is why neither he nor his defenders could take effective refuge in the

legacy of the nation's modern and contemporary art history. To hold on to the arrogance and prerogatives of modern art would not have been a commendable stance in a political environment where the *Hindutva* prejudice against Husain's nudes reflected a larger hostility to the very object of modern Indian art and the licences it enjoyed. To cite the cases of innumerable other more lascivious modernist nudes in the works of Husain's contemporaries, or to argue that 'Hindu' modern artists have as unabashedly unclothed their goddesses as this 'Muslim', would have exposed them all to the same dangers and violations. So, paradoxically, the best defence for this distinctly modernist artist and his peers was to justify his imagery in terms of ancient sculptural precedents and religious iconography. The motivated force and direction of the attacks on him left him few options, and made the claims to 'artistic freedom' a particularly treacherous ground to stand on. With his back to the wall, he could publicly indulge in none of the modernist daring about the inversions of tradition, about laying bare bodies and sexualities, or about playfully mocking one's gods and goddesses. Whatever may have been the artistic intention of these images, the proud options of transgression and irreverence (the founding premises of modernist aesthetics, and of all 'avant-garde' art) were not open to Husain in the face of these attacks.[18] Instead of holding to his modern artistic licence to disrespect or break with tradition, he could only offer up for his detractors his deep 'respect' for the goddesses he had portrayed, and the 'innocence' and 'spirituality' of his erotic representations. He has had to declare, for instance, that the title 'Bharat-Mata' was not one that he had given the painting under attack, but one given without his knowledge by the organizers of the art auction. Worst of all were the string of apologies that Husain had to offer to the Shiv Sena for the offence his paintings had inadvertently caused.

15   In rounding off this discussion of the 'Husain affair', let me pose the problem of transgression on a different register, by pushing it away from the content of Husain's images on to the ontological status of his works within a public domain. What was being violated, all through this controversy, was not only the authority of the 'work of art', but also the all-important boundaries between 'art' and 'non-art'. Husain's paintings were being dragged out of the sphere of modern art practices to answer charges in a public political domain to which they never belonged. It is important to labour the point that Husain's goddesses were 'works of art' that were never intended to serve as religious icons, even as we struggle to demarcate a legitimate public domain that his artworks can occupy, without encountering public wrath or offending the religious sentiments of worshippers. There are generic distinctions to be made between the visualization of goddesses in Husain's art and those in popular print-productions and calendar art, equally between the fields of reception and circulation of these divergent genres of images. While he has worked with a series of popular referents, culled especially from film posters and hoardings, Husain's images have also unsettled these idioms in a way that resist their easy reception by consumers of popular culture.[19] The point to reiterate is that a work of modern art has seldom been able to comfortably inhabit this unbounded domain of the 'popular'. The situation is particularly paradoxical in the case of Husain, who, more than any other contemporary artist, has consciously courted the popular – obsessively drawing on the fantasies and indulgences of Bollywood cinema (as in his famous Madhuri series of paintings and film) and spraying his imprint across prints, posters, tin cans and designer drapes to produce a

Figure 3.7 M. F. Husain, 'Madhuri as Radha' (Lithograph Series, c. 1990). Reproduced Courtesy of the Artist.

'cottage industry' of his own images in the market (Figure 3.7).[20] Yet, in all these citations and interventions, Husain would never have wished to have dissolved the divide that kept his artistic oeuvre securely apart from these many other genres of mass-productions, nor to have given up the vantage position of the 'secular modern' from which he operated. The popular public sphere has claimed him in a way that he could never have bargained for. It has eroded his high ground of autonomy and immunity, leaving him and his art dangerously vulnerable before a hateful and inapposite public.

Goddesses that have become 'art': Notes from the Durga Pujas of contemporary Calcutta[21]

16 If the campaign against M. F. Husain has allowed the new claims of the 'religious' to intrude into the secularized domain of modern art, the field of Durga Puja celebrations in today's Calcutta is marked by a pointedly opposite trend – the conspicuous secularization of a religious festival and its metamorphosis into a public 'art event'. The transforming nature of this public field can be seen to both preserve and erase the markings

Figure 3.8 Remake of the Fort and Palace Architecture of Rajasthan at Suruchi Sangha Puja, New Alipore, 2004. Reproduced Courtesy of the Visual Archive of the CSSSC.

of the ritual occasion within the body of the urban festival, continuously deflecting the ambience of worship into one of display and spectacle. In the context of this article, it is instructive to see how this field of festivity has assumed a special artistic character in recent times, and has generated its own discourse on 'art' production and reception, even as it has remained categorically distanced from the sequestered worlds of contemporary art practices in the city.[22]

17 During the days and nights of the festival, the entire topography of the city undergoes a magical transfiguration, with the streets taken over by myriad shapes and forms of *pandals* (temporary pavilions that are erected to house the images of the goddess). These *pandals* (as all of us who live in this city know) serve primarily as exhibition sites, taking on spectacular forms of architectural replicas, remakes of temples, forts and palaces, theme parks and craft villages (Figure 3.8). For several years now, a defining feature of such spectacles has been an unfettered local licence to copy, reassemble and reinvent whatever monument or site catches the fancy of organizing clubs, producers and publics. From the pre-historic cave sites of Bhimbhetka in central India to distant African villages, from the temples of Orissa or Khajuraho to the Opera House of Paris, all of India and the world are laid open for free 'tours' to the people of the city during the week of the festival (Figures 3.9 and 3.10). In keeping with these tableaux, the images of the goddess and her entourage take on newer and newer forms (Figure 3.11) each icon competing with its rivals as an object for viewing and photography. The ambience is increasingly that of public art installations – so like art exhibitions, Pujas these days are routinely 'opened' by invited celebrities, designed by art school trained artists or set design professionals, often organized by professional event managers, and drawn into competitions for a growing number of awards for excellence of production offered by media groups and commercial houses in the city.

18 At the same time, there is a public, popular and, most importantly, an ephemeral dimension to the field of production that firmly sets it apart from the established enclaves of modern art: its circuit of art galleries, exhibitions, catalogues, critics and

THE BLURRING OF DISTINCTIONS

Figure 3.9 A Ghanaian Village at the Behala Sahajatri Puja, 2004. Reproduced Courtesy of the Visual Archive of the CSSSC.

Figure 3.10 The Facade of the Paris Opera House at a Salt Lake Durga Puja, 2009. Reproduced Courtesy of the Visual Archive of the CSSSC.

collectors. For all its endeavours to innovate, experiment and inculcate new artistic tastes in the spectator, all Durga Puja tableaux must take their place within an unenclosed and unbounded public domain, and must struggle to find popular approbation alongside connoisseurial attention. The locations being the open street and roadside parks, all *pandal* structures, however elaborate, must also come down at the end of the festival week, just as every Durga clay idol, however beautiful, must be ritually immersed at the end of the Puja. The new publicity and prestige that surround this domain of 'festival' art, just like the new artistic identities that are staked around it,

Figure 3.11 The Durga Image-Group in the Style of Pahari Miniature Painting, in Keeping with the Rajasthani Architectural Tableaux, Being Photographed by Television News Reporters – Suruchi Sangha Puja, New Alipore, 2004. Reproduced Courtesy of the Visual Archive of the CSSSC.

tend to be as fleeting and seasonal as the event itself. The lack of durability and permanence gives this body of creations a status that does not brook any easy or sustained equation with the more entrenched worlds of 'art' and 'artists'. So, even as the Durga Puja festivities have taken on the form of a major public art event in the city, there is still a crucial line of distinction to be maintained between the objects of modern art and these Durga Puja productions: a line that keeps blurring but is also continuously renegotiated by artists and publics on either side of the divide.

Of central importance to this discussion is the long-established nomenclature of the Durga Puja as a 'festival': as a time of public congregation, conviviality, and the intricate enmeshing of worship with mass celebration. The process of secularization of the festival in and around the city of Calcutta has a long history that goes back to the early twentieth century, when the Puja moved from elite households to the open streets, from *zamindari* patronage to community sponsorship, and when, in select areas, the community or the *sarbojanin* Puja also became an important platform for anti-colonial nationalist gatherings and mobilization.[23] Over the latter half of the twentieth century, it is this category of the community or the *sarbojanin* Puja, organized by neighbourhood clubs which grew to unprecedented scales, drawing on a growing corpus of funds from subscriptions and sponsorships, jostling with each other to provide the season's most spectacular tableaux of *pandals*, decoration and lighting. The declining weight of the religious within the changing body of the urban festival is now part of a long, familiar lament. The argument can always be pushed both ways. At one level, it can be pointed out that the ritual calendar continues to set the dates for the annual event – that the prescribed icon of Durga, surrounded by her four children, continues to feature as the centrepiece of the ever-new forms of *pandal* designs; and however innovative be the image of the goddess and the structures that house her, what continues is the performance of all the rituals of worship through the five days of the Puja. On the other hand, it can also be shown that the Puja is often no more than an excuse for a huge spurt of consumption, for a flood of new productions and releases, and a mega show of lights, sights and sounds that have increasingly obscured the religious event and the sanctity of its performance. Taking for granted, then, the now longstanding identity of Calcutta's Durga Puja as a secularized festival and the city's most extravagant mass public event, the main contemporary shift that I wish to foreground is the entry into the field of a distinct set of claims and discourses about 'art' production. This artistic identity is one that has had to struggle to assert itself both within the structure of the religious event and within the space of mass display and spectacle.

20   The recent career of a particular genre of production, which is locally termed the 'art' or the 'theme' Puja, provides the main lead for tracking the new artistic profile of the festival. There are multiple markers of 'art' that energize these productions and give them a cognitively distinctive status in local perceptions. One clear marker lies in the kinds of forms given to the iconography of the goddess and the nature of the *pandal* tableaux constructed around the icon. There are broadly two standardized forms – one, the realistic, movie-heroine type appearance of the goddess, with muscle-flexing *Asuras* and growling life-like lions; the other, the large-eyed traditional stylized faces of the goddess ensemble under one frame (*ekchaala*) (Figures 3.12 and 3.13) – against which the newness of conceptions are staged each season. One needs to look more closely, though, into what constitutes the 'new wave' within this genre of productions, and what kinds of licences and novelties find acceptance within this field. Unlike the parallel field of modern Indian art, here, the modernity or contemporaneity of the new productions constantly have to seek out a base in traditional authenticities, whether classical or folk. Examples of distinctly modernist Puja installations or images of the goddess turn out on the whole to be far less effective than the different archaeological and craft ensembles and a flourishing variety of 'folk-art' Durgas that have swept the field (Figures 3.14 a and 3.14b).

21   There is also, often, a distinct contemporary category of the 'secular' (a recognizably political ideology of 'secularism') that is profiled in these Durga Puja tableaux – as

Figure 3.12 Example of the Realistic Style of the Goddess and a Muscle-Flexing Asura – Durga Puja, Barisha, Behala, 2008. Reproduced Courtesy of the Visual Archive of the CSSSC.

Figure 3.13 Example of a More Traditional Stylized Single Unit Durga Pantheon – Durga Puja, Salt Lake, 2008. Reproduced Courtesy of the Visual Archive of the CSSSC.

Figure 3.14 *a* (Left) and *b* (Below). A Typical 'Folk Art' Durga in a Recreated Bhil and Gond Art Village – Behala Club Puja, 2006. Reproduced Courtesy of the Visual Archive of the CSSSC.

we see in the 'Communal Harmony' installation set up in 2002 in a south Calcutta venue, where the designer blended the architectural styles and décor of a temple and a mosque to highlight the 'cross-fertilization of Islamic and Hindu cultures' (Figure 3.15) where the Durga image took on the look of a Mughal miniature painting, and her sari the patterning of Persian carpets, and where the idol at the far end was set off at the entrance by the most famous media photograph of the Gujarat carnage of 2002 (the

THE BLURRING OF DISTINCTIONS

Figure 3.14 Continued.

Figure 3.15 The 'Communal Harmony' Temple-Mosque Fusion Tableau at Hindusthan Park Puja, 2002. Reproduced Courtesy of the Visual Archive of the CSSSC.

face of Mohammad Ansari pleading for police protection). It is in the same contemporary spirit of the 'secular' that that another neighbouring Durga Puja tableau, the same year, laid claims on the early nineteenth-century Muslim millenarian peasant rebel of Bengal, Titumeer (of the Faraizi movement), and reconstructed with great aplomb in a small local park Titumeer's legendary bamboo fortress, one that is said to have been felled in a single night by Bentinck's army (Figure 3.16). For the designer of this Puja, the choice of Titumeer and his imaginary fort was made in a clear-cut

Figure 3.16 Recreation of Titumeer's Bamboo Fortress at Babubagan Club Puja, Dhakuria, 2002. Reproduced Courtesy of the Visual Archive of the CSSSC.

present-day stance of anti-colonialism and anti-communalism – by these terms, by this reading, Titumeer (a militant *Jihadi*, an iconoclast and Islamic puritan) can be non-controversially appropriated as an archetypal subaltern nationalist rebel and his story easily accommodated within the space of a Durga Puja *pandal*.

22 Such overt anti-communal stances apart, the 'secular' dimensions of today's festivities, I would argue, find their most powerful manifestation in the name of 'art'. Even in the traditional milieu of the production and worship, the Durga Puja always involved the work of several Muslim rural artisans, who would supply different elements of the goddess's arms, ornaments or *pandal* decorations. This has long been a part of the inclusive syncretic flavour of the festival. In recent times, this image is given an altogether new 'secular' and 'artistic' orientation by a novel type of creative personnel who have captured the field of Durga Puja designing, side by side with the communities of hereditary idol-makers or the suburban firms of *pandal*-decorators who had long dominated the trade. The field now attracts in growing numbers a diverse group of artists and designers, ranging from the successful art-college trained professionals and film and television set-producers, to local amateurs, to a type who stand ambivalently strung between identities of 'artist' and 'artisan'. Cut off from the cosmopolitan, national and international circuits of modern art activity, deprived equally of access to the worlds of high design or advertising, this provincial group has found in the local sphere of Durga Puja productions a main avenue of earning and acclaim. It is in their conscious capacity as 'modern artists' that they have intervened in this field of public art, and brought with them a new concept of production. Under this new dispensation, the Puja in its entirety – the image, the *pandal*, the surrounding tableaux, the colours, the decoration and even the music – is conceived of and laid out as an integrated 'theme' (hence the nomenclature of 'theme' Pujas) either by an individual artist with the help of artisan labour, or by an art designer and his team, or sometimes by

event-impresarios who mobilize supervising artists and rural craft persons from near and far to work on these projects. There is a close complementarity, here, between these different types of creative personnel, their work processes and their styles of productions, within the rapidly spreading domain of 'art' Pujas in the city.

23 There is today a rich graph to be plotted of artistic careers, authorial styles and design typologies within the phenomenon of the 'art' Pujas, just as there are new maps to be tracked of its spread and proliferation across the extended space of the festival city. We could cite the instance of two of the most prominent of this new creed of young Durga Puja 'artists' of contemporary Calcutta – Sanatan Dinda and Bhabatosh Sutar – both of whom have worked their way up from humble backgrounds to secure an art college training, and have used their rising credentials in the field of Durga Puja productions to carve out aspiring careers in the alternative circuits of gallery art. Sanatan Dinda came to specialize in a particular style of Tantrik iconography of the goddess, imaginatively drawing on the traditions of Pala period stone sculpture and the bronze statuary of the Himalayan Buddhist pantheon (Figures 3.17 a and 3.17b) placing his Durga creations within simulated tree shrines and mixed pagoda and temple ensembles, all of which would be fabricated each year in a narrow alley in north Calcutta.

24 Bhabatosh Sutar, on the other hand, has made his name in the field, by working closely with various local craft and folk forms (like Bankura terracotta sculpture, West Dinajpur bamboo and wood carvings or Shantipur handlooms) to spearhead a form of Puja installation that innovatively cites and subsumes these craft idioms within his own signatorial style (Figures 3.18 a and 3.18b). What holds together their respective

Figure 3.17 a and b Two Durga Creations by Sanatan Dinda at his Hatibagan Pujas. Reproduced Courtesy of the Visual Archive of the CSSSC. *a* (Left) Durga in the Style of a Pala-Period Black Schist Sculpture, 2002. *b* (Right) Durga in the Style of Tibetan Buddhist Bronze Sculpture, 2006.

Figure 3.18a Two Durga Creations by Bhabatosh Sutar: Durga in the Style of Bankura Terracotta Statuary, Barisha Shrishti Puja, 2002.

styles is a tight authorial control over the entire production, a common premium on the centrality of Durga image with which they begin and around which they plan the larger ensemble, and a deep investment in both the artistry and the religiosity of the Durga imagery they sculpt each year. While Dinda has refused to work in any other medium except the ritually prescribed alluvial clay and has declined an offer for the collection and preservation of one of his images in a museum, Sutar has been open to sculpting his Durgas with durable material like wood or baked and lacquered clay, with the conscious intention of the post-Puja preservation of his works, arranging for the rituals to be performed before a small substitute set of clay idols which are to be immersed. Much to the pride of the first Puja club with which he made his name, Sutar stands out as one of the few Puja designers whose images have found their way into collections for three consecutive years (2003–5) – one was acquired by a five-star hotel, another by a private art collector, and a third for a state craft museum.[24]

We are standing, then, in a public field where the Durga images can be seen to simultaneously inhabit their double identities as worshipped icons and works of art. The claims of ritual and artistic productions can comfortably coalesce, here, without

THE BLURRING OF DISTINCTIONS

Figure 3.18b Durga as a Primeval Animistic Force Rising Out of Fire, Naktala Udayan Sangha Puja, 2009. Both Reproduced Courtesy of the Visual Archive of the CSSSC.

any overt sense of violation and transgression. In the new worlds of Calcutta's Durga Puja, the works of 'artists' like Dinda and Sutar can be seen to stand within a spreading wave of such art styles and fashions – of several varieties of Tantrik-art Durgas with *pandals* replete with Yantra symbolisms and motifs, and an even wider array of primitivist, folk-art Durgas – where artistic liberties with form never seem to push against the basic iconographic tenets of the image of the goddess. We need to ask what allows for such overlaps and fluidities between 'artistic' and 'religious' designations in this genre of imagery and disallows them in others. The clues, one can show, lie in the very conditions that differentiate this field of production and display from the exclusive domain of modern art practices.

26 If the contemporary festival presents an upsurge of artistic claims and assertions, it also exposes the ambivalence and fragilities of the identities of 'art' in this ephemeral sphere. The category of the Durga Puja 'artist' is one that struggles to find a firm foothold in a world, where (as I have already stated) recognition and success frequently turn out to be as temporary as the event itself, and where few routes open out for admission into the more exclusive national or international modern art circuits. None of the prestige and glamour, little of the social and cultural capital, and certainly nothing comparable to the kinds of prices that the modern Indian artist commands on the art market are available to this circle of designers and their works. One of the oldest and best-known corporate Durga Puja awards, on offer since 1985 by Asian Paints, still searches out winners under the label, 'Best Artisan of the Year' – a label that merges these artists with the community of traditional idol-makers from whom they wish to stand apart, and denies them the very status of 'artist' that they covet. The same anomalies also hover around the Durga image on view in the *pandals*, or on display in a hotel lawn or a craft museum. Whether or not these images can be accorded, the epithet of 'art' is a much-debated subject in Calcutta's artistic circles. In post-Puja

LITERARY THEORY AND CRITICISM

settings, in particular, these figures seem to lose their animation and lie in a curious state of liminality: as 'icons' whose lives have passed and as 'artworks' whose lives are still to be defined.[25]

Conclusion: A problem of publics

27 I highlight these ambivalences that surround Durga Puja 'art' and 'artists' to mark out, once again, its separateness from the contiguous sphere of contemporary art, where the critical lines of distinction between the 'religious' and the 'art' object still fall powerfully in place. In contrast to the field of the Pujas, the distinctions here need constantly to be reaffirmed and resurrected – to stake claims to a special order of artistic privileges vis-à-vis sacred icons, and to mark out a select public as the target of address. The question of publics, their artistic literacy and initiation in certain languages of representation, is centrally at issue. If, in the unbounded space of mass-viewing, the 'art' of the Pujas can never escape the demands of popular appeal and approbation, and must coexist with a host of more mundane or standardized productions, the modern artwork, on the contrary, thrives within its own circles of exclusion and sets its own clear bounds on the publics it cultivates and the connoisseur community to which it belongs. Despite its investment in the transformation of public tastes, there can be no sealing-off of a niche audience for these new Durga Puja productions in the same ways that are possible for modern avant-garde productions. This has direct bearings on the kinds of iconographies that emerge and thrive in these overlapping but distinctly divergent spheres.

28 In bringing together these two apparently incommensurate worlds of productions and practices, the main intention of this chapter has been to open up a set of oppositional tropes in the kinds of authorities and immunities that 'art' confers on its subjects and objects. One of its broader concerns has been to test the terms and conditions on which 'art' can encode the space of the 'secular' in contemporary India, and the extent to which it can assert its creative prerogatives over images that come out of a supposedly segregated domain of the 'religious'. In its claims on images of divinities, how effectively can modern art deflect the 'religious' into the 'cultural' and produce an alternative category of iconicity? Conversely, how smoothly can images that lie embedded within a different history of worship and popular devotion live out their new lives as objects of 'art'? In engaging with these questions, much is at stake, I have argued, in determining the fields of public location and engagement of these realms of images.

29 The paradoxes that beset Husain's iconographies of Hindu goddesses and the nation, as they are stripped of their designation as 'art' by a hostile and indignant public, are offset by the paradoxes that hover around the new age iconographies of Durga, as they can only partially be transfigured as 'art' in a shifting zone of public tastes and demands. In each case, there are different battles to be waged in securing for these images their desired publics and in defining the limits to the licences they seek. As contemporary Indian art finds itself periodically pushed into a domain of public accountability and thrown open to a new intensity of public adjudication on its freedoms and responsibilities, there is an urgent need to constitute a different sense of proprietorship over cultures, mythologies and iconographies – one that would

THE BLURRING OF DISTINCTIONS

legitimize the representational licences of the veteran Husain, as much as those of his younger counterparts who form the contemporary avant-garde, or those of upcoming Durga Puja designers of Calcutta, while also underlining their widely divergent locations in the contemporary art milieu. We would have to keep asking: what kinds of immunity, protection and authority can they varyingly claim or take for granted? And what are the public domains that these many worlds of art can rightfully and comfortably inhabit?

This chapter has been all about contrasts and anomalies. Let me end by juxtaposing, again, two contrary scenarios of limits and possibilities. In one, we have the self-exiled Husain, his celebrity stature undiminished by the unceasing campaign against him, reaching out to the world with élan while contending with an increasingly shrinking national space of inhabitation of his art. If his Hindu right-wing detractors have made capital out of a deliberate misrecognition and non-comprehension of his iconographies, lambasting them as 'immoral' and 'anti-national', a section of his own community of artists, curators and gallery owners in India has also distanced itself from his art, for the needless political controversy it drags into its secure enclaves. Given the regularity with which Husain's works have been vandalized in galleries and exhibitions, there is a strong fear within this community of further endangering these locations of art and their precious rights and privileges. So, during 2008 and 2009, the biggest modern art fair in the capital – the mega Indian art summit at Pragati Maidan – chose to play it safe by not showing any works of Husain, pointedly excluding the very person who had first brought big money into contemporary Indian art. In the other scenario, we have a host of small-time Durga Puja artists, with none of the fame or cultural capital of a Husain, seeking out new artistic designations and public spaces of viewing for their work and basking under a rising spurt of corporate attention, within the very localized milieu of the city's festival. The safety and prestige of the artistic

Figure 3.19 A Tantrik-Style Unclothed Durga Being Worshipped at Selimpur Pally Puja, 2006. Reproduced Courtesy of the Visual Archive of the CSSSC.

locations that Husain has had to forfeit are being actively claimed by this other group. It is tempting to think of them as playing out, albeit within a very different vernacular forum, Husain's dream of embodying popular tastes and of letting free the modern art object within a more open circuit of reception and consumption. It is specially pertinent to see how the contentious nude, that is rendered into such a vehement target of outrage in Husain's images of goddesses, can comfortably rest within a new register of Tantrik iconography and devotional affect within the ambit of viewing and worship of Calcutta's Durga Puja. So, while Husain's playfully irreverent and erotic Durgas continue to fight the charges of defamation and transgression and live within a precarious politics of risk,[26] a resplendent nude red Durga can unproblematically hold her own as both an aesthetic and worshipped object in a festival that has been able to freely negotiate the boundaries between 'art' and 'religion' (Figure 3.19).

Textual and rhetorical questions

Textual

1. The distinction between artistic and religious objects in the sites of art production and reception has become a matter of sieging culture. Such besieging brings further contestation between sacred and secular (paragraphs 1 and 2). What is Thakurta's thesis on art, religion, the sacred, and the secular? Answer the question considering what she proposes (paragraphs 3 and 4): The spiritual in the Indian art tradition has secular designation. Does she suggest that art is no less sacred and spiritual than religion is? (Similarly, do the defenders of religion also claim that the sacred and spiritual belong to their domain?)
2. The religious nature of Indian artistic tradition is constantly blurred in Calcutta (Kolkata) Durga Puja spectacles (paragraph 4). After presenting and analysing the "Hussain affair" in paragraphs 15 to 25, Thakurta argues how Durga Puja in Kolkata has become a space of the secular, that is, worship performed as spectacle, and festivity performed as artistic. Trace the paragraphs where she writes about "anti-communal harmony" and the "syncretic flavor of the festival" and analyse her arguments which critique the rightist political nature of modern India.
3. The writer critiques the nature of "public accountability," "public adjudication," exile of the artist, and stands taken by the "community of the artists, curators, and gallery owners" (paragraphs 28 to 30). Discuss her conclusions.

Rhetorical

1. Thakurta's criticism of religious fundamentalism is peppered throughout the essay. She uses terms like "redrawn and policed" (paragraph 4), "do not confuse" (paragraph 5), "license and morality of art and norms of Hindu iconography," "extra-artistic factors" (paragraph 8), and "hostile and indignant public" (paragraph 29). Find more words, phrases, and sentences where the writer proposes her arguments and writes back on the opponents of Hussain. Analyse the nature of attack in terms of expression and verbalisation of discourse, which is called style in rhetoric. What do you think about the appeal of the ethos in her writing? Is the

THE BLURRING OF DISTINCTIONS

ethos[27] exerted by her confidence of knowledge over the matter as reflected in the essay and/or is it her stand on art and religion?

2. Where does the writer give the opposition (those who opposed Hussain's paintings) their say? Trace the voices of the opposition. Does she provide occasions for debate? Does she defend herself and Hussain? How does she present her counter arguments?

Discussion questions

1. Goddess Saraswati in The *Matsya Purana* (Chapter IV) as Savitri, Shatarupa, Gayatri, and Brahmini forms evolves as Brahma's daughter. The father is attracted to her exquisite beauty while her brothers (sons of Brahma) felt ashamed by the God's urge for the daughter. Brahma sent them away and copulated with Saraswati. The mythical texts, the Khajuraho temple images, and the strut images of Hindu temples are pervasive with erotic, sexual images and icons. How do such arts represent religion? Is secular art profane in such representations?

2. Art is autonomous, it can threaten social establishments. Vivian in "The Decay of Lying" by Oscar Wilde compares art with nature:

> Art finds her own perfection within, and not outside of, herself. She is not to be judged by any external standard of resemblance. She is a veil, rather than a mirror. She has flowers that no forests know of, birds that no woodland possesses. She makes and unmakes many worlds, and can draw the moon from heaven with a scarlet thread. Hers are the "forms more real than living man."
>
> (664)[28]

What is your stand on the autonomy of art?

3. Jacque Derrida writes,

> everything that concerns the question and the history of truth, in its relation to the question of man, of what is proper to man, of human rights, of crimes against humanity, and so forth, all of this must in principle find its space of discussion without condition and without presupposition, its legitimate space of research and reelaboration, *in* the University and, within the University, above all *in* the Humanities.
>
> (25)[29]

Universities in South Asia, at times, are threatened by fundamental views against liberalisation. Discuss what the idea of university is in terms of questioning and debating everything under the sun and moon.

4. Satan questions servility. What is your perspective on authority?

Free, and to none accountable, preferring
Hard liberty before the easy yoke
Of servile Pomp.

(John Milton: *Paradise Lost: Book II*)

Inter-textual discussions

1. *The Adventures of Huckleberry Finn* was published in 1884. A library in Massachusetts opinionated that it offended conventional morality by the language spoken by Jim and Huck. A New York library removed it from their children's section. It charged, "Huck not only itched but he scratched, and that he said sweat when he should have said perspiration" (Dawn B. Sova. 2006. *Social*, 4).[30] *Alice's Adventures in the Wonderland* was banned in China for offending humans by featuring animals using human language (13). Emile Zola's *Nana* was banned in 1894 for writing "pernicious literature." One of the charges was "nothing more diabolical had ever been written by the pen of man; they are only fit for swine, and those who read them must turn their minds into cesspools," and his heroine is a prostitute (Sova, 234). The English translation by Richard F. Burton and F.F. Arbuthnot of Vatsayana's *Kama Sutra* was called the filthiest book and it was banned from entering into the United States in 1962 (Sova, *Sexual*,132–33). Valadimir Nabokov's *Lolita* was considered '"filth"' and banned in France and England, among other countries.[31] Why should a book or a work of art be banned? If the banning is on moral grounds, who decides the codes of morality? If it is based on the reason of inciting violence and threatening the stability of society, who should take the responsibility, the writer or the reader?
2. The movies of Hollywood and Bollywood are replete with bloodshed and violence and are received well as action movies. But a scene on explicit lovemaking generally goes through the scissors of the censor board in India. From the point of view of moral policing, which is more dangerous to society, scenes of violence or of love making? What may be the psychological factor behind such perspectives?

Critical and creative thinking

1. These sets of terms do not mean the same thing.
   Non-discourse and discourse
   Seeing and visuality
   Sex and sexuality[32]
   Naked and nudity[33]
   Can you see a naked body or is the body always constructed and discoursed and thus seeing the naked is never possible? Read the following anecdote and discuss the oppositions.

   A group of students registered for a class on "Sexuality" hoping that the semester will be full of excitement. The professor focused on Foucaudian notion of power, discussed patriarchy in the next class, American hegemony in the coming week, Russian and American politics in West Asia in the following classes. The students have to discuss on eco-feminism, "me too" movement, and likewise, the class invested on International Relation, Globalization and Feminism, Hijab, Spivak's "Situating Feminism," Marx, Gramsci, and Lucas. There was utter disappointment among the enthusiasts

THE BLURRING OF DISTINCTIONS

because everything under the sun and moon was discussed and very little of or almost nothing about sex. It was a class on sexuality not on sex.

Michael Foucault talks to Alessandro Fontana and Pasquale Pasquino in an interview in 1977. The interview is published as "Truth and Power." The sets of terms can be understood by how Foucault suggests systems of power construct truth and thus become discourse.

2. Kandinsky thinks, "Whither is this lifetime tending?" "To send light into the darkness of men's hearts – such is the duty of the artist," said Schumann. "An artist is a man who can draw and paint everything," said Tolstoi (26).[34] In your opinion, what is the message of the competent artist?

3. Chinnamasta is one of the goddesses of supreme knowledge in Hindu mythology. What is your response to the painting of the goddess? You may try to know the form of knowledge she represents. Write a commentary on a painting of the goddess who has severed her head and at then copulates with the god Shiva.[35]

4. The raindrop wanders and measures the body of the meditating goddess in Kalidasa's *Kumarasambhava*

The first clear rain-drops falling on her brow,
Gem it one moment with their light, and now
Kissing her sweet lip find a welcome rest
In the deep valley of the lady's breast;
Then wander broken by the fall within
The mazy channels of her dimpled skin.

(Griffith Canto V. *Kumarasambhava*) [36]

Philosopher Shankaracharya (9th century AD) known for his celibacy also, in is long poem *Saundarya Lahari* (*The Wave of Beauty*)[37] describes the body of the goddess Parvati. How does a devout religious poet "dare" to depict the beauty of the body of a goddess revered as mother?

Notes

1 A longer version of this chapter was first written as a plenary lecture for a conference titled 'Deus (e)x Historia', organized by the History, Theory and Criticism programme of the Department of Art and Architecture, MIT, USA, in April 2007. The main concern of the conference was with the 'return' of religion as a critical factor in global affairs and the profound challenges this has posed to the secularized practices of intellectual and artistic productions. It has subsequently been presented at seminars at the Centre for Studies in Social Sciences, Calcutta; at the Center for South Asian Studies, University of California, Los Angeles; and at TRAIN (Centre for Transnational Studies in Art, Identity and Nation), London. I am grateful for the comments and questions received at each of these presentations.

2 The text of the Delhi High Court judgement, along with a selection of recent newspaper editorials and petitions in support of Husain, has been published in a booklet, *Maqbool Fida Husain ... Petitioner* (New Delhi: Sahmat, 2008).

3 Somini Sengupta, 'An Artist in Exile Tests India's Democratic Ideals', *New York Times*, 8 November 2008. The current state and predicament of the artist is discussed in my essay, 'Fault-lines in a National Edifice: On the Right and Offences of Contemporary Indian Art'

111

LITERARY THEORY AND CRITICISM

and several other essays in Sumathi Ramaswamy, ed., *Barefoot Across the Nation: Maqbool Fida Husain and the Idea of India* (forthcoming, New Delhi: Routledge, 2010).

4 The categorical distinction between the two is taken for granted in all Western theories of art, from antiquity to the Enlightenment. See, for example, Moshe Barasch, *Theories of Art: From Plato to Winckelmann* (New York: New York University Press, 1985). On the art museum as the main institutional site for the production and perpetuation of this distinction, see, for example, Carol Duncan, *Civilizing Rituals: Inside Public Art Museums* (London and New York: Routledge, 1995), or David Carrier, *Museum Skepticism: A History of the Display of Art in Public Galleries* (Durham: Duke University Press, 2006).

5 I have elaborated on this theme in some of the essays in my book, *Monuments, Objects, Histories: Institutions of Art in Colonial and Postcolonial India* (New York: Columbia University Press, 2004).

6 Ever since its outburst, the 'Husain affair' has been the subject of a lot of journalistic and academic writing. Among the latter, are Monica Juneja, 'Reclaiming the Public Sphere: Husain's Portrayals of Saraswati and Draupadi', in *Economic and Political Weekly*, 25–31 January 1997; Karin Zitzewitz, 'On Signature and Citizenship: Further Notes on the Husain Affair', in Parul Dave-Mukerji, Deepta Achar and Shivaji Panikkar, eds, *Towards a New Art History: Studies in Indian Art* (New Delhi; D. K. Printworld, 2002); and my two essays, 'Clothing the Goddess: The Modern Contest over the Representations of the *Devi*', in Vidya Dehejia, ed., *Devi: The Great Goddess, Female Divinity in South Asian Art* (Washington DC: Sackler Gallery, 1999) and 'Art History and the Nude: On Art, Obscenity and Sexuality in Contemporary India' in *Monuments, Objects, Histories*.

7 The number of books written on Husain has been in proportion to the celebrity stature of the artist. Richard Bartholomew and Shiv S. Kapur, ed., *Maqbool Fida Husain* (New York: Harry N. Abrams, 1972); Geeta Kapur, 'Maqbool Fida Husain: Folklore and Fiesta' in *Contemporary Indian Painters* (New Delhi: Vikas, 1978); Dnyaneshwar Nadkarni, *Husain: Riding the Lightning* (Mumbai: Popular Prakashan, 1996); Rashda Siddiqui, *In Conversation with Husain Paintings* (New Delhi: Books Today, 2001); and K. Bikram Singha, *Maqbool Fida Husain* (New Delhi: Rahul & Art, 2008) provide a good sample, over time, of the field of writing on the artist.

8 Juneja, 'Reclaiming the Public Sphere', and Zitzewitz, 'On Signature and Citizenship'.

9 Md. Shahid Pervez, 'Why Sunderlal Patwa went for Husain's jugular', report from Bhopal, *The Statesman*, 15 October 1996.

10 Guha-Thakurta, 'Art History and the Nude', pp. 245–8.

11 Charges stated in the first criminal case brought against the artist by the Jamshedpur unit of the VHP, quoted in *The Telegraph*, 5 October 1996.

12 'M. F. Husain disrobes even our beloved Bharat mata! See with your own eyes the rogue painter's anti-national act' – Petition circulated by the Hindu Janjagruti Samiti 'to Protect the Pride of the Motherland' on Monday, 6 February 2006. Website: *Viveka-Jyoti* – 'Contributing our bit to Awaken, Unite and Strengthen Hindu Society'.

13 On the legal history of prosecutions of art, and the definitions in law about what constitutes 'crimes by art' as distinct from 'crimes against art', see Rajeev Dhavan, 'Censorship and Intolerance in India' and Akhil Sibal (the young lawyer defending Husain), 'Freedom of Speech and Expression: Constitutional and Legal Provisions' in *Iconography Now* (New Delhi: Sahmat, 2006); also, Lawrence Liang, 'Sense and Censoribility', Lead Essay, *The Art News Magazine of India*, Issue on Censorship, vol. xii, issue iii, no. iii, 2007.

14 One of the strongest expressions of this was carried in the cover story, 'In Defence of Freedom in Art: Against the *Hindutva* Attack on M. F. Husain', *Frontline*, Chennai, 15 November 1996, pp. 4–13.

15 Ibid., pp. 11–12. Citation from an interview with M. F. Husain in London, carried in *Frontline*, Chennai, 17 October 1996.

16 Guha-Thakurta, 'Art History and the Nude'.

THE BLURRING OF DISTINCTIONS

17 Lynda Nead, *The Female Nude: Art, Obscenity and Sexuality* (London and New York: Routledge, 1992), p. 25.
18 Anthony Julius, *Transgressions: The Offences of Art* (Chicago: University of Chicago Press, 2002) delves into transgressions as a constitutive feature of the identity of modernist art, ever since Flaubert and Manet, in an age that he marks as the 'Origins of the Transgressive Period'. Working out a complex typology of transgressions and its charges of offences, the book ends with its own provocative 'Coda: Every Work of Art Is an Uncommitted Crime'.
19 Juneja, 'Reclaiming the Public Sphere', p. 157.
20 Gayatri Sinha, 'Masses of Maqbool', *The Telegraph*, Arts & Ideas, Calcutta, 24 November 1995.
21 This section on Durga Puja in contemporary Calcutta is based on a collaborative research project, undertaken between 2002 and 2008, with my colleague, Dr Anjan Ghosh. It has drawn on the large archive of interviews, newspaper writings, publicity material, and photographs housed in the archive of the Centre for Studies in Social Sciences, Calcutta. The prime focus of my study has been on the changing visual culture and artistic profile of the festival.
22 Some of my main formulations about the new 'artistic' identity of the contemporary festival phenomenon in Calcutta are laid out in my article, 'From Spectacle to Art', *Art India, The Art News Magazine of India*, vol. ix, issue iii, quarter iii, 2004.
23 For a brief history of the changing social and civic character of the festival in nineteenth-century Calcutta, see Tithi Bhattacharya, 'Tracking the Goddess: Religion, Community and Identity in the Durga Puja Ceremonies in Nineteenth-Century Calcutta', *Journal of Asian Studies*, vol. 66, no. 4, November 2007.
24 My research has closely tracked the careers and changing forms of Puja productions of Sanatan Dinda and Bhabatosh Sutar, along with those of other Puja 'artists' in different neighbourhoods of Calcutta, from 2002 to 2008. While Sanatan Dinda ceased working on Durga Pujas in 2007, after ten years in this field, to graduate to a new identity as a painter and a Puja judge, Bhabatosh Sutar continues to be one of the topmost, award-winning Puja designers.
25 Even the most successful of Durga Puja designers, Bhabatosh Sutar, stands disillusioned about the prospects of his Puja productions (on which he invests immense expense, labour and time) finding their deserved place in art collections or corporate spaces. He is also disappointed by the lack of adequate attention and care given to his terracotta Durga Puja ensemble from 2003 that stands largely ignored behind glittering wedding party tableaux on the plush lawns of the ITC Sonar Bangla Hotel in Calcutta.
26 This theme of 'risk' and 'exile' entangling Husain's life and art is powerfully explored by Sumathi Ramaswamy in her Introduction, 'Barefoot across India; An Artist and his Country' in *Barefoot Across the Nation*.
27 See Ethos, Pathos, and Logic which are kinds of artistic proofs according to Aristotle in *The Art of Rhetoric*.
28 Oscar Wilde. "The Decay of Lying" in Hazard Adams (1992). *Critical Theory Since Plato*. Fort Worth, Harcourt Brace Jovanovich (658–70).
29 ("The Future of Profession or the University without Condition (Thanks to the "Humanities," What Could Take Place Tomorrow" in Cohen, Tom. (Ed.). (2001). *Jacque Derrida and the Humanities: A Critical Reader*. Cambridge: CUP. (24–57).
30 Sova, Dawn B. (2006). *Banned Books: Literatures Suppressed on Social Grounds*. New York: Facts On File.
31 Sova, Dawn B. (2006). *Banned Books: Literatures Suppressed on Sexual Grounds*. New York: Facts On File. See also, Karolides, Nicholas J. (2006). *Banned Books: Literatures Suppressed on Political Grounds*. New York: Facts On File.
32 See Foucault, Michael (1990). *The History of Sexuality*. New York: Vintage
33 See Nead, Linda (1992). *The Female Nude: Art, Obscenity and Sexuality*. London: Routledge.

34 Kandinsky, Wassily (2008) *Concerning the Spiritual in Art*. Trans. Michael T.H. Sadler. Floating Press (First published 1911).
35 See Kinsley, David R. (1998). *Tantric Visions of the Divine Feminine*. Delhi: Motilal Banarasidass.
36 Griffith, T.H. Trans. *The Birth of the War-God: A Poem by Kalidasa* (*Kumarasambhaba*). www/gutenberg.org/files/31968/31968-h/31968-h.htm -.
37 The poem can be accessed online.

4

WOMEN AND FREEDOM

Firdous Azim

1   Feminist movements use many strategies and deploy various political and social theories for the attainment of their goals. In the new globalized order, 'third world' feminisms have taken recourse to a language of rights, seeking to bring in processes like the world conferences or conventions such as the Convention for the Elimination of all Forms of Discrimination against Women (CEDAW) for the framing of national agendas and demands. Whilst this has been an empowering strategy, what remains in the background is the notion of 'liberation'. Rights speak a language of equality and fair play, of entitlements and access. From within this arena of a rights-oriented movement, I would like to seek spaces where a redress of women's subordinated position translates not only into a movement for justice and equality, but also highlights the questions of freedom and liberation. These may be the spaces where women's problematic social positioning is highlighted, where the meaning of 'freedoms' as it pertains in a gender-discriminated world can be debated.

2   This paper will look at the way that notions of freedom enter into women's debates in their struggle for the formation of both personal and national identities or identities as citizens of nations. The paper is divided into two sections, which look at how women's voices were deployed to formulate notions of citizenship and statehood at the end of the nineteenth and twentieth centuries. The voices selected from these two eras are from different sources: literary sources from Bengal for the nineteenth and early twentieth centuries, and voices from a particular movement in Bangladesh for an illustration of the debate about women's citizenship in the late twentieth century. It is interesting to see how these very different spheres of struggle and articulation grapple with definitions of national spaces and debate the formation of public and private identities of women.

3   I would like to begin with a well-known essay by Cora Kaplan: 'Pandora's Box: Subjectivity, Class and Sexuality in Socialist Feminist Criticism' (1986). Analyzing the 'split' feminist field, the essay shows the different spaces ascribed to men and women in Enlightenment discourse. Based on an analysis of Mary Wollstonecraft's *A Vindication of the Rights of Woman* (1792), this essay traces the differences in gender to the differentiated terrain of post-revolutionary Europe in the eighteenth century, which had carved out different and more confined spaces for women in the aftermath of the French Revolution. The 'new' post-revolutionary woman could access

DOI: 10.4324/9781003213857-4

115

the rights granted by the new state, only by curbing some freedoms and by bringing herself under the purview of reason and rationality. The freedoms to be sacrificed were psycho-sexual in nature and entailed a curbing of what the eighteenth century had called 'sensibilities' and that Wollstonecraft herself calls 'a romantic twist of the mind'. This 'sacrifice' of passion for reason creates a gender-differentiated position, and as Kaplan points out, men were carving out spaces that could incorporate both 'passion' and 'imagination'. Wordsworth's 'Preface to the Lyrical Ballads' written in 1800 is an impassioned document, which squarely puts passion, emotion and imagination at the centre of creative and artistic work.

4   Taking the *Vindication* as the document that spells out the position of women in the new era, we can easily see that the place of passion and emotion – of what was seen to lie at the other side of sense and reason – is problematic for women. Female sexuality, especially the expression of sexual and romantic desire, is construed as a problem. As Kaplan goes on to say:

> It is interesting and somewhat tragic that Wollstonecraft's paradigm of women's psychic economy still profoundly shapes modern feminist consciousness. How often are the maternal, romantic–sexual and intellectual capacity of women presented by feminism as in competition for a fixed psychic space.
>
> (Kaplan 1986: 159)

Translating these concerns into the language of rights and freedoms, the ease with which 'third world' feminisms deploy the language of rights can be contrasted with the ways in which demands for freedoms are cloaked. Freedom in this gendered construction refers to the larger space ('roomier' – as Kaplan says the male romantics had carved for themselves) where passions and emotions have a freer play.

5   In much of the world, the end of the nineteenth century witnessed a grappling with the issue of freedom from a colonial power. This process was accompanied by a process of self-definition, where nation-states that emerged out of anti-colonial struggles debated and constructed a discourse not just around a set of democratic rights, but around a notion of selfhood and identity. Hence independence meant not only a shaking off of colonial shackles, but coming into one's own – a return to self was seen as part of the process of gaining independence. A hundred years on from that moment, and in the case of the Indian sub-continent, fifty years after the departure of the British, and in the case of Bangladesh, after another war of liberation, it is interesting to look at how those founding concepts have weathered.

6   I will be looking specifically at the notions of independence and freedom as they apply to women. Women played a central role in this process, as both colonizer and colonized took recourse to notions of captured and debased womanhood as justifications of their position or struggles. Thus the colonialist justified his 'civilizing' mission as one that would 'liberate' women from the oppressions arising out of superstition and barbarity, and the colonized mounted their liberation struggles with an appeal to the mother nation, and saw their task as liberating the conquered motherland. The part that women played in this whole process has been highlighted, and it is interesting to see whether the discourse of freedom initiated by the colonized is different when women enter the field as active agents and actors. Women's voices are important in

WOMEN AND FREEDOM

this context, as women are situated at the crossroads, as it were, between struggles for freedom and the definition of self.

7   I will be looking at literary writing in Bengal from the end of the last century to show how the issue of freedom entered women's writings. In contemporary Bangladesh I will look at the struggle for freedom as a part of the women's movement which largely expresses itself as a struggle for rights. I will show how certain demands can be easily expressed and perhaps even hope to be met, whereas other forms of freedom are more difficult to bring into the public discursive arena. The nineteenth-century discourse will be examined through the area of literature, whereas the contemporary struggle will look at women's movements in Bangladesh as they struggle to voice demands for freedom. In both cases, the different sources show women's oblique positioning, and the transformative potential that their presence in any sphere of struggle or discourse contains.

Independence, freedom and a sense of home

8   One of the most striking literary portrayals of the independence struggle against the British is to be found in Rabindranath Tagore's *Ghare Baire* (1985a), translated as *Home and the World*. Written in 1905, this oft-read novel allies its heroine and her longings and desires to the longing and desire for freedom and independence as expressed through the various anti-British movements of the period. Bimala is shown in a typical scene, looking out of her window, at the landscape outside. Her eyes follow the little winding river, and she imagines the river as it finally meets the sea. She is like that tiny river, bound within its banks, with the ultimate desire of merging with the sea. This desire for freedom is also expressed as one of transgressing limitations and boundaries, of travelling vast expanses and of merging with a greater reality. The novel goes on to describe the pitfalls of this journey. Bimala and her desire for freedom are linked to India/Bengal and its struggle for independence and freedom, and the text serves as a warning of the dangers that stalk such desires.

9   While we struggle to understand what we are being warned against – women's desire or the struggle for national independence – we can only come to the conclusion that the two are linked. The notion of freedom itself is perhaps enough to open up a whole new horizon, where different constituencies clamouring for this democratic principle will force emerging nation-states to listen to different voices. Women's demand for freedom is highly significant in this context, linked as it is with the special space women are given within the discourse of independence and the formation of the nation state.

10   Let us just pause for a moment and look at how women formed part of the debate around nationhood through the various movements of the nineteenth century. Partha Chatterjee's 1989 essay spells out for us the place of women in the definition of the nation, and the significant division of the colonial space into public and private, which is echoed in Tagore's novel. The place that women occupied was also perhaps a response to the colonial discourse, which measured the 'development' of a civilization according to the treatment it meted out to its women and the position it accorded them. In this response, a myth of a glorious Indian past was created, and a past that was evoked in order to place women within positions of dignity in an Indian situation.

117

LITERARY THEORY AND CRITICISM

11   We can then look at the way these issues are debated within women's writing. For my example, I have looked at the poetry of Toru Dutt, who was writing in English in the 1870s in Calcutta. Marginalized both by the fact that she was writing in English and also by being a woman, her poetry nevertheless can be seen as part of the project of defining the emerging nationalistic space through a concentration on the figure of the woman. 'Savitri', written in 1877 and published in 1882, is a poem that can be read as part of the reformulation of the figure of the woman as a literary/cultural symbol. It is a long poem that portrays this well-known figure from Indian mythology, a myth which is usually deployed to be the symbol of wifely devotion. Ironically enough, in Toru Dutt's rendition, 'Savitri' becomes a symbol of freedom, of freedoms that were once enjoyed by women in India, but which were now lost. Thus: 'In those far-off primeval days / Fair India's daughters were not pent / In closed zenanas'... ('Savitri', Part 1, lines 72–75).

12   The contrast between the inside and the outside is drawn as between the present and the past. It is in the present that Indian women are confined within their homes. Toru Dutt, however, seeks freedom not only in ancient India, but surprisingly enough, in modern Europe. Were we to read her poetry along with her letters, we would notice in both forms of writing an intense desire for freedom. Indrepal Grewal's *Home and Harem* (1996) has a very good reading of the desire for freedom expressed in Toru Dutt's letters to her English friend. 'Freedom' is not seen as political freedom here, but as freedom of movement, as freedom to wander and roam. Women's entry into this new sphere of writing poses the question of how the nationalistic discourse would accommodate these differing notions of freedom. Savitri wanders 'in boyish freedom', and one of her main freedoms was the choice of life partner. The contrast between an imagined and ancient India and the present sense of confinement finds expression in her letters as the contrast between her confined life in her family home in Baugmaree near Calcutta and the freedoms and friendships she had enjoyed during her sojourn in England. Ancient India is thus compared with contemporary England or Europe. The movement is both backwards in time – to the glories of the classical past – but also outwards – outside – for 'other' images of freedom. The notion of the comforts of the mother-nation is offset by the drawing of other sites and arenas where Indian daughters are more comfortable and crucially enjoy a sense of freedom.

13   If Toru Dutt can be seen as a marginalized literary figure in nineteenth-century Bengal, Swarnakumari Devi, sister of Rabindranath Tagore, is both a 'mainstream' as well as a marginalized figure. She is part of the mainstream that Tagore's literary output stands for in Bengali writing, but she is marginalized in that her personal reputation has always been subservient not only to her brother's, but also to the other literary 'greats' of Bengal, such as Bankim Chatterjee. In her novels, she also examines the concept of freedom via the concept of the new woman. Marriage and the creation of a home are perhaps the main themes in her writing. This home is geared towards the needs of this new woman, a site where all her desires and wishes could find expression. For example, the novel *Kahake* (1898), translated by herself as *The Unfinished Song*, contains long diatribes on the nature of love and whether marital love is qualitatively different from other kinds of domestic love, including that between parents and children. The debate is about women and choice in marriage, and hence hearkens to

118

WOMEN AND FREEDOM

the definition of what constitutes a home, on how women's desires can be contained within the home. Devi follows the traditional nineteenth-century novelistic 'resolution' device, where personal desires and social realities need to harmonize into a neat ending, to avoid personal tragedy, but the irregularities in her writing – the long polemical speeches which disturb the narrrative or the plot – are emblematic of this need to question the contours of the home and women's place within it. Greater rights and freedom of choice for women in marriage seem to be guiding her writing, even at the expense of artistic harmony and balance.

14   Another mainstream yet marginalized voice from the turn of the nineteenth century is that of Rokeya Sakhawat Hussain. Originally from provincial East Bengal, she established a school for Muslim girls in Calcutta, and her writings concentrate on the position of Bengali Muslim women. In 'Sultana's Dream' (1905), she adopts the 'literary' strategy of utopian writing, where she takes the notion of women's power and desire to the plane of fantasy, and through 'air-cars' and fountains etc. an ideal world is imagined. This piece of fantasy takes recourse to the women's movement – flying across worlds – and contrasts strongly with her later work *Abaradh Bashini* or *Secluded Women*, which is a series of humorous essays, written between 1928–1930. These essays concentrate on women's confinement within the home, of the veiling of her body, and through humorous vignettes protest women's lack of freedom. Rokeya Sakhawat Hussain places women between this fantasy of freedom – of soaring to the sky – and the reality of women's confined bodies. Looking at her Calcutta school as the space she created for women, this oscillation between freedom and confinement becomes visible. The girls were transported to school in a horse-drawn carriage that was covered with a sheet according to purdah principles, while the education that they got was geared towards creating the first generation of free-thinking Muslim women in Bengal.

15   How are we to look at these women writers? For this essay, I have just touched on a few writings from women of the late nineteenth and early twentieth centuries, and I would really like to make the case that Bengali literary history needs to be re-read with a concentration on these marginalized literary voices. Such a re-reading would bring to the fore different dimensions of the terrain in which the nationalist ideal was being debated and formulated. Does this mean that there is a real change in the discourse when we include women writers? This takes us not to the question of the autonomy of women's voices, but to whether gendered readings can change the outlines of nationalist formations and discourses. Just by looking at the notion of home as expressed in Toru Dutt or Swarnakumari Devi, we see how definitions change. Toru Dutt opens the discourse wider and further afield, whereas Swarnakumari Devi makes an internal exploration to change the contours of the domestic sphere. A different kind of woman – a more assertive one in the case of Devi, and in Dutt's case, the expression of women's desire, serves to blur the boundaries between the private and the public and issues of freedom are brought into the private domain. Struggles for freedom do not pertain to the national struggle only, but enter into the home and struggle to redefine that sphere.

16   Thus, the blurring of the public/private through women's writings forces a public examination of the domestic terrain, and works towards a refashioning of that terrain.

Women's writing and writing per se, as we know, in the late nineteenth and early twentieth centuries has to be considered within its class constraints, but even this very limited sphere of the emerging middle classes manages to bring out many issues. First, it shows how freedom and the concept of the home are contradictory, and how the woman, meant to be the centre of the home, traverses between her domestic status and her status as an independent citizen of the emerging nation-state. Significantly, it also highlights the transgressive nature of women's desires and opens up a special literary arena in which these desires can find artistic expression. Finally, it seeks to ascribe a kind of constrained freedom to women, a bonded freedom, as it were, in which certain demands can be addressed and others either ignored or suppressed. Women's writings are also interesting in the sense that they show us the emergence of women's voices and, in the period under consideration, the veiled and indirect expression of desires and demands.

17   The tone set by this late nineteenth-century nationalistic discourse persists, and we saw a complete re-emergence of it during the 1971 Bangladesh Liberation War. The nation was again imaged as a woman, and notions of freedom and independence were related to that figure. While doing so the 'real' position of women did not enter the liberation discourse at all, except in the case of rape cases during the war (and even here the discussion has been very weak and fragmentary). It is in the new context of Bangladesh that we now need to examine the way that women's demands are expressed, the notion of women's freedom brought into view and the various arenas and actors involved in this process.

18   The problematic and often oblique positioning of women that the nineteenth-century literary sphere delineated for women persists within the newly independent nations. How women were positioned in India, for example, in the aftermath of the partition and the division of the country has been very well recorded by Urvashi Butalia. Using first-person narratives and interviews, *The Other Side of Silence* (2000) is an account of the displacement of peoples across boundaries, which is the staple of partition studies in South Asia, but a concentration on the displacement of women brings along with it a re-questioning of the borders, a re-questioning of the contours of the newly formed states. Gender and citizenship – stock words of the rights discourse – acquire new meanings when viewed in this light. What are the parameters that define citizenship and how is the state to formulate and advocate for its gender-differentiated citizens? Though this section is not looking at literary renditions, it will be useful to look at Susie Tharu and K. Lalita's introduction to the second volume of their massive anthology of Indian women's writing, for an understanding of the ways in which women are written out of the national imaginary (Tharu and Lalita 1993).

19   Similarly, in the series of interviews put together under the title of *Ami Birangona Bolchi* (1998) by Nilima Ibrahim, the newly emerged nation of Bangladesh is made to look at the status of women victims of war rape. The word birangona (feminine for bir or hero) had been coined in 1972 to give the status of war heroes to the victims of Pakistani rape. The interviews reveal the very anomalous position that these women occupy within the nation for which it has been said they have 'sacrificed their honour'. Thus rights for women follow a sexed and gendered pattern, and movements for the rights of women have actually to grapple with those positions. At both moments of

nation formation, in 1947 and 1971, women's sexual positioning ('vulnerability'/'honour'/'sacrifice') was central in determining their national identity, even their citizenship. Hence it is important to look at how the notion of women's sexuality is debated in women's struggles around citizenship rights and equality within the newly formed national spheres.

20   Here I will be concentrating on the women's movement in Bangladesh, which is manifested in a number of women's groups that seem to be acquiring greater visibility over the last 20 or so years. Without going into the various differences in approach, it can easily be said that the women's movement takes recourse to a discourse of rights and democracy. This seems to be the safest and most acceptable ground from which to operate, but it is interesting to see how even within this basically accepted democratic value, there are certain areas that are considered 'difficult'. The difficulty arises regarding what has already been seen as the psycho-sexual sphere, of the freedom to express desire. Control on women's sexuality at the personal and state levels are translated into a curbing of freedoms – of movement, of expression, of work and employment. The women's movement itself tends to mask its demands for greater freedoms, including sexual freedom, in issues such as violence against women or women's health issues instead of speaking directly of women's sexuality. This strategy is useful and often helps to 'smuggle in' a demand for greater sexual and emotional freedom, but it also has its flip side in that by containing demands for greater freedom, it keeps on curtailing freedoms.

Women's work, sexuality and freedom

21   The literary sphere continues to be the place from where women's desire especially for sexual freedom can be expressed. This is not only in the case of women's writing, but also in the strategies that women's groups adopt for themselves. I would like to take the case of Naripokkho, a woman's group in Bangladesh, which tried to bring the issue of women's desire to the political forefront first through its International Women's Day celebration in 1990. Using a late-nineteenth-century literary text – Rabindranath Tagore's dance-drama *Chitrangoda* (1985b) – notions of femininity and masculinity were highlighted as they played themselves out between the male and female protagonists of the play. Female sexual desire as it finds expression throughout the play is juxtaposed with an assertion of female identity and a demand for equality. However, the production had a limited impact. Though it could be viewed as an example of the way that literature could be brought to the service of women's liberation, it did not have the kind of larger social effect that women's movements need to make.

22   Finally, when the issue of sexuality and freedom did enter the public arena of the women's movement, it was not through these deliberate and subtle literary renditions, but through struggles of marginalized groups of women, whose living depended on sex work. Through a series of campaigns against brothel evictions (from 1993 onwards), Naripokkho, as well as other women's and human rights groups, brought to the public forefront the issues pertaining to women's sexuality, their status and position in society. A common platform, Shanghoti, comprising women's groups, human rights groups, NGOs, journalists, health workers and sex workers' groups, emerged out of

these campaigns. Shanghati is an alliance of diverse groups and has been working formally since May 1999 to struggle for the recognition of the rights of sex workers. One of its most successful efforts was to win a court case against the eviction of a brothel in Narayanganj, where the judge in a historic ruling gave legal status to women residents of the brothel and to their trade.

23   The first change that the alliance brought about was perhaps the change in nomenclature – from prostitution to sex work. Despite the problematic associated with the term sex work itself, this change in nomenclature helped to highlight the issues of women's right to work and also of what constituted women's work. Hence by combining the words sex and work, the rights discourse could be brought into play with an emphasis on the right to work and also an opportunity arose which allowed us to debate the issue of sex. The rights agenda allowed the movement to spell out many demands that found an easy resonance in the larger political arena. The coalition, formed of many diverse organizations, can be seen as the way in which women's demands can be articulated through a diversity of groups, and can be used as an example of platform building, and what is gained and lost in the process. Many organizations in the alliance are lawyers and human rights groups, and maybe the emphasis on rights in the campaign was guided by this fact. However, this essay will look at how this emphasis on rights can be seen to modify the very arena of rights in which it is placed.

24   Despite the presence of multi-interest groups, one of the main strategies used was that of prioritizing women's voices. This had the effect of transforming political spaces, in that it brought voices of sex workers directly into the mainstream of political and social movement, and also gave us a space where again we can look at the 'autonomy' or otherwise of women's voices. Autonomous or not the transformatory effect of the inclusion of women's voices into the political discourse was again made clear. We may have come a long way from the time that Gandhi had expressed 'extreme resentment at the inclusion of prostitutes of Barisaal in the cause of the Congress party' because of their 'immorality' (Sangari and Vaid 1989: 22), but the inclusion of 'immoral' women's voices is still a struggle, and the political mainstream, including the feminist mainstream, is still wary of such an inclusion.

25   Let us now look at some of the main issues that came out of the campaigns. The first one to look at will be that of women's work, as we struggled to change the nomenclature from prostitution to sex work. The contention here was that this change in naming also highlighted the special nature of women's work, linking it to women's position in the job market in general. This pertained not only to lack of occupational options for women, but to how women's entry into the job market is reflective of the domestic roles assigned to her. Her entry into the public world can be seen as a continuum with her private and domestic roles. Prostitution also brings to the fore the notion of sexuality, based on presumed male predatoriness. What remains unexamined within the purview of prostitution is women's sexuality: she is merely a body to give pleasure. Just as women's pleasure is not at issue in prostitution, so is it not in the other sphere where women function as sexual beings – in marriage. Prostitution is work, not pleasure for women (and incidentally brings up the question of whether work and pleasure can mix), but the very feminized nature of the profession, of prostitution as women's work, showed us how women's sexual pleasure is not an issue, even where agency may be.

26   Women perform two major roles within the home – as wife and mother. Both refer to her reproductive functions and hence refer to the arena of sexuality, which includes sexual activity, desire, agency and so on. As women's sexuality is confined to or given legitimacy only within marriage, the question of how sex is organized within marriage remains crucial. Sex is a duty for women, performed to meet the husband's conjugal demands, and in order to produce children – it is sex work. Keeping the continuum between women's domestic duties and the work that is available to her in the job market, prostitution can easily be seen as sex work. Drawing a continuous line between women in public and private spheres helps us to see how women's subordination pertains to both spheres. So while we seek recognition for prostitution and call it sex work, we at the same time need to look at the positioning of women engaged in prostitution.

A question of rights

27   The main thrust of the campaign was on rights. This thrust as mentioned earlier was guided by strategic considerations and it was most helpful not only in keeping the coalition together, but in bringing certain other issues to the fore.

28   Let us look at what this emphasis on rights achieved. One of the main rights evoked, given that it was an anti-eviction campaign, was that to the right to dwelling and called on the sanctity of the home. This had the effect of redrawing the notion of home. Not only were brothels places of work, but homes, where domestic and affective roles were performed. Maternal functions and duties were performed here. Along with the recognition of brothels as homes was the fact that these homes were licensed workplaces.

29   Brothels are demarcated as red light areas by the government and the sexual trade that goes on here is given legal sanction by the laws of the land. Stressing legitimacy also helped to decriminalize the sex trade. Brothel residents emphasized the fact that they paid rent, even at exorbitant rates, and hence reiterated their absolute right to the spaces that they had been living in and working from.

30   Perhaps even more interesting was the demand for state protection. The law-enforcing agencies were blamed for failing to provide protection, as well as for joining hands with the criminal elements involved in the eviction. In this manner, it was the women now who were the legal occupants of these homes and spaces and their evictors the criminals. The government had to answer for their collusion with the evictors and their failure to provide protection. This is again a very significant dimension. The right to demand from government institutions the services and facilities that they are meant to provide is not a very established practice in countries like ours. One of the ways in which feminist groups have been working is to monitor service delivery systems, such as health, or law-enforcement agencies, point out the areas where citizens are not given the services that are their right, and work towards making these systems more effective. The demand for state protection and the institution of the court case are really a part of the same process. This campaign is an illustration of the way that the state and government are responsible for the protection of the rights of all its citizens and the ways in which diverse sections of the citizenry can place its demands.

31   Making the state responsive to women's demands may have a flip side in that it also allows the state to define and determine women's positions. The point that is being

made here is one of demand and assertion – of incorporation and citizenship – and that of definition and control. Somehow women have to play between these poles. Even while they are placed at the centre of state control they have to 'prove' their status as citizens. Just as the post-enlightenment positions for women had called upon a redefinition of women as rational beings and hence fit citizen-subjects, so too the demand for state protection and services is based on a notion of 'deserving' citizens. The question whether by allowing state and law-enforcing functionaries entry into brothels and homes ensures greater security or whether it results in a greater state control (or coercion) is really emblematic of the very difficult positioning as citizens or subjects of the state. In a way we can see how these demands fluctuated between the personal and the public – the personal demands for home and the demand to the state for ensuring the security of that home. Again it is women, placed at the crossroads between the public and the personal, making the personal public, and demanding public recognition of duties and functions, who straddle both spheres. Using the rights discourse was a helpful and empowering strategy as far as the campaign was concerned, helping us to institute a court case for the rights of sex workers to their abode.

The incorporation of women's voices

32 The other and perhaps even more interesting strategic intervention was the active participation in leadership roles of evicted brothel residents and a direct voicing of their own concerns and needs.

33 Let us just spend a minute to look at these first-person voices and to examine a notion of truth or authenticity that may pertain to them. These voices did not function as conduits to the 'truth' of prostitution or sex work, but were strategically used to appeal to the audience. Brothel residents wielded the discourse to put forwards their demands as they thought fit. The recourse to a notion of rights proved very useful and these rights were demanded on the basis of duties performed. The right to the home was justified through the fact that they paid rent, the right to state protection was demanded on the basis of the performance of civic duties, such as voting, paying taxes and being useful citizens of the state.

34 The definition of 'usefulness' was interesting. Brothel residents defined the use-value of their work in terms of a social 'safety valve' and even while they talked about eviction from brothels as a violation of their rights, they did not hesitate to use other arguments to bolster their demands. One strategy of course was the appeal to pity and sympathy – poor women driven out of their homes to walk the streets. The other was an appeal to social order, and the picture of poor women walking the streets was rendered in terms of a spectre that would not only haunt but corrupt social sexual morality. Thus there was no hesitation in using a conservative approach that appealed to the patriarchal status quo, to recover the brothels.

35 It was in the voicing of demands and organizing the campaign that a new form of political empowerment was experienced. This empowerment did not take the form of glorification of sex work as a site where alternative notions of female sexuality may surface, as some postmodernist feminist discourses seem to suggest. On the other hand, the organization of women's sexuality in prostitution rests upon a system of monogamy, and looks at itself as the flip side of marriage. It lays a premium on youth

and beauty and old age appears as a dire fate to many prostitutes. Age sometimes brings its own compensations, and some women may acquire positions of power and decision-making within the brothel set-up. Female sexuality and female sexual desire, amongst prostitutes, seems to rely on a notion of monogamous and heterosexual sexuality. Very little emerges about female relationships, except that the hierarchy established by age and beauty is very palpable. It is difficult to look at prostitution as a site of female sexual emancipation, or even as a site where prevalent norms and rules are subverted. It indeed seems to be the other side of marriage – the other institution in which women function as sexual beings.

36   If we are looking for a 'different' voice within this campaign, it was to be found regarding the question of 'rehabilitation'. The stand normally taken is to 'rehabilitate' these 'unfortunate' women into the mainstream of society and a complete puzzlement ensues when these 'rehabilitated' women protest against the rehabilitation measures. The measures taken in the name of rehabilitation include (a) skill development in traditional female activities, such as sewing; (b) being given inputs, such as a sewing machine, to ease transition into another profession; and (c) marriage. Each of these measures has proved to be ineffective. As far as skill development and training are concerned, these skills do not give enough financial return in the job market. It is also unrealistic to feel that a sewing machine will suffice to set up a tailoring shop and finally, women who have been 'married off' find themselves being used as prostitutes by their new husbands, who now become their pimps. In each case, the special difficulty women who have been known to be sex workers may face are not taken into consideration. Employment in garment factories, for example, may even be protested by fellow workers, not to say of the fresh forms of sexual exploitation to which their past histories could expose these women. And of course it is facile to speak of rehabilitating women in prostitution into the job market, when we know of the limited opportunities available to all entrants into the job market and when we are speaking of a socially disabled group of women. As one brothel worker put it to the person recommending other jobs – 'Would it be all right for me to be working in your husband's office?' Women were sent into vagrant homes by the government, which they found very demeaning and where they were subjected to fresh forms of sexual exploitation.

37   The campaign of 1999 turned the notion of rehabilitation on its head, by demanding rehabilitation into brothels, by claiming rights over that space and by the demand that the women engaged in prostitution need to be recognized as citizens with the full rights of citizens. Earlier, sex workers had talked of 'social rehabilitation' and now we have had a demonstration of the full meaning of that term. Social rehabilitation, at one level, means the ability to hold up one's head; to be given dignity and recognition as a fellow member of society, regardless of who you are and what you do, but now the recognition is for the rights of women who are prostitutes, of recognition as workers, as women who are on their own and earning their own keep. One of the strongest statements to come out of the campaign was – 'We do not depend on anyone for food or lodging, so leave us alone'. This assertion of economic independence immediately places the sex worker in a position of dignity and does not allow the welfare approach that guides rehabilitation efforts to come into operation. The rehabilitation being asked for is recognition as citizens, as subjects of the state.

LITERARY THEORY AND CRITICISM

38   How are we to read these *fin-de-siècle* voices? One obvious way is to read them as an extension of the Enlightenment discourse, as an extension of the constituencies that are to be embraced within the democratic framework. At another level, we can also see these voices as disturbing, not merely clamouring for inclusion, but negotiating change and transformation. Be they the literary voices of the late nineteenth century, or the marginalized groups of today, women seem to be asking for a redefinition of the political and social body, of asking for a redefinition of the nation, so that different ways of inclusion can be envisioned. Ideas and definitions of home and nation are directly effected by the literary voices of the past. Today's women are actually seeking to change not only the private dimensions of what constitutes the 'home', but also asking for a public recognition of the variety of images and institutions that that word evokes. It seeks to force the body politic to take cognizance of the different ways of organizing life and sexuality and to make the nation and state respond to each of these changes.

39   What is also interesting is that in this age of privatization, where all services are being taken away from the state, we found women's groups in Bangladesh coalescing to demand services from the state. With all the prognostications of the demise of the nation-state, it seems that the state remains essential as a last recourse to marginalized groups. This is even true for inter-state situations – as is borne out in the case of migrant female labour and the response to their needs by various women's and human rights groups. It has been to lobby state and government bodies for better legislation and better protection. It is as though in this vast jungle of globalization, disempowered and marginalized groups can only turn to instruments of state for the protection of rights and freedoms. As the world 'opens up', individual states may yet be necessary for the guaranteeing of human rights and liberties, but the negotiations on which these rights are incorporated can be read to highlight the positional differences between citizens within national boundaries and which is then extended to the position that they may occupy in the globalized sphere where these boundaries do not have the same demarcating status.

Notes

1 See Chatterjee, Partha (1989). in K. Sangari and S. Vaid (Eds.). *Recasting Women: Essays in Colonial History*. New Delhi: Kali for Women, 233–53.
2 See Spivak, Gayatri (1998). "Explanation and Culture: Marginalia" in *In Other Worlds*. New York: Routledge.
3 For the phrases used see Millet, Kate (1969). *Sexual Politics*. Urbana: University of Illinois Press, 62.
4 Ibid., 21.
5 Kumar, Radha (1993). *The History of Doing: An Illustrated Account of Movements for Women's Rights and Feminism in India, 1800–1990*. Verso: London, 36.

References

Butalia, Urvashi (2000) *The Other Side of Silence: Voices from the Partition of India*, London: Hurst.
Chatterjee, Partha (1989) 'The nationalist resolution of the women's question' in K. Sangari and S. Vaid (eds) *Recasting Women: Essays in Colonial History*, New Delhi: Kali for Women, 233–253.

WOMEN AND FREEDOM

Dutt, Toru (1882) 'Savitri' in Paul Trench (eds) *Ancient Ballads and Legends of Hindustan*, London: Kegan, 3–45.

Grewal, Inderpal (1996) *Home and Harem: Nation, Gender Empire and the Cultures of Travel*, London: Leicester University Press.

Hussein, Rokeya Sakhawat (1985) *The Complete Works of Rokeya Sakhawat Hussein (Rokeya Rachanabali)*, Dhaka: Bangla Academy Press.

Ibrahim, Nilima (1998) *The Voices of War Heroines (Ami Birangana Bolchi)*, Dhaka: Jagrata Prakashani.

Kaplan, Cora (1986) 'Pandora's box: subjectivity, class and sexuality in socialist feminist criticism' in *Sea Changes: Essays on Culture and Feminism*, London: Verso, 147–176.

Sangari, K. and Vaid, S. (eds) (1989) *Recasting Women: Essays in Colonial History*, New Delhi: Kali for Women.

Tagore, Rabindranath (1985a) 'Home and the World (Ghare Baire)' in *The Complete Works of Rabindranath Tagore (Rabindra Rachanabali)*, Calcutta: Viswabharati Press, Vol. 8, 137–334.

Tagore, Rabindranath (1985b) 'A dance-drama (Chitrangoda)' in *The Complete Works of Rabindranath Tagore (Rabindra Rachanabali)*, Calcutta: Viswabharati Press, Vol. 3, 157–200.

Tharu, Susie and Lalita, K. (eds) (1993) *Women Writing in India: 600 B.C. to the Present*, New York: The Feminist Press.

Textual and rhetorical questions

Textual

1. Third world feminism has taken recourse to the language of rights for the elimination of all forms of discrimination: Rights speak a language of equality and fair play, about entitlements and access. They all lead to the question of freedom and liberation. What are the ways in which Azim's discussion of the notion of freedom enters women's debate? Are they benevolent colonialists, freedom fighters, Tagore's writings, liberation war in Bangladesh, and/or social movements? You may wish to revise your answer after reading the essay again in relation to the Textual and Rhetorical questions that follow.

2. The essayist explores and analyses how freedom entered women's writing in the nineteenth-century Bengali literature and in contemporary women's rights movements in Bangladesh. Regarding women's writing in Bengali literature, Azim comments that the writing was against the "colonial discourse, which measured the 'development' of civilization according to the treatment it meted out to the women and position it accorded them." She then writes about the literary response where "a myth of glorious Indian past was created, and a past that was evoked in order to place women within position of dignity." (paragraph 10). How do women's issues appear in women's writing in the late nineteenth and early twentieth centuries in Bengal? Write about the ways exemplified by the essayist while discussing the poems of Toru Dutta and the novels of Swarnakumari Devi and Rokeya Sakhawat Hussain? (paragraphs 12 to 15).

3. In paragraph 17, Azim critically comments on women's writing and the existing social problems. Paraphrase in two sentences.

4. The desire for the sexual/sexuality and freedom comes into the public arena not by using literature to express the desire (as *Naripokkho* did) but by women's struggle in the public space which changed the perception of women's rights as linked to "immorality" (as reflected in Gandhi's ideology against prostitutes: paragraph 23) to perceiving women's rights as connected to "work" or a "job." Analyse Azim's proposition in paragraph 24.

Rhetorical

1. After critically "examining women's writing and the existing social problems" in paragraph 16 (see Textual Question 3), Azim cites four writers, Urvashi Butalia, Susie Tharu and K. Lalita, and Nilima Ibrahim (paragraphs 18 and 19) before moving on to contemporary Bangladesh. What rhetorical device does she use to end the section? What kind of reading-help does the section provide?
2. Firdous Azim's essay is regularly in conversation with the reader by using phrases like "The paper will look at," "I would like to," "I will be looking," "Let us . . ." etc. Do you think such addresses help readers track a writer's thoughts? Make a list of the phrases she uses and develop a broad thesis of the essay.

Discussion questions

1. There were discourses of freedom for women initiated by the colonisers and colonised. The condition of women in South Asia prompted looking for freedom of the self. Such discourses and desire for freedom can be understood by reformations, movements, and literary expressions. Partha Chatterjee, in "The Nationalist Resolution of the Women's Question,"[1] critiques how nationalism "could not resolve" women's issues despite assuming that once India gets freedom, other problems will be gradually solved. Do you think nationalism, or any such grand narrative, can be the elixir to end the problems of casteism and inequality? Argue with examples (1000 words).
2. In the last two sections of the essay, "A Question of Rights" and "The Incorporation of Women's Voices," Azim talks about the transformation of brothels as homes (both ethical and moral spaces), as protected space, as possessing empowerment, and as the space of the citizens. Answer any one of the following two questions in this context of transformation.
   a. Do you think it is the state that ultimately guarantees rights? What is the nature of state and how does it disseminate its function to protect the marginalised?
   b. Discuss the crisscrossing of religious and artistic spaces with sexual spaces in relation to groups of women like the Devakis or the Badis, and the temple dancer traditions found in India and Nepal.
3. Kora Kaplan points out how women in the post-revolutionary period had to access their rights only under the purview of reason and rationality. What were sacrificed according to Kaplan? (paragraphs 3, 4). Do you think emotion and passion are the attributes of the weak?

WOMEN AND FREEDOM

Inter-textual discussions

1. The Nupi Lan (Women's War) movement in Manipur, India and the Shahada movement in Maharashtra, India, were two of the most powerful early- and mid-twentieth-century women's struggles, respectively. Likewise, the women's "revealing dress code" resistance and the anti-triple *talak* movements are also recent examples of struggle by women. Gayatri Spivak warns,

> In the interest of the effectiveness of the women's movement, emphasis is often placed upon a reversal of the public-private hierarchy. This is because in ordinary sexist households, educational institutions or workplaces, the sustaining explanation still remains that the public sector is more important, at once more rational and mysterious, and generally more masculine, than the private. The feminist, reversing this hierarchy, must insists that sexuality and emotions are, in fact, so much more important and threatening that a masculine sexual politics is obliged, repressively, to sustain all public activity. The most "material" sedimentation of this repressive politics is institutionalized sex discrimination that seems the hardest stone to push.[2]
>
> (1998 139–40)

Do you think that women's movements in South Asia may "oblige" masculine sexual politics? (3000 words).

2. There are many organisations in Nepal that work for women's rights, equality, and freedom. Some of them work to solve the problem of sex trafficking in South Asia and other countries. The problem can be addressed in multiple ways like giving sex education, solving poverty and ignorance problems, reforming the penal system to deter the victimisers, critiquing the universal success of patriarchal ideology,[3] and freeing women from economic dependency.[4] The problems persist despite many such efforts. What is your critical position? (Write an essay in five to seven paragraphs.)

Critical and creative thinking

1. Radha Kumar writes:

> First attempts to reform prostitutes were made in Calcutta by Michael Madhusudan Dutta, a member of the young Bengali group, who proposed to rehabilitate them by turning them into actresses, and got the Bengal theatre committee to accede to his proposal. This appears to have been the point at which women began to replace men in playing female roles in commercial theatres: several prostitutes turned actresses, and one of them, Binodini, shot into stardom.[5]

Nagarbadhus like Amrapali of Ujjain in ancient India had "star" status and are now glamorised in movies and fictions. Vatsyana's *Kamasutra* elaborately prescribes the art of seduction and sex that a woman like Amrapali had to be

129

trained in. Does social history provide texts and documents about the unglorified conditions of women like Binodini and Amrapali? If not, how do you read such unglorified instances within the glorified historical accounts and literary narratives? Foucauldian historiographical methods and Saidian "contrapuntal reading" may help you conceptualise and critique stardom and glorification.

2. What do you think about the rights of women within the systems like Uniform Civil Code, Hindu Law Reform, Brahminical rules, Muslim personal law, Hindu marriage, and *Nikahanama*?

3. Select episodes and scenes from Bollywood movies and South Asian TV serials (soaps) that validate or oppose polygamy, child marriage, dowry, *sindoor*, *vivaham hom*, *saptapadi*, *kanyadan*, *sati*, women within the ideologies of marriage as a holy union, and prostitution/sex work as sins of society. How do you conceptualise women's status within such beliefs and attitudes? Prepare a debating session.

4. Property-inheritance and the status of a wife in polygamous relationship are not only the issues of present economic and legal debates but have instances in Hindu mythical narratives like the *Puranas* and epics. Documenting such instances can be helpful to tracing women's history in Hindu societies, texts like the *Manusmriti* and the *Mahabharata* are especially revealing.

5

HYPHENATED POST-COLONIAL

A divergent perspective[1]

Tariq-Amin Khan

1   Renewed interest in state theory beginning in the 1970s sparked scholars and activists to question the nature of the capitalist state and led to the famous Miliband-Poulantzas debates in the pages of the *New Left Review*. It was in the context of these debates that Hamza Alavi penned his strident critique of state theorists' failure to account for the divergent histories of state formation in post-colonial societies, which he said should be differentiated from the Western state.[2] Alavi's critique fell on deaf ears, however, because the idea of the 'normal' European nation-state form was already considered the model for emerging post-colonial societies to emulate. Thus, theoretical advances in understanding the state since this time have really been about the Western capitalist state. Only recently, scholars with a poststructuralist orientation—postcolonial theorists, critical ethnographers, and some social geographers—have started to more intently examine the post-colonial state. Among these, many have theorized the post-colonial state based on empirical ethnographical studies, but the nature of the postcolonial state, its foundational character, remains elusive and is confounded by its characterization in either largely ambivalent cultural terms as a "cultural artifact"[3] (Gupta and Sharma) and as a "series of cultural acts and material production" (Joseph and Nugent) or in terms of "technologies of spatial power" (Radcliffe).[4] Before I discuss these confounding problematics in state theorization, I will clarify my use of the hyphenated form of the term 'post-colonial' in contradistinction with the non-hyphenated form widely used by poststructuralist/postcolonial studies scholars.

2   The term 'post-colonial' is used here to periodize from the colonial era the decolonization of the former colonies into supposedly sovereign states. However, the term's use also underlines the prevailing status of *inter*-national relations: colonialism may have formally ended only to be reinscribed by dependency, subordination, and underdevelopment in post-colonial societies. The term is thus used to represent both continuity with and a distinction from the colonial state form in the period since decolonization. 'Post-colonial' is therefore not deployed in a poststructuralist sense signalling the linguistic turn as it tends to in literary theory, postcolonial studies, or ethnographical studies of poststructuralist scholars.[5] On the contrary, the hyphenated form is used here to signal the start of another era of quasisovereignty, dependence, and subordination introduced (and now intensified) since decolonization and is based in a nuanced reading of the diverse set of states comprising the post-colonial world. In the context

DOI: 10.4324/9781003213857-5

131

of the reinscription of dependency, I have avoided the term 'neocolonial' as it has been historically surrounded by controversy and its usage can be distracting.[6]

3   The term 'post-colonial' also helps to distinguish African and Asian states that emerged after the formal demise of colonial rule at the end of the Second World War from the 'normal' (European) nation-states. With respect to Latin American states, however, this distinction creates a dilemma: should Latin American states be considered post-colonial? If the broad description of post-colonial states mentioned previously—in the sense of the reinscription of subordination and dependency on the US and Western states, Western transnational corporations, and international financial institutions—then Latin American states share a similar reality. At the same time, these states have a different colonial and contemporary history than states of Africa and Asia (especially in relation to the emergence of nationalism and the presence of the Aboriginal population that still largely lives at the margins). Indeed, Latin American states were decolonized between 50 and 100 years before the African and Asian states. Moreover, the Iberian powers that colonized Latin America were marked by a very different, non-capitalist history (one typified by the rise of latifundia, minifundia, and other social differences based on Indigeneity/race and class rather than ethnicity/nationalism) as compared with much of Africa and Asia. As such, the application of the term post-colonial in the case of Latin American states is questionable. In distinguishing Latin American states from postcolonial states, my position is not very different from scholars involved in ethnographical studies of the state, although our reasons for doing so are divergent.[7] Nonetheless, this raises further questions about the relevance of using 'post-colonial' for states in the Americas. Thus, I confine the term here to the states within Africa and Asia that emerged during the post-1945 era of decolonization.

4   I should also clarify that the terms the 'Third World' and the (global) 'South' are used here interchangeably to signal and refer to states of Africa, Asia, and Latin America. In saying this, I recognize that the idea of the 'Third World' should be critically assessed as its usage could result in an easy slippage into generalizations that do not reflect the enormous differences between the various regions of the South, let alone the differences among states within the same region. Indeed, the idea of *tiers monde* was originally constructed to "define the structures of disadvantage" which echoed those of the peasantry (part of the 'Third Estate') within the social order of pre-revolutionary France;[8] therefore, the term Third World has been a descriptor deemed to identify 'inferiorized' parts of the world. But this description has not gone unchallenged. The leaders of the Non-Aligned Movement, not very long after decolonization, appropriated the idea of the Third World (not without complications) to invert its demeaning representation and to symbolize the notion of resistance against imperialist domination—as reflected in the idea of Third Worldism.[9] Thus, inherent in the use of the term here is the underlying concept of Third Worldism. However, by characterizing African, Asian, and Latin American states as the global South and as the Third World, I do not mean to gloss over the vast differences between them. Therefore, these two terms are used interchangeably, albeit sparingly.

5   Similarly, in using the term 'the West', or the 'Western world', my intention is not to reduce to a unitary entity the differences in language, culture, and/or history of the different states of Europe, North America, and Australasia. Rather, the terms' usage signifies for the different Western states a common broad commitment to capitalist

culture ('Western values') and a determination to pursue common imperialist interests around the world. The 'West' as a construct also posits itself as the superior identity to its racialized and gendered 'other', the 'non-West' or the Third World.

Writing the post-colonial

6   The linguistic turn in the social sciences and humanities has undoubtedly challenged the more essentialist and reductionist understanding of racialized, gendered, and class-based (among other) identities, although class (and even race)[10] has been blurred through interpretations of colonialism as more than a one-sided act of sheer dominance over the colonized—without dealing with the issue of class exploitation as such and the link between racism and capitalist accumulation/domination. Many postcolonial theorists instead view colonization as an *'encounter'* between an oppressive and a resistant force, thus signifying resistance and 'empowerment' of the colonized as well. This understanding is articulated by a host of postcolonial and subaltern studies writers, most notably Ranajit Guha, and Edward Said in trying to address the criticism against his *magnum opus, Orientalism*.[11] This is not the place to enter into a polemic with postcolonial or poststructuralist scholars on whether the resistance of the colonized was coeval with the power and domination of the colonizers or whether these scholars' understanding of colonialism introduces into the debate a degree of ambivalence and contingency that has, in the process, effectively disabled a more complete conception of power and domination. Even a cursory glance at the colonial 'encounter' uncovers the sad reality of resistance: of all the slave revolts, which were very violently put down, only Haiti's was successful. This 'success' only made hope turn into sorrow, however, because the imperialist powers ensured that Haiti's aspiration to *freeness* would be made into a terrible example that would never be repeated (France and the US not only placed a naval blockade around Haiti, they forced the liberated colony to pay reparations to France for freeing itself. Then the US decided to briefly occupy Haiti at the turn of the last century to ensure its subservience, which has continued into the present era making Haiti into a veritable neoimperial prison).[12] In raising this issue, I *do not* contend that resistance is futile; some national liberation struggles were initially quite successful, such as in Algeria, Indonesia, and Vietnam. On the contrary, Haiti's example highlights that the discussion of resistance—without an understanding of the structural composition of the colonial state and a political economy understanding of power—is incomplete and unable to explain how a handful of colonizers or settlers could effectively occupy and control (albeit imperfectly) vast numbers of colonized people. Incidentally, this structural legacy of the colonial state is deeply imbricated with the post-colonial state (see the discussion on the book's main argument next and Chapter 3). In other words, the Foucauldian perspective on power that informs critical ethnographical ideas of the state overlooks a structuralist understanding of power and resistance. This outlook can therefore celebrate resistance without a considered analysis of why examples of successful resistance to colonial or imperial power and even post-colonial state power are merely a few etchings on an enormous canvas.

7   In contrast to the contributions of critical ethnographers studying the post-colonial state, I attempt its more nuanced structuralist comprehension, which is rooted in social history and involves a political economy of the post-colonial state and critical

understanding of power and resistance. The latter entails a recognition of how imperialist imperatives in the Third World and the clientalist role of most post-colonial states continue to underwrite the social and cultural fragmentation and economic dependency of post-colonial societies. That being said, I am sympathetic to Akhil Gupta and Aradhana Sharma's critique of an instrumentalist reading of the state, which they note has been so focused on the state's "structuralist and functionalist aspects as an instrument in the hands of the capitalist class"[13] that it ignores the "cultural dynamics of the modern state."[14] In focusing on culture as an antidote to instrumentalism, the gaze of critical ethnographers is directed by a poststructuralist reading that derives from an almost exclusive emphasis on local specificities, such as corruption, 'everyday practices', the bureaucracy or governmentality, and culture at various local institutional sites. However, the attention to these specificities, as objects of knowledge, and these scholars' empirical, cultural, and transnational approaches become so pervasive and intense that they ignore the external impulse and the structural dynamics of power, and pay scant attention to the need for mobilizing broader societal resistance against the oppressive power of the dominant classes and imperialist states—in order to move beyond the individualized stories of resistance. In this way, critical ethnographers reaffirm the state *not* as a pivot embodying the social relations of power but rather as "a dispersed ensemble of institutional practices,"[15] reflecting the dispersal of power against which they claim that resistance remains fertile. Such a perspective enables critical ethnographers to claim in Foucauldian terms that the "modern state is not the source of power but the effect of a wider range of dispersed forms of disciplinary power that allow 'the state' to appear as a structure that stands apart from, and above, society."[16] Mitchell goes on to suggest, "[w]e must analyze the state ... not as an actual structure, but as the powerful, apparently metaphysical effect of practices [of control]."[17] Ignoring the intrinsic role of structures foregrounds the notion that power is dispersed in institutions and events rather than in classes. This negation of structure assumes that power is socially (or even ideologically) neutral. As such, this outlook benefits the state-framed and state-propelled class projects by neither analyzing nor interrogating their structural framework or questioning who benefits and who loses out.

8   In contrast, Poulantzas too did not view the state as a repository of power or as a subject or thing (unlike Hegel's idea of the state); rather, in contradistinction with Foucault, Poulantzas regarded the capitalist state as a relationship of forces or, more precisely, as the "material condensation of such a relationship among classes and class fractions."[18] For Poulantzas, this specific materiality of the state (embodied in state structures) is critical; otherwise, the state can be viewed as an instrument that is simply reducible to state power—that is, the class that can manipulate this instrument can capture the capitalist state.[19] Preceding Poulantzas, Marx and Engels originally argued against this instrumentalist view of the state when analyzing the failure of the Paris Commune to capture state power.[20]

9   This critical appraisal helps distinguish my own work and issues that are important to my research as I discuss some elements of a poststructuralist theorization of the post-colonial state. However, my critique of critical ethnographers does not entail complete rejection of their ideas: some generalizations made by these ethnographers about the post-colonial state have merit. What their research lacks is an effort to

address more substantive questions about the state including the following: what is the nature of the post-colonial state in relation to the capitalist Western state; is the state apparatus autonomous or relatively autonomous of competing class, bureaucratic, and other interests (in other words, who rules, what forces control the state, and what are their roles in post-colonial states with respect to setting economic, political, and social priorities vis-à-vis imperial imperatives); how does the external impact the internal apparatus of the post-colonial state; and how is underdevelopment reinscribed in the post-colonial era—simply put, how is neoliberal globalization different from the first three or four decades of post-World War II capitalist development/domination?

10   In focusing on the nature of the state, my goal is not to attribute singularity to form and function of the post-colonial state. Instead, the assumption underlying questions about the nature of the state is that the post-colonial state is *not* a 'material condensate' of a dominant class in a classic sense like the Western capitalist state. As a result, the post-colonial state cannot be fully understood unless the players who wield power and influence on the state are identified. This brings us to the question of who rules and what is the form of the state; that is, is the post-colonial state capitalist, protocapitalist, non-capitalist, or a combination?

11   Mobilizing efforts to make the state more representative requires the identification, as foes or allies, of contemporary players who control or influence the direction of policy and development in post-colonial societies. For example, if feudal elites have an abiding influence in controlling the functions of the state (a situation that is prevalent in many post-colonial states and societies), how can resistance be mobilized and extended when these same elites pretend to champion progressive transformative agendas and pay lip service to issues of democratization, alleviation of poverty, and land redistribution? Critical ethnographers are less interested in the nature of the state than in post-colonial state formation, which they claim is more encompassing in examinations of culture, territorial sovereignty, and the "mappings of state and citizenship [that are seen] as moving out of the state's hands and increasingly into a transnational space informed by indigenous social movements and multilateral development agencies."[21] Critical ethnographers and some geographers also suggest that there is much current 'rethinking of the state'. This process involves questioning the perceived role of the state in regulating social life while state sovereignty and its 'cultural legitimacy' face potentially undermining challenges from a variety of forces: ethnic/national movements, neoliberal globalization, and movement of people as migrants and refugees.[22] As I will discuss later, this type of theory rests on an assumption that the state is 'weak' in an era of rising transnationalism, an assumption whose validity needs to be critically assessed in the first instance.[23]

12   Anthropologists involved in critical ethnographic explorations view the post-colonial state, therefore, as a 'cultural artifact' or work towards the adoption of a 'denaturalized' attitude towards the state. This attitude stems from an avoidance of attributing a certain 'natural' essence to the state, and yet these same scholars often end up lamenting that the "paradox of inadequacy and indispensability has robbed the state of its naturalness."[24] Hansen and Stepputat noted that contributors to their edited volume, *States of Imagination: Ethnographic Explorations of the Postcolonial State*, such as Akhil Gupta, David Nugent, Sarah A. Radcliffe, and others

all share this denaturalizing approach to state and governance in the postcolonial world; they all study the state, politics, and notions of authority empirically from a variety of ethnographic sites; and they all position themselves in
the space between a Gramscian and Foucauldian position on power, government and authority where much of the reconceptualization of the state has
been taking place.[25]

Investigating the post-colonial state using this approach involves two problems. First,
it assumes what needs to be explained: whether the post-colonial state is actually a
'natural' embodiment of sovereignty and a source of social order. In other words,
what are the naturalizing processes that generate awe and make people see the post-
colonial state as a bastion of power, authority, and sovereignty? Conversely, what
would a 'denaturalizing' process entail, and what would be the consequences not just
for the state but especially for society? Furthermore, given that critical ethnographers
are ambivalent about the nature of the state (viewing the state as a paradox or a cultural artifact), it is odd that a 'denaturalizing approach' does not involve an exploration of *how* (and why) the "institutionalized sovereign government remains pivotal
in our very imagination of what a society is."[26] In the context of the post-colonial
state, the assumption about state sovereignty has more to do with its roots in the
Western imagination—propelled by the ideas of Hobbes and fed by the writings of
ethnographers—without much appreciation of the external imposition that has most
post-colonial states in a vice-like grip. Ordinary residents/citizens in *most* post-colonial
societies are aware that sovereignty is actually wielded outside their respective states—
by imperial and corporate political and economic powers that influence internal and
external outcomes with respect to their state and society.

13   Second, this approach of striving for that in-between space that is populated by
Foucauldian and Gramscian ideas may be the source of much confusion about the
poststructuralist perspective of the state and consequent ambivalence about the nature
of the state. Foucault and Gramsci take antipodal positions in examining a phenomenon which, I would argue, cannot be easily reconciled. Foucault begins with a discussion of the microphysics of power and its immanence in all social relations; because
he considers that power solicits resistance it is easy for him to overlook the structural
dimension (and pervasiveness) of power and imagine the diffusion of power in institutional and cultural practices. Gramsci, in contrast, begins at the macro level of class
power and outlines how the state is a class hegemonic project, which is materialized in
relatively autonomous state structures. For Gramsci, if the working class is to success-
fully overthrow the bourgeois state, it will have to be successful in the counter-hegem-
onic 'war of movement' and 'war of position'. Gramsci did, however, recognize (based
on his involvement in the council movement in the Risorgimento) that resistance may
be ambiguous when carrying out these 'wars': the subaltern may be progressive on
some issues and reactionary on others.[27] So, if critical ethnographers situate themselves between Foucauldian and Gramscian perspectives, their position will not just
be immersed in contradiction (as noted by Hansen and Stepputat);[28] rather, the force
of the opposing polarities is such that mediation will eclipse either the micro or macro
registers of power. But, because we are dealing with a poststructuralist understanding
of the state, and because Gramsci's radical materialist notions contradict Foucault's

HYPHENATED POST-COLONIAL

micro-level ideas of power and resistance, it is quite conceivable that the latter will prevail over the former.

14   Beyond the poststructuralists, it is also disconcerting that other writers from both Weberian and orthodox Marxist perspectives articulate the postcolonial state as an undifferentiated entity that is largely indistinguishable from the 'modern' Western nation-state. Specifically, these scholars, and even developmental state theorists, have failed to account for the divergent histories of state formation in post-colonial societies (poststructuralist ethnographers excepted), the peculiar make-up of the bureaucracy, and the function of the post-colonial state in asserting the internal control of society while facilitating the external domination by Western states and metropolitan capital.[29] In contrast, ethnographic explorations have addressed the issue of colonialism in their inimitable style of an 'encounter', and although they have not distinguished the post-colonial state from the Western nationstate, they have argued quite correctly that the idea of the 'normal' nationstate was embraced by post-colonial elites at the time of decolonization.[30] Little attention has been paid, however, to the acquiescence of political and bureaucratic Third World elites to the demands of imperialist powers and their expectations that the former would fall in line on international issues, within the so-called community of nations. I will address some of these issues, as well as the significant historical differences between post-colonial states and Western nation-states, in the next chapter to provide context for the subsequent discussion of post-colonial states and why they cannot be classified as nation-states.

Why theorize the post-colonial state?

15   In post-colonial societies, the state remains the most powerful force of political order and is the basis of multilateral, regional, hemispheric, and now supranational organization of the world. The power of this force notwithstanding, various kinds of proclamations have been made about the 'weakness' or the 'demise' of the nation-state to include post-colonial states.[31] This language of 'weakness', which was in vogue until recently,[32] had to be disentangled from the notion of transnationalism and demystified from the project of globalization to clarify the imperial imperatives that underlie both these ideas. "[A]lthough contemporary globalization has complicated the nation-state form, it has not rendered it obsolete as a form of political organization."[33] However, clarification of the character of the post-colonial state is difficult because theories are greatly divergent and are becoming more complicated as new modes of analysis are developed to theorize about the post-colonial state. For instance, the idea of transnationalism has emerged along with the project of globalization, enabling scholars to focus on social processes such as migrancy and social movements that are rooted in, and transcend, nation-states. But increasingly, the term 'transnationalism' is also casually employed by many poststructuralists to link the local with the global, where global becomes synonymous with globalization as a transhistorical idea—largely undistinguished from the ideological, political, and imperial projects that underlie contemporary globalization.[34] Marxists have long recognized that local struggles have an international dimension in the era of imperialism (some have termed the current conjuncture a period of 'new imperialism').[35] However, imperialist powers also consistently attempt to short-circuit this international dimension in order to prevent and

subvert efforts to widen the span of local struggles on the international plane. As Petras and Veltmeyer pointed out, support for local struggles in the era of globalization has been effectively thwarted by the process of *NGOization*.[36] It would be imprudent to paint all non-governmental organizations (NGOs) with a broad brush, but if NGOs mostly rely on Western donors or Western development agencies and corporate philanthropy for their survival, then it is not inconceivable that they will be influenced by their benefactors. Also, the rise of NGOs accompanied the intensification in social dislocations caused initially by International Monetary Fund's (IMF) structural adjustment measures throughout the 1980s, and the process was accelerated by the rise of globalization since the early 1990s. As a result, although some NGOs do meaningful work, organizing resistance on a society-wide platform—which is really a political imperative—for most of the NGOs, their work gets reduced in the current conjuncture to a fragmented and extremely localized social work initiative. Therefore, the term 'transnational' needs to be problematized to prevent mechanistic and casual labeling of any program, policy, or struggle as 'transnational'. In other words, application of the notion of transnationalism should be context-specific. In this way, the idea may become an organizing principle that can inform, coordinate, and conceivably organize internationally the local grassroots resistance and the work of indigenous social movements against imperial impositions, the neoliberal globalization project, and other forms of racial and gender oppressions and class exploitation. Realization of this potential, as opposed to rendering the idea of transnationalism into a mere rhetorical device, requires vigilance in two key areas: (i) the historicism inherent in not distinguishing contemporary globalization from capitalism's historical international trajectory since its infancy and (ii) the tendency to read mechanically a transformative potential to a program, policy, movement, or action and thus read its global (international) links without also identifying the ultimate beneficiaries (ordinary people versus the imperialized and imperialist holders of privilege).

16   The title of this book suggests that it uses a post-colonial perspective to analyze critically the imperatives of capitalist globalism, that is, its propensity of external domination of the post-colonial state. Based on this understanding, as I have argued elsewhere,[37] the project of globalization could only be realized once nationalist and independent-minded leaders in many post-colonial societies were overthrown or eliminated through the Central Intelligence Agency's (CIA) 'dirty tricks' and military coups, the developmental project was shelved, and the 'new' international division of labour was adopted in the late 1970s.[38] These measures subsequently opened the doors of most Third World states to the transfer of labour-intensive operations from the North, the establishment of Free Trade Zones and sweatshop assembly lines, the acceptance of the export-orientation bind on the economy with the consequent loss of an internal market, and the dismantling of the public domain for privatization and market access through the IMF's structural adjustment programs and World Trade Organization policies. These changes have not been part of some transhistorical process as Gupta and Sharma have alluded;[39] rather, the globalization era marks a qualitative shift involving a power transfer from the national (the nationstate/post-colonial state) to the global (meaning capital and corporations), a move in which, paradoxically, the post-colonial state has been fully complicit. In accepting this shift and the new reality of capitalist globalism, states in both the North and the South have worked hand-in-glove, not as

'weak' entities; rather, the proto-capitalist post-colonial states (weak in the sense of their client status) have been relatively strong vis-à-vis their own populace in enforcing the neoliberal shift in state and society. Before capitalist globalism came to pass, the national was paramount: the US with the support of most Western nation-states started to elevate the nationstate to mythical heights, beginning at the Bretton Woods conference in 1944, and the narrative of the all-powerful state has since navigated both imagined and real paths. Therefore, the challenge for theorists of the state is to make sense of the external impulses of the hegemonic Western state and international financial institutions and to analyze why and how the post-colonial and Latin American states have acquiesced in delimiting their power in relation to capital. For the post-colonial state, however, this dramatic turn to self-imposed delimitation of power vis-á-vis capital has created the dilemma for indigenous elites to create 'normal' nation-states—an idea that was internalized with the appearance of the colonial state and the eulogizing of the Western nation-state as the most effective vehicle of territorial representation and internal management of the populace. However, this self-imposed delimiting of state power has been realized by the force of external domination, a fact that state theorists have ignored in favour of analyses of internal state imperatives. This separation of external and internal state dimensions is one of the important issues addressed in this book and one of the key arguments for a theory of the post-colonial state. Incidentally, the case for integration of internal and external dimensions is specifically made in Chapters 2 and 3.

17   A post-colonial state theory can also explicate the ongoing impact of the colonial legacy on the state in post-colonial societies. However, these links cannot be articulated in an ahistorical manner. If we merely focus on the current era of capitalist globalism when most post-colonial states are trying to outdo and outbid one another in offering a favourable corporate climate for privatization and investment capital from transnational corporations, then we will miss examining the historical developments of the 1960s and 1970s. During this period, it was Western capital that was clamouring to get into post-colonial states and having much difficulty because of the restriction imposed on foreign direct investments. In the past 60 years or so of decolonization, links have been forged between the adoption of the capitalist path of development and the evolution of the post-colonial states in their current form. Even on a longer time horizon, admittedly, forms of Euro-US domination have changed over the past two and a half centuries, but the maintenance of a subordinate and dependent South is still the paramount imperialist goal with respect to states in the Third World. The identification of dependency as the common disabling tendency among Third World states should not become the basis of homogenizing the situation to all states of Africa, Asia, and Latin America. For the purpose of theorization, this generalization of dependency needs to be made more specific based on categories of post-colonial states' social and economic formation: as capitalist or proto-capitalist. Alongside, capitalist exploitation and race construction/racialization need to be understood as complementary social processes. These social processes even had some White people becoming racialized at one point in history (Irish, Southern and Eastern Europeans, and Ashkenazi Jews) who were subsequently deracialized as they became part of the dominant Northern European communities in Europe and North America, whereas the historically racialized peoples, the Aboriginal and non-White from Africa, Asia, Australasia, and Latin

America, continue to be oppressed and exploited in complex and contradictory ways for capital's benefit. However, even between the two broad variants of capitalist and proto-capitalist formations offered in this volume, a range of differences can be analyzed, including the composition and role of class forces, the differences in the nature of the state's relative autonomy, the question of whether understanding the power of dominant class forces should focus on the economic or political, or on their dialectical interplay. There is also considerable difference between capitalist and proto-capitalist categories that symbolize the incredible difference between the treatment of South Korea and sub-Saharan African states. Further, variations exist *within* each of these two respective categories. For instance, in the case of capitalist formations there are differences between India and China on the one hand and South Korea and Brazil on the other. Ultimately, these complexities are integrated in a meaningful theorization of the post-colonial state in Chapter 3, this volume.

Theorizing the post-colonial state

18 My primary argument in this book is that the post-colonial state has been the key mechanism in the global South's subordination (internally, by undermining civil society, and externally, by facilitating its imperialist domination) such that its populace remains largely fragmented and powerless as it is forced to yield to a unified front of mobile metropolitan capital that has the support of Western and client post-colonial states. The explanatory framework for this argument, which I introduced in the last section, can be synthesized as part of three complementary conceptual categories: (i) the *capitalism–nation-state nexus* and how it unfolds for Western nation-states and becomes the *capitalism–imperialism nexus* in colonial and post-colonial contexts, (ii) the problems with separating internal and external moments in state theory, and (iii) the primacy that state theorists have placed on either the economic or the political dimension without distinguishing the capitalist state from the proto-capitalist state. Most post-colonial states fall into the proto-capitalist category, whereas a few are capitalist entities. Distinguishing proto-capitalist from capitalist post-colonial states makes it possible to theorize the two variants of postcolonial states. In Chapter 3, I will begin with a broad theorization of the post-colonial state and then, in the final two chapters, shift to a concrete examination of state formation in India and Pakistan to clarify the capitalist and proto-capitalist variants, respectively.

19   I was motivated to conduct this research partly because of a resurgent interest in the post-colonial state and partly by witnessing how existing theorization has proceeded without either problematizing the ideological nature of neoliberal rule or foregrounding the external impulse of contemporary imperialist interventions and domination of the South. I also wanted to address the following significant omissions in post-colonial state theory: the differing natures of post-colonial states and the incompleteness of nation-building (failure to address the 'national question'), the impact of the colonial state, and the structures of internal and external domination. These omissions appear not only in the work of ideologues of neoliberalism and liberal social scientists but also in scholarship by various types of state theorists, including those of critical ethnography and of the developmental state. Three main limitations can be identified in the

current 'discourse' on the post-colonial state: (i) a 'flattening of history', especially the history of the colonial state, whose imprint is deeply etched on the post-colonial state; (ii) a lack of comprehension of the capitalism–imperialism nexus and of the nature and role of the post-colonial state in facilitating the external imperialist domination of state and society; and (iii) an emphasis on culture, paradox, and ambiguity in identifying the state at the expense of a more nuanced structuralist understanding of the state.

20   Against this backdrop, my political economy and social history perspective is meant to critique the prevailing orthodoxy, which universalizes Western ideas and remains committed to a Eurocentric reading of the 'non-European' world. There is an apparent refusal to understand, or even notice, how colonial legacies shape the histories of post-colonial states; a characteristic current imperialist response is to demand post-colonial states to do more to support imperialist projects, while remaining silent about the North-South divide and the increasing dependency of the South on the North. Currently, this involves a formal push for 'good governance' and democracy in the Third World within a privatized social framework that does not empower ordinary people and leaves the state relatively removed from issues related to the well-being of its populace including health, education, and gainful employment. Instead, Western states are eager to see a greater involvement of NGOs in local issues in Third World states and want an even bigger push towards privatization and the dismantling of the public domain in this age of neoliberalism. These observations underpin much of the work in the first two chapters.

21   I will begin Chapter 1 by foregrounding the conceptual framework of the *capitalism–nation-state nexus* and by addressing the larger historical context of capitalist development and the rise of the nation-state in Europe, which led to the extension of colonialism to Africa and Asia. This link demonstrates the very different context of the European nation-state formation compared with that of the post-colonial state. I will also contest the idea of the 'normal' nation-state and clarify how this notion was imagined by post-colonial ruling classes as they emulated the European experience of nationalism and nation-states formation. Similarly, I will critically assess theories of nationalism, most of which universalize the European nationalist experience to post-colonial state and society. I will address the problems inherent in Eurocentrism and distinguish my critique of universalization from Partha Chatterjee's so that I can analyze Benedict Anderson's celebrated work[40] and critically assess his ideas of nation and nationalism. My analysis of the colonial state's manipulative social policy will reveal that the nature of identity construction in the colony and its debilitating impact for the colonized have produced antagonistic conflicts, which continue in the post-colonial era. This chapter shows how the capitalism–nation-state nexus was central for the capitalist development of Europe and North America and how a new capitalism–imperialism link emerged as soon as capitalists (with full support of their respective nation-states' militaries) begin their search for new colonies from the mid-18th century. As the capitalism–imperialism nexus re-emerged in the post-colonial era, subordination was reinscribed on state and society through clientelism and US imperialist domination.

22   Chapter 2 provides the historical context to post-colonial state's re-subordination, and the analytical framework will assist in developing a theory of the post-colonial state in Chapter 3. Critical to this framework is the *capitalism–imperialism nexus*, which

emerged during colonialism and has become the key instrument of re-subordination of post-colonial states. Because modernization theorists have played a pivotal role in introducing developmentalism to the global South and in encouraging post-colonial and Latin American states to serve as clients for the post-World War II capitalist/imperialist superpower, I will examine the ideas of two key modernization theorists. I will also briefly examine how the Cold War between the US and the Soviet Union became a hot war for post-colonial and Latin American states. This happened with the formation of the US security state and the CIA, which resulted in the elimination or removal of nationalist post-colonial and Latin American leadership. I will then show how the developmental state was an effort to resist the capitalism–imperialism nexus but that the indigenous bourgeoisie began to dismantle the inward-oriented developmental state because of the economic stagnation and corruption accompanying this statist model and embraced the market-oriented path of capitalist development. The US, its Western allies, and international financial institutions took the developmental state's failure as an opportunity to pressure Third World states to privatize the public domain and introduce economic liberalization. At the same time, because the peasantry was being displaced from rural areas as mechanization and Green Revolution technology was introduced, Western states lost no time in introducing the 'new' international division of labour—effectively transferring labour-intensive production to the global South to take advantage of this captive reserve army of displaced and unemployed workers. With the demise of the Soviet Union, the priority for Western states was to extend neoliberalism for the eventual re-subordination of proto-capitalist post-colonial states. The combined effect of these changes and the pauperization of the urban working class that followed led to the emergence of the urban informal sector as the most exploited form of self-employment—in effect, the work of a disguised proletariat. The idea that families who are involved in the informal sector are complicit in their own *self-exploitation* is a relatively unexplored concept in the context of capitalist globalism; therefore, I will examine how self-exploitation is realized within the current capitalist framework. Finally, I will analyze how the division between North and South has been cemented by the new international division of labour, whereas the capitalism–imperialism nexus has intensified the re-subordination of post-colonial state and society in the period of neoliberal globalization.

23   The historical and social analyses of colonialism, nationalism, and the capitalism–imperialism nexus that I present in Chapters 1 and 2 provide part of the foundation for my theorization on the post-colonial state. Chapter 3 builds on this background by first examining the nature of the economic system and social relations that were dominant in the colony, as these have a bearing in the post-colonial era; most post-colonial states adopted the structures of the colonial state, which were quasi-capitalist or protocapitalist. My theorization about the post-colonial state, therefore, includes three inter-related issues: the impact of the colonial state structure, the role of internal class relations, and the force of external imperialist domination of post-colonial state and society. In addressing these three issues, I am able to integrate the external and internal dimensions of the post-colonial state, which I consider to be central to a more comprehensive analysis of the character of the post-colonial state. By critically engaging with Alavi's theorization of pheripheral capitalism, I will examine colonial

India's social conditions in order to demonstrate that, although the colony may have been a periphery of the metropolitan capitalist colonial power, its social relations, contra Alavi, were not capitalist or even peripherally capitalist. I will argue that the 'overdeveloped' bureaucracies of most proto-capitalist states have so encumbered and shackled their societies that feudal relations did not significantly weaken. As a result, capitalists and the working class are weak in proto-capitalist societies and, barring a few exceptions, do not enable the release of productive forces for capitalist, socialist, or some other form of social transformation. Following this, I will examine the nature of the post-colonial state more broadly by analyzing the character and roles of the bureaucracy and the propertied classes and how they contributed to managing the affairs of post-colonial state and society. Throughout much of this analysis I address the external meddling of imperialist power, integrate the external and internal moments, and discuss the need for a dialectical interplay between the economic and the political dimensions.

24   In addressing the nature or character of the state, I offer two variations of the post-colonial state: the capitalist and the proto-capitalist variant—the latter typifying most states of Africa and Asia. In this context, my research contributes to a new understanding of the post-colonial state in the era of capitalist globalism. There are very different implications for the post-colonial state depending on whether the state is analyzed as capitalist or proto-capitalist; hence the two case studies on state formation in India and Pakistan (Chapters 4 and 5, respectively) are my attempt to ground theory in practice.

25   Much of what I offer in Chapter 4's social analysis of early post-colonial India and its transition to a capitalist state is omitted in current ethnographical studies of the post-colonial state: an examination of the land question, an analysis of social relations in India, an assessment of the benefits derived by the propertied classes from the early social and economic policies of the Nehruvian state, and an examination of the role of the Indian bureaucratic elite. As the external dimension is an essential part of my broad analysis of India's state formation, I integrate it within this chapter. Moving from this integrated analysis, I will then examine the post-Nehruvian era: Indira Gandhi's stint with populism, the rise of regionalism, and how Hindu fundamentalism/nationalism gained prominence and captured state power. Through a careful analysis of the Indian bourgeoisie's aggressive moves to adopt neoliberalism and attack on the inward-oriented state-led developmental model in favour of economic liberalization, I demonstrate how India shook off the 'failed' developmental state label, rebranding itself 'incredible India'. Despite tremendous economic expansion and consistent high growth rates in the past decade, however, India's social fissures have not decreased, poverty has not been reduced, and the rural-urban divide is glaring. As a result, there is broad internal resistance to neoliberalism in India. In the final section, I will examine this resistance, which has taken the form of armed action of radical groups and *adivasis* (Indigenous people) to oppose corporate mining interests, the Indian state, and its paramilitary thugs. The challenge to neoliberalism, along with the nationalist movement in Kashmir, Assam, and elsewhere, has also led to the rise of the security-obsessed Indian state.

26   My case study of Pakistan's state formation in Chapter 5 will reveal that, in contrast to what happened in India, once the civil and military bureaucrats had taken

firm control of the state apparatus in the immediate aftermath of decolonization, they completely aligned the country with the US. This decision made Pakistan captive to US demands and eventually led the country to become a client state of its US patron. My critical assessment of Pakistan's formative years shows that its very basis of existence as a homogenous Muslim *'nation'* was challenged from the moment of its inception by the assertion of ethnic and national identity claims. The demands for subnational rights and provincial autonomy were made by Baluch, Bengali, Pashtun, and Sindhi nations against the dominance of the bureaucratic elite from the Punjab and their junior partners (migrants from North India, who later chose to also identify themselves as the *Mohajir* [migrant] nation). I undertake an extended socio-political analysis of Pakistan's first three decades since decolonization, integrating internal and external dimensions. External factors affecting Pakistan were much more complex than those for India. The first three decades marked two long periods of military dictatorship between which was the civilian rule of Z.A. Bhutto. General Ziaul Haq's military dictatorship was extremely damaging for Pakistani society; its reverberations are being felt to this day. Haq not only deepened Pakistan's clientelist relationship with the US, in the context of the Afghan War against the Soviet Union, he also unleashed the forces of militant Islam. In a separate section of the chapter I will address the Pakistani state's role in enabling a rightward ideological shift and the radicalization of militant Islamists. The further intensification of Pakistan's clientelist relationship with the US and the consequent rise of the Taliban against the US and North Atlantic Treaty Organization forces in Afghanistan and Pakistan, has also resulted in the Taliban attacking Pakistani state and society, which has made public safety and security in the country a number one concern. The Haq regime was also pivotal to the military's expanded involvement in the economy and impeded private industrial capital investment, whereas the power of the feudal elite has remained unchallenged. Consequently, the capitalist class has become weaker, as the civil and military bureaucrats, and now the civilian political leadership, have wreaked havoc with the already fragile economy. The result is that Pakistan remains a very dependent proto-capitalist state.

27   In the final section of the chapter, I will analyze the social and economic constraints, and investigate why economic liberalization in Pakistan has not received the kind of enthusiasm that it has in India. The rudderless Pakistani economy and the *rentier* nature of its key players' activities mean that the country is essentially on life support. Because the US has largely provided this economic support, even if it has been through the IMF and the World Bank, clientelism has become deeply entrenched, and Pakistan now is even more beholden to the US. The result of this dependency and subordination has been more intensively reinscribed in the period of capitalist globalization.

28   The importance of identifying the character of a post-colonial state as capitalist or proto-capitalist provides valuable clues about the internal makeup of society and the effect of external imperialist forces on both state and society. As the case studies of India and Pakistan reveal, there are serious implications for state sovereignty for *proto-capitalist states* in relation to the *capitalist post-colonial state*. The latter may still be dependent on Western capital and to a degree on Western nation-states, but it has more room to manoeuvre. In contrast, the sovereignty of *proto-capitalist states* is seriously compromised because they are made up largely of client states and dependent on the imperialist power. This dependency also has significant consequences for

economic independence and for autonomy in developing appropriate social and political policy frameworks. The concluding thought here is that by returning to the larger structural questions and the legacy of the colonial state, by re-establishing the relationship between imperialism and capitalism, and by reintegrating the separations, the expectation is for a fresh understanding of the post-colonial state in the age of capitalist globalization.

Textual and rhetorical questions

Textual

1. After mentioning the problem of theorising postcolonial state and discussing it further in his essay (paragraph 1), Khan takes on the hyphenated term "post-colonial" and associated terms like the "Third World," and the "global South" (paragraphs 2, 3, and 4). Does the writer take the terms contestably? Clarify his position.

2. Khan's position regarding post-colonial state is "rooted in social history and involves a political economy of the post-colonial state and critical understanding of power and resistance." His position is different from the structuralists and functionalists who ignore cultural dynamics of post-colonial state. Furthermore, he sees problem in how critical ethnographers view the post-colonial state. He also alludes to Poulantzas's position to support his idea. Explain the debate on post-colonial state developed in paragraphs 7 and 8. Read paragraph 9 and 10 to further understand Khan's position.

3. What do you understand by a "denaturalizing approach to state and governance in the postcolonial world" in relation to "post-colonial state as a 'natural' embodiment of sovereignty and source of social order?" Why are Foucauldian and Gramscian positions "the source of ... confusion?" Is it because a "denaturalizing approach to state" and a "variety of ethnographic sites" "position themselves in the space between" the ideas of Foucault and Gramsci? Read paragraphs 12, 13, and 14 to understand Khan's arguments.

Rhetorical

1. Khan's language in paragraph 11 is of advice, suggestion, and criticism. Mark the words and phrases "requires," "pretend," and "pay lip service." A similar tone is evident in paragraph 16 when he uses the phrase like "'dirty tricks'." How is the language of criticism both subtle and harsh in these two paragraphs?

2. Khan reasons the need of theorising the post-colonial state in the context of the existing world orders of globalisation and transnationalism. Analyse his argument in terms of how he problematises globalisation and transnationalism (paragraph 15).

3. How do you understand the following two terms as complementary to one another: Theorisation and problematisation? Furthermore, two significant terms used frequently in academic research are "statement of problem" and "hypothesis." Why does a researcher lead from the "statement of problem" to the "hypothesis" and

not the opposite way around while writing a proposal for research? Do you think that the "statement of problem" is problematisation of the object of research/knowledge?

Discussion questions

1. Paragraph 17 is a critical commentary on the existing political and economic nature of the West and its subordinated post-colonial states. Khan writes, the "forms of Euro-US domination have changed over the past two and half centuries, but the maintenance of a subordinate and dependent South is till the paramount imperialist goal with respect to the Third World." The trade war between China and the US, migrant policies of Europe, and conflicts in West Asia have further complicated the forms. Paraphrase the paragraph and present a critical commentary on the contemporary global situation in your own modes of argument (1500 words).
2. If a state is an institutionalised-organised space of authority and sovereignty, there were/are similar concrete states and proto-states like city-states in Mesopotamia and Greece, tribes in Asia and Africa, empires, and papacy in Europe. Elaborate and analyse the nature of such socio-political organisations (1500 words).
3. Nation/nationalism is an illusive and abstract term and yet a double bind of emotion and realisation stronger than state. Nationalism is authoritative, expansive politically, emotional in literatures, tearful in poetry, militarily commanding, fascist in rhetoric, militant in emotion, patriarchal in power, motherly in love and affection, aggressive in territoriality. Elaborate on this statement[41] (1000 words).

Inter-textual discussions

1. Ashis Nandy writes[42] about three images of Indian state: "*The state as a protector* [...] to protect society against arbitrary oppressor; " the "*state as a moderator or liberator* ... to introduce Indian society to the modern world" initiated by the modern elites of the country, and the "*state as an arbiter*" "where social relationships can be renegotiated." In relation to the images of a state (Indian or other), consider the following propositions by Nandy[43] about the culture and state: "One way of the state and culture relation is 'to look for the means by which culture can be made to contribute to the sustenance and growth of the state'. The state here is seen as operating according to certain fixed, universal and sociological rules." The other way is to see "the state as a protector, an internal critique of thermostat ... to serve the needs of or contribute to the enrichment of the culture." Paraphrase Nandy's concepts of state, culture, and responsibility and put forwards your thesis to critique Indo-Pak relations (2000 words).
2. *Do Bigha Zamin* (*Two Acres of Land*) is a film by Bimal Roy which was released in 1953. The film represents the plight of the common people against the state mechanism. Moorthy in Raja Rao's novel *Kanthapura* (1938) does not resign as Shambu and Parvati do in the *Do Bigha Zamin*. How do ideologies of the state mechanism function in the two narrative contexts? These two narratives belong to two difference times in India (1500 words).

HYPHENATED POST-COLONIAL

Critical and creative thinking

1. Gujarati poet Jaya Mehta's "Lokshahiman" ("In a Democracy")[44] is ironical in tone about democracy and freedom. Discuss.
2. *Desh*, *Mulka*, *Watan*, *Matrabhumi*, *Janmabhumi*, *Rajya*, *Nāṭṭin* (Tamil), and *Dēśanlō* (Telgu) are both physical and emotional spaces. Ronald Grigor Suny[45] writes about nationalism using the metaphors of "Sleeping Beauty" and the "Bride of Frankenstein." The former is "the kiss of freedom," and the later is the "'invented" and 'constructed' nature of nation and nationality" (3, 4) by assembling parts and trying to make a whole. How can Suny's ideas be appropriated to understand such terms?

Notes

1. Prof Khan has suggested the title from the Introduction chapter of his book.
2 See Hamza Alavi, "The State in Post-Colonial Societies: Pakistan and Bangladesh," *New Left Review* 74 (July–August 1972): 59–81.
3 This was one of the ways that Benedict Anderson originally identified *nationness* and nationalism; see Benedict Anderson, *Imagined Communities: Reflections on the Origin and the Spread of Nationalism* (London: Verso, 1991) 4.
4 Akhil Gupta and Ardhana Sharma, "Globalization and Postcolonial States," *Current Anthropology* 47.2 (April 2006): 278; Sarah A. Radcliff e, "Imagining the State as a Space: Territoriality and the Formation of the State in Ecuador," *States of Imagination: Ethnographic Explorations of the Postcolonial State*, ed. Thomas B. Hansen and Finn Stepputat (Durham: Duke University Press, 2001) 125; Gilbert Joseph and Daniel Nugent, *Everyday Forms of State Formation: Revolution and the negotiation of rule in modern Mexico* (Durham: Duke University Press, 1994), cited in Radcliff e, "Imagining the State as Space" 123.
5 For a poststructuralist understanding and definition of 'postcolonial', see Ania Loomba, *Colonialism/Postcolonialism* (London: Routledge, 1998).
6 Although Kwame Nkrumah was probably the first one to use the term neocolonial, it soon became embroiled in controversy between the 'pro-Chinese' and the 'pro-Soviet' camps in the late 1960s and 1970s. Avoiding the use of the term, therefore, is a way of not wanting to revisit this debate.
7 See Thomas B. Hansen and Finn Stepputat, eds., *States of Imagination: Ethnographic Explorations of the Postcolonial State* (Durham: Duke University Press, 2001) 13.
8 John Dickenson et al., *Geography of the Third World* (London: Routledge, 1996) 4.
9 See Vijay Prashad, *The Darker Nations: A People's History of the Third World* (New York: New Press, 2007).
10 The work of critical race theorists tends to focus so narrowly on identity, difference, 'whiteness', and representation that the political economy or structural elements of race and racism, which pertain to the theoretical and material significance of race and colonialism, especially in relation to capitalism, remain untheorized. As an example, see the breadth of articles using critical race theory in a special issue of *Critical Sociology*: see Rodney D. Coates, "Introduction to Special Issue of Critical Sociology: Critical Race and Ethnic Theory, Researchand Process," *Critical Sociology* 29.1–2 (2002): 7–11.
11 See Ranajit Guha, *Elementary Aspects of Peasant Insurgency in Colonial India* (Delhi: Oxford University Press, 1997); and Edward Said, *Culture and Imperialism* (New York: Knopf, 1993).
12 See Michel-Rolph Trouillot, *Haiti, State Against Nation: The Origins and Legacy of Duvalierism* (New York: Monthly Review Press, 1990).
13 Poulantzas's adherents would probably disagree with such a characterization but that is another discussion.

14 Gupta and Sharma 279.
15 Hansen and Stepputat 14.
16 The interpretation of Foucault is from Timothy Mitchell, "Economy and the State Eff ect," *State/Culture: State Formation After the Cultural Turn*, ed. George Steinmetz (Ithaca: Cornell University Press) 89, cited in Hansen and Stepputat 4.
17 Mitchell 89, cited in Hansen and Stepputat 17.
18 Nicos Poulantzas, *State, Power and Socialism*, trans. Patrick Camiller (London: New Left Books, 1978) 128.
19 Poulantzas, State 129.
20 See Karl Marx and Frredrich Engels, *On the Paris Commune* (Moscow: Progress Publishers, 1971).
21 The quote is from Radcliffe 124.
22 See the edited volumes of Hansen and Stepputat.
23 Hansen and Stepputat claim the opposite, that is, the state is not weak in the 'era of transnationalism' less conclusively – rather than critically assessing whether such an assumption is valid in the first place; Hansen and Stepputat 16.
24 Hansen and Stepputat 2.
25 Hansen and Stepputat 3.
26 Hansen and Stepputat 2.
27 See Antonio Gramsci, *Selections from the Prison Notebooks of Antonio Gramsci*, ed. and trans. Quintin Hoare and Geoff rey Nowell Smith (New York: International Publishers, 1991).
28 Hansen and Stepputat 3.
29 For instance, see the work of the writers on the developmental state, such as Vivek Chibber, Peter Evans, Aseema Sinha, and Jorgen Pedersen; their views are flagged in Chapters 3 and 4.
30 Hansen and Stepputat 9–11.
31 Clyde Barrow tackles the claims of the weakness or the demise of the state in Clyde Barrow, "The Return of the State: Globalization, State Theory and the New Imperialism," New Political Science 27.2 (June 2005): 123–145.
32 See William Robinson and Jerry Harris, "Towards a Global Ruling Class: Globalization and the Transnational Capitalist Class," Science & Society 64.1 (Spring 2000): 11–54; Robert Burbach and William Robinson, "The Fin de Siecle Debate: Globalization as Epochal Shift," *Science & Society* 63.1 (Spring 1999): 10–39. For a debate on whether the nation-state has weakened, see A. Sivanandan and Ellen Wood, "Globalization and Epochal Shifts: An Exchange," *Monthly Review* 48.9 (February 1997): 19–21.
33 Pheng Cheah, "Given Culture: Rethinking Cosmopolitical Freedom in Transnationalism," *Boundary* 2 24.2 (Summer 1997): 159.
34 For example, Gupta and Sharma identify the Integrated Child Development Services program of the Indian government that was started in 1975 as "part of a transnational set of ideas and policies that were global in their reach and effects" contending that it would be hard to argue that before the 1991 market reforms "the Indian state was outside an arena of globalization" (emphasis in original). It is this casual invocation of the transhistorical notion of globalization that is being contested; Gupta and Sharma 278.
35 As an example of this understanding see Amiya Kumar Bagchi, "Parameters of Resistance," *Monthly Review* (July–August 2003): 136.
36 James Petras and Henry Veltmeyer, *Globalization Unmasked: Imperialism in the 21st Century* (Halifax: Fernwood/Zed, 2001).
37 Tariq Amin-Khan, "Is Corporate Globalism an Epochal Shift?" Gala Conference of Marxism 2000 and the Association of Economic Research, University of Massachusetts, Amherst, July 2000.
38 On the role of the Central Intelligence Agency (CIA) in eliminating nationalist leaders in the Third World, see William Blum, *Killing Hope: US Military and CIA Interventions Since World War II* (Monroe: Common Courage Press, 2004); on the dismantling of the developmental project in order to implement the globalization project, see Philip McMichael, *Development and Social Change: A Global Perspective* (Thousand Oaks: Pine Forge, 2004)

143–177; and on the "new" international division of labour see F. Fröbel, J. Heinrichs, and O. Kreye, *The International Division of Labour: Structural Unemployment in Industrialised Countries and Industrialisation in Developing Countries*, trans. Pete Burgess (1977; Cambridge: Cambridge University Press, 1980).

39 See Gupta and Sharma.

40 See B. Anderson, *Imagined Communities*.

41 I have translated in English the section of my Nepali article "Gundruk-ko Saino" ("Gundruk and Bond") in "Fursad" *Annapurna* (Jan 21, 2017). Gundruk is a food item popular in the Nepali hills. My argument in this article is how rootedness evolves out of the vernacular and is different from nationalism. My idea of rootedness is inspired by Gayatri Spivak (2010) *Nationalism and the Imagination*. London: Seagull.

42 See Nandy Ashis (2007). "Democratic Culture and Image of the State: India's Unending Ambivalence" in *Time Warps*. Delhi: permanent black, 36–60.

43 See Nandy, Ashis (2004). "Culture, State and the Rediscovery of Indian Politics" in *Bonfire of Creeds: The Essential Ashis Nandy*. New Delhi: Oxford University Press, 89–107

44 Check Tharu Susie and K. Lalita. (Eds.).(1995). *Women Writing in India: 600 B.C. to the Present. Vol. II: The 20th Century*. Delhi: Oxford University Press, 366. The poem is translated by Shirin Kunchedkar.

45 Ronald Grigor Suny. (1993). *The Revenge of the Past: Nationalism, Revolution, and Collapse of the Soviet Union*. Stanford: Stanford University Press.

6

GRASSROOTS TEXTS

Ethnographic ruptures and transnational feminist imaginaries

Piya Chatterjee

"**Trans-**, trânz-, trâns-, pfx. across, beyond.——Also tran-, tra-. [L. trāns, across, beyond.]" (Geddie, 1167)

"**Translate**, trâns-, trânz-, træns-, trrænz-lāt', v.t. to remove to another place: to remove to heaven, especially without death; to enrapture: to render into another language: to express in another artistic medium: to interpret, put in plainer terms, explain: to transfer from one office (esp. eccelesiastical) to another: to transform: to renovate, make new from old.——v.i. to practice translation: to admit of translation—— adj. **Tran-slā'table**.——n. translā'tion, the act of translating: removal to another place, see, &c.: rendering into another language: a version: the working up of new things from old materials: change of place (distinguished from rotation): the automatic re-transmission of a telegraphic message."(Geddie, 1167)

"**Translation** n., conversion, paraphrase, version, transformation, change, rendition." (Microsoft Word 200 Thesaurus, U.S. version)

"The traditionally desired invisible translation of the original text misreads, replaces and displaces the text—erases it, in fact. But an opaque translation, drawing attention to its own presence in the text, foregrounds the difference between original and reproduction. This is a self-reflexive translation, a thick translation, drawing attention to its own presence and the ideological nature of translation as a colonizing act." (Karamcheti, 193).

Introduction: Tangles and provocations

1   Sometimes, I confess, when I am asked to write about the "transnational feminist" implications of my work around Indian tea plantation women's lives, I get mired in a dense thicket of anxieties and questions. How could my ethnographic work located in

the hinterlands of eastern India be "transnational"—apart from my own bi-national, diasporic subjectivity and movement? And how can I make legible the feminist commitments and lessons I learn from this space when the primary discussions about the "transnational" and "feminism" appear to be rather firmly located in – or aimed towards the – imperial centers of the North? Almost immediately, I recognize the limiting – but also productive aspects – of these questions, as much as I understand that they gesture to thick, knotty tangles which will be hard to smooth out and braid neatly.

2   First, as Chandra Mohanty and others have argued, the presumption that a feminist ethnography of tea plantations is a local "case study" which does not impact broader "global" theory is problematic – especially if one implicitly assumed that truly "global" theories are produced first in imperial centers (Mohanty 333–358). The "local" ethnographic case informs "global" theory, at best. Surely, a critical and plural understanding of "transnationalities" break across these epistemic assumptions and binary inequalities. The plantation case is, for example, already global, formed in specific sites by historical transnational processes.

3   Second, despite de-centering interventions, some might still posit that hegemonic constructions of the "transnational" continues to rest on such an enduring axes of reference – North to South, and vice versa. The imperial vectors of knowledge formation are difficult to dislodge. In that case, feminist ethnographies which seek to wrench the "transnational" away from this bi-lateral trajectory can suggest knowledges that are "otherwise" constituted, otherwise "centered."

4   Third, there is the presumption that 'feminist' sensibilities that emerge from these local places (out there in the peripheries of the so-called Third World) are not so relevant to the question of difference and power in the feminist preoccupations of the so called First World. Postcolonial and antiracist feminist scholarship, produced in the past three decades, has certainly revealed these geopolitics of difference and power in the study of women, gender and sexualities, here/there/here. Many feminist scholars/ activists have persuasively argued about the "third" in the "first", and for additional critical scrutiny on displacement and poverty in its many forms, mobile, across borders – in the North as much as the South.

5   This destabilization has helped to produce "transnational feminisms" as a powerful catch-all rubric within which many kinds of feminisms can be grouped. While these destabilizations do highlight multilateral engagements between women, the geopolitical binaries of imperial knowledge circuits still informs transnational projects in enduring ways. As an anthropologist who writes from places which don't have an immediate relevance to this imperial geography, I am concerned with how transnational feminist projects, based and produced in the United States might still obscure these implicit stances of "relevance" and significance.

6   Why does it matter at all – politically and ethically – to offer stories about plantation women if I choose not to fit them into a South-to-North axes? What if the lack of proximity to Northern preoccupations continue to render such analysis as merely one more entry into the old encyclopaedia of difference that is really still an index for distant strangeness made somewhat familiar? Such provocations open up a rather large Pandora's Box. This is a box that might be stuffed with ethnographic curiosities. They gesture to provisional explorations. They beg grounding.

7   In this essay, I explore these difficult knots by sharing, with humility and care, some grassroots lessons that I learned from the tensions and fissures of fieldwork in tea plantation country.[1] These are lessons that destabilize. They only begin to explore the big provocations I have set up. The braid I will weave will still have many knots, still remain messy – though that is perhaps the point: producing text through ethnographic methods is a snarly and messy business.

8   In staging the plantation, and presenting these ethnographic ruptures, I use "translation" as a tool with which I can engage the full "play" of power and ethics that are involved in each set of encounters. The phrase, "to remove to another place" begins one dictionary definition of translation, (offered in the introductory epigraph), is particularly appropriate for meditations on "transnationalities" – all their betweennesses, movements, border-crossings. Afterall, anthropological fieldwork, and the ethnography it produces, does always move us to "another place."

9   What might such "dis-placement" mean to the "texts" that are produced especially between women, elite researcher and her subaltern interlocuters? What do these "grassroots texts" suggest about the questions of difference/power/ethics always entailed in such encounters? What can be said about the "collaborative" aspirations involved in revealing the deeply collective nature of all anthropological fieldwork?

Staging the transnational plantation, historically

10   First, let us briefly tackle the ethnographic "case" problem by asserting that both the plantation and tea, the commodity that is its raison d'etre, were constituted by deeply historical transnational processes. In the world histories of capitalism and imperial trade this little bit of leaf has played an enormously vivid role: think of the Boston Tea Party, the Chinese trade (which created a balance of payments problem for England) and the Opium Wars (which involved a rather critical triangle trade between Indian opium and Chinese tea). In the heyday of the Chinese tea trade, one third of the East India Company's profits were due to tea. The East India Company was the first and most powerful multinational conglomerate in the world.

11   The labor of indigenous (adivasi) and Nepali women workers in Indian plantations (set up to battle against the Chinese control of the trade) continued to build the fortunes of the British plantocracy, and tea merchants in India, and then Ceylon. I have explored elsewhere how the "feminized fetishism" of labor and consumption simultaneously, in empire and colony, became vital to the story of tea. This "violence of the fetish" is racially and sexually embodied within the sign of the woman – bent low over the tea bush, or appearing colorfully on the packages which sell tea. Such are the exotic currencies of a star commodity as it circulates in a global and transnational trade.

12   Second, the "plantation" itself is one of the enduring models of bondage and a catalyst for 'diaspora' in the most profound ways. The dialectical tensions of labor bondage, and the need for labor itself, has given shape to the emergence of both settler colonialism in the Americas as well as the allied impetus for mercantile expansion and commodity trade – through the growing demand for products like sugar, coffee, tea and so on. From slavery to indentureship, from the Americas to Asia and Africa, the "plantation" becomes the crucible of a "diasporic imaginary." This is a crucible

GRASSROOTS TEXTS

created by the brutal, alienating and annihilating waves of human migration in a scale hitherto never seen in world history. Consider the forced horrors of the Middle Passage across the Atlantic, or the coolie ships that plied their indentured cargo from Calcutta to Fiji, Madras to Trinidad, and Bombay to Natal.

13   Third, let us locate a "transnational" migration within eastern India where these specific stories are located. Let us consider, provisionally, the codes of "nation-ness" to which they might speak. Indeed, what is the "nation" for an adivasi ("original inhabitant"/indigenous) villager who, due to famine, is desperate for food and livelihood? When a kinsman – a sardar (labor contractor) commissioned by British planters desperate for labor – tells her stories of easy cultivation and free plots of land, she goes.

14   She and her fellow "recruits," as they were known, probably don't understand where this journey as "coolie" batches will lead them. They leave their desh (country, the word that translates closely to the Hindi, "nation") for a place that will become their new "home." This is what the "nation" probably meant to them – that homeland, desh, so suddenly far away. If such a notion of the desh can be viewed as a kind of "pro-tonation," then we might view these labor diasporas as transnational. Simultaneously, labor recruitment from the Kingdom of Nepal also ensured a steady supply of future workers into the Darjeeling hills and the Dooars. Such are the trans-"national" travels in the histories of plantation settlement in eastern India. Translations (and Speaking "Transnationally"): "To Render Into Another Language" (Geddie, 1169)

15   The tea plantation resonates with a play of tongues, a play that reflects other "nations," other places. It is a polyphony, a cross-cutting chatter of patois and power. The North Bengal plantation's linguistic diversity is worked through a historical economy in which the procurement and disciplining of women and men into regimes of work constitutes a primary thread of articulation: of utterance, speech, the command over the written word, the many commands over bodies in labor. That is, they speak out the underlying "scripts of power," understood in the broadest sense. The languages spoken flow through the arteries of the plantation system, indexing the ranks of field and factory, coursing through clusters of labor quarters and hutments which make up its villages. It is in these villages, that such a "play of tongues" enters into layered, semi-autonomous planes of social action: community and caste exclusions and inclusions, racialized practices, and gendered rankings speak through the polyvalent chatter of a multilingual landscape.

16   Let us begin with a mixed, and incomplete list, of what is spoken in a North Bengal plantation: Kurukh (the language of the Oraon), Nepali, Sadri, Bengali, Hindi, Santhali, English. Sadri, a variation of the lingua franca of the Chotanagpur, the homelands of many working communities in the Dooars, is used and understood by all communities. A Nepali woman worker will speak to her Oraon friend in Sadri; a Bengali burra sahib (senior manager) will shout at a Santhali woman for plucking leaf carelessly. Neither speaks his or her "mother-tongue." Sadri, inscribed sometimes into Hindi script, is primarily an oral tradition from the Chotanagpur Plateau.[2] It flows between caste and so-called tribal divisions to create cohesion in what is otherwise a dazzling plural cultural landscape. It acts as social gel within the villages. In other moments of use, as when the planter shouts at a woman worker, Sadri is transformed into a verbal act of command and power.

153

17   However, following the caste, class and ethnic patterns of power in North Bengal, Bengali – the mother-tongue of many upper echelon staff and managers – is a primary language of dominance. Significantly, it is not used as commonly as Hindi within regimes of work, because the latter's linguistic markers are more kindred to the lingua franca of the plantation, sadri. However, as the language of the surrounding social and political elite, members of the labor elite – overseers, factory workers, and union leaders – are conversant in the language. Some, particularly union leaders, will serve as political brokers, indeed translators of power, between the planter elite, ordinary workers, and regional political party bosses, most of whom are Bengali.

18   Bengali also remains the dominant language of instruction in government-run public schools and colleges. The language of education and educational policy in general, continues to exclude Sadri and Nepali speakers in significant ways. On the whole, Sadri speakers would prefer to be instructed in Hindi. While government-run Hindi schools till Class Ten proliferate in the plantation area, the first threshold examination at the end of that class, to gain entrance into junior colleges and for further undergraduate training, is written in Bengali or English. The resulting disenfranchisement of an important sector of the population in North Bengal, which includes non-plantation communities as well, has resulted in serious political unrest and social movements around language issues and educational policy. Despite some campaigns by trade unions and town-based adivasi social organizations, curricular instruction and examination issues have not led to policy shifts within regional educational administration. Because of support from a powerful political movement for ethnic based regional autonomy, the Gorkhaland movement, the Nepali community has been more successful in constructing Nepali-medium schools in the area.

19   Within the plantation precincts, primary schooling, and the only basic training in literacy that most plantation children will receive, is sparse. In the British period, many schools were run by the plantations but with Indian independence, the government took over its administration. As a result, tea companies do not carry, and seldom exercise, any responsibility around basic education. Curricular instruction is in Hindi, and classes run up to Class Four. Young girls will wait for plantation jobs that they may inherit, if they are lucky, search for casual work, or get married and move into another plantation. If their family has resources and some permanent employment in the plantation, a boy will move into the local Hindi high-school. For the few Catholics and other missionya (Christians), admission to the local Catholic-run schools are a real possibility. Though non-Christian families will also attend these schools, missionya children will be helped by parish priests to gain admission. These schools offer both Hindi and English instruction.

20   For most women, debates about language policy and basic literacy, and the promise of some upward mobility, is a moot point. However, many remain attentive, and critical, of an educational policy which keeps most of their children from succeeding in higher education, even if they may have the economic resources to educate them beyond Class Ten. Because of customary patriarchal and patrilocal norms of marriage shared by all communities, and because of their potential bodied value as future field-workers, most girls and women are denied basic education. In the classificatory norms of the literacy-education-development paradigm, they are defined as "illiterates." (Freire 1969).

21 Yet, following Paulo Freire's general contention, that the syntax of the literacy-development paradigm situates those without formal, or text-based, education within a place of essential lack, I will argue that women are the primary translators of the historical and cultural knowledges of the plantation. (Freire 1969). Theirs is a polyphonic oral mastery of a knowledge base that they reproduce, critique and create anew in their kitchens, rituals and fields of labor. Though marginalized from the formal educational system and from socio-economic mobility, theirs is a cultural literacy that cannot be defined by lack. Certainly, the conditions leading to non-literacy radically diminishes the chance of socio-economic betterment and upward mobility, but it is not a primary sign of their sense of social being. Indeed, their remarkable facility with languages, in various sites of power, constitutes an ontology of personhood, and sociality, which is necessary, powerful and creative.

22 In important ways, their subordination within the plantation system necessitates their knowledges of what are the dominant languages of rule: Bengali, Hindi, and even a smattering of English. This is in addition to Sadri, Nepali, and perhaps the old mother-tongues of their homelands in the Chotanagpur. Munnu Kujoor who understands four languages and speaks two (Nepali and Sadri) fluently, is Oraon. Her language is Kurukh which, she tells me, is still spoken in the Purana (Old) Line, one of the villages where many Oraons live. "It is not like Hindi, didi (elder sister), the words are totally different. You know, like the inter-menter that they speak in south India. Have you heard Tamil bhasa (language)? I think it sounds like that. I don't speak it but my parents could."

23 I speak to Munnu Kujoor in a basic colloquial Hindi/Bengali mix. My own education in an international English-medium school in northern Nigeria and India, and subsequent undergraduate and graduate education in the United States, has resulted in linguistic loss. It is typical of a certain bourgeois, postcolonial and diasporic experience. Taught Hindi until Class Ten, and with enough skills to write in simple Hindi, I have adequate conversational skills in that language. I was never taught to write in Bengali, my mother-tongue, though speak it better than Hindi. I learned early that the loss of literate facility in my mother-tongue, marked me as firanghi (foreign) even before I had left India for higher education.

24 However, ironically, such a loss of literate privilege enabled me to enter the oral worlds of women in important ways. Indeed, they recognized that while I embodied upper-caste, upper-class privilege, my broken facility with both dominant languages of rule (including my own mother-tongue) resulted in an awkwardness that they could help me with as I searched for a word from Bengali to translate into Hindi. It was an awkwardness that made me enter the "outside" places of linguistic belonging.

25 Certainly, their confidence in various linguistic traditions was more significant than my self-conscious search for the "correct" syntax and linguistic useage in two. Though my English marked clearly the privileges of Amriki-ness (American-ness), and the ultimate sahib-language,[3] those quick shifts between Hindi-Bengali-Hindi created the necessary patois of communication – one which I, in some embarrassment, called my kichdi bhasa (mixed-curry language).

26 Such are the vagaries and possibilities of translation of experience to language: of scripted loss, reaching beyond worlds into new kinds of words and arrangements, a

calligraphy of what is spoken, what is wrenched from memory, what is not said. The presumed intimacy that my knowledge of Hindi could bring to bear to our basic communication was always fractured, but it was a fracturing that created other forms of connection. Loss was also, in this instance, possibility.

27   Simultaneously, let us not forget how these movements between languages, and the new languages created, constitute a new kind of trans-understanding. This sketch reinvigorates our understandings of the dazzling pluralities of linguistic mix which continue to 'remember' the other places – the desh – many left, never knowing whether they would get back, or where they were going.

Authorship: "Conversion, paraphrase, version, transformation, change, rendition" (Microsoft Word 2000 thesaurus, U.S. version)

Make Something and Show Us
Everyone thinks I am illiterate.
I am going to be an author and show them.
Everyone thinks I am incapable of anything.
I will do something and show them.
Everyone thinks I am bad.
I will show them by doing good.
Everyone thinks I am the land's grass.
I will show that I am the sky's stars.
Everyone thinks I don't have a mind.
I will show them that I am a poet.
Rita Chhetri (1999)

Rita Chhetri writes this poem as part of a collection of essays, poems, and testimonials that she has been collecting for some years. She works at Debpara Tea Estate, a plantation neighboring the plantation which is my primary fieldsite, New Dooars Tea Estate. We met first in 1993 but have started a conversation about her writing only in 1998. She writes from her memory of an alphabet learned last in Class Five, the extent of her participation in formal education. Because of her family's small resources, her brother continued his education while she took permanent employment as a tea plucker. She keeps loose pages in a thick cardboard folder, in a plastic bag, so that the monsoon rains which seep through the ceiling of her labor quarter, her home, do not damage the papers.

28   When we meet again in 1998, after a five year hiatus, she tells me that she has never lost her fire for writing; that she wrote on any scrap of paper, even the scratch paper used to make packets of channa (snacks). I asked her whether she kept these scraps, stained by the residue of lemon juice and spices, and she nodded, "some, but many times I would rip them up and throw them away. I was so angry, so angry..." I asked to see some of her saved work and told her to keep collecting whatever she wrote, that one day I would try and help to turn them into a book.

29   We sit together on some monsoon days in the summer of 2000, talking about a collaborative project in which her writing might be produced in situ, as a book. After xeroxing her work so we each have separate copies of her writing, we work

GRASSROOTS TEXTS

on translations. She writes in Nepali, in Hindi script. I don't understand Nepali so she translates each line into Bengali, and sometimes Hindi words that I might understand. Since I can read the Hindi, we read each line out together. I scribble out initial translations of each line in English, repeating them back to her in Bengali. It is a long process and she does not have much time to offer away from household and labor responsibilities.

30   The poem presented is dated as being written on March 10, 1999. She tells me she wrote it as a response to a man's mockery of a small sewing business she had begun with a few unemployed women in the plantations. She says, "He mocked me and said, 'how do you think you will run this? You don't even know how to read and write." I want to give it to this man who said this to me. I want to give him a book" (*Complicities*: Marcus, 1997).

31   Rita Chhetri's poem, the conditions of her writing and her translating some to me, begs a scrutiny of another politics of translation – not only the process of "conventional" translation as sketched above but the translation of this encounter and experience into an ethnographic text. The specific translation of her written Nepali into English, and into this particular text of English, is an act that transforms the enabling effects of oral dialogue (Rita speaking her meaning and intent to me in Hindi/Bengali) into a language, congealed into text, that she will not read, and which will circulate in article book-form, across other borderlines of power.

32   I will offer only some of her written samples as breaks, or punctuations of a dream which I envision about some women-led community organizing efforts taking place in the area. Though we plan to work on an entirely separate project which will make her, singularly, an author, this possible collaboration will depend on more consistent meetings. The book never happens, though we end up collaborating[4] in grassroots organizing from 1999–2007, a collaboration that is equally fragile and burdened by the messy ethics of inequality of status and power between us.

33   The aspirations around this collaboration of book production and authorship is mediated through a politics of value: time, wages-lost, bodied energies. Its immediate political economy will depend on how she can get time "away" from her necessary wage-labor and how we can both ensure that she incurs no losses, material or otherwise. These are sets of tricky ethical calculations and need to be underscored within any narrative claims of ethnographic collaboration. In the few days she spends with me discussing her writing, she takes hours from her weekly holiday to meet. Though she does not lose daily wages in this process, she does give me time that she might spend in household chores. These hours offer a bit of rest, she assures me. With the usual ambivalences, I learn to accept her will and her desire to spend time sharing her other work.

34   Within this preliminary stage of narrative presentation, I appropriate her "voice" for a specific kind of analysis about translation. It is a task of translation and insertion, which is central to ethnographic production. Yet, despite its fragmentations and its reflexivities, the future ethnography cannot escape the issues of ethical accountability to one's interlocuters and to the analysis produced. Claims of textual transparency through self-referential moments around ethnographic collaboration, and efforts of collaboration within actual social practice are connected within a political, epistemological arc that should show these faultlines of inequality clearly.

35 Let me ask you, then, to revisit the place within which Rita and I are sutured into a particular web of social power. Beyond the actual symbol of languages we inscribe into our rough and lined paper, our encounter folds into another page about the neo-feudal politics of rural India. It is one that inscribes, continuously and consistently, our politics of location: her Nepali working class and gendered personhood; my Bengali upper-caste, bourgeois self, connected by kinships of class privilege to the postcolonial plantocracy, and far-flung cosmopolitan diasporas. Our encounter crosses certain boundaries of power, but also underlines those terms of inequality. These are oppositional positions.

36 My act of "appropriation" is, let's push it further, also an act of thievery even as I expose the faultlines of our encounter. As Jigna Desai, Danielle Bouchard and Diane Detournay suggest at the end of their essay on transnational feminist praxis, "admitting one's culpabilities and naming the transaction as stealing allows for "honorability."[5] (Desai et al., 51–52) In other words, the assertion that epistemological claims of the text itself are implicated in the snarls of accountability and ethics within field encounters is now a given, but perhaps we need to push into the ethical questions a bit more, start tracing out something we might imagine as a system of ethical-narrative-accountability.

37 "Honorable thievery" might be one way to thread these forms of epistemic violence – that which is "done" to make this "text" come into being. In that light, self-referencing, reflexivity and postmodern textual strategies are not being used here as a magic trick, a sleight of hand that might actually obscure the more obvious terms of feudal power that define relationships in a North Bengal plantation. It is not intended to obscure the fact that the act of translation, like any act of power, begs for an honest web of ethical accountability.

38 Why did I think, when first stepping into the Labor Lines in 1991 that here was something kindred to apartheid? Why did I think that we, postcolonial sahibs and memsahibs, wore (to paraphrase Franz Fanon) Brown Masks? Any claims of "transnational sisterhood" from such epistemic sites have to be made, then, very carefully. Yet, the politics of claim, however, might not be the same as the politics of the imagination – the imagination can embrace these faultlines, the thieving, and still stretch towards fragile solidarities. These kinships, unlike liberal understandings of "sisterhood," begin with the undeniable recognition of structural power. Understanding intention, hers and mine, is important in this recognition for it allows the possibility of encounter. But it is always sutured tightly to the nets of privilege and subalternity which fling us in opposing directions.

39 But I am still hopeful about the possibilities that can seed within transnational feminist imaginaries. When the imagination remains in dialectical connection to the bodied and the immediate, others possible kinships (containing the tensions and fissures within) might be crafted. The maw of representational politics do not need to stop us from imagining, dreaming and acting.

40 I don't think of this consciously when Rita and I sit, trying to thread together some common language of understanding. I don't think of this consciously when I try to find her in the hospital where she works as a nurse's aide, many years after I met her in plantation country. Will she remember me? Our "relationship" is fractured by territorial and temporal distance. Our sessions, sometimes a few days long, are interrupted

by her work demands, my other research and organizing efforts, and the inevitable departures to Calcutta and California. Does she experience these interruptions, particularly the long absences, as a certain betrayal? Does she weigh my rhetorics about such textual, and other, possibilities with caution?

41 These are reflections, now translated in California, born from privileged travel, a cosmopolitan migration. There is only some sharp historical irony when she tells me of how two generations ago, her kinsmen came here from the harsh slopes of the Nepal Himalayas in search of work. Some went to Darjeeling, some came to Dooars. These are not co-eval travels. I do not imagine them as such.

Patriarchal recordings: "The automatic re-transmission of a telegraphic message"

42 (Geddie, 1169)

43 It is late 1992, well into the first year of fieldwork. I have bought a small tape recorder and mini-cassettes though am hesitant to use the machine. To use it feels more extractive than conversations (which I have without taking notes), and I don't want to jeopardize the fragile trust of the few women who have befriended me. But I am also keen on hearing life stories, in detail, and though I take notes at night, trying to remember what was said from memory, I often forget details – a turn of phrase or a sigh. Finally, I mention this to Munnu Kujoor, an Oraon woman-worker with whom I have a consistently close relationship. She has told me of the songs that women sing while in the field, as they pluck the tea. I would like to hear these songs, and perhaps even tape them. I tell Munnu that I will give her the tape recorder and she can decide, with the women, what they would like to say. She asks her dol (labor gang) about this and they agree but ask that I not accompany Munnu into the tea field. She tells me that they will feel inhibited and shy. The subsequent recordings are hilarious: songs, fragments of songs interspersed with dialogue about the crazy memsahib's project. I transcribe some but have never published these.

44 Munnu keeps the tape recorder with her and she tells me that she uses it at night, speaking into it like a daily journal. She asks that I don't ever write it down, that it is between her and me. I listen to some of what she shares, we talk about it and I never transcribe it. Then, one day she tells me that she has been speaking to a Nepali woman in her natal village and she wanted to speak into the tape recorder, give me her life story. Munnu says, "She has had a very hard life, didi, (elder sister) you have to hear it: her father beat her, her husband is terrible. He is a drunkard and beats her. She lost many children and she works and works despite everything. She knows many things about history too. She wants to speak to you." Delighted at this opportunity to meet someone who actually wants to talk to me, and also into the tape recorder, we make arrangements to meet. I ask Munnu repeatedly if it will be okay to take the tape recorder with me. She knows that people suspect I work for the U.S. or Indian government, that I am considered a spy, so I insist that she clear this again with her friend. I am told that all is well. One late afternoon, we head over to the little liquor shop which her friend, Maya, runs with her husband. Maya, Munnu and I go up a rickety flight of stairs to a small room in the store itself. We are introduced, I give Maya the tape recorder, show her how to start and stop the machine and tell her that if at any

moment she feels uncomfortable with the process, she can turn it off, and also that I will give her the tape.

45   She says she is excited to tell the story because "we women have been too long under the men's feet and Munnu has explained why you are here." Though I am not expecting this moment of proto-feminist analysis, the three of us begin a discussion about women's status in the villages and in plantation work. It is a sharp and exciting discussion. After about fifteen minutes, I hear some shouting downstairs and then a wiry Nepali man bursts into the room. Maya's husband has arrived.

46   He shouts at Maya, glares at me with anger, and grabs the tape recorder. "What is going on, memsahib," he shouts, "how dare you come here to talk to my wife with this?" I stumble into an explanation, apologizing profusely while Munnu and Maya look aghast. I explain to him that I am interested in "women's stories" and that is all and Munnu had said it would be okay to do so. I know, instinctively, that I cannot mention Maya's keen interest in our meeting. Munnu lives in another plantation and members of her family in this, her natal plantation village, are also powerful union members. Munnu also tries to placate him. Finally, I ask him to listen to what his wife has said. It is clear to me that if he does not, she might be harmed. Thankfully, she has spoken generally about the plantation, and had not yet begun to share any of her own personal predicament. As he rewinds the tape, I realize, with some horror, that I am using an old cassette which I had tested earlier and had an acquaintance speak into. As luck would have it, Maya's husband started the tape as this acquaintance said in English: "I am the son of a judge." Hearing the English, Maya's husband lost his equilibrium again and this time he was shaking with anxiety: "Who is this speaking in English? Where is the judge?" Once again, we placated him. He asked me bluntly which government I was spying for. He told me that he was a trade union leader, as well as a field overseer, and that I must now come and speak to his union about what I was doing in the plantation. I told him I would be happy to talk to the entire union about what I was doing because I had nothing to hide. Then with some dramatic flourish, I took the cassette out of the recorder and handed it to him. I said, "Look, I have no intent of taking something away that upsets you so. Please be assured that I won't do this again and keep the cassette." We set up an appointment with the union leaders and I left with Munnu. Maya kept her eyes down as she said goodbye.

47   The attempt to "get" a woman's life story, in a collaborative way (through a friend of hers) was ended summarily in a dramatic moment of patriarchal disruption. It was an important "failure" on several levels, but in that moment of non-fruition, (of the narrative interrupted, of the narrative-that-could-not-be told) much can be learned about the politics of translation.

48   First, it underscored the problematic nature and use of machines in "getting" a narrative. Certainly, Maya's husband may have viewed her "captured talk" as revealing his treatment of her. But he was most explicitly incensed, and troubled, by the English fragment which suggested the power of a state, which might capriciously rule his life. Indeed, his recognition of the English word "judge" suggests recognition of a distant, but present, governing apparatus. In his eyes, I was certainly a representative of a ruling elite, and language, which organized plantation feudalisms. That moment of machined error revealed the highly problematic, and complex, ways that the oral is

GRASSROOTS TEXTS

"caught" into text. Though I had given Maya the tape recorder, it was still read as a tool of the state, and also a certain colonizing access to their lives.

49   Second, my deferral to him (in effusive apology) might have been read by Maya, and Munnu, as an acquiescence to his bullying, and indeed, the blatant patriarchal interruption of a fragile feminized solidarity that was coming into play. Since we had met to discuss, among other things, the subordination of women, my easy capitulation to his anger may have been read more ambiguously by the two other women. However, at that moment of rupture, I perceived the dangerous effects of my own gendered privilege upon them. Though I explained to Munnu why I had not responded to his bullying, I was left with a nagging feeling that she thought I had capitulated too easily.

50   Third, I recognized – yet again – how fragile moments of a proto-feminist solidarity, and intimacy, can easily collapse into the maw of ethical failure. Munnu had told me that Maya was regularly beaten by this man – why did I not insist that we meet in a safer, private place? Did I jeopardize her physical safety despite the fact that I turned everything over to him? Though Munnu assured me that Maya was fine, I was left with a nagging sense that I should have never come with that tape recorder.

51   Certainly, this small incident can be read in other ways too: The fact is that both Munnu and Maya knowingly invited me to speak with her; the fact is that they wanted to speak into the recorder in a collective and powerful way. Despite my own ambivalences, I cannot deny their agency, the force of their conscious will.

52   The fact of patriarchal disruption offers, again, a moment of surrender to the immediate experience – to recognize that the interruption of one woman's attempt to speak her life presented a powerful narrative about ethnographic "failure." If the session with Maya had been taped without interruption, the choices of transcription and translation would have opened other kinds of questions. In this instance, I learn again that many lessons are cohered in the tasks of translation. In those moments of rupture, I need to abandon myself to these lessons, and to the shadow of the narrative aborted.

Conclusion: Messy braids

53   Feminist anthropologists have explored, for some time now, the ethics and geopolitics of representation in a discipline founded on colonial expansion and its knowledges. Following their critical scholarship and lead, through these "grassroots texts," I reveal some faultlines of power which mediate the production of ethnographic narratives. From the outset of fieldworks, these texts were catalyzed by a basic feminist desire to highlight plantation women's lives, experiences and "voices." In both these episodes, there was an attempt at "collaboration" (in the dialogical process of creating the narratives, through writing and recording). Certainly, both episodes offer the "collective" and "dialogical" moments at the center of the process.

54   In the encounter with Rita Chetri, I begin with an assertion of voice which quickly demonstrates her astute and critical sensibilities: a moving example of one subaltern woman's claim to authorship, to the power of writing itself. Indeed, I was eager to translate Rita's collection but never managed to do so, for reasons that were "transnational" as much as they were about the fissures of social status and material power which separated us. It also involved grassroots organizing that took off from 1999,

that engaged our energies and our "collaborations in other ways. But that is another, linked story, beside the immediate concerns of this essay.

55   Our encounters offer a flickering attempt at "collaboration" in the production of text, which does not really come to fruition. I still have copies of all her material – translated into English but cannot get myself to publish them as an example of innovative fieldwork collaboration, and a feminist text of plantation subalternity. This refusal is already a refusal of "power" – Rita simply does not have the access to put her work forwards in the circuits of written, print capital. I refuse to broker her words and this creates a tangle, a set of knottings, which I need to attend to with more ethical nuance. For now, the ethical issues – which also include an eight-year-old relationship around organizing which also fractured badly– means that the copies of her stories and poem rest on a dusty shelf.

56   In the second episode I shared involving Munnu, Maya, and Maya's anxious and disruptive husband, I offer a "ruptural moment' that appears most obvious in terms of the "impossibilities" of the narrative. Yet, what interests me here is that the sense of ethical "failure" can be seen in more nuanced ways. Indeed, this sense of "failure" of "getting" Maya's story was in my inability to "lift" what she wanted "displaced" – relayed – to others. That is, her tale of endurance and perhaps resistance to patriarchal violence. But I was also learning sharp lessons about the deeper context of the plantation, and the scrutiny of planters and union leaders as I meandered through these spaces and spoke, primarily, to women workers. My quick capitulation to the husband's intimidation also had everything to do with the pedagogies of isolation in which my own gender and status was so definitively marked by the geopolitics of privilege as an insider/outsider, regionally and transnationally. More importantly, I did not try to meet her again because of my concern that my presence had already made her more vulnerable to intimate violence. That remained the final punctuation for the story that never-made-it, but which also birthed another one.

57   Through exploring these difficult issues of power and ethics within ethnographic production, (and narrative-making) I have also sought to create a capacious space within which I/we can call out the plural and the paradoxical, the difficult and the joyous in all our epistemic work – and everything in-between as well. Perhaps we can create an unbounded space using our "transnational feminist imaginaries," – a liminal zone, crafted (and freed) by ethical and honest critiques and the belief in the importance of solidarities that can still be built across the crevasses of power and difference which separate us. Here. There. Here.

Notes

1 My involvement with plantation communities and politics started in the early 1990s with my more conventional field research phase in the early 1990s. This shifted to grassroots organizing from 1999–2007. The small narratives of "ethnographic rupture" that I share in this essay come from the early phase of fieldwork, not from the direct experience of organizing.

2 Sadri, also known as sadhani, is a patois used in the Chotanagpur Plateau by diverse and distinct linguistic adivasi and caste-communities. I surmise that this is a kind of bridge-language that combines aspects of several other languages in this highly plural linguistic landscape.

3 By this phrasing, I merely gesture to the urban-elite English spoken in some managers' (sahibs') parlours. Increasingly, though, this "public school" Indian English is being replaced by managers who are more comfortable with Hindi or Bengali.

4 It is important here to flag the problematic of "collaboration" which can assume co-evalness. I am suggesting something far more problematically nuanced and unequal. Other authors in this excellent collection also parse out the claims and problematic of collaboration in very similar ways to what I am attempting in this brief essay.

5 Jigna Desai, Danielle Bouchard and Diane Detournay use the work of Helen Hoy to offer this very important line of thinking. Helen Hoy looks at the "collaborations between Metis Canadian artist, activist and writer Maria Campbell and white Canadian performer and writer Linda Griffiths and her own production of scholarship on Native Canadian literature as a white woman . . . as maybe framed by stealing" (61–62).

6 "Perspectives on observation have changed. . . . Inquiry within geography can fruitfully be viewed as the interplay between theory and observation. Theory consists of ideas about how the world is structured and how it works. Observation, in the most general sense, involves human interaction with the world. Its objective is to obtain information about the structure and dynamics of the world so that this information can be compared with human ideas, or theory. The comparison of observational information with theoretical ideas constitutes the core of scientific inquiry and represents the process by which scientific knowledge is generated. Regardless of the differing opinions that have emerged about the interplay between theory and observation, most geographers accept that this interplay is central to geographic inquiry" (28). "Observing Our World" by Bruce L. Rhoads and David Wilson in *Research Methods in Geography: A Critical Introduction*. Basil Gomez & John Paul Jones III. (Eds.). Singapore: Wiley-Blackwell.

7 See Lane, Richard J. (2013). *Global Theory: An Anthology*. London: Routledge.

8 Spivak, Gayatri Chakravorty. (2012). *An Aesthetic Education in the Era of Gloabalization*. Cambridge: Harvard University Press.

9 Cultural Studies is engaged in three different senses: First, in the sense that it is not neutral in relation to the exclusions, injustices, and prejudices that it observes. It tends to position itself on the side of those to whom social structures offer least, thus engaged means to be political and critical. Second, it is engaged in that it aims to enhance and celebrate cultural experiences: To communicate enjoyment of a wide variety of cultural forms in part by analysing them and their social underpinnings. And third, and this marks its real difference from other kinds of academic work, it aims to deal with culture as a part of everyday life, without objectifying it. In fact, Cultural Studies aspires to join, to engage in the world itself (1). Another useful way of approaching Cultural Studies is by considering the debates about method and interest that have divided the field internally. Of these, the three most important are (1) the debate over the claim that culture (and hence Cultural Studies) has strong political force; (2) the debate over the determining power of economic structures on cultural formations; and (3) the debate over the role that individual experience should play in Cultural Studies analysis. (Simon During, (2005) *Cultural Studies: A Critical Introduction*. Oxon: Routledge, 38).

10 (1973). *The Interpretation of Cultures: Selected Essays*. New York: Basic Books: 5.

11 Spivak, Gayatri Chakravorty. (2005). "Scattered Speculation on the Subaltern and the Popular" in *Postcolonial Studies*. Vol. 8, No, 4, 475–86.

12 Rhoads, Bruce L. and David Wilson. (2010). "Observing Our World" in *Research Methods in Geography: A Critical Introduction*. Ed. Basil Gomez and John Paul Jones III. Singapore: Wiley-Blackwell (26–40).

References

Desai, Jigna, Danielle Bouchard and Diane Detournay. "Disavowed Legacies and Honorable Thievery: The Work of the 'Transnational' in Feminist and LGBTQ Studies." *Critical Transnational Feminist Praxis*. Eds. Amanda Lock Swarr and Richa Nagar. Albany: SUNY Press, 2010. 46–62. Print.

Freire, Paulo. *Pedagogy of the Oppressed*. Trans. Myra Bergman Ramos. New York: Herder and Herder, 1970; New York: Continuum, 2001.

Geddie, William. Ed. *Chambers Twentieth Century Dictionary*. London, Edinburgh: W.&R. Chambers, 1901.

Karamcheti, Indira. "Aimé Césaire's Subjective Geographies: Translating Place and the Difference It Makes." *Between Languages and Cultures: Translation and Cross-Cultural Texts*. Eds. Anuradha Dingwaney and Carol Maier. Pittsburgh: University of Pittsburgh Press, 1995. 181–197.

Marcus, George. "The Uses of Complicity in the Changing Mis-en-Scene of Anthropological Fieldwork." *Representations* 59 (Summer 1997), 85–107.

Mohanty, Chandra. 1986. "Under Western Eyes: Feminist Scholarship and Colonial Discourses." *Boundary 2* XII/XIII (1, 3), 333–358. Print.

Nagar, Richa and Amanda Lock Swarr. "Introduction: Theorizing Transnational Feminist Praxis." *Critical Transnational Feminist Praxis*. Eds. Amanda Lock Swarr and Richa Nagar. Albany: SUNY Press 2010. 1–20. Print.

Textual and rhetorical questions

Textual

1. How does Piya Chatterjee read the local issue (ethnography of tea plantation) within the global transnational theoretical discourse? Focus on three more questions the essayist asks to answer the above question: What informs global theory, who rests on the references, and what have postcolonialist and antiracist feminist scholarship done? (paragraphs 1–4).

2. Why does the essayist want to share her experiences with the readers by using translation as a tool? What are the "difficult knots" she wants to "explore?" (paragraphs 7, 8).

3. Bondage, migration, and diaspora are related to plantation according to Chatterjee. What are the instances of such labour movement she is referring to? Give examples of other than tea plantation as "crucible of a 'diasporic imaginary'". You can trace the labour history, for instance, of Indians in Africa and Africans in the West Indies (paragraphs 12, 13, 14).

4. Chatterjee writes about her interactions with three women workers, Munnu, Rita, and Maya. Relate these women's accounts with what the essayist writes:

> I will argue that women are the primary translators of the historical and cultural knowledges of the plantation. (Freire 1969) Theirs is a polyphonic oral mastery of a knowledge base that they reproduce, critique and create anew in their kitchens, rituals and fields of labor. Though marginalized from the formal educational system and from socio-economic mobility, theirs is a cultural literacy that cannot be defined by lack. Certainly, the conditions leading to non-literacy radically diminishes the chance of socio-economic betterment and upward mobility, but it is not a primary sign of their sense of social being. Indeed, their remarkable facility with languages, in various sites of power, constitutes an ontology of personhood, and sociality, which is necessary, powerful and creative.
>
> (Paragraph 21)

Do you think that the focus of the above quote is the essayist's thesis? Give reasons for your answer.

Rhetorical

1. Do you think that the essayist's observation is theoretically informed? Theory and observation and their interaction are significant research purposes of a geographer (Rhodes and Wilson, 28).[6]
2. What is the cultural status of the writer? How does translation as a tool help avoid bringing her cultural baggage of being an academic coming to study planation labourers in East India to the experience? How familiar is she with the languages of the region?
3. How do you justify Chatterjee's writing as a combination of personal experience and as Richard J. Lane writes, "the complexities of representing that lived experience" (724).[7] Read her "Conclusion: Messy Braids" to analyse the combination of personal narrative and representing the other.

Discussion questions

1. What do you think about the ethnographic approach of the essayist to write about other's culture? Since ethnography developed from anthropology, Gayatri Chakravorty Spivak's definition of Cultural Studies can be a platform to discuss the difference between anthropological research and that of Cultural Studies:

> The Cultural Studies position can be roughly summarized this way: colonizers founded Anthropology in order to know their subjects; Cultural Studies was founded by the colonized in order to question and correct their masters. Both disciplines study culture, the first culture of others as static and determining, the second the culture of one's group – as dynamic and evolving. As a result of this polarization, anthropology has launched a comprehensive auto-critique.
>
> (*An Aesthetic Education in the Era of Globalization*, 120)[8]

In this context, tea plantation is the material production by the women and men of Eastern India and Chatterjee explores the behaviour as she identifies the women in terms with "an ontology of personhood, and sociality, which is necessary, powerful and creative" (paragraph 21). According to Simon During, cultural studies "tends to position itself on the side of those to whom social structures offer least." Furthermore, Chatterjee looks at the politics too. During writes about one of the methods of cultural studies by defining culture with "a strong political force" (1).[9] After comprehending the quoted statements above, do you think that anthropology/ethnography can be coupled with Cultural Studies? Mark the phrase "humility and care" (paragraph 7) while discoursing the question. Write a five-paragraph essay (1500 words).

LITERARY THEORY AND CRITICISM

2. Discuss tree-worship as ethno-environmental study or ethno-environmentalism. In Nepal, around the Hindu festival of Diwali (called Tihar in Kathmandu), Newa, or Newar, the community worships crows and dogs. Find out about similar examples from your location and develop a methodology informed by ethnographic studies and/or cultural studies (3000 words).

Inter-textual discussions

1. Chatterjee's essay reads tea plantation as a significant cultural sign. The meaning of a sign is context bound. Sign, significance, and context are related. Referring to Max Weber Clifford Geertz writes that[10] culture is understood as a "web of significance" man "himself has spun" and interpretation of culture is thus done in terms with meaning. About the semiotic approach, Stuart Hall writes, "since all cultural objects convey meaning, and all cultural practices depend on meaning, they must make use of signs." Observe the cultural signs human beings have spun (to borrow from Geertz and Hall together) and interpret signs like "Kabbadi" which has moved from countryside to urban spaces as a pop cultural sport. Have the meanings changed in such a movement? Similar movement can be traced in ethnic foods which have become delicacies in the cities. Select "Kabbadi" or any ethnic food and provide a semiotic interpretation (500 words).
2. Munnu, Rita, and Maya can compose poems and tell stories about their plights. Are they "removed from all lines of social mobility"[11] and hence Rita may compose a poem and Maya may tell her story but they are not heard in the sense that they are outside the "lines of social mobility." What does Gayatri Spivak mean by "Can the subaltern speak?" Rita and Maya speak but they are still the subaltern. Observe the woman Bhanumati in Goutam Ghose's film *Moner Manush* (*Soul Man*) to develop a comparison. Discuss the term subaltern in relation to the women in the essay and the woman in the movie (500 words).

Critical and creative thinking

1. Is it necessary to connect the local issue within the Western theory? Do you think theorisation is possible only from Western academic locations to legitimise and globalise issues like "subaltern," "identity," and "feminism"? Form a debating session in the class.
2. Logical positivism or the inductive method is different from the deductive method. A priori or a theory-laden approach is independent of experience, and thus is deductive, which is to conceive a general theory and move towards testing the theory (Rhodes and Wilson 28). There, however, are post-positivist arguments:

> Differences between these perspectives depend on the degree to which observation is viewed as "theory-dependent." If observation is highly dependent on theory, especially a theory under test, information derived from the observation may be biased and unhelpful in evaluating the theory. Thus, whenever theory-dependent observations are used to evaluate theory,

the research process can be said to be somewhat circular. This view laid the ground for relativistic conceptions of science which maintain that the relative value of theoretical ideas must be judged on the basis of social criteria since observation, which is biased by theory, cannot be used to adjudicate among different ideas. A corollary of relativism is that objectivity no longer is preserved in any absolute sense; all ideas fall or stand based on their relative merits as defined within a social context.[12]

(28)

The other end of post-positivism is realism:

Realism, in fact, argues that the theory-ladenness of observation is *necessary* for objectivity: only by viewing the world through the lens of theory can we hope to discern what the world is really like. In other words, science without concepts is blind and the notion of building knowledge from theory-neutral observations, even if such observations could be obtained, is fundamentally misguided. This necessitates that both background knowledge and observational information serve as forms of evidence in the testing of a theory; empirical data are not ignored, but neither are they viewed as the absolute arbiter when a theory is evaluated. Viewed in this light, theory-dependence does not threaten objectivity, but instead provides the basis for collection of appropriate observations for theory testing (Rhoads and Thorn 1996).

(Rhodes and Wilson, 29)

How does a student of literature negotiate with social science theoretical stands? How do tropes work in empirical studies?

Part II

CRITICISM

7

OF MIMICRY AND MAN

The ambivalence of colonial discourse

Homi Bhabha

> Mimicry reveals something in so far as it is distinct from what might be called an itself that is behind. The effect of mimicry is camouflage... . It is not a question of harmonizing with the background, but against a mottled background, of becoming mottled – exactly like the technique of camouflage practised in human warfare.
>
> Jacques Lacan, 'The line and light', *Of the Gaze*.[1]

> It is out of season to question at this time of day, the original policy of a conferring on every colony of the British Empire a mimic representation of the British Constitution. But if the creature so endowed has sometimes forgotten its real significance and under the fancied importance of speakers and maces, and all the paraphernalia and ceremonies of the imperial legislature, has dared to defy the mother country, she has to thank herself for the folly of conferring such privileges on a condition of society that has no earthly claim to so exalted a position. A fundamental principle appears to have been forgotten or overlooked in our system of colonial policy – that of colonial dependence. To give to a colony the forms of independence is a mockery; she would not be a colony for a single hour if she could maintain an independent station.
>
> Sir Edward Cust, 'Reflections on West African affairs ... addressed to the Colonial Office', Hatchard, London 1839

1   The discourse of post-Enlightenment English colonialism often speaks in a tongue that is forked, not false. If colonialism takes power in the name of history, it repeatedly exercises its authority through the figures of farce. For the epic intention of the civilizing mission, 'human and not wholly human' in the famous words of Lord Rosebery, 'writ by the finger of the Divine'[2] often produces a text rich in the traditions of *trompe-l'œil*, irony, mimicry and repetition. In this comic turn from the high ideals of the colonial imagination to its low mimetic literary effects mimicry emerges as one of the most elusive and effective strategies of colonial power and knowledge.

2   Within that conflictual economy of colonial discourse which Edward Said[3] describes as the tension between the synchronic panoptical vision of domination – the demand for identity, stasis – and the counter-pressure of the diachrony of history – change,

DOI: 10.4324/9781003213857-7

LITERARY THEORY AND CRITICISM

difference – mimicry represents an *ironic* compromise. If I may adapt Samuel Weber's formulation of the marginalizing vision of castration,[4] then colonial mimicry is the desire for a reformed, recognizable Other, *as a subject of a difference that is almost the same, but not quite.* Which is to say, that the discourse of mimicry is constructed around an *ambivalence*; in order to be effective, mimicry must continually produce its slippage, its excess, its difference. The authority of that mode of colonial discourse that I have called mimicry is therefore stricken by an indeterminacy: mimicry emerges as the representation of a difference that is itself a process of disavowal. Mimicry is, thus the sign of a double articulation; a complex strategy of reform, regulation and discipline, which 'appropriates' the Other as it visualizes power. Mimicry is also the sign of the inappropriate, however, a difference or recalcitrance which coheres the dominant strategic function of colonial power, intensifies surveillance, and poses an immanent threat to both 'normalized' knowledges and disciplinary powers.

3   The effect of mimicry on the authority of colonial discourse is profound and disturbing. For in 'normalizing' the colonial state or subject, the dream of post-Enlightenment civility alienates its own language of liberty and produces another knowledge of its norms. The ambivalence which thus informs this strategy is discernible, for example, in Locke's Second Treatise which *splits* to reveal the limitations of liberty in his double use of the word 'slave': first simply, descriptively as the locus of a legitimate form of ownership, then as the trope for an intolerable, illegitimate exercise of power. What is articulated in that distance between the two uses is the absolute, imagined difference between the 'Colonial' State of Carolina and the Original State of Nature.

4   It is from this area between mimicry and mockery, where the reforming, civilizing mission is threatened by the displacing gaze of its disciplinary double, that my instances of colonial imitation come. What they all share is a discursive process by which the excess or slippage produced by the *ambivalence* of mimicry (almost the same, *but not quite*) does not merely 'rupture' the discourse, but becomes transformed into an uncertainty which fixes the colonial subject as a 'partial' presence. By 'partial' I mean both 'incomplete' and 'virtual'. It is as if the very emergence of the 'colonial' is dependent for its representation upon some strategic limitation or prohibition *within* the authoritative discourse itself. The success of colonial appropriation depends on a proliferation of inappropriate objects that ensure its strategic failure, so that mimicry is at once resemblance and menace.

5   A classic text of such partiality is Charles Grant's 'Observations on the state of society among the Asiatic subjects of Great Britain' (1792)[5] which was only superseded by James Mills's *History of India* as the most influential early nineteenth-century account of Indian manners and morals. Grant's dream of an evangelical system of mission education conducted uncompromisingly in the English language, was partly a belief in political reform along Christian lines and partly an awareness that the expansion of company rule in India required a system of subject formation – a reform of manners, as Grant put it – that would provide the colonial with 'a sense of personal identity as we know it'. Caught between the desire for religious reform and the fear that the Indians might become turbulent for liberty, Grant paradoxically implies that it is the 'partial' diffusion of Christianity, and the 'partial' influence of moral improvements which will construct a particularly appropriate form of colonial subjectivity. What is suggested is a process of reform through which Christian doctrines might collude with

172

OF MIMICRY AND MAN

divisive caste practices to prevent dangerous political alliances. Inadvertently, Grant produces a knowledge of Christianity as a form of social control which conflicts with the enunciatory assumptions that authorize his discourse. In suggesting, finally, that 'partial reform' will produce an empty form of 'the *imitation* [my emphasis] of English manners which will induce them [the colonial subjects] to remain under our protection'.[6] Grant mocks his moral project and violates the Evidence of Christianity – a central missionary tenet – which forbade any tolerance of heathen faiths.

6   The absurd extravagance of Macaulay's 'Minute' (1835) – deeply influenced by Charles Grant's 'Observations' – makes a mockery of Oriental learning until faced with the challenge of conceiving of a 'reformed' colonial subject. Then, the great tradition of European humanism seems capable only of ironizing itself. At the intersection of European learning and colonial power, Macaulay can conceive of nothing other than 'a class of interpreters between us and the millions whom we govern – a class of persons Indian in blood and colour, but English in tastes, in opinions, in morals and in intellect'[7] – in other words a mimic man raised 'through our English School', as a missionary educationist wrote in 1819, 'to form a corps of translators and be employed in different departments of Labour'.[8] The line of descent of the mimic man can be traced through the works of Kipling, Forster, Orwell, Naipaul, and to his emergence, most recently, in Benedict Anderson's excellent work on nationalism, as the anomalous Bipin Chandra Pal.[9] He is the effect of a flawed colonial mimesis, in which to be Anglicized is *emphatically* not to be English.

7   The figure of mimicry is locatable within what Anderson describes as 'the inner compatibility of empire and nation'.[10] It problematizes the signs of racial and cultural priority, so that the 'national' is no longer naturalizable. What emerges between mimesis and mimicry is a *writing*, a mode of representation, that marginalizes the monumentality of history, quite simply mocks its power to be a model, that power which supposedly makes it imitable. Mimicry *repeats* rather than *re-presents* and in that diminishing perspective emerges Decoud's displaced European vision of Sulaco in Conrad's *Nostromo* as

> the endlessness of civil strife where folly seemed even harder to bear than its ignominy ... the lawlessness of a populace of all colours and races, barbarism, irremediable tyranny... . America is ungovernable.[11]

Or Ralph Singh's apostasy in Naipaul's *The Mimic Men*:

> We pretended to be real, to be learning, to be preparing ourselves for life, we mimic men of the New World, one unknown corner of it, with all its reminders of the corruption that came so quickly to the new.[12]

Both Decoud and Singh, and in their different ways Grant and Macaulay, are the parodists of history. Despite their intentions and invocations they inscribe the colonial text erratically, eccentrically across a body politic that refuses to be representative, in a narrative that refuses to be representational. The desire to emerge as 'authentic' through mimicry – through a process of writing and repetition – is the final irony of partial representation.

LITERARY THEORY AND CRITICISM

8   What I have called mimicry is not the familiar exercise of *dependent* colonial relations through narcissistic identification so that, as Fanon has observed,[13] the black man stops being an actional person for only the white man can represent his selfesteem. Mimicry conceals no presence or identity behind its mask: it is not what Césaire describes as 'colonization-thingification'[14] behind which there stands the essence of the *présence Africaine*. The *menace* of mimicry is its *double* vision which in disclosing the ambivalence of colonial discourse also disrupts its authority. And it is a double vision that is a result of what I've described as the partial representation/recognition of the colonial object. Grant's colonial as partial imitator, Macaulay's translator, Naipaul's colonial politician as play-actor, Decoud as the scene setter of the *opéra bouffe* of the New World, these are the appropriate objects of a colonialist chain of command, authorized versions of otherness. But they are also, as I have shown, the figures of a doubling, the part-objects of a metonymy of colonial desire which alienates the modality and normality of those dominant discourses in which they emerge as 'inappropriate' colonial subjects. A desire that, through the repetition of *partial presence*, which is the basis of mimicry, articulates those disturbances of cultural, racial and historical difference that menace the narcissistic demand of colonial authority. It is a desire that reverses 'in part' the colonial appropriation by now producing a partial vision of the colonizer's presence; a gaze of otherness, that shares the acuity of the genealogical gaze which, as Foucault describes it, liberates marginal elements and shatters the unity of man's being through which he extends his sovereignty.[15]

9   I want to turn to this process by which the look of surveillance returns as the displacing gaze of the disciplined, where the observer becomes the observed and 'partial' representation rearticulates the whole notion of *identity* and alienates it from essence. But not before observing that even an exemplary history like Eric Stokes's *The English Utilitarians and India* acknowledges the anomalous gaze of otherness but finally disavows it in a contradictory utterance:

> Certainly India played *no* central part in fashioning the distinctive qualities of English civilisation. In many ways it acted as a disturbing force, a magnetic power placed at the periphery tending to distort the natural development of Britain's character.[16] (My emphasis)

What is the nature of the hidden threat of the partial gaze? How does mimicry emerge as the subject of the scopic drive and the object of colonial surveillance? How is desire disciplined, authority displaced?

10   If we turn to a Freudian figure to address these issues of colonial textuality, that form of difference that is mimicry – *almost the same but not quite* – will become clear. Writing of the partial nature of fantasy, caught *inappropriately*, between the unconscious and the preconscious, making problematic, like mimicry, the very notion of 'origins', Freud has this to say:

> Their mixed and split origin is what decides their fate. We may compare them with individuals of mixed race who taken all round resemble white men but who betray their coloured descent by some striking feature or other and on that account are excluded from society and enjoy none of the privileges.[17]

OF MIMICRY AND MAN

Almost the same but not white: the visibility of mimicry is always produced at the site of interdiction. It is a form of colonial discourse that is uttered *inter dicta*: a discourse at the crossroads of what is known and permissible and that which though known must be kept concealed; a discourse uttered between the lines and as such both against the rules and within them. The question of the representation of difference is therefore always also a problem of authority. The 'desire' of mimicry, which is Freud's 'striking feature' that reveals so little but makes such a big difference, is not merely that impossibility of the Other which repeatedly resists signification. The desire of colonial mimicry – an interdictory desire – may not have an object, but it has strategic objectives which I shall call the *metonymy of presence*.

11   Those inappropriate signifiers of colonial discourse – the difference between being English and being Anglicized; the identity between stereotypes which, through repetition, also become different; the discriminatory identities constructed across traditional cultural norms and classifications, the Simian Black, the Lying Asiatic – all these are *metonymies* of presence. They are strategies of desire in discourse that make the anomalous representation of the colonized something other than a process of 'the return of the repressed', what Fanon unsatisfactorily characterized as collective catharsis.[18] These instances of metonymy are the non-repressive productions of contradictory and multiple belief. They cross the boundaries of the culture of enunciation through a strategic confusion of the metaphoric and metonymic axes of the cultural production of meaning.

12   In mimicry, the representation of identity and meaning is rearticulated along the axis of metonymy. As Lacan reminds us, mimicry is like camouflage, not a harmonization of repression of difference, but a form of resemblance, that differs from or defends presence by displaying it in part, metonymically. Its threat, I would add, comes from the prodigious and strategic production of conflictual, fantastic, discriminatory 'identity effects' in the play of a power that is elusive because it hides no essence, no 'itself'. And that form of *resemblance* is the most terrifying thing to behold, as Edward Long testifies in his *History of Jamaica* (1774). At the end of a tortured, negrophobic passage, that shifts anxiously between piety, prevarication and perversion, the text finally confronts its fear; nothing other than the repetition of its resemblance 'in part': '[Negroes] are represented by all authors as the vilest of human kind, to which they have little more pretension of resemblance *than what arises from their exterior forms*' (my emphasis).[19]

13   From such a colonial encounter between the white presence and its black semblance, there emerges the question of the ambivalence of mimicry as a problematic of colonial subjection. For if Sade's scandalous theatricalization of language repeatedly reminds us that discourse can claim 'no priority', then the work of Edward Said will not let us forget that the 'ethnocentric and erratic will to power from which texts can spring'[20] is itself a theatre of war. Mimicry, as the metonymy of presence is, indeed, such an erratic, eccentric strategy of authority in colonial discourse. Mimicry does not merely destroy narcissistic authority through the repetitious slippage of difference and desire. It is the process of the *fixation* of the colonial as a form of cross-classificatory, discriminatory knowledge within an interdictory discourse, and therefore necessarily raises the question of the *authorization* of colonial representations; a question of authority that goes beyond the subject's lack of priority (castration) to a historical

175

LITERARY THEORY AND CRITICISM

crisis in the conceptuality of colonial man as an *object* of regulatory power, as the subject of racial, cultural, national representation.

14   'This culture ... fixed in its colonial status', Fanon suggests, '[is] both present and mummified, it testified against its members. It defines them in fact without appeal.'[21] The ambivalence of mimicry – almost but not quite – suggests that the fetishized colonial culture is potentially and strategically an insurgent counter-appeal. What I have called its 'identity-effects' are always crucially *split*. Under cover of camouflage, mimicry, like the fetish, is a part-object that radically revalues the normative knowledges of the priority of race, writing, history. For the fetish mimes the forms of authority at the point at which it deauthorizes them. Similarly, mimicry rearticulates presence in terms of its 'otherness', that which it disavows. There is a crucial difference between this *colonial* articulation of man and his doubles and that which Foucault describes as 'thinking the unthought'[22] which, for nineteenth-century Europe, is the ending of man's alienation by reconciling him with his essence. The colonial discourse that articulates an *interdictory* otherness is precisely the 'other scene' of this nineteenth-century European desire for an authentic historical consciousness.

15   The 'unthought' across which colonial man is articulated is that process of classificatory confusion that I have described as the metonymy of the substitutive chain of ethical and cultural discourse. This results in the *splitting* of colonial discourse so that two attitudes towards external reality persist; one takes reality into consideration while the other disavows it and replaces it by a product of desire that repeats, rearticulates 'reality' as mimicry.

16   So Edward Long can say with authority, quoting variously Hume, Eastwick and Bishop Warburton in his support, that: 'Ludicrous as the opinion may seem I do not think that an orangutang husband would be any dishonour to a Hottentot female.'[23]

17   Such contradictory articulations of reality and desire – seen in racist stereotypes, statements, jokes, myths – are not caught in the doubtful circle of the return of the repressed. They are the effects of a disavowal that denies the differences of the other but produces in its stead forms of authority and multiple belief that alienate the assumptions of 'civil' discourse. If, for a while, the ruse of desire is calculable for the uses of discipline soon the repetition of guilt, justification, pseudo-scientific theories, superstition, spurious authorities, and classifications can be seen as the desperate effort to 'normalize' *formally* the disturbance of a discourse of splitting that violates the rational, enlightened claims of its enunciatory modality. The ambivalence of colonial authority repeatedly turns from *mimicry* – a difference that is almost nothing but not quite – to *menace* – a difference that is almost total but not quite. And in that other scene of colonial power, where history turns to farce and presence to 'a part' can be seen the twin figures of narcissism and paranoia that repeat furiously, uncontrollably.

18   In the ambivalent world of the 'not quite/not white', on the margins of metropolitan desire, the *founding objects* of the Western world become the erratic, eccentric, accidental *objets trouvés* of the colonial discourse – the part-objects of presence. It is then that the body and the book lose their part-objects of presence. It is then that the body and the book lose their representational authority. Black skin splits under the racist gaze, displaced into signs of bestiality, genitalia, grotesquerie, which reveal the phobic

OF MIMICRY AND MAN

myth of the undifferentiated whole white body. And the holiest of books – the Bible – bearing both the standard of the cross and the standard of empire finds itself strangely dismembered. In May 1817 a missionary wrote from Bengal:

> Still everyone would gladly receive a Bible. And why? – that he may lay it up as a curiosity for a few pice; or use it for waste paper. Such it is well known has been the common fate of these copies of the Bible... . Some have been bartered in the markets, others have been thrown in snuff shops and used as wrapping paper.[24]

Textual and rhetorical questions

Textual

1. Mimicry is about parodying the coloniser and not representing them in totality. Mimicry is defined as an ironic compromise between "conflictual economy of colonial discourse" as "the tension between synchronic panoptical vision of domination" and "the counter-pressure of diachrony of history." Hence mimicry is threatening and a menace (read paragraph 8 to understand menace) because the coloniser fails to make the colonised follow him. What is the relation of mimicry to the civilising mission of the colonisers? (paragraphs 1 to 3).
2. Why does Bhabha think that the effect of mimicry is threatening, and is a menace? Explain why mimicry is ambivalent and why European effort to appropriate the East is an inappropriate and partial subject formation? (you may revisit Textual Question 1).
3. Bhabha writes (in paragraph 1) that English colonial discourse after the Enlightenment speaks with a "forked" tongue, "not false." Why does he think that the authority of colonialism is exercised "through the figures of farce"? Do you think forked tongue and figures of farce are the strategies of the civilising mission? Elaborate in two paragraphs.
4. Conflictual economy of colonial discourse is, in the words of Edward Said, "the tension between synchronic panoptical vision of domination" of fixing the identity of the colonised and the realities of differences and multiplicities. But though the East or non-Europe is full of diversity and difference, the European discourse about the colonised people is to accept the other of Europe not as different, not quite different, not quite the same. Hence to be effective, does the colonial discourse have to construct the East as something else, as other, as "almost the same" (paragraph 2)? Discuss what Bhabha suggests? Questions 1 and 2 are related.
5. Where do we find Grant and Macaulay's designs exemplified? Homi Bhabha cites examples from Joseph Conrad's *Nostromo* and V.S. Naipaul's *The Mimic Man*. Elaborate and explain what Ralph Singh anxiously reveals (read paragraph 7) and reason in the light of Grant and Macaulay. A related question is who is "the authorized version of otherness" and why? (paragraph 8).
6. Read the passage (paragraph 9) and explain how the constructed colonial "partial" identity writes back on the essentialist motive of the empire? Explain who

the actor is and who is acted upon? Does Bhabha answer the questions he raises by the end of the passage?

> I want to turn to this process by which the look of surveillance returns as the displacing gaze of the disciplined, where the observer becomes the observed and "partial" representation rearticulates the whole notion of *identity* and alienates it from essence. But not before observing that even an exemplary history like Eric Stokes's *The English Utilitarians and India* acknowledges the anomalous gaze of otherness but finally disavows it in a contradictory utterance:[25]

> Certainly India played *no* central part in fashioning the distinctive qualities of English civilization. In many ways it acted as disturbing force, a magnetic power placed at the periphery tending to distort the natural development of Britain's character. (My emphasis)

Consider answering the following questions too: What is the nature of the hidden threat of the partial gaze? How does mimicry emerge as the subject of the scopic drive and the object of colonial surveillance? How is desire disciplined, authority displaced?

Rhetorical

1. Do you think the essayist merely defines mimicry? Where does he talk about the dynamics of mimicry in terms of the purpose, effect, and power of mimicry? Discuss how the essay is structured along these dynamics? (1000 words).
2. Collect the definitions on mimicry from the essay and analyse how terms in general are defined. You should avoid citing those paragraphs and lines where he writes about the effect and power of mimicry though you can discuss them separately by reading paragraphs 3 and 13.
3. Bhabha's method of reading mimicry is deconstructive. Give reasons that support this statement after reading the following passages:
   i.   colonial mimicry is the desire for the reformed, recognizable Other, *as a subject of difference that is almost the same, but not quite*. Which is to say, that the discourse of mimicry is constructed around an ambivalence; in order to be effective, mimicry must continually produce its slippage, its excess, its difference (paragraph 2).
   ii. The *menace* of mimicry is its *double* vision which in disclosing the ambivalence of colonial discourse also disrupts its authority. And it is a double vision that is a result of what I've described as the partial representation/recognition of the colonial object (paragraph 8).

Discussion questions

1. Bhabha's essay presents a theory of mimesis. The nature of mimesis is complex and indeterminate in the context of the relationship between the coloniser and the colonised. Write a paper in 3000 words. Provide a thesis sentence for the paper and topic sentences for subsequent paragraphs to prove your point.

OF MIMICRY AND MAN

2. Postcolonial theory in its initial phase focused on the ideas of representation and resistance. Elaborate. You may like to include the arguments put forwards in Discussion Question 1, but you probably require a different thesis sentence to deal with this question. The answer may look similar for both the questions, provided you have separate theses sentences for both the questions (2000 words).

Inter-textual questions

1. Naipaul's main character in *The Mimic Men* is Ranjit Kripalsingh who changes his name to Ralph RK Singh and goes through transcultural experiences. Bhabha characterises such men (women) as "'partial' presence"(123): In his early young days, he lives in his native land in emptiness, and then when he moves to London, he mimes metonymically [(or mimicry is *"metonymy of presence"* (Bhabha 128)], imitates the coloniser's ways as part of the whole but never the whole, not the metaphor, not the substitute, never the real. "We pretend to be real, to be learning, to be preparing ourselves for life, we mimic men of the New World" (Naipaul: *The Mimic Men*: 146).[26] Analyse Bhabha's "Of Mimicry and Man" from the point of view of Naipaul's *The Mimic Men*? The question is not about the application of Bhabha's theory of mimicry to the novel but reading Bhabha in the light of the novel.
2. Discuss mimicry in the following:
    a. The song and scene "Mera Juta Hai Japani" from Hindi movie *Shree 420*.[27] Look for a translation of the song.
    b. The image where a Nepali Gorkha soldier displays his valour and honour with the Victoria Cross.
3. How is Jacques Lacan helpful in understanding mimicry? Bhabha begins his essay with a quote from Jacques Lacan's "The Line and Light."[28] Lacan describes how aquatic animals like crustaceans camouflage and mimic the surrounding to protect themselves:

> But, in mimicry, we are dealing with something quite different. Let us take an example chosen almost at random – it is not a privileged case – that of a small crustacean known as *caprella*, to which is added the adjective *acanthifera*. When such a crustacean settles in the midst of those animals, scarcely animals, known as briozoaires, what does it imitate? It imitates in that quasi-plant animal known as the briozoaires is a stain – at a particular phase of the briozoaires, an intestinal loop forms a stain, at another phase, there functions something like a coloured center. It is to this stain shape that the crustacean adapts itself. It becomes a stain, it becomes a picture, it is inscribed in the picture. This, strictly speaking, is the origin of mimicry.
>
> (99)[29]

Postcolonial discourses have emphasised concepts like resistance, mimicry, adaptation, appropriation, "revisionism," and "reconciliation."[30] Discuss these concepts to comprehend the development of postcolonialism as resistance, the earlier discursive phase, to revisionism and reconciliation, as discoursed in the present times.

LITERARY THEORY AND CRITICISM

Critical and creative thinking

1. What is the relationship of mimicry with hybridity? Manicheanism, a term popularised by Abdul JanMohammed, however, contestably corresponds with the idea of mimicry and hybridity.[31] Discuss with your colleagues.
2. Phantom in the cartoon series *Phantom* by Lee Falk is a Western hero who adopts and imitates African modes of life in a jungle. What kind of mimic hero character is Phantom? Can you elaborate on this mode of mimicry by reading at least one or two comic strips? Analyse the popular comic cover where Phantom mounts a horse wearing his traditional mask and suit while the skull cave opening depicts an exotic African interior.

Notes

1   J. Lacan, 'The line and the light', in his *The Four Fundamental Concepts of Psychoanalysis*, Alan Sheridan (trans.) (London: The Hogarth Press and the Institute of Psycho-Analysis, 1977), p. 99.
2   Cited in E. Stokes, *The Political Ideas of English Imperialism* (Oxford: Oxford University Press, 1960), pp. 17–18.
3   E. Said, *Orientalism* (New York: Pantheon Books, 1978), p. 240.
4   S. Weber, 'The sideshow, or: remarks on a canny moment', *Modern Language Notes*, vol. 88, no. 6 (1973), p. 112.
5   C. Grant, 'Observations on the state of society among the Asiatic subjects of Great Britain', *Sessional Papers of the East India Company*, vol. X, no. 282 (1812–13).
6   ibid., ch. 4, p. 104.
7   T.B. Macaulay, 'Minute on education', in W. Theodore de Bary (ed.) *Sources of Indian Tradition*, vol. II (New York: Columbia University Press, 1958), p. 49.
8   Mr Thomason's communication to the Church Missionary Society, 5 September 1819, in *The Missionary Register*, 1821, pp. 54–5.
9   B. Anderson, *Imagined Communities* (London: Verso, 1983), p. 88.
10 Ibid., pp. 88–9.
11 J. Conrad, *Nostromo* (London: Penguin, 1979), p. 161.
12 V. S. Naipaul, *The Mimic Men* (London: Penguin, 1967), p. 416.
13 F. Fanon, *Black Skin, White Masks* (London: Paladin, 1970), p. 109.
14 A. Césaire, *Discourse on Colonialism* (New York: Monthly Review Press, 1972), p. 21.
15 M. Foucault, 'Nietzche, genealogy, history', in his *Language, Counter-Memory, Practice*, D. F. Bouchard and S. Simon (trans.) (Ithaca: Cornell University Press, 1977), p. 153.
16 E. Stokes, *The English Utilitarians and India* (Oxford: Oxford University Press, 1959), p. xi.
17 S. Freud, 'The unconscious' (1915), SE, XIV, pp. 190–1.
18 Fanon, *Black Skin, White Masks*, p. 103.
19 E. Long, *A History of Jamaica*, 1774, vol. II, p. 353.
20 E. Said, 'The Text, the world, the critic', in J. V. Harari (ed.) *Textual Strategies* (Ithaca: Cornell University Press, 1979), p. 184.
21 F. Fanon, 'Racism and culture', in his *Toward the African Revolution*, H. Chevalier (trans.) (London: Pelican, 1967), p. 44.
22 M. Foucault, *The Order of Things* (New York: Pantheon Books, 1971), part II, ch. 9.
23 *Long, History of Jamaica*, p. 364.
24 *The Missionary Register*, May 1817, p. 186.
25 Check footnote of Bhabha's essay.
26 For reference, see footnote 12 in Bhabha's essay.
27 *Shree 420* is an iconic Indian movie of 1955 directed by Raj Kapoor. The main character, Raj sings: "My shoes are Japanese, these trousers are English, a Russian red cap on my head,

180

OF MIMICRY AND MAN

but my heart still is an Indian" (my literal translation of the first two lines). You may also watch a Hindi movie *Love Marriage* (1959) where the lead character sings "Teen kanaster peet peet kar galaa phadkar chillana, yar mere mat burana mano, ye gana hai na bajana hai!" The literal translation of the song is: "Lancing tin and can, and shouting is not music! Don't mind dear, this is neither singing nor playing music." The song continues, "By rocking waist and jumping like in the circus instead of dancing, its your mistake to think the world is full of idiots." Notice how the hero of the movie, Sunil Kumar, played by Dev Anand, sings and criticizes Western song and music while wearing a formal Western suit which he does on other occasions in the movie. Criticizing Western values were popular movie themes of the time though such themes would not necessarily be the major storyline.

28 See Jacques Lacan (1973). *The Four Fundamental Concepts of Psychoanalysis. Book XI* in Jacques-Alain Miller. *The Seminar of Jacques Lacan*. Trans. Alan Sheridan. London. W.W. Norton.

29 Ibid.

30 For a discussion on postcolonialism as revisionism and reconciliation, see Graham Huggan (2013). "General Introduction" in *The Oxford Handbook of Postcolonial Studies*. New Delhi: Oxford University Press.

31 JanMohammed, A.R. (1985). "The Economy of Manichean Allegory: The Function of Racial Difference in Colonialist Literature" *Critical Inquiry* 12 (1).

8

EPILOGUE

The tantra of contemplative cultural critique

Lata Mani

1 Tantra is arguably the most misunderstood term in the spiritual lexicon of Hinduism. It may therefore seem curious that it is being introduced in the essay that brings this volume to a close. Yet, it is precisely its contentious status that has led me to refrain from naming its relevance to this project until the synthetic vision and goals of a tantric orientation have been demonstrated in the range of subjects here explored.[1] If my intention in undertaking this work has succeeded to any degree, it will have become clear to readers that no aspect of the social world can be deemed to be outside of the proper purview of a contemplative analysis. Equally, it is hoped that I have illustrated in some measure the value to social inquiry of a contemplative framework – the questions that it draws to our attention, the answers that it refuses to foreclose, and the tools it provides us in our analysis.

2 A key aspect of tantra is that it fundamentally honours embodiment and the potential of humans to live harmoniously with each other and with nature. The realm of matter is thus of intrinsic interest to it. Nothing is so profane and nothing so sacred that it precludes critical inquiry from a tantric standpoint. Within tantra, knowledge of the potential of humanness is counter-balanced with awareness of the actuality of the human condition and of the many means by which human potential is thwarted or nourished, whether by individuals themselves or by the contexts in which they live. As a consequence, the sociocultural, the economic, the political and the behavioural are squarely within its compass. They are that which must be understood if one is to live consciously and skilfully. Conflict, frictionality, contradiction and misperception are as much a part of the raw material of tantric knowing and being as the yearning to cultivate stillness, compassion, dharmic wisdom and non-duality. Tantra calls upon one to witness and be present to the fullness of all that one encounters within and without. One witnesses knowing that one's view is inevitably partial and that no overview of infinity is possible. This realisation inspires modesty, not so much as a virtue but as a natural consequence.

II

3 All this makes for a close affinity between tantra and the project of progressive, secular cultural criticism. Both take the phenomenal world as inherently worthy of attention.

182

DOI: 10.4324/9781003213857-8

Both are interested in the relationships between people and the social worlds that they inhabit, inherit, imagine and/or create. Both pay attention to the positive as well as the negative, the affirmative as well as the conflictual. For both, culture is not just generative of the meaning systems that make existence intelligible, but also of the semiotic grid that gives rise to misperception and illusion. Both are passionate in their engagement of the world: neither pretends to a distanced objectivity. Each has its own vocabulary and conceptual tools.

4   But there are differences. Although the phenomenal world is a central concern for both, progressive, secular cultural critique brackets everything outside of a narrowly conceived notion of materiality. Indeed, secular criticism assumes that nothing other than matter exists. By contrast, tantra sees the material and the so-called non-material as existing and unfolding by means of a complex dance of mutual determination. In the tantric view, spirit is integral to matter. But even more, it is the very cause of matter, its creator. It thus follows that the tantric posture toward matter is that of an attentive, loving, adoration.

5   Notwithstanding popular misconceptions, however, tantric adoration is not unqualified or hedonistic in nature. It is, rather, disciplined by the sense that the purpose of life is to discover one's inevitably local place in the cosmic scheme of things, and then learn how to occupy that place in a manner congruent with karma, dharma, and the reality of interbeing within and across species, within and across planets. By this point, our secular comrades may be seen to be receding, so to speak, in the tantric rear-view mirror. And from a secular standpoint, erstwhile tantric colleagues are fast disappearing into a vortex of what to the former appear to be undemonstrable claims.

6   While I have not sought to deny the points beyond which a tantrically based spiritual wisdom forcefully parts company from a progressive secular perspective, I have striven to indicate the substantial ground shared by both. This seems to me to be crucial for at least two reasons. First, we live in a time when public debate on matters pertaining to religion frequently seems to consist of duelling abstractions which obscure more than they reveal. Inflated by little more than hot air and the tragic history of bigotry, such discussions often exclude a vast 'middle ground' (at times better described as 'other ground') of lives lived outside the plot lines of miasmic narratives of nation, religion, race and civilisation, with their myths of purity, separation, hierarchy and injury. Challenges to such abstractions need to be anchored in the dense complexity of lived relations, and on this point both secular critics and tantric philosophy would agree. However, a further step needs to be taken.

7   A philosophical ecumenicism toward religion *per se* is necessary. Even though not everyone is drawn to a religious or spiritual perspective or way of life, those secular in inclination must embrace the fact that the sacred is a vital resource for most of humanity. This is a reality to be reckoned with, not merely a concession to be granted. Indeed, the facts being what they are, it is secularism, not religion, which is in need of explaining itself. Accepting the importance of religion does not, however, disarm critique of its regressive aspects. Rather, it renders such challenges all the more convincing to those, usually in the majority, who despite their religious practice or affiliation, nonetheless frequently disagree with the discourse of the conservative minority that claims to speak for and about them.

8   One secular strategy for dealing with religion has been to insist that it is a personal affair that should be kept out of the public domain and in particular that of the state. This position is neither theoretically viable nor even practical. Religion is inescapably part of the public domain. Religious rituals and celebrations span public as well as private spaces. Religious institutions are active in society. At a very minimum, then, the regulation of religion is a law and order issue for the state. However, the problem with taking the stance that religion is personal is even greater than this. For, philosophy, music, dance, art and myriad aspects of everyday cultural practice in India derive from its religious traditions. Where is one to draw the line?

9   Finally, this position is theoretically unsustainable. As secular cultural critics will readily agree, there is no such thing as a personal space that is beyond social determination. Seeking to limit religion to the private sphere, especially when so many other dimensions of personal conduct are routinely regulated by the state, merely evades the problem of ensuring that religious practice conforms to law, and that all religions and all practitioners are deemed equal before the law. Unless the irreducibly social character of religion is fully recognised, one fails to grasp how it is interwoven in almost every aspect of the life of its practitioners. Worse, one leaves the door open for a special claims argument about religion, in which it is erroneously held to be outside of history and above critical assessment by humans.

III

10   Many people of faith also claim religion to be a personal matter. In taking this view, they too fail to confront the important interpretive and practical issues just noted. However, there is an additional concern. Such a position also evades profound questions of a spiritual nature. Who are we as individuals? Who are we as a human collectivity? What is our relationship to each other, to the rest of nature? What is interconnectedness and how are we to experience it and cultivate it? What is dharma in our time/space? How are we to apply it to every facet of our existence, breath by conscious breath?

11   Unless we are willing to enter into this kind of active process with the traditions in which we practice, we will be treating them as if they were dead relics, not live inheritances. We will accept as given, assumptions and practices that manifest or have sedimented into them past and/or present prejudices. We will, in effect, be evincing fear of our potential as humans to learn as well as err, to be kind as well as cruel. Such an orientation makes us averse to the reality of life as a complex, not always controllable, process. The desire for a measure of protection against the unpredictable generates discomfort with the ambiguous, the messy, the contingent, the ever-changing. All of this can lead us toward a rigidity of religious or philosophical perspective. As a consequence, we can create conceptual fortresses, arming ourselves with circular logics intended to repel all theoretical incursions. We can, in short, shirk our ethical and interpretive responsibilities as humans by taking cover in what we claim to be the eternal certitudes of our faith.

12   Tantra precludes this option. It does this by requiring us to take as the very stuff of our practice, that which a fearful or rigid framework would rather dismiss. It urges us to attend to matter in all its aspects, and to embodiment in all its dimensions. This is

EPILOGUE

the context in which the essays gathered here address subjects not usually considered in the same text: neoliberal globalisation, the web of life, fundamentalism, Western Advaita, trash, the anatomy of faith. The tantric refusal to countenance a clear division between the sacred and secular realms has required one to draw on the analytical resources of both, although, depending on the topic, concepts from one or other knowledge tradition have predominated. Given the breadth of a tantric orientation, an exclusivist approach makes no sense. And while neither sacred nor secular knowledge can by itself be deemed sufficient, together their insights deepen and extend our analysis.

13   The tantric embrace of the concrete is especially significant in a period when dominant discourses manifest utter disdain for facts. Whether it is the dubious economic promise of globalisation for the majority of people, the representation as 'a global elite' of a professional class essentially subordinated to the logic of First World capital, or the plundering of yoga and meditation in order to extend the body's capacity to work longer and faster, fantasy seems to prevail over reality. It is as if desire and will can together confidently order, 'let it be so', and make good their proclamation. But, as common sense, history and tantric wisdom teach us, disharmonious action generates disharmonious consequences. Over time, fantasy when unchecked can mutate into psychosis. When elemental facts are thus ignored, the repercussions cannot but be in proportion to our adharma.

14   Short-cuts beget adharma. When, as in Bangalore, we fill tank beds and generate high value real estate with no concern about where the rainwater will drain, we create the conditions whereby in time we will be flooded out of our homes. Indifference to process and consequences leads to adharma. When we celebrate urban growth without planning for the increased need for sewage disposal, we invite our toilets to overflow. And if we then simply pump untreated sewage into local lakes we create health hazards for us all. Privileging profit over human needs valorises adharma. And when the slaughter of tens of thousands of poultry in context of something called 'avian flu', brings more attention to restaurant menus than to the affected birds and poultry farmers, we witness the normalisation of adharma.

15   Matter matters. Process is critical. Karma rules. Adoration of Creation, compassion toward self and all others, and living by the actuality of our interconnectedness are the way of wisdom. These are not mere claims but actual principles whose functioning can be observed in our lives as also in that of the world around us. While the language used here borrows from the sacred, these ideas are congruent with some of the deepest aspirations of a progressive secular vision. Regardless of where we begin any inquiry into our predicament as a species at this time in history, we will probably all agree that there is much that is out of balance in the way we as a collectivity are living and acting. We seem to be careening our way into the future either unconsciously or wantonly indifferent to the consequences of our actions.

16   Mercifully, consequences have a way of catching up with us. With each passing day, evidence mounts of the deleterious effects of our irreverence and disregard, whether for the environment, for each other, or for our potential as humans. Such estrangement sustains the sense of duality. Awakening ourselves out of the delusion of separation, shaking off alienation, becomes an urgent necessity. Tantra charts a way forward. It proposes a coherent means of uncovering duality as a deadly misperception, and

offers practices that assist us in our journey toward embracing self, other, Creator and Creation.[2]

Textual and rhetorical questions

Textual

1. Lata Mani writes about tantra in terms of "potential" and "actuality," "knowing," and "yearning," and finally, in terms of the impossibility of "overview." Clarify what she means by the features and functions of tantra (paragraph 2).
2. Tantra and secular criticism are similar in many aspects according to Mani, and she further writes about the tantric view that "spirit is integral to matter." What does she conclude by proposing the tantric view? (paragraphs 3 and 4).
3. Do you think tantra has "undemonstrable claims?" If such claims are made, who may claim this? (paragraph 5).
4. Is there anything personal in the context of the proposition that everything is public and hence political, and hence religion too is public and political? What is Mani's critical view about religion in paragraphs 8, 9, and 10?
5. Lata Mani's ideas of tantra, sacred, and secular are appropriated in contemporary times influenced by globalisation in urban lifestyle because tantra, for her, is not a "rigid frame work." Her concluding remarks in paragraphs 12, 13, and 14 contextualise tantra in a wider framework of understanding modern times. Do you agree?

Rhetorical

1. In paragraph 11, the essayist uses the pronoun "we" fourteen times. Give textual reasons for using "we, us, our" frequently in this paragraph? Trace the language of the previous paragraph. Who is the intended audience or personae for using the pronoun "we?" Why does she use "we" in the middle of her writing?
2. Lata Mani gives methodological significance to tantra, instead of defining tantra per se to critique the present social condition. Tantra is strategically discoursed; it is a point of view. Explain how she uses tantra as a methodology.
3. The title suggests that it is a reflective piece of cultural criticism. Locate instances where Mani reflectively critiques existing psychological postures of contemporary culture.

Discussion questions

1. The division between secular and sacral is pervasive, which postcolonial discourse reads as an orientalist project (in a Saidian sense). The secular for Eurocentric ideology is rationalist, reformist, and progressive whereas the sacral is mythical as well as superstitious,[3] and anarchical. Western colonialism in general had and still has this overarching ideology to distinguish the West and the East. The secular is similar to the Arnoldian idea of the Age of Europe which reflects "sweetness and light" as against "anarchy."[4] Lata Mani is not overtly postcolonial in

EPILOGUE

this essay but the way she discourses tantra is suggestive of subtly writing back on the European/Western ideology of reason as the instrument of being a civilised human. Develop a sustained argument to write an essay on the problems of the Western idea of the secular. Edward Said's seminal books *Orientalism* and *Culture and Imperialism* will help you to develop your arguments (3000 words).

2. "Restoring tantra to human consciousness" is "restoring humans" (Frankenberg & Mani, 1).[5] Discuss the above statement in the light of Ajit Mokherjee's *Tantra Art: Its Philosophy & Physics*.[6] Mukherjee's proposition is

> Tantra is the experience of life to bring out spiritual power within us by inward contemplation of the centers of energy or chakras. Human body is the expression of that energy that we can realize by inward contemplation, and the ultimate goal of such contemplation is to seek truth. This is Tantra-yoga.[7]

Inter-textual discussions

1. Lata Mani's text is methodologically parallel to Ashish Nandy's essay "Shamans, Savages and the Wilderness: On the Audibility of Dissent and the Future of Civilizations."[8] Nandy understands the shaman as a voice of dissent from the past, and one who articulates the "values of freedom" (177). Mani implies in her essay that Tantra has to be understood in a wider framework in the times of globalisation and consumerism. Similarly, shamanism is a possibility to understand multiple social ideas and actions like a voice of dissent, a person of healing, of therapy, and a leader in his or her own ways. Both writers appropriate or contextualise tantra and shamanism, respectively, in the modern-day world. How can one appropriate "sacrifice" methodologically to understand contemporary times? To appropriate mythical characters, themes, and objects, you can think about Prometheus, Sisyphus (from Greek mythology), and Kirttimukha (from Hindu mythology).

2. Do you think that the tendency to divide sacred with secular is the problem of binarism which ignores the double bind inherent in conceptual thinking? Neat binary categorisation is a dangerous academic practice. Do you agree?

Critical and creative thinking

1. Ajit Mukherjee defines the three associated concepts tantra, tantra yoga, and tantra Art in the following terms, they are paraphrased here:[9]
   - Tantra is both an experience of life and a method to bring out one's inherent spiritual power.
   - Tantra helps discover the locations of the centres of energy or the *chakras* in the human body.
   - Human beings are the expression of that energy.
   - Humans try to understand the essence within them and the universe by inwards contemplation to seek truth.

187

- The way to seek truth is through tantra yoga by which the dormant in the unconscious is developed.
- Tantra art is one of the essential forms of yoga which uses images and symbols, geometric shapes, and contours.

2. There are primarily two tantra systems of belief: Mentally constructed (*Daksinacara* school of belief) or literally manifested (*Vamacara* school of belief). Collect information and write a brief note on the two schools of belief.

3. James Joyce's *Ulysses* is a Homeric epic set in Ireland. The allusions are appropriated – though not in a realistic mode – with intense floating ideas, multiple narrative points of view, and by challenging the reader in every episode. Mythical narratives and characters are appropriated in contemporary contexts. Can you write a short story with *Ulysses* as your model?

Notes

1 The place of tantra within the Hindu tradition is a contradictory one. While on the one hand it is recognised as an integral dimension of Hindu philosophy, it has also falsely come to be associated with black magic and occult sexual and ritual practices.

2 For a sustained exposition of tantra as philosophy, practice and vital wisdom for humanity, see the teachings compiled by Ruth Frankenberg and Lata Mani in www.thetantrachronicles.com.

3 The statement is paraphrased from Ashcroft, Bill et al. (2008). "The Sacred" in *The Post-Colonial Studies Reader*. Routledge: London (517).

4 See Mathew Arnold's *Culture and Anarchy*.

5 For more detail see Frankenberg, Ruth & Lata Mani (2013). *The Tantra Chronicles: Original teachings from Devi, Shiva, Jesus, Mary, Moon*. www.thetantrachronicle.com.

6 Mukherjee, Ajit. (1977). *Tantra Art: Its Philosophy & Physics*. New Delhi: Rupa & Co.

7 See Gupto, Arun (2018). *Goddesses of Kathmandu Valley: Grace, Rage, Knowledge*. 2nd ed. London: Routledge.

8 Nandy, Ashis (2007). *Time Treks: The Uncertain Future of Old and New Despotisms*. Bangalore: permanent black.

9 See Mukherjee, Ajit. (1977) *Tantra Art: Philosophy and Physics*. New Delhi, Rupa and Co. (11–37).

9

POST-COLONIAL HYBRIDITY

Midnight's children

Harish Trivedi

Introduction

1   Salman Rushdie is perhaps the best-known contemporary writer in the world, famous not only for his literary works but also for the controversy caused by his novel *The Satanic Verses*. He has given a new turn both to the Indian novel in English and to the long literary relationship between India and Britain by inaugurating a new 'post-colonial' phase of it, and by exercising a pervasive influence on several younger Indian novelists, such as Amitav Ghosh, Rohinton Mistry, Mukul Kesavan and even a Hindi novelist such as Alka Saraogi (see p.159 below). Ambitious in scope, his novels not only represent individual characters or even a society as a whole, as fiction traditionally had done, but also attempt to 'narrate the nation', in Homi Bhabha's formulation (see *Nation and Narration*, ed. by Homi Bhabha, London: Routledge, 1990). This chapter focuses on his first major work, *Midnight's Children*, to suggest several (con)textual and theoretical ways of engaging with it.

Text and bibliography

2   *Midnight's Children* was published in 1981 in London and has subsequently been reprinted in paperback editions in both the UK and the USA, but not in India. (All references here are to the Vintage paperback edition, 1982.) It was the second novel by Rushdie; the first was *Grimus* (1975), a curious fantasy set outside of space and time, which got savage reviews on publication and has not been rescued by Rushdie's later success. *Midnight's Children* won the Booker prize and instantly established Rushdie as a major novelist. His third novel was *Shame* (1983), a satirical account of an unnamed country much like Pakistan; it is considerably shorter than all his other sprawling novels. His fourth novel, *The Satanic Verses* (1988), was largely about Indian characters in England but also contained, as indicated in the title, an account of the early period of Islam and of some supposedly apocryphal verses in the Koran thought to have been interpolated by the Devil. His irreverent treatment gave offence to many Muslims, leading to riots and deaths; the book was banned in several countries including India and Pakistan, and, in February 1989, the Ayatollah Khomeini of Iran issued a *fatwa* calling for the execution of Rushdie, upon which he had to go into prolonged hiding with the help of state security. (The *fatwa* was officially lifted in 1998.)

DOI: 10.4324/9781003213857-9

LITERARY THEORY AND CRITICISM

3   Undaunted, Rushdie continued to publish throughout the 1990s. *Haroun and the Sea of Stories* (1990) was a book for children which has a story-teller who loses his voice. A substantial collection of his essays followed, *Imaginary Homelands* (1991), as well as a collection of his short stories, *East, West* (1994). *The Moor's Last Sigh* (1995), a big novel again, returned to Bombay for its setting though it also took in south India, where the first contact between India and the West had taken place, and Moorish Spain. His latest work, *The Ground Beneath Her Feet* (1999), is again international in range, encompassing India, England and the USA, and incorporating a notable component of rock 'n' roll through a reworking of the myth of Orpheus.

4   Much of what has been published so far on Rushdie and on the 'Rushdie affair' has been in newspapers and periodicals, and given his contemporaneity and his still unfolding career, critical discussions of his work are to be found largely in scholarly journals. A useful guide to this material is the extensive *Salman Rushdie Bibliography* by Joel Kuortti (New York: Peter Lang, 1997); it lists works by Rushdie as well as those about him. Of the books published on Rushdie, Timothy Brennan's *Salman Rushdie and the Third World: Myths of the Nation* (London: Macmillan, 1989), which categorizes him as a 'Third World cosmopolitan', provides a stimulating account in a framework especially relevant to this course. Three introductory monographs are each titled *Salman Rushdie*: these are by Catherine Cundy (Manchester: Manchester University Press, 1996), who also offers a comparison of Rushdie and V.S. Naipaul; by D.C.R.A. Goonetilleke (London: Macmillan, 1998), who seeks especially to explicate the Indian context and references; and by Damian Grant in the British Council's Writers and their Work series (Plymouth: Northcote House, 1999). *Reading Rushdie: Perspectives on the Fiction of Salman Rushdie*, ed. by M.D. Fletcher (Amsterdam: Rodopi, 1994), and *Critical Essays on Salman Rushdie*, ed. by M. Keith Booker (New York: G.K. Hall, 1999), both contain a wide range of essays on his works. A more specifically focused selection is *Rushdie's 'Midnight's Children': A Book of Readings*, ed. by Meenakshi Mukherjee (Delhi: Pencraft International, 1999), comprising ten essays on the novel and an early interview; this is of special interest as besides the editor, six of the contributors are Indian.

5   Rushdie's novels contain perhaps an exceptionally high proportion of real historical events, directly represented or readily recognizable public figures, and constant resemblances to the known facts of his own life. The most extensive and reliable biographical account so far is by Ian Hamilton, 'The First Life of Salman Rushdie' (*The New Yorker*, 25 December 1995–1 January 1996), which stops at the publication of *Midnight's Children*.

Approaching midnight's children

Rushdie and India

6   Reportedly, when Martin Amis, one of the prominent British novelists of Rushdie's own generation, was once asked what Rushdie had and what he had not, he succinctly answered: 'India'. India has been not only the setting but the grand theme of Rushdie's fiction so far, a theme which he has exploited like no Indian novelist before; but at the same time, the space India occupies in the Western literary world has been considerably

enhanced through his representation of it. For many Western readers, in fact, Rushdie speaks for India in a way which seems not only representative but authoritative, and his version of India is often taken to be the 'real' India. The publication of *Midnight's Children* was 'like a continent finding its voice' (*New York Times*) – as if the three thousand years of continuous literary tradition had not existed; the novel was 'a fascinating history lesson as well as an engrossing story' (*Philadelphia Enquirer*); and its story 'was nothing less than that of modern India' (*Publishers Weekly*; all quoted on the covers of the paperback editions). Even an academic specializing in Indian Studies, Robin J. Lewis, has stated that Rushdie has 'altered our vision of the Indian sub-continent', to the extent that all the previous literary representations both by British writers such as Kipling and Forster and by Indians such as Raja Rao and R.K. Narayan have been 'simultaneously subsumed into, and surpassed by, Rushdie's passionate evocation of the recent history of India and Pakistan' (in *Masterworks of Asian Literature in Comparative Perspective*, ed. by Barbara Stoler Miller, Armonk, NY: M.E. Sharpe, 1994, pp.178–9).

7 Rushdie's relationship with India and the nature of his affiliation with it thus become critically significant issues in themselves. He was born in Bombay on 20 June 1947, close enough to 15 August 1947, the day India became free, when his hero in *Midnight's Children* Saleem Sinai and his 1,000 coevals are born. His parents were Westernized middle-class Muslims who migrated to Pakistan seventeen years later and subsequently to England. Meanwhile, unlike his fictional hero, Rushdie himself was sent at the age of thirteen to England to attend Rugby School, and later went to Cambridge where he did a degree in history which included an optional course on the history of Islam. He has said that he faced racial discrimination at school where he was unhappy, but also that his pale skin and pukka British accent later made him more or less indistinguishable from Englishmen. His upper-crust English education may have come about due to parental inclination and affluence, but he himself seems to have been keen enough and quite ready for the move:

> I grew up with an intimate knowledge of, and even a sense of friendship with, a certain kind of England; a dream England ... I wanted to come to England. I couldn't wait. And to be fair, England has done all right by me.
>
> (*Imaginary Homelands*, p.18)

Even if modulated by a tone of self-deprecating irony, the statement reveals a significant truth. Rushdie went back briefly to Pakistan after Cambridge, found the country distinctly uncongenial, came back, and has stayed in England ever since as a British citizen.

8 Recently, Rushdie has spoken of himself as having been 'exiled' by India, and in 1998 he expressed his own resolve to turn even imaginatively away from the country: 'I will never write about India again' (quoted in Mukherjee, p.15). Earlier, when he was fully engaged as a writer with the subject of India, he had, speaking on behalf of 'those of us who write from outside India', seemed to contemplate the question of ethical responsibility: 'are we just dilettantes in such affairs, because we are not involved in their day-to-day unfolding, because by speaking out we take no risks, because our personal safety is not threatened? What right do we have to speak at all?' (*Imaginary*

Homelands, p.14). But these turned out to be merely rhetorical questions, for the answer Rushdie went on to provide was that from the outside, a writer like himself had a privileged double vision: 'we are not willing to be excluded from any part of our heritage ... Our identity is at once plural and partial ... If literature is in part the business of finding new angles at which to enter reality, then once again our distance, our long geographical perspective, may provide us with such angles' (*Imaginary Homelands*, p.15).

9   As can be seen, though he continues to be widely regarded in the West as the chief literary spokesman for India, Rushdie in fact stands at an acute angle to the country of his birth, perhaps even at a tangent. His growing vexation with India is quite the opposite of the yearning and nostalgia with which Raja Rao, for example, regards India (see Chapter 8 above). Rao's continuing if wishful project even now to write in an Indian language such as Kannada or even Sanskrit is in fact directly to be contrasted with Rushdie's editorial comment in his introduction to *The Vintage Book of Indian Writing*, ed. by Salman Rushdie and Elizabeth West (London: Vintage, 1997), brought out to mark the fifty years of Indian independence, that Indian writing in English during this period had been 'stronger and more important' than what had been produced in all the other eighteen Indian languages. Besides being an aggrandizement of his own kind of writing, this sweeping statement is also remarkable, as Meenakshi Mukherjee puts it, for 'the aggressiveness' of his 'empty claim based on ignorance' (Mukherjee, p.26).

10   In fact, such erasure of the indigenous literary culture is reflected widely in the present critical discourse on post-colonial literature which almost by definition is literature written in English, the language of the erstwhile colonizers, by the colonized even after the moment of political (if not cultural) decolonization. Some of these writers come from a social background which was so Westernized that they lost the local language as they acquired more and more English and would not have been able to write in it even if they wanted to, as in the case of Rushdie himself and probably most of the younger Indians writing in English. But some others, who remained effectively bilingual, still wrote in English in order to have the benefits of addressing a larger global audience. Incidentally, the use of English has been an issue of contention also among African writers. The Kenyan writer Ngugi wa Thiong'o actually switched in mid-career to begin writing and publishing in his native Gikuyu but in his case, this could be no more than a symbolic or even paradoxical gesture, for he then proceeded to translate his own Gikuyu works into English. (See the extract from his book, *Decolonising the Mind*, and also a contrasting moderate statement on the question of language from another African writer, Chinua Achebe, both reprinted in *Colonial Discourse and Post-Colonial Theory*, ed. by Patrick Williams and Laura Chrisman (London: Harvester Wheatsheaf, 1993, pp.428–55.) In India the decision to write in English looks quite different inside the country from the way it may look in the West. Where over 70 per cent of the population is now literate but where knowledge of English is still confined to not more than 5 per cent of the people at a generous estimate, few would even begin to doubt that the eighteen major Indian languages still have a viable and vibrant literary culture – though his anglicized upbringing and his recent constrained circumstances may not make Rushdie the best-placed person to know this.

POST-COLONIAL HYBRIDITY

Hybridity

11   Rushdie's stance, his works, and – if one may bring in the personal in the case of so patently autobiographical a writer – his own formation are an embodiment of the extent and the depth to which a colonizing culture can penetrate that of the colonized. While the colonizer and the colonized are both infected by each other through their historical conjunction and mutual cultural discovery – for example, the British in India up to the eighteenth century were often seen to 'go native' and were (even in English) called 'nabobs' – the coercive weight of assimilation ultimately falls rather more on the colonized. As each interacts with the Other (in the deeper psychic sense of the word expounded by Jacques Lacan; see Chapter 1 above, p.24), each ceases to remain what it previously was and becomes 'hybrid'. There is of course a philosophical sense in which everything is always and already hybrid, for (as the deconstructionist Jacques Derrida has argued) the pure and pristine origin is a myth and the search for it must grow ever more recessive or deferred. The profoundly complex political, racial and cultural transaction that takes place between the colonizer and the colonized and the several distinct phases of nationalism that it goes through, from imitation and assimilation to resistance and finally to post-colonial internationalization, was expounded with passionate engagement by Frantz Fanon in his widely influential works *Les Damnés de la terre* (1961; trans. by Constance Farrington as *The Wretched of the Earth*, London: Penguin, 1967) and *Peau noire, masques blancs* (1952; trans. by C.L. Markmann as *Black Skin, White Masks*, London: Pluto Press, 1986). One contemporary post-colonial critic who has reformulated with exceptional sophistication the concepts of colonial hybridity, 'mimicry', 'sly civility' and 'in-betweenness' is Homi Bhabha, in his collection of essays *The Location of Culture* (London: Routledge, 1994), which also includes a piece containing a discussion of Fanon. (Extracts from both Fanon and Bhabha appear in Williams and Chrisman, pp.36–52, 112–23.)

12   The persistence of the colonial intermixed with the post-colonial is reflected in *Midnight's Children* in a number of ways. The conditions on which the 'departing Englishman' William Methwold sells his 'Estate' in Bombay by partitioning it among four ethnically varied Indian families are that they must retain all his furniture and fittings and carry on just as he did; to make the self-proclaimed 'allegory' (*Midnight's Children*, pp.95–7) even more explicit, he later turns out to be one of Saleem's several fathers. When Ahmad Sinai's skin begins to turn pale and he is presently 'transformed into a white man', he is secretly rather pleased for, as he explains: 'All the best people are white under the skin; I have merely given up pretending'. A 'theory' which the narrator advances here is that in the first decade of India's independence, 'the gargantuan (even heroic) efforts involved in taking over from the British' had similarly turned the businessmen of India 'white' as well (p.179). Another instance of continued post-colonial anglicization in the novel is the narrator's upbringing and education: 'In India we've always been vulnerable to Europeans ... I was being sucked into a grotesque mimicry of European literature ... Perhaps it would be fair to say that Europe repeats itself, in India, as farce' (p.185).

13   Perhaps it would be fair to add that these statements are made by exceptionally Westernized characters who seem only too willing to be 'sucked into' a reverent imitation of Europe. There are, of course, other contrasting versions of the way the West

LITERARY THEORY AND CRITICISM

has impacted on large segments of the postcolonial Indian society which were not as completely hybridized as Saleem Sinai's world seems to be, or whose hybridization produced a different and more resistant effect on them. For these, we may turn to some instances of writing in the Indian languages. Those dependent on translations might begin to get a sense of this very rich field through my translations of Hindi writings such as Sharad Joshi's story 'Who Isn't Afraid of Virginia Woolf?' (see Text 11.2) or Kamaleshwar's 'The Nose of King George the Fifth' (see Text 11.1). Nirmal Verma's stories are also available in *The Crow of Deliverance: Stories*, trans. by Kuldip Singh and Jai Ratan (London: Readers International, 1991). More recently, and still only partially, translated is Alka Saraogi, *Kali-katha: Via Bypass* (see Text 11.3).

14   Even lower down in the colonial cultural order and more widespread was the social stratum which remained relatively exempt from the range of colonial permeation, comprising the 'subalterns' who could not speak, or who spoke in very different modes and languages which could not be registered in the discourse of their colonial masters. (See 'Can the Subaltern Speak?', 1988, by Gayatri Chakravorty Spivak, repr. in Williams and Chrisman, pp.66–111). As Spivak clarifies in a revision and elaboration of her argument, the subaltern is distinguished from the 'elite' precisely by his/her 'inhabiting a space of difference' (see her *Critique of Postcolonial Reason*, Cambridge, MA: Harvard University Press, 1999, p.271, n.118).

15   Rushdie's fictional world in *Midnight's Children*, even if presented with intermittent irony, remains the world of the Indian elite, who are not only more 'vulnerable' to being hybridized but who perhaps are the elite because they have been so hybridized in the first place. The term 'hybridity' here may in fact stand as a euphemism for aspiration to Englishness. As Richard Cronin has argued in an unsettling comparative reading of *Midnight's Children*:

> Salman Rushdie has more in common with Rudyard Kipling than with Premchand or Bankim Chandra Chatterjee. It is an ancestry that he resists as energetically as Saleem resists the notion that his real father is an Englishman ... but, for all his efforts, *Midnight's Children* is better seen as a post-independence version of *Kim*.
>
> ('The Indian English Novel: *Kim* and *Midnight's Children*', *Modern Fiction Studies*, 33.2 (Summer 1987); repr. in Mukherjee, pp.134–48)

History as fiction and magic realism

16   As has been seen, *Midnight's Children* has been read at least in the West as being not only a novel but also a 'history lesson'. Nor can such a reading be called a wilful misreading, for the hero Saleem claims on the very first page that he was born 'mysteriously handcuffed to history' (p.9) at the precise moment that India attained freedom. This is the governing trope of the novel and is kept up throughout with a device whereby the novelist cuts back to Saleem's life to show what was happening to him whenever a historical event of national significance occurred. On the whole, though, this results in simple juxtaposition; the nation does not intersect, much less determine, the lives of the characters here in any important way. Nor is *Midnight's Children* really

comparable with traditional historical novels, from *A Tale of Two Cities* and *War and Peace* to *Gone with the Wind*, where the focus is largely on the personal relationships between individual characters as their lives are played out against the backdrop of momentous historical events but are at crucial junctures interrupted and disrupted by them. In *Midnight's Children*, Saleem's life and the life of the nation run rather as two parallel streams, each on its own fairly watertight course.

17   Interestingly, Rushdie himself later claimed that he never intended his novel to be read as history:

> [Saleem's] story is not history, but it plays with historical shapes. Ironically, the book's success – its Booker Prize, etc. – initially distorted the way in which it was read. Many readers wanted it to be the history, even the guide-book, which it was never meant to be.
>
> (*Imaginary Homelands*, p.25)

This sounds very much like E.M. Forster's claim that *A Passage to India* is not a political novel: 'the book is not really about politics, though it is the political aspect of it that caught the general public and made it sell' (*The Hill of Devi and Other Indian Writings*, ed. by Elizabeth Heine, London: Edward Arnold, 1983, p.298). But a book is in effect just how it is read; what the author wished it to be has been called 'the intentional fallacy'. In any case, we know that Rushdie wrote some passages of his novel more or less out of Stanley Wolpert's *A New History of India*, and many other parts apparently came out of newspaper reports and other documentary sources; in fact, at one point, the narrator even challenges the reader: 'If you don't believe me, check' (quoted by Neil ten Kortenaar, '*Midnight's Children* and the Allegory of History', *Ariel*, 26.2 (April 1995), repr. in Mukherjee, pp.28–48).

18   A radically different way of looking at the correlation between history and fiction is the post-structuralist one, according to which nothing exists naturally or objectively but everything is 'constructed' through and in language. Thus, neither history nor fiction is simply 'given'; rather, both are 'narratives' with their own procedure of selection, omissions and biases, according to the 'subject-position' of the person who narrates them. To hold that anything can exist outside its representation is to be an 'essentialist', i.e. to believe that things have an unmediated essence. It is in this sense, for example, that nations are not real but 'imagined communities' (see Chapter 1, p.14) and are no more or other than what they are narrated to be: 'Nations, like narratives ... fully realize their horizons in the mind's eye ... To study the nation through its narrative address does not merely draw attention to its language and rhetoric; it also attempts to alter the conceptual object itself' (Homi Bhabha, 'Introduction' to *Nation and Narration*, pp.1, 3). As if all this were not 'ambivalent' enough, the language in which the nation is narrated is held to be equally a construction: 'It is the project of *Nation and Narration* to explore the Janus-faced ambivalence of language itself in the construction of the Janus-faced discourse of the nation' (Bhabha, p.3).

19   There has over the years evolved an uncanny intertextuality between the theoretical articulations of Bhabha and the fictional narratives of Rushdie which may make it particularly apt to read Rushdie in terms of Bhabha. But such a reading will have to

leave out of account all those other reading practices according to which General Dyer in this novel has more of a verifiable historical reality to him than Ahmad Sinai, and Jawaharlal Nehru is not a construction in the same sense as is Saleem. For many readers, the fact of India becoming free at the stroke of midnight of 14/15 August exists not on the same plane of credibility as Saleem being born at just that moment (the midnight being more historical than the children), and the Emergency which Indira Gandhi imposed is simply more real than anything Padma can do or say. Curiously, Rushdie himself has attempted to conflate the ambivalences of post-structuralism with the contingencies of post-colonialism; he speaks of himself as someone 'forced by cultural displacement to accept the provisional nature of all truths, all certainties' (*Imaginary Homelands*, p.12). This would seem to imply that for those not culturally displaced like him, truth is still truth and certainty is still certainty.

20   When *Midnight's Children* first came out it was often described as a work of magic realism. This term had earlier been used to describe the mode of fictional representation adopted by some Latin American novelists, most notably Gabriel García Márquez, author of *One Hundred Years of Solitude* (1967; trans. 1971), and also by some European novelists such as Milan Kundera. In this mode, the largely realistic tenor of the novel is punctuated with episodes and descriptions which are clearly fantastic; an obvious example from *Midnight's Children* would be the characteristics and function of Saleem's nose. Related to this is the bending of reality achieved through the use of the grotesque, an eminent example of such a work being Günter Grass's *The Tin Drum* (1959), which is narrated by Oskar, a dwarf who has physical deformities quite comparable to Saleem's. Rushdie's fiction can be seen to bear the clear influence of both these styles: '*Midnight's Children* owes its magic', as Patricia Merivale has stated, 'to García Márquez and its realism to Günter Grass' ('Saleem Fathered by Oskar: Intertextual Strategies in *Midnight's Children* and *The Tin Drum*', *Ariel*, 21.3 (July 1990), repr. in Mukherjee, p.116). Rushdie himself has acknowledged the importance for him of both Márquez and Grass, by suggesting that Márquez's kind of magic realism 'expresses a genuinely "Third World" consciousness', and by recalling that his reading of *The Tin Drum* when he was twenty gave him 'permission' to become the kind of writer he had it in himself to be (*Imaginary Homelands*, pp.301, 276).

Style and form

21   There are thus many close non-Indian literary antecedents for *Midnight's Children*, and some more have been adduced, such as Sterne's *Tristram Shandy*. The style of the novel is marked by constant word-play, especially punning, and this, together with the thin line dividing his fiction from autobiography, has reminded many readers of James Joyce. In fact, Rushdie himself has described the style of his early fiction as 'sub-Joyce' (quoted in Hamilton, p.100). Yet the novel reads distinctively Indian as much in form and style as in theme, mainly because it is marked on almost every page with a confident unselfconscious deployment of Indian words and phrases and social and cultural allusions. Rushdie's use of a mixed, hybridized English has been seen as a liberating strategy not only for himself but also for numerous subsequent Indian writers, some of whom have also attempted similarly to narrate the nation. This has

POST-COLONIAL HYBRIDITY

marked a departure from earlier modes of Indian writing in English, though it must not be forgotten that novelists such as Raja Rao and Mulk Raj Anand had even earlier attempted to appropriate English in their own ways (see Chapter 8 above). G.V. Desani, a writer whose example Rushdie acknowledges, made comparable appropriations in his novel *All About H. Hatterr* (1948), where the initial in the hero's assumed name stands for '*Hindustaniwalla*' (G.V. Desani, *All About H. Hatterr*, repr. Harmondsworth: Penguin, 1972, p.33).

22   With characteristic exuberance and radical bravado, Rushdie has claimed that his use of English is a form of a final fight against colonialism:

> Those of us who do use English do so in spite of our ambiguity towards it, or perhaps because of that, perhaps because we can find in that linguistic struggle a reflection of other struggles taking place in the real world ... To conquer English may be to complete the process of making ourselves free.
>
> (*Imaginary Homelands*, p.17)

There is, of course, another way of looking at it, which is that to go on writing in the language of the colonizer, however inventively and 'subversively', is still to remain colonized and to enlist oneself 'in a foreign if not enemy camp, that of the colonizer' (John Updike, review of *The God of Small Things* by Arundhati Roy, *New Yorker*, 23–30 June 1997).

23   If Rushdie's extensive use of Indian allusions and Hindi-Urdu words does not quite 'conquer' English, it does serve at least to 'chutneyfy' it. It also underlines the fact that his intended reader is clearly a Westerner and not an Indian, for many of his habitual stylistic devices do not work equally well for someone who knows any Hindi or Urdu. One of the most frequent of these is the use of a Hindi word as a kind of authenticating strategy, to show that Rushdie knows his India from the inside as the reader does not and has the reliability of a native informant. (This is a familiar literary practice; for example, in their oriental tales Robert Southey, Thomas Moore and Lord Byron had all used Eastern words and allusions, supported by scholarly authorities cited in the footnotes, to heighten their credibility.) Though Rushdie does not have footnotes or a glossary, he often does stop to provide the English equivalent immediately afterwards. 'Godown, gudam, warehouse, call it what you like' (p.71) is a characteristically prolix example, in which the first word is from Indian English, the second from Hindi, and the third from British English (rarely used in India), all to describe the same object. Even more remarkable is his strategy in a sentence such as 'I do not need to tell you that aag means fire' (p.71) or the following passage:

> Talaaq! Talaaq! Talaaq!
> The English lacks the thunderclap sound of Urdu and anyway you know what it means.
> I divorce thee, I divorce thee, I divorce thee. (p.62)

But this is disingenuous, for if the reader knew what it meant Rushdie wouldn't need to provide the translation.

24   In another category altogether are the many palpable and elementary errors in Rushdie's use of Indian words and allusions which were pointed out after the novel was published. Resourceful as ever, Rushdie then wrote an essay to explain that these errors had been planted by him in the novel to establish that his narrator Saleem was an 'unreliable narrator'! (See 'Errata: Or, Unreliable Narration in *Midnight's Children*', in *Imaginary Homelands*, pp.22–5.) But unreliable narrators usually are unreliable, as with Nelly Dean in *Wuthering Heights* or Marlow in *Heart of Darkness*, because we are not supposed to endorse their perceptions and judgements, and not because they get their 'facts' wrong.

25   Rushdie was born an Indian and has grown to be an Englishman – by education, place of residence and work, and in terms of his national affiliation. His books have been differently (and generally better) received in the West than in India. For example, while *Midnight's Children* has been read by many in the West as an affectionate celebration of India, *India Today* described it as 'one of the most ferocious indictments of India's evolution since independence' (this is quoted – ironically, to market the book – on the cover of the Picador paperback edition). In wider terms, he represents the postcolonial globalization of the world through migrancy and assimilation in a new phase of neo-colonialism. By the same token, perhaps, work like his does not represent that other larger, but proportionately under-represented, segment of the post-colonial peoples of the world who are not migrants and who, though necessarily affected by colonization (or hybridized) in their own way, continue to be rather more local than global where they are.

26   In the long history of the national and literary interaction between India and Britain, Rushdie, born on the post-colonial cusp like his midnight's children, expresses acutely the almost intractable complexity of both colonization and decolonization. He perhaps also marks the end of an era, the span of two hundred years in which Britain was the most important nation for India in the English-speaking world, as the generation of Indian writers in English after Rushdie have tended to migrate more to the USA and Canada than to Britain. Rushdie's latest novel, *The Ground Beneath Her Feet*, offers some symbolic moments here. It is the first of his novels where the story brings together events in India, Britain and the USA. The novel comes to the reader with an endorsement by Toni Morrison, the Nobel prize winning Black American writer, who describes the book as showing Rushdie 'at his absolute, almost insolently global best'. Just as British literature is not likely in the future to be as concerned, or even as little concerned, with India as it may have been in the past, so Indian literature, especially Indian writing in English, looks like moving beyond Britain and the colonial connection to attempt to address a new readership in the new neo-colonial centre of the world, the USA. This signals a post-colonial realignment of positions for Britain as well as India.

Questions and exercises[1]

1   Trace the manifestations of post-colonial hybridity in Rushdie's work, beginning with *Midnight's Children* and going on through *The Satanic Verses* and *The Moor's Last Sigh*.

POST-COLONIAL HYBRIDITY

2 Examine Rushdie's fictional representation of modern Indian history with reference to historical works or works by other novelists, e.g. Shashi Tharoor, Rohinton Mistry and Mukul Kesavan.
3 Analyse Rushdie's style, especially in terms of innovation and accessibility.
4 Examine the ways in which Rushdie can be considered an 'Indian' writer, especially when compared with other Indian writers in this course, including those who write in the Indian languages.
5 Develop a comparison between Rushdie and V.S. Naipaul as postcolonial writers, beginning, if you like, with the analysis offered by Catherine Cundy in *Salman Rushdie* (Manchester: Manchester University Press, 1996).

Textual and rhetorical questions

Textual

1. The idea of representation is critiqued by Harish Trivedi when he discusses Salman Rushdie's *Midnight's Children* (see paragraph 6 "Reportedly . . .").[2] Analyse his ideas in relation to what Trivedi further interprets the novel in the light of the 'personal' and the 'historical' (see paragraph 16 "As has been . . ."). The mode of representation, on the one hand, is "authoritative," "altered," and "passionate evocation," (paragraph 6), and on the other hand, the mode is magical realism (paragraph 16 "As has been . . ."). Does Trivedi present a contradictory view of representation as authoritative as well as magic realistic or are both these modes of depiction of India complementary? Analyse these two paragraphs.
2. Trivedi explains hybridity and purity,

> "There is of course a philosophical sense in which everything is always and already hybrid, for (as deconstructionist Jacques Derrida has argued) the pure and pristine origin is a myth and the search for it must grow over more recessive of deferred."
>
> (paragraph 11)

Do you think hybridity presupposes purity even if the presupposition is mythical? Argue whether the desire for the myth is the quest of purity. Your argument should be related to the ideas from the passage (50–70 words).

Rhetorical

1. Trivedi rarely leaves his arguments, interpretations, and explanations unsubstantiated. He frequently cites writers and critics. While writing about *Midnight's Children*, Trivedi quotes Rushdie's *Imaginary Homelands*. Discuss how these quotes are relevant for the essayist. How do the quotes support his ideas?
2. One of the key phrases of the essay is "post-colonial hybridity." Give two examples from the text where the writer explains the phrase. Does he define the phrase explicitly?

199

3. Interesting information, allusions, and the use of simple language keep readers engaged. Is the writer successful in such an engagement? Compare the methods that are used to attain the reader's engagement in Homi Bhabha's and Trivedi's essays.

Discussion questions

1. There has always been a debate in India about the quality of English writings versus that of *Bhasabhasi*, vernacular, or regional writings. What are the reasons for Salman Rushdie's claim that English writing in India is "stronger and more important?"[3] Do you think that "stronger" is a qualitative term and "important" is an abstract one? Amit Chaudhuri comments in "Modernity and the Vernacular,"[4] "Can it be true that Indian writing that endlessly rich, complex and problematic entity, is to be represented by a handful of writers who write in English . . .? (2001, xvii). What is your critical stand from your cultural location?
2. Read passage 17 and argue on the postcolonial resistance through English writing: Trivedi mentions, "Rushdie has claimed that his use of English is a form of a final fight against colonialism:" (paragraph 22)

> Those of us who do use English do so in spite of our ambiguity towards it, or perhaps because we can find in that linguistic struggle a reflection of other struggles taking place in the real world . . . To conquer English may be to complete the process of making ourselves free.[5]
>
> (*Imaginary Homelands*,17)

Trivedi adds,

> There is, of course, another way of looking at it, which is that to go on writing in the language of the colonizer, however inventively and "subversively", still to remain colonized and to enlist oneself "in a foreign if not enemy camp, that of the colonizer. . . "

3. Postcolonial theorists discuss the term "appropriation" as a kind of resistance of language. Bill Ashcroft et al write about the adaptation of "standard" English language to be appropriated in local contexts of, for instance, India or Nigeria, to give local colouring (2008, 261–62).[6] Appropriation is followed up by abrogation of the standard language (and culture). Elaborate abrogation and then appropriation by discussing Jean Rhys's *Wide Sargasso Sea* and V.S. Naipaul's *The Mimic Men*.[7]

Inter-textual discussions

1. Hybridity is both a consequence of the encounter between coloniser and colonised and also a mode of resistance by "writing back" on the empire by using the

coloniser's language (English in this case). Read the passage and write a response by bringing in various examples,

> Most post-colonial writing has concerned itself with the hybridized nature of post-colonial culture as a strength rather than a weakness. Such writing focuses on the fact that the transaction of the post-colonial world is not a one-way process in which oppression obliterates the oppressed or the colonizer silences the colonized in absolute terms. In practice it rather stresses the mutuality of the process. It lays emphasis on the survival even under the most potent oppression of the distinctive aspect of the culture of the oppressed, and shows how these become an integral part of the new formation which arise from the clash of cultures characteristic of imperialism. (Ashcroft, Bill et al, 2008, 137)[8]

2. Creolisation is indigenisation. Do you think cricket in the West Indies was indigenised as language was creolised in Jamaica? What have "doosra" spin bowling and "helicopter shot" batting done as the indigenisation of cricketing style in South Asia?

Critical and creative thinking

1. Ipshita Chanda in "The Tortoise and the Leopard, or the Postcolonial Muse" alludes to a story. The Old Man of Abazon tells the story of the leopard that had been stalking the tortoise for a long time.

> Finally, he caught up with him and said, "prepare to die". The tortoise asked for some time to prepare himself. The leopard saw no harm in granting this wish. Then the tortoise went into strange action on the road scratching with hands and feet and throwing sand vigorously in all directions. "Why are you doing that?" asked the puzzled leopard. The tortoise replied: Because even after I am dead I would want anyone passing by this spot to say, yes, a fellow and his match.[9]

> What is the nature of resistance by the use of English language in the works of Chinua Achebe, Salman Rushdie, and/or Arundhati Roy? Does context determine the use of English language to write back on the empire? Does Roy surrender to the nuances of "pure" English whereas Rushdie toys with the "purity" by vernacular idioms? What does Achebe do in his writings, coming from Nigerian Igbo culture?

2. Think about the nature of resistance by Mahatma Gandhi in the struggle for Indian independence. His weapons were folk in nature: Walking, *lathi*, *dhoti*, and *charkha*.[10]

3. Nkisi Kozo or Minkisi (in plural) is an object, particularly a double-headed dog believed to possess spirits in Congo, became a symbol of African resistance.[11] Similarly, mid-nineteenth-century *Chapati* (what the local bread is called in India

201

or Pakistan) distribution was another mode of resistance against the British. Find out the narratives related to these items.

4. Do you think the modes of creativity and collective actions like anarchism are also types of resistance?[12]

Notes

1 The questions and exercises are given by Harish Trivedi.

2 I have provided the first word of the paragraph in this particular essay so as to avoid confusion regarding counting the paragraphs.

3 www.indiatoday.in/magazine/interview/story/19970714-indian-writers-in-english-seem-to -have-been-doing-most-interesting-work-salman-rushdie-830364-1997-07-14 or See (1997) *The Vintage Book of Indian Writing: 1947–1997*.

4 See Chaudhuri, Amit (2001) *The Picador Book of Modern Indian Literature*. London: Picador.

5 Rushdie, Salman. (1991) *Imaginary Homelands: Essays in Criticism, 1981-1991*. London: Granta.

6 See information in footnote 5.

7 For more detail see Stephen Slemon's "Post-colonial Critical Theories" in *Postcolonial Discourses: An Anthology*. Ed. Castle, Gregory. (2001) Malden: Blackwell. 107–08.

8 Ashcroft, Bill et al. (Eds.). (2008) *The Post-Colonial Studies Reader*. 2nd ed. London: Routledge.

9 For Chanda's essay see *Comparative Studies of South Africa, Africa and the Middle East* 23.1–2 (2003) 128–140. My question is based on the idea Chanda proposes in the essay. See Achebe's *Anthills of the Savanah*.

10 The first three lines of a famous Hindi songson Gandhi freedom struggle is "Dedi hame ajadi bina khadga bina dhal / Sabarmati ke Sant tune kar diya kamal" (You bestowed us freedom without sword and disc / O Saint of Sabarmati, you wove magic." The lyricist is Ramchandra Baryanji Dwivedi or Kavi Pradeep who wrote the song for the movie *Jagriti* (1954).

11 See Mirzoeff, Nicholas (2009) "Imperial Transcultures: From Kongo to Congo" in *An Introduction to Visual Culture*. 2nd ed. London: Routlege (126–46).

12 See Stephen Duncombe (Ed.). (2012). *Cultural Resistance Reader*. Indian Ed. New Delhi: Adarsh Books. The book is a comprehensive discourse on the nature and kinds of resistance.

10

FRAGMENTING NATIONS AND LIVES

Sunlight on a broken column

Vrinda Nabar

Introduction

1 Attia Hosain's *Sunlight on a Broken Column* appeared in 1961, long after India and Pakistan became independent countries in 1947. It is thus a historical novel, grounded in the issues of nation and identity that had always simmered beneath the surface during colonial rule and even earlier. The history of India has always been one of localized loyalties and regional kingdoms or fiefdoms. Even the much-touted unification of India, attributed to the British, can seem no more than a whitewash effected through the dubious, self-promoting policies of conquest and annexation. Divisive forces arising from economic, religious, class and land-ownership issues were at work even during the British presence in India, but their disruptive potential was by and large kept under control. The British were forceful enough when these threatened to disturb the administrative peace. They were less assiduous, however, about interfering in issues once they were able to convince themselves that Indians were following their own religious practices. Thus, for example, British decisions about sati (or widow-burning) were motivated not by notions of gender injustice but by discriminations as to what was or was not proper according to Hindu law. An East India Company circular of 1813 declared sati prohibited if it infringed Hindu law because, for example, the widow was less than sixteen, pregnant or coerced into immolating herself (see L. Mani, *Contentious Traditions: The Debate on Sati in Colonial India*, Berkeley: University of California Press, 1998, pp.18ff.). The guise of political expediency or respect for other religions made it possible to be selective about which issues needed the tempering influence of British fair play. In this introductory section I want to touch briefly on four aspects of this social and historic context for a reading of *Sunlight on a Broken Column*: the struggle for independence; communalism, and the partition of colonial India into independent India and East and West Pakistan; the social structure of India; and the specific situation of women.

2 Following on from the unsuccessful revolt of 1857 in which rulers from different parts of India, in a rare and unprecedented show of solidarity, tried to overthrow British dominion, power was transferred from the East India Company to the Crown. As we have seen in earlier chapters, the 1850s also saw the initiation of moves to 'educate' the natives through the setting up of universities and the introduction of Western

DOI: 10.4324/9781003213857-10

systems of thought into the syllabuses (see Gauri Viswanathan, *Masks of Conquest: Literary Study and British Rule in India*, London: Faber, 1989).

3   Meanwhile, the struggle for freedom proceeded in a series of phases. The most significant among these was the launching of the Indian National Congress in 1885. This was perhaps the first organized effort to bring together people from all over India and prepare an agenda that would seek to focus the government's attention on various social and national problems.

4   The freedom struggle was far from homogeneous. Fairly early on, it was embroiled in tussles between the so-called 'extremists' and the 'moderates' (see the references to Tilak and Gokhale in the section 'An analysis of India?' in Chapter 7 above). Another factor was the setting up of the Muslim League in 1905. This began as a reaction to the Partition of Bengal by the British but soon became a national body aiming to protect the future of Indian Muslims in a free India. From soon after 1900, then, the independence movement was marked, turn and turn about, by attempts to create a united front and by schisms between conservative Hindus demanding a truly Hindu state and those in the Muslim League insisting on a protected status for India's largest minority group. The annual Congress of 1928 was marked by particularly fierce division which meant that most organized Muslims stood aloof from the Civil Disobedience campaign begun in 1930 (see Judith Brown, *Modern India: The Origins of an Asian Democracy*, 2nd edn, Oxford: Oxford University Press, 1994, Chapter 5). Attia Hosain's novel, set mostly in the 1930s, draws on the ways in which these various splits eventually had friends and even families divided along very bitter lines.

5   In spite of these tensions, the freedom movement gathered momentum. The growing discontent with what the moderates had called the 'economic drain' of the country under colonial rule was buttressed by the extremist effort to translate this discontent into political form. The First World War brought home to Indian leaders the near impossibility of a fair and equitable solution on the part of the British towards India and her people. This hardened the attitude of those who had agreed to support Britain's war efforts in the belief that this would lead in turn to Britain giving greater autonomy to India. Even Indian industrialists, disillusioned with Britain's post-war prioritizing of British industries, threw themselves behind the call for *swaraj*, or self-rule.

6   From there to non-cooperation and, eventually, the demand that the British 'Quit India' was a progression that took a more or less predictable course. That it took so long to reach a point when independence was more or less certain (1920–42) perhaps in part reflects the fact that both British colonialists and Indians demanding independence realized the complexities of the situation. It also bears witness to the fact that the terms of independence were negotiated with extreme tenacity by both sides. However that is, with Gandhi's growing appeal the British juggernaut became increasingly aware of the impossibility of administering India as merely another colony, or as an extension of its dominions. The economic problems experienced back home in Britain after the Second World War made independence for India a more or less natural corollary – as P.J. Cain and A.G. Hopkins remark, 'from being one of Britain's major debtors, India emerged in 1945 as her largest single sterling creditor' (*British Imperialism: Crisis and Deconstruction, 1914–1990*, London: Longman, 1993, p.16). To gain a full sense of the context of Indian writing after 1940 you would need to explore the situation in more detail than space allows here, beginning for example with the account by Judith

Brown or that given in Chapters 15–17 of Sugata Bose and Ayesha Jalal, *Modern South Asia: History, Culture, Political Economy* (London: Routledge, 1998).

7   What is unambiguous is that Independence was a milestone that has always been remembered with mixed emotions in the Indian subcontinent. Independence meant not just freedom from colonial rule but the division of British India into India and Pakistan (the latter comprised West Pakistan, now Pakistan, and East Pakistan, now Bangladesh). It also meant communal violence, bloodshed, and, for vast numbers of people, a permanent rootlessness arising out of their forced migration from places where they had spent entire lives to new homes in a different country. In the weeks preceding and following 15 August 1947, bands of refugees crossed over the new borders: some accounts suggest that as many as ten million people were displaced from where they had lived before Partition. Some people had the luxury of freely and willingly settling anew according to their religion, but for the vast majority it was an exile – a choice without alternatives that simply took them to a refugee camp.

8   Implicit also in the history of this period were the several socioeconomic changes that became part of free India's move towards what was called a 'socialistic' pattern of development. New laws made the old feudal structures impotent, though more than fifty years of freedom have not wiped out the more insidious operations of feudal power, especially in the countryside. The more tangible changes were the new land laws, the curbing of landlord and princely privileges, and the gradual emergence of other hegemonic forces in the socioeconomic and sociocultural structure. The beginnings of these changes can be seen in *Sunlight on a Broken Column*. In the novel, they affect the way power groups aligned themselves even before Independence.

9   In India, family and the community have always played a central role. In spite of the changing life-patterns in urban India, lifestyles remain moulded by traditional notions of social roles. Individualism as a way of life has not yet penetrated Indian mores. Individual choices are often conditioned by the demands of family loyalty and 'honour' (*izzat*). Added to these constraints are those of caste, religion, region and class. These are particularly manifest in matters of marriage, arranged marriages still being the accepted norm. *Sunlight on a Broken Column* can only be properly understood against such a background.

10   Readers today, particularly non-Indian readers who see the 1990s in India described as a period of economic and social reform, might assume that the representation of women in *Sunlight on a Broken Column* can be considered now as safely historical and that 'modern' India has moved away from these traditional notions. To my mind this would be wrong; I would emphasize rather the need to look at the Indian women's movement in a sociocultural context that remains by and large conservative and orthodox, and in which tradition has been consistently and variously used to oppose individual freedom. You can follow up these arguments in more detail in Vrinda Nabar, *Caste as Woman* (Delhi: Penguin, 1995), especially in the introductory chapter, 'Our Women, their Women'. While the focus of my study has been Indian womanhood, I argue there that this constraint on individual freedom also applies to men.

11   It would be far more accurate to describe contemporary Indian social life (again, to most non-Indians this would mean its urban manifestations) as superficially Westernized but fundamentally loyal to traditional indigenous priorities. Awareness of the importance of such loyalty and rootedness was particularly strident in the most

LITERARY THEORY AND CRITICISM

recent national elections (1999), which had Sonia Gandhi contending for membership of the Lok Sabha (the Lower House of Parliament). Throughout her campaign, Ms Gandhi's primary electoral message had been that she was a loyal wife (*patni*), widow (*vidhawa*), and daughter-in-law (*bahu*) of the Gandhi family.

The author and the text

12   *Sunlight on a Broken Column* was first published in 1961. As its title (borrowed from T.S. Eliot's *The Hollow Men*) indicates, the novel is heavy with memories. Attia Hosain's life, by all accounts, closely paralleled that of the protagonist. Like Laila, Hosain belonged to an orthodox Muslim feudal class, that of the Taluqdars, who enjoyed near princely privileges. Anita Desai's introduction to the Virago Modern Classics edition of Hosain's novel tells us the little we know about Hosain's life (Attia Hosain, *Sunlight on a Broken Column*, London: Virago, 1988; all page references are to this edition, but the Penguin India edition of 1994, which also includes Desai's introduction, uses a similar pagination).

13   Hosain was born in 1913, and migrated to England in 1947, the year India became independent. The years in between were largely spent in Lucknow, a city which even today retains some of the old nawabi ambience of the Mughal period. Lucknow has always been associated with the culture and mannered patterns of behaviour that marked a life lived in courts and feudal Muslim households. In keeping with this lifestyle, Hosain was taught Persian, Urdu and Arabic at home. As the daughter of the Taluqdar of Oudh she was a person of some status. (A sense of the nuances of feudal life in that once princely state can be had from Satyajit Ray's film *Shatranj ke Khiladi* ('The Chess-Players') based on a short story by Premchand.) Her father died when Hosain was eleven, and she and her siblings were brought up by her mother according to a curious mix of orthodoxy and liberalism. At home she experienced life more or less in purdah. The women's quarters were separate, the way they are in *Sunlight on a Broken Column*, and though she and her sisters did not observe the practice of purdah when they went out, we are told that their car had silk curtains at the windows, which was in fact a form of purdah (p.viii and cf. also p.88; the literal meaning of purdah is 'curtain'). Outside the home, however, Hosain studied in the elite La Martiniere school and, later, at the Isabella Thoburn College. She was also influenced by the nationalist movement and the Progressive Writers' Group in the 1930s. Although after 1947 she lived abroad, Hosain continued to be associated with India, dividing her time between her country of birth and her country of residence, and anchoring her own women's programme on the BBC Eastern Service.

Approaching sunlight on a broken column

14   Hosain's early life coincided with the years of the freedom struggle. Virtually all educated middle-class Indian homes were affected by the ideological issues contouring this struggle. The call for *swaraj* and *swadeshi* goods (goods manufactured in India) had an especially emotive appeal to large numbers of people, and Gandhi's efforts to mobilize people into spinning their own cloth had also captured the imagination of patriotic

FRAGMENTING NATIONS AND LIVES

Indians. Hosain's novel describes how Laila and her friends took to wearing coarse hand-spun cotton saris – a symbolic gesture of protest, which offended the sensibilities of women like her aunt Saira and the hawk-nosed Begum Sahiba (p.130). Laila's idealism is balanced by her ability to look at those around her objectively and not be swayed by rhetoric and jingoism. She survives the terrible years of Partition, when the family is divided much the way the country was, so that in retrospect Hosain is able to offer a hope for sanity that is particularly relevant to the troubled relations between India and Pakistan today.

Writing women's lives

15   The autobiographical nature of *Sunlight on a Broken Column* makes it very appropriate to pursue further discussion of it within the context of women's writing about their own situation in India. While the compositions of early Indian women writers were known and read through the ages, recent feminist scholarship has attempted to organize these in a more disciplined manner and to show how women in India have, for a long time, documented their lives and experiences. A valuable source here is *Women Writing in India*, ed. by Susie Tharu and K. Lalita (2 vols, Delhi: Oxford University Press, 1993). This groups these women according to historical period and the prevalent social mores and movements of the time. In my own *Caste as Woman*, I use some of these texts to highlight the fact that revolt against the traditional roles of Indian womanhood is not a new thing. At the same time, however, my case is that these accounts and these rebellions were sporadic rather than indicative of any sustained ideological conviction or struggle.

16   Such writing took varied forms, from the the early bhakti poets who wrote popular verse in various regional languages from the eighth to the sixteenth century, to the autobiographical and fictive efforts of women – again in regional (bhasa) languages – in the nineteenth and early twentieth centuries. In spite of the occasional presence of poets such as Toru Dutt (1856–77) and Sarojini Naidu (1879–1949), it was only in the 1950s and 1960s that Indian women writers in English began to gain any real reputation. Nayantara Sahgal's *Prison and Chocolate Cake* (London: Gollancz, 1954) is autobiographical, and her novels have frequently drawn on her life. Other more contemporary women writers – Anita Desai, Shashi Deshpande, Rama Mehta (whose autobiographical novel *Inside the Haveli*, London: Women's Press, 1994, is an interesting example of life in purdah in an orthodox Hindu household) and, most recently, even Arundhati Roy – have written fiction where the personal is central to the main issues and conflicts.

17   It could of course be argued that this is true of all writing and that autobiographical fiction cuts across cultures. Why it becomes a point of interest in women writers in India is because conventionally women have not been given to public displays of their private lives. If one looks at the work of the early bhakti poets in India, what is significant is the unambiguous presence of the 'I' factor and the sense it gives of communities of women. The compositions narrate, with remarkable irreverence, the minutiae and trivia of their daily lives and their personal conflicts (Bahinabai, for instance, talks of how her fame and renown have made her husband jealous, see *Women Writing in India*, I, 107ff.).

LITERARY THEORY AND CRITICISM

18   In later autobiographical writing, while home and family continue to play an important part, writers will still talk of learning to read and write in secret. The Bengali
writer Rassundari Devi (1810–?), author of *Amar Jiban*, describes how she wrote out
the characters of the alphabet on the charcoal-blackened walls of the kitchen. Women
such as Binodini Dasi (1863–1941, author of the Bengali work *Amar Katha*), and
Hamsa Wadkar (1923–72, author of the Marathi work *Sangatye Aika*), both performing artists, are explicit about the way women like them were manipulated by men.

19   Other writers have written of their lives and, indirectly, of women's lives. The
Bengali novel *Nabankur* by Sulekha Sanyal (1928–63) describes how the little girl
Chobi was censured and discriminated against for being a daughter, but shows Chobi
leaving home. All these writers feature in Volume 1 of *Women Writing in India*. Also
included there is a story by Lalithambika Antharjanam (b.1909). Her account of
her determined bid for an independent existence as a writer is told in 'Childhood
Memories' (see Text 9.1). The poet Indira Sant (b.1914), writing in Marathi, uses
the personal to project a politics very similar to that of feminism. Finally in these
examples, writing in Bengali, Mahasweta Devi (b.1926) puts the lives of tribal
women into her fiction, often using the all-pervasive influence of Hindi cinema and
its insidiously exploitative lyrics to highlight sexual atrocities and oppression as in
her novel *Stanyadayani* ('The Wet-Nurse/Breast Giver') of 1980. Three stories by
Devi can be found in translation in *Imaginary Maps* (translated and introduced by
Gayatri Chakravorty Spivak, London: Routledge, 1995). Another, 'Shishu', appears
in Volume 2 of *Women Writing in India* along with three poems by Indira Sant (see
pp.236–51, 123–6).

The personal and the political

20   In this section I want to focus specifically on the way fiction is a means of telling wom-
en's lives, and a means of autobiography, in relation to *Sunlight on Broken Column*.
For me, Anita Desai's introduction offers an interesting way into such questions. It is
tempting to see this introduction as a relatively innocent affair. The presence of any
kind of introduction is of a piece with the fact that the novel is published as a 'Modern
Classic', but the publishers are keen to avoid too scholarly an appearance: the introduction is more like a recommendation from a friend than the kind of thing one finds
in an edition of Jane Austen. Students might see a consonance between this and the
'personal' nature of the fiction. That said, the opening sentences do touch on an important aspect of the political nature of the novel; Desai writes,

> In India, the past never disappears. It does not even become transformed into
> a ghost. Concrete, physical, palpable – it is present everywhere. Ruins, monu-
> ments, litter the streets, hold up the traffic, create strange islands in the moder-
> nity of the cities. No one fears or avoids them – goats and cows graze around
> them, the poor string up ropes and rags and turn them into dwellings, election
> campaigners and cinema distributors plaster them with pamphlets – and so
> they remain a part of the here and now, of today.

(p.v)

FRAGMENTING NATIONS AND LIVES

The opening lines of Desai's introduction to *Sunlight on a Broken Column* are almost an echo of what Naipaul had attempted to convey in *An Area of Darkness* nearly thirty years earlier, when he spoke of the remnants of Indian relics in the Trinidad home of his boyhood: string cots, brass vessels, images of deities, one ruined harmonium, wooden printing blocks which were never used, all brought from India by his grandparents (V.S. Naipaul, *An Area of Darkness*, Harmondsworth: Penguin, 1979, p.29). Naipaul had been amazed at the tendency to cling to this dilapidated past, symbolized by objects, rituals and customs, and, as he grew up, had become obsessed enough with what he did not understand to travel to India and attempt to decipher the mysteries of this area of darkness.

21   Desai's introduction uses the observations about the past quoted above to comment on Hosain's writing. Hosain's novel and her collection of short stories 'are monuments to that past', Desai suggests, but while monuments are often 'grey, cold and immutable', Hosain's books are 'delicate and tender, like new grass, and they stir with life and the play of sunlight and rain ... To read them is like wrapping oneself up in one's mother's wedding sari, lifting the family jewels out of a faded box and admiring the glitter, inhaling the musky perfume of old silks in a camphor chest' (p.vi).

22   These remarks are obviously meant to be complimentary, but I think they are revealing in ways that perhaps Desai did not intend. It is true that the past is very central to Indian life, but if cattle and goats graze around monuments it is not a peculiarly Indian attribute of that past that makes them do so. Rather, it is because in a country overrun with so many living creatures, their presence in the most unlikely places is almost natural. The seeming harmony between man and beast is not so much mystical as part of a larger, and very real, chaos of poverty and deprivation, of contradictions and irrationalities that coexist with pragmatism, making India the kind of enigma that defies simplistic description.

23   However, Desai's romanticized assessment of Hosain's writing (the comparisons to old saris and family jewels) does not just risk merely trivializing the past but also, perhaps unwittingly, colours it with shades of Orientalism. Developments in postcolonial criticism and literature make *Sunlight on a Broken Column* a difficult novel to talk about, and my reservations about Desai's statements arise out of the overtly exotic ambience they give to a novel already replete with it. (I return to this theme in the last section of this chapter.)

24   A simple way into the issue is through the very beginning of the novel:

> The day my Aunt Abida moved from the zenana into the guestroom off the corridor that led to the men's wing of the house, within call of her father's room, we knew Baba Jan had not much longer to live.
>
> (p.14)

Death, the zenana and the men's wing. In just one sentence, Hosain brings in three elements that make for the dramatic. From this point onwards, the filling in of exotic details never stops: the quarrelling maid-servants, the men-servants, the sweepers, the gardeners, the washerman and the old faithful family retainer Hakiman Bua, with her quaint and colourful turn of phrase – 'Your books will eat you. They will dim the

LITERARY THEORY AND CRITICISM

light of your lovely eyes, my moon princess, and then who will marry you, owl-eyed, peering through glasses?' (p.14). But as the story develops, these exotic details often carry political resonances. The exotic details do not form a comfortable shell because Independence and its aftermath are overriding concerns in the novel. The decision to stay on in India or migrate to Pakistan becomes a major subject of conflict in the family, with opinions and personalities sharply polarized on the issue.

25   Within these political resonances, the nature of the family and the stranglehold it can have on individual lives are at the centre of the novel. In India, the family is at once the source of much strength and of the near-total loss of individual freedom. It can make issues like loyalty, honour, respect for one's elders, and for the tried power of tradition override all concerns of individual happiness. Laila's grandfather Baba Jan is important to the novel because he holds the old feudal family together. This becomes clear from the conversation Laila has with her cousin Zahra, the one who 'said her prayers five times a day, read the Quran for an hour every morning, sewed and knitted and wrote the accounts' (p.14). Zahra is worried that Baba Jan's death will change the old ways, that their Uncle Hamid with his 'English ideas' may not want them all to stay together.

26   The role of the zenana is stronger in the first part of the novel, but diminishes once Baba Jan dies. Hosain's description conveys the sense of female bonding that is endemic to Indian life and constitutes so much of its strengths and weaknesses. It is through the zenana that the lives of women like Hakiman Bua, Saliman Bua and Nandi are also incorporated into the novel's canvas, but though Hosain touches on their exploitation, they remain shadowy appendages to a household defined by class privilege.

27   Though segregated, the women of the household form interesting contrasts: the fiery and sensitive Aunt Abida who had been rebel enough to spurn Uncle Mohsin's interest in her; her more subservient sister Aunt Majida, a quiet if somewhat whiny woman given to preying on people's sympathies and making a fetish of her religious absorption; and Aunt Majida's daughter Zahra, who fits the role of the dutiful young girl described in the passage quoted above. Interestingly, through the conventional Zahra, Hosain seems to allow the reader at least to think about the idea that liberation might mean a range of things depending on social class and education. Once married, Zahra seems to Laila a quite different – and physically assertive – person: 'Another year', she tells Laila, 'and you will have finished your studies, you will be taken everywhere, you will probably be married. Don't shake your head, you cannot always live an unnatural life.' Listening to her Laila observes how, as Zahra stretched her arms above her head, 'her blouse was tight across her breasts. No more loose, shapeless clothes, no more stooping and hunching of shoulders to conceal and deny one's body' (p.141).

28   Zahra even takes the differently rebellious Laila under her wing, bringing her out of purdah and dressing her up, dragging her to public events in defiance of their Aunt Saira's reservations. The orphaned Laila had been brought up by Aunt Abida in a relatively less constrained manner. But in contrast to Zahra, Aunt Abida, once married, is totally robbed of the spark she had always possessed. When she visits, Laila notices that she looks withdrawn, and that 'The two days her husband had stayed she had centred all attention on his care and comfort, as if everyone and everything else was secondary' (p.138). Much later, paying her a visit, Laila experiences the tensions and

210

jealousies of a zenana very different from the one she had grown up in. There is no bonding here, only ingrowing pettiness and spite:

> In the days that followed I grew to sense the extent of their antagonism against Aunt Abida. They resented the sensitiveness of a character beyond their reach and understanding. They attacked what was bigger than their comprehension with petty thrusts.
>
> The jealousies and frustrations in that household of women were intangible like invisible webs spun by monstrous, unseen spiders.
>
> And yet without each other they had no existence. Physically and mentally their lives crushed each other. (p.251)

When the time comes for Laila to leave, Aunt Abida breaks down and weeps, something she had also done the night before she was married. This is the only real display of emotion she allows herself, and she is dry-eyed when she says goodbye in front of the other women. Yet, even in these moments of intimacy, complete intellectual honesty is impossible. Laila knows that she would not be able to tell her about her love for Ameer because of the distance of tradition.

29   Her fears are not unfounded, for Aunt Abida is consistent throughout the novel in her insistence on the rightness of the elders. The woman who had argued that Zahra and Laila needed to be present when Zahra's future is discussed had, even in that unusual moment, held on to the inviolability of duty and obedience. In reply to Uncle Mohsin's sarcastic query as to whether she would have Zahra choose her life partner, she admits that this would be unwise since the girl had had neither the upbringing nor the opportunity for such a choice. She could, however, 'be present while we make the choice, hear our arguments, know our reasons, so that later on she will not doubt our capabilities and question our decisions. That is the least I can do' (p.21).

30   Marriages had to be arranged because individual choice suggested a preference for love which is equated with sin over a love oriented to one's family and duty: 'love between man and woman was associated with sex, and sex was sin' (p.312). To Aunt Abida's way of thinking, Laila's decision to marry Ameer was unforgivable: 'You have been defiant and disobedient. You have put yourself above your duty to your family ... You have let your family's name be bandied about by scandal-mongers and gossips. You have soiled its honour on their vulgar tongues' (ibid.).

31   The notion of family honour, or *izzat*, and its hold on social behaviour remains strong even today. It informs the cinema of Bollywood as much as it does day-to-day life. As I emphasize in *Caste as Woman*, while *izzat* in many instances is particularly circumscribing of women's lives, it also makes individual action difficult for both men and women, particularly in relation to marriage and codes of behaviour. It was these considerations that had made marriage between Laila's cousin Kemal and her childhood friend Sita unthinkable. Though Laila rejects the old pressures of class and background when she marries Ameer, the past remains important to her, and it is to exorcize the ghosts of the past that she eventually returns to the old family home in Hosanpur in Part Four of the novel. The reflective tone here surely prompts the reader

LITERARY THEORY AND CRITICISM

beyond a romanticized view of the past into the same kind of concerned feeling and thinking about its meaning and values.

Nationalism and the politics of partition

32   Attia Hosain's novel describes the middle-class dilemma as many of her Muslim characters debate whether to stay on in India or move to Pakistan. The trauma of Partition haunts the Indian subcontinent even today and has found expression in literature both in English and in the regional languages. Among the better-known novels representing the humanitarian crisis of the time are Khushwant Singh, *Train to Pakistan* (London: Chatto & Windus, 1956); Amitav Ghosh, *The Shadow Lines* (London: Bloomsbury, 1988); and Bapsy Sidhwa's *Ice Candy Man* (London: Heinemann, 1988, but republished as *Cracking India*, Minneapolis: Milkweed Editions, 1991). There is also a large number of short stories about Partition. Bhisham Sahni, 'The Train Has Reached Amritsar', and Ajneya [S.H. Vatsayan], 'Getting Even', convey the feelings of those on the evacuee trains that have become a symbol of the horror of the time (see Texts 9.3 and 9.4). Lalithambika Antharjanam's story 'A Leaf in the Storm' (see Text 9.2) is particularly interesting because although it graphically depicts the reality of events it was written in Kerala by a woman who had never been to the areas of India most affected by the violent events of Partition; in this respect, it shows the power of these events in the Indian consciousness. Saadat Hasan Manto, on the other hand, was born in the Punjab, the area most affected. Perhaps his best-known story, 'Toba Tek Singh' is, however, distinct among those I refer to here in taking a more oblique stance in relation to the violence – it begins 'A couple of years after the Partition of the country, it occurred to the respective governments of India and Pakistan that inmates of lunatic asylums, like prisoners, should also be exchanged' (see Text 9.5, p.351). Another collection is *Writings on India's Partition*, ed. by Ramesh Mathur and Mahendra Kulasrestha (Calcutta: Simant Publications, 1976). Writings on Partition are not confined to prose, however. In India poems depicting the feelings and mood of the time, such as Amrita Pritam's 'Ai Akan Waris Shah Nu' ('To Waris Shah I Say'), are regularly anthologized; Anju Makhija and Menka Shivdasani have recently edited an anthology of Sindhi poetry on Partition.

33   Partition has also become an important theme in Indian cinema with a number of films being based on novels and stories, including *Train to Pakistan* based on Kushwant Singh's novel and *1947-Earth* based on *Ice Candy Man*. Mention might also be made here of the film *Garam Hava*, which has a script by the well-known writer Ismat Chugtai based on an unpublished short story of her own, and the influential television serial *Tamas* (based on Bhisham Sahni's novel first translated as *Kites Will Fly*, Delhi: Vikas Publishing House, 1981, and now as *Tamas*, Delhi: Penguin, 1988).

34   Comparison of *Sunlight on a Broken Column* with any of these texts would be valuable not least because it is likely to highlight the way that although the 'family' – with its varied connotations, of love, belonging, duty, loyalty and *izzat* – forms the centre of the novel, it is the politics of the time that gives the book its flavour. Much of the novel is set in the years preceding Independence. It ends with the way Independence affected Laila's family and mirrors the complex events that shaped the nationalist struggle.

212

FRAGMENTING NATIONS AND LIVES

35   Laila's family, which represents the Taluqdars, or the landed gentry, is rooted in the mannered courtesies of a class that was to become socially redundant very soon. There is a period touch to Hosain's descriptions of Baba Jan and his three loyal friends (pp.33–4). As Laila observes,

> Baba Jan had ostensibly little in common with his three friends ... Yet they had in common a strange arrogance and a will to exercise power – always to be in a position which forced men to reach up to them; and if they ever stepped down themselves, it was an act of grace. In varying degrees they had been helped by birth, privilege and wealth to assume such a position; but without some intrinsic quality they could not have maintained it.

(p.34)

This feudalism, intrinsic to Indian society since at least 1200, still survives though in a less assertive form. It may be seen in the insistence on division of labour as being a sign of social and caste status, because certain tasks are perceived as demeaning.

36   Laila also hints at the growing nexus between men like these and political power. The Raja of Amirpur, a patron of the arts and of philanthropic causes, was 'politically powerful, able to influence the elections of councillors and the decisions of ministers'. In spite of the privileges that the four men enjoyed, their commitment to their little world was complete. They 'loved the city to which they belonged, and they lived and behaved as if the city belonged to them' (p.35). Implicit here is the old feudal notion of *mai-baap* (the paternalistic face of feudalism, in which the feudal lord was seen as father and mother) that was also cleverly used by the British in India to manipulate the loyalty of the 'natives'.

37   The freedom struggle and its milestones affect individual lives in much the same way that family loyalties do. Laila's cousins Asad and Zahid had lost their father in the cause of the Khilafat movement. This movement was triggered off by the British betrayal of their promise made to Indian Muslims during the First World War, that the position of the Sultan of Turkey (who was the Khilafa, or religious head of Muslims the world over) would remain unaffected by the outcome of the war. Gandhi was associated with the leaders of the movement almost from the beginning, helping them devise a Khilafat Day and encouraging them to share in the idea of non-cooperation. Not surprisingly, Asad and Zahid had been brought up to wear hand-spun cloth and to hate all things that were foreign. A firebrand idealist, Asad is repeatedly in trouble and is the first to defy Uncle Hamid, who succeeds Baba Jan as the family patriarch, and leave home. It is interesting – as Hosain allows Laila to be more liberated – to compare how she presents the possibility of a relationship with Asad as somehow still impossible as compared to the relationship that develops with Ameer. How, for example, are we to understand the fact that the man Laila loves joins the British Army, while the man held at a distance is the one involved in Indian politics?

38   While Zahid leaves for Pakistan only hours before Independence, on the ill-fated train that arrives at its destination filled with corpses, Asad stays on in India. He grows increasingly involved in the freedom struggle, but then the tone of the narration shifts after Ameer's death when he gets to be Laila's source of comfort and hope:

We had dreamed when we were young of Independence; he was now part of it with all its undreamt-of reality – its triumphs and defeats, its violent aftermath, the breaking-up of our social order, and the slow emergence of another.

(p.318)

Laila's student days are peppered with protests, black-flag demonstrations against the Viceregal visit, and riots in which her young cousins are repeatedly injured, but from which Hosain keeps Laila herself aloof. The Civil Disobedience movement initiated by Gandhi meets with a mixed response from members of the family. The uncle of Laila's childhood friend Sita has been a freedom fighter, but Sita herself is shown as disillusioned with idealism (pp.186–7). Her college friend Nita is rusticated for her involvement in what was to be a non-violent protest. She dies two days after reaching home as a result of head injuries received during a police lathi-charge.

39   Laila, Asad, and Kemal are important in the context of Independence and the period following because they debunk fundamentalist distortions about the Hindu-Muslim divide. While it would be simplistic to pretend that irrational suspicion and hatred do not colour attitudes on either side of the border, significantly large numbers of Indian Muslims think of India as 'home', a choice made without any apparent mental conflict.

40   The period covered by the novel sees the freedom movement reach maturity, and ends with the creation of India and Pakistan. The communal political divide had begun as far back in 1905 with the setting up of the Muslim League and the division of Bengal along communal lines. (Lord Curzon, then Viceroy, had hoped this would undermine the strong nationalist movement in the province but in fact it had almost the opposite effect.) Relations between Hindu and Muslim nationalists, however, became more tense and heated as freedom came to seem a less nebulous goal. *Sunlight on a Broken Column* has characters repeatedly questioning the possibility of Hindus and Muslims being able to coexist in a free India. As students, Laila's college friends Nita and Nadira had argued fiercely about their differing ideologies and political convictions, but these had been arguments between two individuals belonging to different faiths. As Partition becomes an imminent event, such divisions become bitter as even members within families find themselves aligned differently.

41   Uncle Hamid represents the interests of the feudal Taluqdars, but his basic loyalty is specifically to the values of an India formed under British rule. He feels betrayed when Saleem confesses his love for Nadira and campaigns for the Muslim League which she and her mother are wholly committed to. Laila talks of the courteous city of Lucknow being invaded by harsh voices raised in dissent. At home, Saleem's demagoguery accuses the Congress of 'a strong anti-Muslim' bias which would surface once the British had left: 'The majority of Hindus have not forgotten or forgiven the Muslims for having ruled over them for hundreds of years. Now they can democratically take revenge', says Saleem during an argument about the creation of Pakistan. His father, Uncle Hamid, and later his brother Kemal, do not subscribe to Saleem's paranoia. 'I always found it was possible for Hindus and Muslims to work together on a political level', Uncle Hamid says in reply to Saleem, 'and live together in personal friendship' (p.234). You might like to take a passage like this and try to see whether Hosain aims to press the reader to take one side or another.

FRAGMENTING NATIONS AND LIVES

42   The harsher realities of the political arena are present in the way friends betray one another. Uncle Hamid finds himself let down by his old friend Waliuddin, who joins the Muslim League and actually agrees to contest the election against him. He is even supported in this move by Agarwal, Sita's father, a staunch Congress supporter, because the Congress and the Muslim League momentarily agree to sink their differences to fight the bigger enemy, the British. Uncle Hamid is compelled to withdraw his political nomination and represent the Taluqdars.

43   Though caught up in their own private dilemmas of love, freedom, and individual choices, Laila and her cousins and friends find the larger world of national politics affecting their lives. Zahra more or less ignores the freedom movement, while Sita is caught up within it. Eventually, and in her own way, Laila allies herself with the nationalist cause, and at the end of the novel finds her freedom through Asad, the cousin she had been close to while she was growing up.

44   The final showdown of the main period of the story takes place a month before Independence. At the family reunion, the intended rational discussion to decide the future ends in anger, reaching a point of no return despite Kemal's plea for peace. Saleem and Nadira migrate to Pakistan with the fervour of new converts. As Laila observes, 'it was easier for them thereafter to visit the whole wide world than the home which had once been theirs' (p.289). On a first reading it perhaps comes as a surprise that the story does not stop here; certainly if it had done so the political messages of the book would have been different. As it is, Part Four takes the reader even closer to Laila's less politically involved point of view. The effect is heightened by the fact that many of the characters are absent from the physical location in which the story now takes place. In this last part, back home, those who elect to stay on find that the changed order and political choices have far-reaching implications. Besides the loss of the privileges of taluqdari, Laila's Aunt Saira has to come to terms with the fact that Saleem's share of the family property will be treated as evacuee property, and that it will be given over to complete strangers. Laila's retreat into the hills has not protected her from the terrible violence before and after Partition, and she reacts sharply to Zahra's accusation that that she had chosen the softer option:

> 'Where were you, Zahra, when I sat up through the nights, watching village after village set on fire, each day nearer and nearer? ... Do you know who saved me and my child? Sita, who took us to her house, in spite of putting her own life in danger with ours. And Ranjit, who came from his village, because he had heard of what was happening in the foothills and was afraid for us. He drove us back, pretending we were his family, risking discovery and death.'
>
> (p.304)

Purdah; the past and the future

45   Attia Hosain's place in the canon of Indian writing in English appears assured. She cannot be said to have star quality, the way Nayantara Sahgal, Salman Rushdie, Vikram Seth, Amitav Ghosh, Arundhati Roy, or even Anita Desai do, but she has been studied, talked about, included in overviews, and, more recently, rehabilitated within

the genre of gender studies. She figures sporadically in anthologies that deal with women's writing and focus on themes such as purdah. *Margins of Erasure: Purdah in the Subcontinental Novel in English*, ed. by Jasbir Jain and Amina Amin (Delhi: Sterling Publishers, 1995) contains two articles on *Sunlight on a Broken Column*.

46   In the first, 'Beyond Purdah: *Sunlight on a Broken Column*', Sarla Palkar speaks of the novel's 'empathy and compassion for all the marginalised groups ... it seeks to go beyond the boundaries or purdahs created by the considerations of gender, race, religion, class, and also nation' (p.118). According to Amina Amin, the second essayist, 'The novel rests on a tightly controlled balance between a life within the household, ordained, enclosed, warm and secure but restricted by demands of modesty, and a life outside, free but insecure and confusing' ('Tension Between Restriction and Freedom: The Purdah Motif in Attia Hosain's *Sunlight on a Broken Column*', p.119).

47   In both these essays, the emphasis is on the element of purdah as a metaphor for women's lives. The men do not figure in the analyses except in passing, as appendages to Laila's ups and downs in her zenana-contoured life. It is tempting to dismiss these omissions as an overemphasis on women's concerns by women, except that my own reading of the novel also suggests that it is the women that hold the story together and are, to a greater or less extent, 'characterized'. It is in the world of the zenana that Hosain is most at ease, and though a large part of the story deals with perhaps the most tumultuous period of Indian history, it never really absorbs our interest as much as the other little world within which Laila and her aunts live.

48   This can take us back, but in a more qualified way, to the issue of the exotic raised above (see p.128). For all Laila's idealism and strength I would argue that the exotic element threatens to overwhelm our sense of this political side to her character. This is perhaps natural at one level, since these details define Laila's world. It is when they seem chosen for effect that it becomes difficult not to remember that this novel was first published in Great Britain and that it was perhaps an early post-Independence effort by a 'native' at capturing the nuances of those years. Part of the problem may be the novelist's own weakness for local colour of the more exotic kind, relevant enough in the normal scheme of things but just a little too laid on in the overall context of the novel. Whether it is the lush description of festivals (pp.40–1), or the cries and colours of the vendors of sweets, vegetables and bangles (pp.58–9), or the way cows, buffaloes, curds, ghee, and the smell of acrid dung are all present in one amazing paragraph on page 98, the predilection for the 'Indian' detail is obvious. There is nothing fundamentally wrong in an Indian novel being obviously filled with the sights and sounds of India. My reservations have to do with a sense that a certain past is, overall, selectively presented in a way that is nostalgic and even sentimental. The larger, and more violent, reality which at times seems really important in the novel thus risks, ironically, appearing irrelevant.

49   Meenakshi Mukherjee comes closest to my own sense of unease. For Mukherjee, the trouble, particularly with the last section of the novel,

> lies in the confusion of purpose. Does the novelist intend to present from Laila's point of view a picture of men and manners in a particular period of Indian history, or does she intend to present one individual's groping towards

FRAGMENTING NATIONS AND LIVES

self-realisation? If it is the former, then the case history method of the past has some validity; but if the novel is taken as a personal document the last chapter becomes extraneous.

(*The Twice-Born Fiction: Themes and Techniques of the Indian Novel in English*, Delhi: Heinemann India, 1971, p.53)

Mukherjee in fact sees the end as an 'orgy of sentimentalism' (p.81), whereas I would suggest that sentimentalism is intrinsic in the whole depiction. Where it works (as in the intricate descriptions of women's lives in that household), such sentimentalism is camouflaged by the fictive strength of personal emotion at its best. It is less successful when the canvas expands to take in the larger world of political uncertainty and the way it affects the lives and careers of the men in the family.

50   While the rhetoric of political debate weaves its way through the novel, the personal and the political interconnect in a loosely knit, somewhat unsatisfactory manner. As already stated, the issues with which the novel is concerned appear rather differently in the post-colonial context. There is virtually no attempt at anything more than a mere narration of details, hardly any criticism, explicit or implicit, of the old ways or of the politics of the freedom movement. None of the actual violence preceding Independence touches the lives of the characters. Neither do the harsher paradoxes of displacement affect Hosain's characters as they do the characters of Amitav Ghosh's more recent *The Shadow Lines*.

51   In spite of Asad's occasional bloody clothes and wounds, the sweat and gore of the freedom struggle or the nightmare of Partition do not really find a place in the story. The men fail to become much more than a forum for intellectual debate. The novel's chief interest lies in its women, particularly Laila, who struggles against her class background and conditioning. Having said that, one should be wary of seeing the picture in too black and white terms. A good many novels and stories which do attempt to depict the actual violence of Partition seem to be shot through with a kind of melodrama which equally fails to engage the reader with the complexity of the situation. Comparison of the novel with the Partition texts referred to in the section 'Nationalism and the politics of Partition' above would be interesting here: for example, setting a 'direct' account of events such as is contained in one of the train stories against Manto's 'Toba Tek Singh' and against Part Four of *Sunlight on a Broken Column*.

52   I would like to end by suggesting that for an Indian reader like myself the novel's underlying themes – the freedom struggle, the loss of an old feudal, semi-aristocratic order, life and love behind the purdah, and the other details included in this family saga – add up eventually to an exotic story, charming primarily for its remoteness from its audience. Nevertheless, this cannot take away the historical interest of the story, both for the development of the Indian novel in English and as a representation of a way of life that is unknown to most of its readers. Laila stands as a metaphor for that middle state – an isthmus between larger and almost overwhelming forces – that many Indian women found themselves in during the 1930s and 1940s. For many Indian women readers now, the interest, however, goes beyond the historical; in its imagining of Laila, they see their own situation today.

LITERARY THEORY AND CRITICISM

Questions and exercises[1]

1 From the histories of India that you have been reading, trace the key events in the development of the Indian independence movement as one demanding separate Hindu and Muslim states. What role would you expect literature to play in this process?

2 On the basis of your reading of works by contemporary Indian women writers (including at least one writing in India about India), consider the evidence for the notion that in India the sociocultural context ... remains by and large conservative and orthodox' (p.124 above).

3 'In considering Indian women's accounts of how they have struggled for freedom we should be particularly conscious of the need to consider cultural difference.' Discuss this comment, drawing on as wide a range of examples of women's writing from India as you can.

4 Compare the representation of Partition in Bhisham Sahni, 'The Train Has Reached Amritsar', Saadat Hasan Manto, 'Toba Tek Singh', and Part Four of *Sunlight on a Broken Column*. Consider overall how far these texts provide evidence for the view that imagining the events of 1947 was very difficult for writers.

5 Compare the presentation of the social structures of India in *Sunlight on a Broken Column* and *Kanthapura*. Can these structures be seen as an important element in the structure of 'the nation' as it was imagined by those seeking independence?

Textual and rhetorical questions

Textual

1. Before critically approaching Attia Hosain's novel, *Sunlight on a Broken Column*, Vrinda Nabar provides some background context. What are those references to context and explain their significance in engaging with a criticism of the novel? (Paragraphs 1–12.) Reason in 150 words.

2. Nabar discusses the issues of family in a traditional South Asian society and the roles of men, the women's wing in a house, *purdah*, women's bonding, family honour, the men's wing in a house, and marriage. What are the traits of feminist criticism that the essayist focuses on and how does the novel oppose traditional patriarchal ideology? You can bring in Marxist critical viewpoints by discoursing male ideology which seems to be the concern of the essayist (200–50 words).

3. Two terms bind the entire essay: "Fragmenting" is corresponded with the novel's key term "broken." What is the conceptual relationship between "fragmenting" and "broken"? Are they synonymous? Argue in around 50 to 60 words.

Rhetorical

1. Discuss how Nabar uses the technique of precedence to put forwards her analysis of Attia Hosain's novel. Do you think that the use of comparison is another related key technique? Explain. (100 words).

218

2. There are many details and references used in the essay which may give the impression that Nabar has a particular community of readers in mind. Who are they? Provide examples to answer the question (50 words).

Discussion questions

1. Read paragraphs 9 ("In India ..."), 23 ("However ..."), and 31 ("The notion...").[2] Nabar discusses the role and nature of family: The dominance of family loyalty, honour, and communal source of strength, over individual freedom. How is family presented by her interpretation of the novel? Do you think the nature and role of family have not changed much in countries like Pakistan, India, Nepal, Sri Lanka, and/or Bangladesh?
2. Transformation of historical memory into material memory (or into art, literature, and media) generates mental memory (culturally defined ways of thinking).[3] Through such transformations, Attia Hosain's novel *Sunlight on a Broken Column* does not remain a document of the individual, but the autobiographical traces are mediated. Reading such nuances of memory, discuss Hosain's work as witness documentation in the context of the history of Partition of India and Pakistan (1000 words).
3. Kaiser Haq sees a pervasiveness of historical voice as memory all around us. Read the part of the poem selected from "How many Buddhas Can They Destroy?" and write your response (500 words).

When you cling to things you have
Or crave a little you don't
And a voice whispers
Let go
For everything is impermanent
It's the Buddha speaking

When your mind is a medley
Of wayward thoughts
And a voice whispers
Get a grip on yourself
It's the Buddha speaking

When your vocal cords are taut and ready
To hurl a volley of abuse
Your fists are itching to fly
And a voice whispers
Take it easy
It's the Buddha speaking

When your hand reaches
Under the table
For a wad of banknotes

And you hear a cautionary voice
It's the Buddha speaking

When you are panting around the maze
Of the rat race
And you hear an amused voice tell you
What a waste of energy it is
It's the Buddha speaking

When you have given up all hope for the world
And place a fantasy finger
On a nuclear button to blow it up
And a gentle voice
Counsels love for all there is
It's the Buddha speaking.

Inter-textual discussions

1. Read Hosain's *Sunlight on a Broken Column* and discuss the world of men depicted in terms of loyalty and honour (150 words).
2. The law of the father[4] is the law inside the threshold of a house where traditional Indian and Pakistani families live around the metaphors like *ghunghat*, *purdah*, *lajja*, *sindoor*, *bhabi*, *chunari*, *sari*, and *salwar-kamij* (find such terms in your cultural locations). The law of the father functions outside the threshold as masculinity. Compare the metaphors of inside and outside. Or are there such overriding metaphors for the male? (1000 words).
3. Bollywood Hindi movies like *Jab Jab Phool Khile* and *Raja Hindustani* demand a lot from women. Such movies were box office hits that exploited the traditional family ideology. Contemporary Hindi movies have questioned and rejected such demands on women and are box office hits. Do you think the times are changing?

Critical and creative thinking[5]

1. Eliot argues in *Tradition and Individual Talent*, " the more perfect the artist, the more completely separate in him will be the man who suffers and the mind which creates."[6] Write a story or a poem based on your experience on any issue of your interest and apply subtle rhetorical strategies to be neutral. You may like to read about English Romantic poet John Keats's idea of "Negative capability" mentioned in the letter to his brothers George and Tom.[7]
2. Surrealist painter, Salvador Dali's *Persistence of Memory* documents the brutalities of war. Observe the painting and discuss what forms memory persists in. Does he take recourse to dream and the unconscious to depict violence? It is not a realist painting. What does he achieve by taking such an unrealistic detour?
3. The passages below are on memory and representation, about pausing and thinking about past experiences. The lines are related to the Western Romantic theory

FRAGMENTING NATIONS AND LIVES

of art of nineteenth-century England. William Wordsworth writes in the *Preface to the Lyrical Ballads*,

> I have said Poetry is the spontaneous overflow of powerful feelings: it takes its origin from emotion recollected in tranquility: the emotion is contemplated till by a species of reaction the tranquility gradually disappears, and an emotion, similar to that which was before the subject of contemplation, is gradually produced, and does itself actually exists in the mind.[8]

S.T. Coleridge in *Biographia Literaria*, defines and categorises imagination as primary and secondary. About primary imagination he writes, "I hold to be the living power and prime Agent of all human Perception, as a repetition in the finite mind of the eternal act of creation in the infinite I Am." He further writes, "The Secondary Imagination I consider as an echo of the former, co-existing with the conscious will, yet still as identical with the primary in the *kind* of its agency and differing only in *degree* and in the *mode* of operation. It dissolves, diffuses, dissipates, in order to re-create; or where the process is rendered impossible, yet still, at all event, it struggles to idealise and to unify. It is essentially *vital*, even as all objects (as objects) are essentially fixed and dead."[9]

The two celebrated passages talk about the idea of memory as recollection when after the experience memory is thawed, softened, and thus recreated as a work of art, an autobiography, a life writing, and a diary. Do you pause and think and recreate?

Notes

1 The questions and exercises are given by Vrinda Nabar.
2 I have provided the first word of the paragraphs in this particular chapter so as to avoid confusion regarding paragraph counting.
3 See Erill Astrid. (2008). "Cultural Memory Studies: An Introduction" in Erill, Astrid & Ansgar Nunning (Eds.). *Media and Cultural Memory: An International and Interdisciplinary Handbook*. Berlin: Walter de Gruyter. (1–18).
4 The meanings I have given are cultural connotations. I have not provided any dictionary meaning but tried to familiarize non-South Asian readers about the cultural norms and ideologies associated with the terms. All these objects also have stylistic and fashionable uses and significance too. *Ghunghat* (veil or headscarf to cover the full or half of the face by Hindu women to show respect to males or strangers), *purdah* (literally screening or cover with the similar reason for use as that of *ghunghat*), *lajja* (literally shame, and it is suggestive of an attribute of especially women to keep family honor), *sindoor* (red or orange vermillion powder put on the forehead as a mark of being a married woman), *bhabi* (is elder brother's wife, an ideal and respected member and yet it also means a demanding term of suffering and sacrifice in South Asian cultures), *chunari* (scarf), *sari*, and *salwar-kamij* (they are traditional dresses worn by women to show womanly moderation and sophistication unlike some Western dresses which reveal a woman's body).
5 The information and questions are not directly related to the essay. The terms 'tradition' and 'memory' in this section can also be understood within literary discourses I have cited.
6 T.S. Eliot (1920). "Tradition and Individual Talent" in *Sacred Wood: Essays on Poetry and Criticism*. London: Methune (25–30).

221

LITERARY THEORY AND CRITICISM

7 John Keats writes to his brothers George and Tom Keats, "What quality went to form a Man of Achievement, especially in Literature and which Shakespeare possessed so enormously – I mean *Negative Capability* that is when man is capable of being in uncertainties, Mysteries, doubts, without any irritable reaching after fact and reason." See Scott, Grant F. (1958). *Selected Letters of John Keats*. Revised Edition. Cambridge: Harvard University Press: (59–61).

8 Owen, W.J.B. (Ed.). (1969). "Preface [1800]" in *Wordsworth and Coleridge: Lyrical Ballads 1798*. Oxford: Oxford University Press (153–79).

9 See Samuel Taylor Coleridge (1817) "Chapter 13" in *Biographia Literaria*. Ed. Shawcross. (1907) 2nd Vol. London: Oxford University Press.

11

PUNYAKANTE WIJENAIKE

Spectral spaces

Minoli Salgado

My body is everywhere: the bomb which destroys my house also damages my body insofar as the house was already an indication of my body.
Jean-Paul Sartre, *Being and Nothingness*[1]

1   In 1977 Alastair Niven claimed that Punyakante Wijenaike was 'one of the most underestimated fiction writers currently at work in the English language'.[2] Thirty years later she still remains almost unknown in the West. Yet in her writing we find some of the most powerful registers of the relationship between identity and place, belonging and homelessness in Sri Lankan literature in English. What is more, her exploration of a subjectivity under threat of erasure in a shifting landscape bears direct correspondences with political and demographic changes that have taken place in the country over the past fifty years. Unlike Arasanayagam, whose literary resurgence is directly linked to the start of the civil war, Wijenaike's work spans forty years and registers a wide range of cultural shifts, all of which are mediated through an exploration of the link between the individual, the home and the land. As a result it is possible to read her work in a multitude of ways: as nationalist inscriptions of belonging and exclusion, as psychological studies of the effects of dislocation, as feminist affirmations of women's claims to inheritance and as literary explorations of the uncanny or the unhomely. The strength of her work lies in the fact that it invites all these readings while being resistant to appropriation by any one of them, demanding a fluid and flexible reading strategy that is informed by the political events of the time of writing. A spatially mediated study of her work not only accommodates the multiple approaches, allowing movement between them, but also simultaneously reveals the ways in which literary responses to demographic and geopolitical changes serve to create and reconstitute the connections between cultural and territorial boundaries over a significant length of time. As will be seen, hidden behind Wijenaike's ephemeral construction of 'home' lurks the contestatory and materially inflected discourse of territorial control and land rights.

2   Through an extensive oeuvre that encompasses five novels as well as novellas, children's books, autobiographical pieces and over a hundred short stories, Wijenaike's focus has remained on the individual's relationship to his – or, most usually, her – dwelling place, and she has unsettled the construction of 'home' by focusing on the

DOI: 10.4324/9781003213857-11

223

individual's displacement within it. Her first novel, *The Waiting Earth* (1966), explores the estrangement between a peasant farmer and his wife and represents their eventual rehabilitation through physical resettlement. In later novels identity is even more firmly located in domestic space. In *Giraya* (1971) and *Amulet* (1994) the walauwe, or family manor, and the urban ancestral home (both of which are patriarchal, intergenerational domestic spaces) constitute a central character – a formidable, spectral presence that excludes and alienates the main protagonists. In many of her texts homes determine the boundaries of human experience while, at the same time, absorbing the mental and physical energies of their occupants; they contain both forbidden zones and family secrets, such that Wijenaike's exploration of home is configured by that which is unhomely, unhiemlich or uncanny.

3   The spatial configurations of these textual homes are replicated in the formal compression, episodic fragmentation and temporal density of her work. In *Giraya*, for example, events are temporally segmented into the form of an annual journal and spatially confined to a walauwe, and in *An Enemy Within* (1998) the collective home of the city of Colombo is spatially reconfigured through multiple narratives that map the city in a telescoped spatio-temporal zone of a single morning in 1996 at the Central Bank of Colombo. Much of Wijenaike's writing also contains elements of melodrama – a feminine, domestic genre[3] characterised by 'emotion, immobility, enclosed space, and confinement'.[4] It registers a claustrophobic configuration of space that serves to test and menace the limits of social order. Mental illness, incest, homosexuality, child abuse, suicide and murder all lie secreted in the homes of a fading aristocracy and an emergent upper class – a space in which a woman, often a new bride, serves as the unwitting interloper. She is an outsider in her own home – a paradigm of an 'unhomely home', which is used to dramatic political effect in the novella '*An Enemy Within*'. Thus, as will be seen, Wijenaike's work, more than that of any other anglophone writer, explores Freud's formulation (borrowed from Jenstch) of the uncanny or unhomely as the manifestation of an absent presence that serves to menace the represented order.

4   Wijenaike is also notable in being the only anglophone writer of her generation (and perhaps of later generations too) whose work has gained regional mainstream popularity. Her novels have been translated into Sinhala and Tamil (as well as Russian) and *Giraya* has been made into a popular teledrama by Sri Lanka's leading film-maker, Lester James Pieris. The unembellished prose, emotional intensity and dramatic charge of her work have certainly been important factors in contributing to this popularity, but these elements alone – evident in all too many anglophone texts – do not set her work apart. Rather it is in her spatialised representation of otherness, of what Anthony Vidler has called 'the architectural uncanny', that reveals Wijenaike's keen sensitivity to cultural changes and her communication of a broader social malaise and anxiety. For the uncanny or unhomely, as Vidler has shown, is a 'psychoanalytical and aesthetic response to the real shock of the modern' arising out of the transformation of something that seemed homely and familiar into something that is definitely not so. It is, he suggests, a product of postindustrial culture, reflecting the insecurity of a newly established class that is 'not quite at home in its own home'.[5]

5   When relocated to postcolonial Sri Lanka, the exploration of the unhomely in anglophone writing can be seen, through Wijenaike's work, to register the cultural

dislocations suffered by the privileged class whose loss of material wealth was marked by loss of land and by a series of territorially inscribed government policies. The colonising resettlement projects that took place from the 1940s to the 1960s, the land reform movement of the 1970s, rural development and urban expansion, and the civil war itself, serve as the social and political backdrop to Wijenaike's texts linking the shift in class relations to the reterritorialisation and deterritorialisation of the times. Indeed the development of her work, charting as it does a movement from a parable of rural life set in an unspecified location, to personalised fictions of the metropolitan capital where Wijenaike lives, delineates the restless search for habitation of an alienated, female, disenfranchised subjectivity. A chronological consideration of her four main texts thus reveals the ways in which literary representations of subject–space relations reflect, re-evaluate and feminise territorially inscribed cultural transformation.

The lust for land

6   When Wijenaike wrote *The Waiting Earth* in 1966 the literary preoccupation with rural life was still flourishing.[6] Like her Lankan contemporary James Goonewardene, and her Indian precursors Raja Rao and Kamala Markandaya, she sought in rural life and traditions the models of being and thinking that would authenticate the experience of living in a newly independent nation – a concern that might in turn serve to ground and legitimit her writing in English and thereby obviate possible charges of 'cultural treason'.[7] Yet despite this thematic link, *The Waiting Earth* cannot be read as a nationalist novel in the way that Rao's *Kanthapura* and Markandaya's *Nectar in a Sieve* can. There is no sustained, self-conscious effort to indigenise the language or develop a political consciousness as there is in Rao, and neither does Wijenaike engage in the polarising presentation of East–West relations that serves to situate and define the nation in opposition to its former colonial master as Markandaya does. In addition Wijenaike does not simultaneously endorse and interrogate rural life in a bid to focalise the nation's gaze on nationalism in the making, as her counterpart Goonewardene chooses to do.

7   Instead, Wijenaike's novel draws on the unhomely state of landlessness to define and legitimit a model of territorial ownership that has direct bearings on our reading of the spatially situated discourse of otherness that has gained currency since the war. While for most postcolonial writers village or peasant life serves as marker of pannational experience – one that integrates the life and traditions of the rural majority of the nation with the knowable communities of the novel – Wijenaike presents rural life as an ambivalent state of disinheritance in which landless peasants are denied the right to own the land they live and work on. It is a manoeuvre which, as will be seen, has serious repercussions when translated into the politics of the present – a step that Wijenaike has already taken in her writing of a short story sequel to the novel, 'Living on the Edge' (2002). Drawing upon a clearly defined moral terrain, *The Waiting Earth* subtly distinguishes between legitimate and illegitimate ownership. When set within its historical context of peasant resettlement, a symptomatic reading of the novel reveals the contradictory political drives of ethnically engineered socialism – a central plank of the ethnic nationalism that emerged in the late 1950s. In this sense the novel, at once moving and measured in its lyricism, persuasively endorses

LITERARY THEORY AND CRITICISM

controversial territorial measures.[8] The unhomely takes two forms in the novel. First it is characterised by the disorientation and uncertainty of the central characters and is abstracted into an historical condition in which the impact of modernity (in the form of the erosion of class barriers, women's independence, consumerism and Western modes of behaviour and dress) is gradually being felt, along with the material insecurities and cultural uncertainties attendant upon the homeless condition. More specifically, however, the unhomely constitutes the condition of landlessness itself, in which the desired and absent land becomes obsessively fetishised and destabilises the mental equilibrium of the central character, alienating him from his wife and family. Thus while it is important to recognise and applaud Wijenaike's socialist sympathies and humanitarian impulses in foregrounding the grinding poverty and homeless condition of the landless peasant, it is equally necessary to analyse the implications encoded in the ways in which such homelessness is resolved and the unhomely domesticated.

8   *The Waiting Earth* narrates the story of a landless farmer, Podhi Singho, and his wife, Sellohamy, and the former's desire to own land in his native village. This desire expresses a need for security, the fulfilment of which would serve, according to Podhi Singho, to legitimate his belonging to the village; he wishes for

> A small piece of land with roots running deep within it, a piece of earth whose yields will belong to us by right and on which, perhaps, a small house too, a house the wind of misfortunes cannot blow away, because the earth on which it stands is mine by right.
>
> [p. 65]

Owning any other land would be to him 'like living with another man's wife' (p. 66).

9   Yet Wijenaike directly challenges the legitimacy of these 'natural rights' by presenting Podhi Singho's desire for land ownership in his native village as a sexual obsession – one that affirms his need for male sexual mastery in the face of his increasing, but entirely unfounded, distrust of his wife:

> he filled his mind with thoughts of the land and the land alone which Rappiel Appu would get for him. This one thing he had yet to live for, this dream to keep him sane. He made his mind see this land now, made it lie open and naked for him and he saw his own body bend over it and his hand thrust the seed into the waiting earth; felt the warm brown moistness against his flesh as it received the seed with a hungry mouth. He even felt the sweat of his body as he worked and then his pleasure and his pride as he watched the first sprouting of the seed he had sown and the great joy he would feel in the final reaping. This land was his and his alone and it would remain so, for always, faithful to him and him alone. It would never turn and twist this way and that with the change of the wind. Unlike a woman, whatever way the wind blew this land of his would lie flat and straight and always in the same place.
>
> [p. 190]

The unspoken obsession drives husband and wife apart, leading directly to his loss of control and rape of Sellohamy – 'it was the land that had driven him to her' (p. 220)

226

– and to her sense of competing with the land as with a mistress, an 'evil that possessed his body' (p. 264). Podhi Singho's land lust is thus not merely linked to his poverty; his desire to own land is, in a curious reinscription of the patriarchal forces of colonial territoriality which feminised the alien landscape in order to control it, associated with his desire to achieve mastery over his wife. (It is also aggravated by her own landlessness as her unendowered state upon marriage serves to fuel his obsession (p. 27).) Thus Podhi Singho's land lust is both ethically and territorially coded, inscribed into a model of patriarchal, colonial territoriality that serves to de-legitimate it.

10   Against this compelling personal drama is set the government land distribution programme of the 1960s, which offered gifts of uncultivated land in the dry zone to landless peasants on the understanding that they clear and work the land themselves and pass it on, undivided, to a single family heir. It was a program that involved significant demographic and cultural shifts: the rupture of settled communities, the division of families, the migration of southerners to the east, the relocation of Sinhalese to land that separatist Tamils laid historical claim to on the basis of ancestral occupation, and new rights of inheritance that effectively enforced long-term occupation by the Sinhalese in these areas. It is a programme described by Farmer as 'an imposed solution [to poverty and landlessness] which has not grown from indigenous society'.[9] Podhi Singho's resistance to the government offer registers the cultural schism caused by resettlement as it is made on the basis that this alien soil would be akin to marital infidelity (p. 66). By setting up a contrast between Podhi Singho's irrational lust for ownership over local land and his rationalised rejection of alien territory on the basis that it is not legitimately his, Wijenaike reinscribes the connection between territorial boundaries and marital rights and makes a compelling case for the legitimacy of the colonisation scheme. The scheme comes to be justified through the text's neutralisation of Singho's land lust within the ambit of government policy.

11   His views are directly challenged by a fellow villager who has chosen to accept the offer; the latter claims that not only will resettlement on new land end his poverty but also that the legal ownership ties him to the land in perpetuity in a blood bond stronger than marriage:

> A man can be parted from his wife, aiya [older brother], but not from this land. A promise I made that when I die this land must go to my wife, or if she too dies, then to my eldest son and if he too dies, to the second son. If all my sons die then it must go to my eldest daughter and so on down the line. [. . .] This land has been so closely tied to my blood that nothing can part it from me. I also had to promise that I would neither sell nor borrow on this land even if my seven children lay starving during a bad time.
>
> [p. 151]

The novel thus not only legitimates the colonising policies of the newly Independent nation but openly acknowledges the ways in which internal colonisation is naturalised, adopted land indigenised, made native and 'tied to blood'. The movement of the novel, charting Podhi Singho's reconciliation to the government project and his corresponding reconciliation with his wife, serves to justify this government policy of Sinhala resettlement and internal colonisation; Podhi Singho, we are told, 'could send his old roots into the new soil without fear of their dying' (p. 321).

12   It is a perspective that Wijenaike seems to continue to endorse. In 2002 she published a short story sequel to the novel, 'Living on the Edge', in which she depicts Podhi Singho's life some forty years on. The correspondence between Podhi Singho's perspective and the narrator's suggests that Wijenaike does indeed share her central character's views. Podhi Singho's home is now under attack from Tamil Tiger rebels, Sellohamy (whose moral courage and resilience in the novel elevated to her to a symbol of female endurance analogous to the motherland itself) has been killed by terrorists and the possibility of dispossession looms. The legitimacy of the colonisation programme is comprehensively affirmed:

> Even though this new land was dry and hard it was his own through the colonisation scheme. [. . .] The giant water tanks built by his own Kings of the past, stood by to irrigate his new land pulled out of the jungle. [. . .]
> The 'tigers' they called themselves and came to drive him from his own land claiming it as theirs by right.[10]

While the novel's claims to territorial legitimacy and ownership of the new land were endorsed through the socialist message that the ownership was, in part, gained through the peasant's physical investment in it – a message reiterated in the claim that 'the land should belong to those who work on it' (p. 68) – the short story disinvests in such political niceties. By 2002 there appears to be no need to question the historical rights of the Sinhalese to these lands; the legitimacy of the colonisation scheme is unquestioned and the land is further reclaimed through a direct link with the ancient irrigation system of Sinhala kings – one of the nation's historical treasures – which stands as an enduring physical marker of ancestral control and ownership, sanctioning Podhi Singho's settlement in the region. While historical evidence does indeed suggest, as this story does, that the appropriated land was neglected and going to waste, 'pulled from the jungle' and tamed, the ideological imperatives of Wijenaike's story suggest a specific political affiliation when situated within the context of war. The overassertion of territorial legitimacy in the later work corresponds to the territorial unease of a nation in which land rights are being violently contested by armed force. Wijenaike's story also powerfully registers how the landless who have been resettled are themselves victims of land disputes and are threatened with dispossession once more. With no counter-narrative of Tamil dispossession to balance it, the unhomely in Wijenaike's representation of rural life can thus be seen to register the cultural and social ruptures attendant on an ethnicised national politics – a social vision that is telescoped into a reflection of class dynamics in her novels *Giraya* and *Amulet*. In these novels, as will be seen, Wijenaike shifts the site of the unhomely from the deterritorialised land to the defamiliarised house.

Unhomely homes

The uncanny would always, as it were, be something one does not know one's way about in. The better oriented in his environment a person is, the

less readily will he get the impression of something uncanny in regard to the
objects and events in it.

Sigmund Freud, *The Uncanny*[11]

I grew up in apprehension, always anticipating something to happen. What
exactly would happen, I did not know. Sometimes the fear would grow into
such large proportions that I would be compelled to seek the safety of my bed.

Punyakante Wijenaike, *A Way of Life*[12]

13 In the opening page of her memoir, *A Way of Life* (1987), Wijenaike attests to the
influence of her childhood home in shaping her personality, wondering 'whether it is
the house that played the most important part in molding people who lived in it' (p.
1). Raised in a sprawling urban mansion run by an affluent Christian grandfather and
a Buddhist grandmother, the home disorientated as much as it fed the imagination.
Regularly terrified by a sadistic personal ayah who 'practices different kinds of torture,
knowing I will never tell on her' (p. 20), Wijenaike sought refuge in a dream world in
which 'long winding verandahs turned into streams of water along which I could swim
or paddle my own boat [and] the open balconies, three in number, turned into sea beds
[where I would lie] believing myself a beautiful mermaid with a long tail and golden
hair' (p. 19). The memoir constitutes a reminiscence of a lost and leisured way of life
at the heart of which stands the unhomely home, one which promises security but is
open to intrusion and terror thus allowing for the development of phobic tendencies
such as spatial fear, 'house-bondage' and the desire to create sanitised, safe zones.[13]

14 All these elements are to be found in *Giraya* and *Amulet*. *Giraya* is set during the
time of the land reform movement of the 1970s (a fact not mentioned in the novel but
which Wijenaike draws attention to in her preface: 'Land Reform was knocking on
the door of people accustomed to living on inherited wealth') and *Amulet* registers
the development of urbanisation and the subdivision of inherited property and land
characteristic of the 1970s and 1980s.[14] The novels offer complementary and contras-
tive readings of the unhomely in their anthropomorphistic representation of home
and detailed consideration of agoraphobic sensibility, but they do so within a clearly
defined social context. The unhomely was, according to Walter Benjamin, born out of
the rise of the great cities, where 'what was once walled and intimate, the confirma-
tion of community [. . .] has been rendered strange by the spatial incursions of modernity'.[15] In Sri Lanka, where land reform served to drastically undermine the economic
power of the landed class,[16] urbanisation was linked to radical social and demographic
shifts. Migration to the city, for example, was exacerbated by the loss of ancestral
lands, and the rise in an educated but often unemployed working class undermined the
power and status of the feudal landlords of ancestral estates who lived in walauwes –
dwelling places that figure prominently in both novels. *Giraya* uses anthropomorphic
markers to register social change, siting the unhomely or uncanny in the social reincar-
nation of the times, in its opening description of the walauwe:

The Walauwe, the old manor house, waits in silence. Is it awaiting death
with courage? Why must anyone need courage to face death? Surely death
is but another change and are we not accustomed to that in life as well? The

walauwe may be pulled down, brick by brick, and then it will rise again with new bricks and new tiles. It will live again under a new name, a new coat of paint and a new way of life. [. . .]

Yes, a house retains its personality only so long as its inmates live within its walls. When they die, or run away, the house must change. If it is not pulled down, it must at least assume a second personality. It must be reborn. Like a human being a house must die before taking life again. The old ebony furniture will be sold as valuable antiques and the yellowed lace curtains pulled down. The old walauwe will die, but the house will live on. [p.1]

These changes to the walauwe that mark a 'new way of life' are grounded in a gothic tale in which an educated woman from a farming background (a member of the rising middle class) increasingly becomes alienated from her dwelling space and its principal occupants – her silent husband Lal, the heir apparent, her mother-in-law Adelaine, a distant matriarch, Manel, her sister-in-law, and the sinister maid Lucia Hamy. The house itself constitutes a central character, its labyrinthine sequence of sealed interconnecting rooms embodying both the frustrated communication between its occupants and the complex relationships of blood and marriage between them. Its panoptic gaze extends beyond its physical confines to the estate itself so that the narrator feels perpetually under surveillance. The house contains several family secrets that are not divulged until the end – Lal's homosexuality and illegitimacy directly imposing the threat of dispossession and homelessness on the narrator. Perpetually on the threshold, outside locked doors or standing by a partially drawn curtain between rooms, she occupies a liminal space, neither mistress nor servant. This social indeterminacy is also registered by changes taking place outside the home: the building of the biscuit manufacturer's mansion that rivals the fading opulence of the walauwe, the construction of a new road to link two villages that divides the estate in two and the clandestine affair between the estate superintendent and Manel, all of which presage the gradual erosion of power of the landed gentry and further destabilise the social positioning of the narrator.

15 Indeed it is in the strangeness of personal and social relations – their uncanny manifestation – that much of the power of this novel resides. The appearance of wealth, status and legitimacy, is revealed as just that: an illusion of power and privilege. The logic of ownership and possession is undermined on more than one level and it is this layering of appearances, their doubling, that gives density to duplicity in the text. Indeed the opaqueness of this novel lies not only in the powerful representation of spectral space in the labyrinthine, unhomely walauwe, but also in the slippage and gaps in the narrative itself, between the epistemologically driven unfolding of plot in the disjointed journal that constitutes the text and the ontologically based construction of events of which this plot forms a part – between in other words, the narrator's quest for meaning and the writer's construction of it in the text. The former involves the presentation of Adelaine as a dominant matriarch, owner and mistress of the walauwe, who is dependent upon her female servant – the sinister custodian of the giraya (areca nut-cutter) – and Lal, her effeminate son, for support. Such narrative emplotment presents the instability of feudal power as the primary social framework for the text,

and it simultaneously locates the feudal system of inheritance and patronage as the model through which social relations are mediated and negotiated. The inevitability of its demise and the uncertainty of precisely what will replace it unsettles the narrator who, reflecting on her husband's snobbery, is prompted to locate herself in opposition to him:

> The day will come when you will have to step down from your walauwe and walk among us the common people. How will you fit in Lal? If you do not make yourself change now, you may in the future stand in a position that is lower than that of the man who now stands humbly before a table loaded with your money, receiving his pay.
>
> [p.110]

Such 'intellectual uncertainty' is fundamental to the structuration of the uncanny according to Freud[17] and the reader's experience of this uncertainty replicates and reinforces the loss of orientation of the narrator.

16   This intellectual uncertainty is exacerbated when, at the end of the novel, the full extent of Adelaine's powerlessness is revealed. Adelaine and Lal, we learn, are only keeping up appearances – conforming to a model of legitimate feudal ownership. Adelaine, it is disclosed, had an affair with a cousin and therefore her illegitimate off-spring, Lal, will not in fact inherit the walauwe – this will pass instead to Manel and her lover, the socially inferior estate superintendent. The threat of dispossession that haunts both the central characters in *The Waiting Earth* thus manifests itself in a new form, that of upper class female dispossession and homelessness, but with an important twist: the very basis of class legitimacy is called into question. Not only is the heir apparent now revealed to be nothing more than an apparent heir, but the estate workers themselves are presented as the product of the numerous affairs of Adelaine's late husband. Blood lines are confused and the very legitimacy of the landed class is subject to scrutiny.

17   Within this context, the position of the narrator, as the resident outsider, the social interloper who has married into the old feudal order, is uncannily legitimated and centred by the author. A farmer's daughter married to the illegitimate son of the wife of a feudal landlord, her ambivalent social position acquires, at the novel's end, a normative status and her homelessness is neutralised. Unlike her inlaws, she is able to converse with servants in a language they recognise, and her easy appropriation of the accoutrements of modernity (such as powdered milk and imported medicine) serves, in the reversed social logic of the text, to legitimate her position. The duplicity of social perspective – the mediation of a feudal order from the perspective of a social outsider – produces an uncanny dislocation of space and residence in the text. It is impossible to locate 'home' in the mobilised presentation of class confluence and class conflict. It is a world in which the individual perspective gains supremacy, where the temporal is mediated through mental states and fluctuations of the lunar calendar (the journal that constitutes the text is written on *poya* – or full moon – days) and where the spatial is constructed through the imaginative mapping of unhoused domesticity. Thus the mobile social positioning of the unhoused narrator serves as more than just a marker

of social change; it also embodies an ontological condition whereby displacement and homelessness prove to be embedded in the very structure of social relations. The narrator, Adelaine, Lal and Manel are all socially unfixed. Far from having nothing in common, they have all transgressed, breaking, variously, class, community and sexual codes, and, what is more, are known to have done so. The walauwe that accommodates them is thus a spectral presence, a construction of spatialised otherness, whereby the inhabitants are rendered strangers not only to one another but also to themselves as they try to maintain the appearance of conformity:

> Here in the walauwe, despite iron bars, Alsatian dogs, padlocks and gates we have to lock room doors as well. And here we lock them, not against people who come and go, but against those living within its very walls.
>
> [p. 75]

As a defamiliarised symbol of the ruling class, the walauwe is destined to die, but, as the opening lines of the novel remind us, 'the house will live on'. Wijeniake's dramatic mobilisation of social relations in this text serves to clear space for new ways of dwelling on the borderland, and in *Amulet* she returns to the theme of the unhomely home in order to reveal the ubiquity of defamiliarised dwelling by focusing her attention on an urban house. The fact that in this later novel the walauwe is presented as a place of light and freedom, 'spacious and cool', where 'birds flew freely in and out of the centre courtyard' (p. 8) and 'people had been free to come and go' (p. 29), indicates that a reading that privileges the walauwe *per se* as the embodiment of the unhomely is misplaced. Rather Wijenaike's work demands that we consider the way in which dwelling itself is negotiated in relation to space, and the ways in which space is resconstructed as a series of displacements in her work.

18   *Amulet* was written in response to the popular demand for Wijenaike to produce a sequel to *Giraya*.[18] Set in an old Colombo house, the novel is, in many ways, haunted by its predecessor. Like *Giraya*, *Amulet* is a first-person, temporally segmented, narrative, that focuses on the experiences of a newly wed woman, Shyamali, married to a relative stranger from a different background and class. The house in which they live is also dominated by servants (including a particularly unpleasant female servant) and contains family secrets that are gradually divulged as the narrative unfolds: the physical abuse of the narrator's husband, Senani, and his sister, Anula, in childhood, incest between Senani and Anula, the suicide of Senani's mother, and Senani's murder of his sister. These secrets are partially revealed in Anula's diary, which Shyamali discovers in her retreat to the attic, and gain physical presencing in the form of Anula's restless, unhoused spirit.

19   It could be argued that family secrets here, as in *Giraya*, constitute that which has been repressed, for Freud's formulation of the uncanny, drawing upon Schelling's idea that the '*unhiemlich* is the name for everything that ought to have remained . . . secret and hidden but has come to light',[19] claimed that the unhomely constituted 'the return of the repressed'.[20] It could also be claimed, as Wijenaike has herself done, that the focus on taboo subjects such as incest and homosexuality constitute 'a confrontation with reality'.[21] Incest, in particular, is rarely addressed in anglophone literature and

Wijenaike has focused on it twice.[22] In Sri Lanka, incest is not just a social phenomenon, it is both a symbolic structure of moral violation that has helped to regulate kinship ties[23] and a central element of Sri Lankan mythological history. In foregrounding it in the context of mobilised class and community relations (the incest between Senani and Anula is after all induced by their nanny), Wijenaike reveals the link between transgressive social and sexual relations.

20   *Amulet* intensifies the key themes of the earlier novel by duplicating symbols, situations and characters internally in the text, thereby creating not only the haunting attendant upon intertextual referentiality with its predecessor, but also the recurrent presencing of key ideas and events within the text itself. Duplication abounds in several forms: first, the uncanny doubles of some of the characters (the servant Pinchamma is strategically linked to Nonchi, the nanny who was responsible for child abuse; Anula's spirit – itself a double of her earthly self – inhabits Shyamali's body); second, the correspondences of circumstance and situation (both Shyamali and her husband had unfaithful fathers and belong to divided homes; both fathers had illegitimate offspring; both Shyamali and her mother are dispossessed, physically constrained in their own homes and finally ejected from them; both Shymali and Anula are denied an inheritance); third, the repetition of events (Shyamali is thrice dispossessed: first in being disinherited from her family home, then in her loss of authority and control in her marital home where a servant 'seems the mistress and I, a house guest' (p. 68), and finally in being unhoused when her husband decides to destroy the home; Senani's murder of his sister is replicated in the ominous confrontation with his wife that ends the novel); fourth, the textual replication (Anula's diary repeats and revises the narrator's script); and finally the dual narrators (Shyamali and Senani). This duplication is entirely in keeping with both the structuration of the uncanny[24] and the legal dilemma that underpins the text: the issue of joint ownership – the issue, in other words, of a duplicated occupation of space, the mutual sharing of living room, which foregrounds the question of territorial control. Thus while disinheritance is central to the narratives of her earlier novels, in *Amulet* the issues attendant upon the disinheritance of the female narrator from her family home and her displacement in and from her marital home are replicated by the conflictual dynamic embedded in joint ownership. Shyamali's exclusion from the family legacy is shown to create as many problems as the legacy of joint ownership inherited by Senani and his sister. What is more, by focusing her attention on the ownership of the home (rather than land ownership as in *The Waiting Earth*), Wijenaike is encoding her reading of the unhomely within a specifically (but not exclusively) female space. For a woman, as one object relations analyst has shown, the home can reflect an expanded boundary of the self.[25]

21   Here then, once again, dispossession, and more specifically the gendered homelessness of women, is foregrounded. The Deega system of marriage (in which a newly married woman goes to live in her husband's home) is analysed as a trope of both physical estrangement and cultural situatedness through the experience of Shymali and her mother in *Amulet*, the narrator of *Giraya*, and Sellohamy in the *Waiting Earth*. It is a system that mobilises women's identities in relation to their dwelling place and marks an area of experience rarely considered in English literature from Sri Lanka.[26] In *Amulet*, however, Wijenaike goes further in naming it and comparing it

with the alternative of joint ownership. Both are found wanting. Shyamali is effectively disinherited by her parent's decision to write the ancestral property to her brother – a man who clearly does not work for a living though he is qualified to do so – on account of the need to keep it in the family name; and the joint ownership of Shyamali and Senani is presented as an embodiment of an unnatural relationship cemented by their incest, a corrosive arrangement that can only lead to family division and estrangement. The only feasible alternative to these two modes is, the text suggests, the creation of separate dwellings, a proposition that Senani – an architect who claims 'I had structured my marriage like I structure buildings' (p. 91) – puts into place. But this marker of modernity destabilises the social conventions under which an earlier generation of women live and effectively serves to unhouse Shyamali. Like the walauwe in *Giraya*, the old Colombo house and the intergenerational family are synonymous, the very structure of dwelling space informing the structure of relationships. Its destruction and replacement with separate dwellings and 'a concrete fortress, a block of apartments [that] will sit heavily on the past so that it will never rise again' (p. 134) presages a fundamental, irreversible shift in interpersonal relations, a radical change in the structuration of community in terms of separation and segregation.

22   In linking the social conditions of uncanny experience to their psychological effects, Wijenaike's work clearly draws attention to the 'disturbances of identity, time and place'[27] generated by the disjunctive temporalities of a society that, while tied to traditional beliefs and customs, is also registering the disintegration of traditional social bonds. The social, cultural and personal alienation attendant upon this shift is increasingly gendered in her work as women – the narrators in *Giraya* and *Amulet* – are shown to gain their identity through and from their dwelling space. If, as Bachelard claims, 'the house image would appear to have become the topography of our intimate being',[28] then Wijenaike's exploration of the unhomely home registers the difficulties of settling into new modes of being and dwelling in the world. Old structures of living are shown to cohabit the present, haunting and unsettling the sites of regeneration and expansion so that territorial security is rendered impossible. This is true of all Wijenaike's work, but what gives *Amulet* the edge over its predecessors is its clear investment in the uncanny: not only in the doubling and repetition noted earlier, nor in the spectral spaces of dispossession informing experience, but also in two other elements that are not present in *Giraya* or *the Waiting Earth*. The first is its focus on what Hamid Naficy has described as a 'phobic partner' and the other is the intellectual uncertainty that pervades the ending.

23   According to Naficy the experience of the unhomely leads the victim to draw comfort from '"phobic partners", such as a trusted person, or object (such as an umbrella and a suitcase)'.[29] While Wijenaike does focus on an uncanny object in her earlier novel, the giraya which gives the book its name, it is presented as an alien and alienating instrument that diminishes rather than empowers the narrator, who feels herself caught between its blades. It is a symbol of exorcism which, in the hands of Adelaine and Lucy Hamy, threatens to divide her from herself. In *Amulet*, however, multiple phobic partners present themselves: Anula's diary (and the spirit of Anula contained herein) and the amulet itself which Shyamali fingers when she is uncertain. There is also a space that offers Shyamali sanctuary – the attic – separate from the house and

yet attached to it, which constitutes what Naficy would describe as a 'safe zone' but one constantly under threat of intrusion.[30]

24   In addition the ending of the novel, with its impending confrontation between Shyamali (now emboldened by her communication with Anula and wearing the amulet) and Senani (who is intent on 'destruction of Shyamali, destruction of house' [sic] (p. 132)), carries the reader to the edge of resolution, the cusp of connection and a kind of suspended logic with the final lines: 'I knock. Shyamali opens the door to me' (p.134). Senani, who has been propelled by images of the future to seek out his wife – 'I can already see in my mind the beautiful new building towering over the two small houses of my children' (p. 134) – is also confronting the future in his wife, who feels protected by the uncanny amulet and is 'prepared for whatever or whoever is coming up the stairway' (p. 88). Her communication with Anula, or rather the spirit of Anula, reconfigures her identity into a doubling of selfhood, a presencing of a simultaneous past and future, for as Royle notes (in relation to Derrida) 'ghosts don't belong to the past, they come from the future'.[31]

25   It is this haunting of an unstable present by an uncertain future, a present that registers the impact of rural displacement, gendered dispossession, class migration and urban emigration, that gives potency to the representation of psychological disturbance in Wijenaike's work. Through historically and socially situated reflections on the unhomely, *Giraya* and *Amulet* offer a reading of the way in which migrations across culture, class and territory affect and influence the structuration of identity, and they reveal how identity itself comes to be spatialised and mobilised in its search for bearings and a home. As Rapport and Dawson have noted, as home becomes more mobile so it comes to be seen as more individuated and privatised.[32] Wijenaike's spatialised structuration of gendered identity carries us to the threshold – the open door of *Amulet* – where transformation occurs. Yet in '*The Enemy Within*', Wijenaike retreats from this position. Here, in a novella that explores the experience of death in the city, the alienation of the protagonists is ethnically and politically coded and boundary marking is foregrounded once more.

The fortress city

26   In *An Enemy Within*,[33] 'home' constitutes the city of Colombo, conceived by its residents as 'a fortress' that grants immunity from the war. The text is part of a collection of the same name comprising two novellas and two short stories, and it focuses on the experiences of the victims of a major suicide bomb attack of January 1996 that extensively damaged Sri Lanka's business centre – in particular the Central Bank, the target of the attack – killing over 90 people and wounding some 1400 others. For the first time in her long career, resident space is both fragmented *and* sanctified, and place is explicitly shown to be socially and communally (de)constructed. While her earlier novels registered a nostalgia (a word that literally means 'homesickness') for settlement and security, this novel is at pains to demonstrate the close connections already existing between the city dwellers, presenting the city as an active and thriving community of individuals and the very hallmark of modernity. Buildings are animated by the activity they engender, and the multiple narratives that structure the text are narrated

from above, at and below ground level, creating a powerful, spatialised sense of community and connection. The eight narratives of the novella are themselves fragmented; but this fragmentation does not describe an alienated subjectivity as it does in her earlier work, rather it works towards a collective mapping of urban life in Colombo. The spatialised presentation of the city as a network of human relationships is contained and constrained by the temporal linearity of narrative emplotment that focuses sequentially on events prior to, during and after the bomb blast. The collectivity of voices thus promote a compelling image of security in residence, of homeliness and of individuals at home in their own narratives.

27   Yet in focusing her attention on a real political event that took place in her home city, Wijenaike's own political persuasions come to the fore, resulting in a personal response to ethnic violence that inscribes boundaries in the process of appearing to interrogate them.[34] The 'enemy within' refers to both the terrorists living in 'safe houses' – ironically the only houses that appear safe in the text – to the trauma induced by the blast itself.[35] Unlike her earlier powerful evocation of the uncanny or unhomely as a marker of social and cultural displacement, here the uncanny is personalised and politicised, given material shape in the insidious form of the Tamil suicide bomber. This personalisation of the uncanny occurs in and through a corresponding anthropomorphisation of the city which 'like a traumatised person [. . .] awaits re-building' (p. 49). Indeed the depiction of Colombo is symbolically saturated, both masculinised and feminised, as military fortress (the dominant metaphor in the text) and maternal nurturer, both mobile and situated – elements that compete for authority in the following passage:

> Colombo in the past, had, from time to time, been a beleaguered city. The Dutch, the Portuguese attacked and raped her virginity. During World War II when she lay in submission under the British, she had been turned into a fortress. But apart from an air raid or two, a bomb or two dropped from the air into the harbour and that too after a warning siren signal, she had not suffered too much.
>
> Today she faced a different situation. The enemy coming from within, from the womb of her own mother. How could she guard against herself? Checkpoints, cordoning off with barrels and barb wire [sic] how could they stop the earth exploding under her feet? The enemy could not be identified, separated. He moved among citizens, he lived among the people of Colombo. [p. 49]

This excess use of metaphoric and symbolic registers to describe a territorially defined space substantiates Featherstone's observation that a geographically bounded space is 'sedimented with symbolic sentiments'.[36] Here community is constructed by the sharing of this symbolic space, whose very excess of registers resists easy categorisation. Rather it is through a clearly defined structuration of belonging that the city gains coherence and definition in Wijenaike's text, for, as Sibley has contended, social space is shaped by our sense of belonging – who does and who doesn't.[37] The contradictory pull of registers siting the city as fortress and maternal source reveals an uncertainty in Wijenaike's placing of the Other. The Other or 'enemy' has both a blood bond to the city and a clear wish to ravage or 'rape' it as the colonisers had done earlier, thus placing him as both insider and outsider, both native and alien. Such uncertainty reflects a fundamental need, in my view, to demonise the enemy through domesticating him; an enemy who, inverting the logic of Wijenaike's earlier texts, constitutes the resident outsider. This ethical elision that grants outsider status through residence has serious ideological implications. As Neloufer de Mel has observed, 'Wijenaike's book shares an ideological affinity with those who cannot/do not wish to separate the Tamil civilian from the militant', foreclosing 'any possibility of reconciliation between the two communities or a just solution to the underlying causes of the ethnic war'.[38] What is more, as de Mel and others[39] have pointed out, Wijenaike's failure to address the issue of army atrocities on Tamil civilians results in a onesided presentation of the conflict; the 'enemy within' – both suicide bomber and the embodiment of trauma – is clearly an external force that needs to be resisted and overcome, never the Sinhala citizens (and readers) who are complicit in fuelling the war nor the Sri Lankan army itself. What is more, while the novella does present two Tamil victims of the bombing, their deaths serve to heighten the betrayal implicit in the suicide bomber's actions, whose thoughts are included in the collective memory that constitutes the city.

28   The biomorphic presentation of the city as a bodily organism thus repeats and revises the anthropomorphic presentation of unhomely homes in Wijenaike's earlier work, reversing the presentation of the resident outsider and revealing a dramatic reversal in her reading of subject–space relations. Wijenaike's uncompromising presentation of the resident outsider does not so much destabilise the boundaries of belonging as reinforce them, inviting a univocal and unifocal response. Unlike her explorations of women's private experience within the marital home, Wijenaike's politically situated texts are territorially deterministic, presenting 'human species as self-markers'[40] and reveal the way in which the ethnic conflict has constrained and codified representations of belonging in a writer who has been fearless in her exploration of the cultural repressed. As Don DeLillo has observed:

> What terrorists gain, novelists lose. The degree to which they [terrorists] influence mass consciousness is the extent of our decline as shapers of sensibility and thought. *The danger they represent equals our own failure to be dangerous.*
>
> [my emphasis][41]

Textual and rhetorical Questions

Textual

1. Why does Salgado by the end of the first paragraph write, "As will be seen, hidden behind Wijenaike's ephemeral construction of 'home' lurks the contestatory and materially inflected discourse of territorial control and land right?" Read paragraphs 7 to 12 where the writer discusses Wijenaike's novel *The Waiting Earth*.
2. Salgado writes that in Wijenaike's novels *Giriya* and *Amulet*, "unhomely home," and "phobic tendencies" (paragraph 13) of the residents can be seen. Salgado elaborates her proposition in her subsequent discussions of the two novels. While

discussing Wijenaike's work *Giriya* what does the essayist mean by "anthropo-morphic markers" (paragraph 14), "frustrated communication" (paragraph 14), "spectral space in the labyrinthine, unhomely walauwe,"and "instability of feudal power as the primary social framework for the text" (paragraph 15)?

3. Salgado's "unhomely home" is presented in a different vein in the novel *Amulet*. Read paragraphs 18 to 25 and explain the essayist's analysis of the novel.

4. Wijenaike's *An Enemy Within* is a collection of novellas and short stories, which focuses on ethnic violence. The essayist interprets the "fortress" and "enemy" in double bind (read the section "The Fortress City"). Elaborate and explain her discussion.

Rhetorical

1. Wijenaike's *The Waiting Earth* and the sequel "Living on the Edge" depict the story of Podhi Singho and Sellohamy who struggle to own land. Salgado mentions three times what Podhi Singho wishes (paragraph 8), how he wishes for the land to the level of sexual obsession (paragraph 9), and a property bond stronger than marriage bond (paragraph 11). The three citations are the proper strategy to present the central tension of the story without summarising it much. Discuss how Salgado appropriates citation to develop her views.

2. The space of the home is qualified by three major terms used by the essayist: "Lust," "unhomely," and both "immunity" and vulnerability. How do they define the idea of "Spectral Spaces," the subtitle of the essay? Analyse the essay in relation to these three terms (100 words).

Discussion questions

1. Home is the private location discursively related with identity. How is the issue of identity different in gendered terms? How is home different for men and women in South Asian cultures? Develop an argumentative thesis statement to answer the question of identity in relation to family and heritage (1500 words).

2. Home is both contrasted and associated with exile, for instance, Jewish exodus, *Nakba* (Palestinian exodus), migration, and diaspora. Displacement from home has been tragic phenomena from West Asia to Rohingya crises in Myanmar. Edward Said writes:

> The exile knows that in a secular and contingent world, homes are always provisional. Borders and barriers, which enclose us within the safety of familiar territory, can also become prisons, and are often defended beyond reason or necessity. Exiles cross borders, break barriers of thought and experience.
>
> (278)[42]

Exile is perceived as a form of punishment, but upon an exile, is the pun-ished trapped or freed? What does exile do to the exiled? Does it deprive them of home or grant them a freer one, enabling them to explore the actions they were exiled for performing in the first place?

3. James Goonewardene's *One Mad Bid for Freedom* is a story of conflict between a Sri Lankan self-taught scientist, Korala and Van Hulft, a university-trained Dutch scientist. The novel presents two different views about nature and marine life. The conflict is between two different approaches. Discuss the novel as a conflict between West and East on the ground of the nature of knowledge. (2000 words)

Inter-textual discussions

1. Derek Walcott's "Ruins of a Great House" depicts home in a dilapidated state, "leprosy of Empire" which is metonymic, if not metaphoric, of the last remains of colonial glory. Time wears out even powerful people and magnificent buildings. P.B. Shelley's poem "Ozymandias" depicts the collapse of an empire "Two vast and trunkless legs of stone," "half sunk a shattered visage" in the desert where once a civilisation stood. Read these two poems. In the context of the ruins of civilisation, construct a postcolonial argument with symptomatic reading of ruined monuments, Raj Bungalows, and neglected cemeteries. The suggestive idea is that the houses are sites of memory[43] (3000 words).

2. Write an argumentative essay on memory and the materials of the past in relation to colonialism, empire, loss of glory, and history of atrocity. Here are some key words for a general reference to past materials: Colonial museums, Heritage hotels, Palace Hotels, Railway/Palace of Wheels, Hill Stations, Bungalows, Raj memsahibs, Chowkidars, Gymkhanas, Cemeteries, Raj ghost stories, and Kipling narratives. Footprints, echoes, and traces can also be discoursed for memory and nostalgia studies.[44]

Critical and creative thinking

1. Home is a favourite issue for poets and novelists. Here are the first two lines from "Home" by the Victorian writer Anne Bronte: "How brightly glistening in the sun/The woodland ivy plays!" Read the poem.

2. What is your idea of memory? The following stanza conceptualises memory in discursive terms:

> Memory is a complex phenomenon that reaches far and beyond what normally constitutes a historian's archives, for memory is much more than what the mind can remember or what objects can help us document about the past. [. . .] Memory, then, is far more complicated than what historians can recover, and it poses ethical challenges to the investigator-historian who approaches the past with one injunction: Tell me all.
>
> (Dipesh Chakrabarty, "Memories", 2006: 115)[45]

3. Gaston Bachelard in *The Poetics of Space* writes,[46]

> This being the case, if I were asked to name the chief benefit of the house, I should say: the house shelters daydreaming, the house protects the dreamer,

LITERARY THEORY AND CRITICISM

the house allows one to dream in peace. Thought and experience are not the only things that sanction human values. The values that belong to day-dreaming mark humanity in its depths. Daydreaming even has a privilege of auto valorization. It derives direct pleasure from its own being. Therefore, the places in which we have experienced daydreaming reconstitute themselves in a new daydream, and it is because our memories of former dwelling-places are relived as daydreams that these dwelling-places of the past remain in us for all time.

(1964: "Introduction:" 6)

4. Moving to a city from the countryside has always been a movement into ambivalent space, a journey to alienation in Kathmandu. Abhi Subedi in "Get Lost," from his collection of poems *Chasing Dreams*[47] presents the very loss of the pristine nature the traveller has left. Contemplate on memory and ambivalence.

Get lost!
The sky spreads its storm
into the open palms
of the gods in the city
and descended upon it
I sat like the shattered sun
in your dooryard
spreading my own words,
my time woven in them

Get Lost!

That was yesterday.
I came to the city
lost like a minuscule sky
in the lanes,
crept out of my own
lanes of memories
and broke into a dawn
under the collapsing roofs
of the houses of the gods.

Notes

1 Cited in A. Vidler: *The Architectural Uncanny: Essays in the Modern Unhomely*, Cambridge, MA: MIT Press, 1992, p. 69.
2 A. Niven, 'The Fiction of Punyakante Wijenaike', *Journal of Commonwealth Literature*, August 1977, XII: 1, p. 55. Niven's essay focuses on evaluating Wijenaike's first novel, *The Waiting Earth* – a text denigrated by D.C.R.A. Goonetilleke as a 'one-key romantic story with a stale Victorian villain, written as an unsophisticated third person narrative'. D.C.R.A. Goonetilleke, *Sri Lankan English Literature and the Sri Lankan People 1917–2003*, Colombo: Vijitha Yapa, 2005, p. 259.

3 H. Naficy, 'Phobic Spaces and Liminal Panics: Independent Transnational Film Genre' in R. Wilson and W. Dissanayake (eds), *Global/Local: Cultural Production and the Transnational Imaginary*, Durham, NC: Duke University Press, 1996, p. 128.

4 Laura Mulvey cited in Naficy, ibid.

5 Vidler, op. cit., pp. 9, 6, 3–4.

6 P. Wijenaike, *The Waiting Earth*, Pitakotte and Padukka: State Printing Corporation, 1993. All references are to this edition.

7 See L. Wikkramasinha, 'Note' in *Lustre: Poems*, Kandy: privately published, 1965, p. 51, cited in Goonetilleke, *Sri Lankan English Literature*, op. cit., p. 49.

8 It could be claimed that my reading here is anachronistic – that these measures have only become controversial since the war. But even B.H. Farmer, whose study of the colonisation programme is commendatory, noted in 1957 that that the scheme caused communal tensions. B.H. Farmer, *Pioneer Peasant Colonization in Ceylon*, London: Oxford University Press, 1957, p. 300.

9 Ibid., p. 291.

10 P. Wijenaike, 'Living on the Edge', *Daily News*, 17 July 2002, p. 22.

11 Cited in Vidler, op. cit., p. 23.

12 P. Wijenaike, *A Way of Life*, Nugegoda: Deepani, 1987, p. 18.

13 A. Vidler argues that spatial fear, leading to paralysis of movement, and temporal fear, leading to historical amnesia, are symptoms of the uncanny; Vidler, op. cit., p. 6. H. Naficy, in his transnational reading of spatial fear and phobic space, has claimed that agoraphobia and claustrophobia both manifest themselves in house-bondage and the need to withdraw into safe zones; Naficy, op. cit., p. 130.

14 P. Wijenaike, *Giraya*, Nugegoda, Panaluwa and Padukka: State Printing Corporation, 1990; P. Wijenaike, *Amulet*, Wellampitiya: Godage International Publishers, 2002. All references are to these editions.

15 Cited in Vidler, op. cit., pp. 4, 11.

16 The Land Reform Act of 1972 put a ceiling of 50 acres on privately owned land, and it was amended in 1975 to also cover plantations owned by joint-stock companies.

17 Ibid., p. 23.

18 M. Salgado, conversation with Punyakante Wijenaike, Colombo, 11 December 2002.

19 Cited in Vidler, op. cit., p. 26.

20 Ibid.

21 Salgado, op. cit.

22 In her award-winning short story 'Anoma', Wijenaike explores the incestuous relationship between a daughter and a father who was a migrant labourer in the Middle East.

23 I am referring here to the practice of cross-cousin marriage that works on the one hand to conserve blood lines while on other to regulate family ties. Gananath Obeyesekere has shown, in his fascinating anthropological analysis of Oedipal myth, how this form of marriage has been idealised in both Lankan myth and familial life, and he has further suggested that the incest taboo is weaker in relation to the sister in Sri Lanka. See G. Obeyesekere, *The Work of Culture: Symbolic Transformation in Psychoanalysis and Anthropology*, Chicago, IL: Chicago University Press, 1990, pp. 145–80, 63.

24 The point has been made well by Nicholas Royle: 'To repeat: the uncanny seems to be about a strange repetitiveness. It has to do with the return of something repressed, something no longer familiar, the return of the dead, the "constant recurrence of the same thing", "a compulsion to repeat".' N. Royle, *The Uncanny*, Manchester: Manchester University Press, 2003, p. 84.

25 E. Rochberg-Halton cited in David Sibley, *Geographies of Exclusion*, London: Routledge, 1995, p. 10.

26 G. Obeyesekere has observed that it is not given much attention in Sri Lankan folk song either, thereby suggesting that it may be an area that is generally unmarked in Sri Lankan literary and oral culture as a whole. He points out 'I have not come across one Sinhala folk song directly indicating the woman's trauma of leaving the parental home for the alien

LITERARY THEORY AND CRITICISM

home of the husband, a genre almost universal in Hindu India, especially in the north', Obeyesekere, op. cit., p. 161.

27 Royle, op. cit., p. 192.

28 Bachelard, G. (1964). *The Poetics of Space: The Classic look at how we Experience Intimate Places*, trans. by M. Jolas, Boston: Beacon Press.

29 Naficy, op. cit., p. 130. Naficy's reading is specifically on phobic space rather than on the evaluation of the broader unhomely.

30 The attic is of course a characteristic locus for containing madness in the nineteenth century novel. Wijenaike herself has said that *Jane Eyre* was one of her favourite novels; Salgado, op. cit.

31 Royle, op. cit., p. 67.

32 N. Rapport and A. Dawson, 'Home and Movement: A Polemic' in N. Rapport and A. Dawson (eds), *Migrants of Identity: Perceptions of Home in a World of Movement*, Oxford: Berg, 1998, p. 27.

33 P. Wijenaike, 'An Enemy Within' in *An Enemy Within*, Ratmalana: Vishva Lekha, 1998. All references are to this edition.

34 Wijenaike's daughter was traumatised by the bomb attack. Her story – along with others that Wijenaike herself investigated – appears as one of the narratives. Salgado, op. cit.

35 This is fleetingly referred to in the text when Siromi 'did not know how to convey that she was held in a grip of anxiety and fear she could not account for. She had no more control over herself, over the enemy within'. Wijenaike, 'An Enemy Within', op. cit., p. 65.

36 M. Featherstone, 'Localism, Globalism, and Cultural Identity' in Wilson and Dissanayake, op. cit., p. 53.

37 D. Sibley, *Geographies of Exclusion: Society and Difference in the West*, London: Routledge, 1995, p. 3.

38 N. de Mel, 'Fixing Uncertainties: Producing "National" Culture in an Era of Globalization – The Terrain of Sexuality in Sri Lanka', *Asian Women*, July 1999, 8, p. 90.

39 See T. Jayatilaka, 'That Day of Horror and Humanity' (book review), *The Sunday Times*, 25 April 1999. Available online: www.lacnet.prg/suntimes/990425/plus6.html.

40 E. Gordon Ericksen, *The Territorial Experience: Human Ecology as Symbolic Interaction*, Austin, TX: University of Texas Press, 1980, p. 113.

41 D. DeLillo, *Mao II*, London: Jonathan Cape, 1991, p. 157, cited in A. Brink, *Reinventing a Continent: Writing and Politics in South Africa 1982–1995*, London: Secker and Warburg, 1996, p. 157.

42 See Edward Said. (2000) "Reflections on Exile" in *Reflections on Exile and Other Essays*. London: Granta.

43 See a critically written article by Elizabeth Buettner, "Cemeteries, Public Memory and Raj Nostalgia in Postcolonial Britain and India" *History and Memory*. 18.1 (2006) 5–42.

44 I collected terms like museums, Palace hotels, Palace on Wheels, Memsahibs, Chowkidars, Cemeteries, Footprints, and Echoes from Buettner's footnotes from the essay. See footnote 60 of his book.

45 . See D. Chakrabarty. (2006). "Memories of Displacement: The Poetry and Prejudice of Dwelling" in *Habitations of Modernity*. Delhi: permanent black. (115–37)

46 Bachelard, Gaston. (1964). *The Poetics of Space*. Boston: Beacon Press

47 Abhi Subedi. (1996). *Chasing Dreams: Poems*. Kathmandu: Mandala Book Point.

12

CHOKHER BALI

The novel of the new age

Radha Chakraborty

1 In *Chokher Bali*, modernity takes the shape of a new interiority, an attempt to psychologize the modern Bengali subject. 'The literature of the new age seeks not to narrate a sequence of events, but to reveal the secrets of the heart', Tagore declares in his preface to the second edition. Such is the narrative of *Chokher Bali*' (Tagore 2012: vi).

2 Serialized in the periodical *Bangadarshan* from 1902 to 1903, *Chokher*

3 *Bali* appeared as a book in 1903. Tagore had been working on the novel for a long time; he had been writing the draft version in 1898 or 1899. In 1901, he completed the draft in his notebooks. From his letters, it is apparent that he began with the working title *Binodini*, but changed it to *Chokher Bali* not long before its publication in *Bangadarshan*. Certain passages were excised from the original serialized version when *Chokher Bali* was published as a book in 1903. In the first edition of Tagore's collected works, *Rabindra Rachanabali* (1941), several of these deleted passages were restored, with Tagore's consent. Some more were rainserted in the independent Visva-Bharati edition of 1947. Most significant, perhaps, is the original ending, restored here with Tagore's approval after being dropped from the book version of 1903.

4 The plot centres upon the complications that ensue when an attractive young widow called Binodini enters the lives of a happily married couple, Mahendra and Asha. Also entangled in the undercurrents of forbidden desire that develop between the key characters is Mahendra's bachelor friend Bihari. Mahendra's possessive mother Rajalakshmi and the widowed aunt Annapurna are other key players in the intensely charged narrative which unfolds the trail of devastation created in their lives by Binodini until her departure into self-exile in Kashi at the conclusion of the novel. Order is restored at the end and the estranged couple are reunited, but the reader is left with the feeling that the experiences narrated in the text have left no character unscathed.

5 When it was published, *Chokher Bali* drew mixed reactions from the literary establishment. In the 10 Jyeshtha 1310 be issue of the journal *Rangalaya* for instance, Panchkori Bandyopadhyay says: '*Chokher Bali* has many flaws; for it also has many merits. Rabibabu has demonstrated his true genius indeed; but it has not proved worthy of our taste. An English novel has been composed in Bengali.' He then concedes, in English, 'But it is a masterpiece' (Bhattacharya 2007: 133).

6 Despite the reservations expressed by various critics at the time of publication, *Chokher Bali* left a lasting impression on the history of the modern Bengali novel. On 26 December 1931, addressing a literary gathering at an event organized in the Calcutta

DOI: 10.4324/9781003213857-12

243

LITERARY THEORY AND CRITICISM

Town Hall to mark Tagore's birth anniversary, novelist Saratchandra Chatterjee reminisced about the days when *Chokher Bali* was being serialized in *Bangadarshan*: 'It was as if the language and mode of expression dazzled our eyes with a new radiance'. In *Rabindranath: Kathasahitya*, Buddhadeva Basu lists many flaws that he perceives in Tagore's novel, but acknowledges its modern appeal, conceding that it is precisely in the imperfections of the characters that Tagore's realism may be detected (1983[1955]: 129–30). He points out that when *Chokher Bali* was first published, it required great audacity to write such a book (ibid.: 129). According to him, the book remains significant for the modern reader as the first Bengali novel that is primarily psychological (ibid.: 14).

7   Yet, this psychological element is not identical with Western literary paradigms. Tagore's representation of Binodini's sexuality, for instance, does not replicate the Freudian paradigm. Binodini is both subject and object of desire, but this desire is fanned by the repressive social practices of nineteenth century Bengal, which do not match the Freudian narrative of the emergence of sexuality thorough the triangular relationship of father, mother and child. About *Chokher Bali* and *Naukadubi* (1906), Santanu Biswas declares, '[I]n spite of Tagore's description of these novels as "analytical" and psychological respectively, Freudian thought could not have influenced their composition at all' (2003: 729). Biswas argues that in Tagore's letters written during and soon after the composition of these novels, there is no mention of the term *manobikalanmulak* (Bengali for 'psychoanalytical'); in fact, Tagore coined the term later, in the 1920s. Biswas also points out that *Binodini* (the draft version of *Chokher Bali*) was completed in 1899, the year Freud published his first psychoanalytical work, *The Interpretation of Dreams*. It is unlikely that Tagore would have read Freud's book at that time. It was in the 1930s that Tagore read Freud's work with more interest. In April/May 1940, he wrote a preface to *Chokher Bali* for the first edition of *Rabindra Rachanabali*, in which he described his approach as 'analytical'. In November/December of the same year, he wrote a preface to *Naukadubi*, in which he alluded to contemporary literary trends: 'These days the curiosity about stories has become psychoanalytical [*manobikalanmulak*]. The weaving of incidents has become redundant'.[1] About Tagore's retrospective accounts of these earlier works, Biswas observes: '[T]he use of the equivalent term for "psychoanalytical" in this case brings out the influence of Freud on the manner in which Tagore read some of his own evidently non-psychoanalytical literary works around this time' (2003: 730). Yet, though *Chokher Bali* cannot be read as a 'psychoanalytical' novel in Freudian terms, it remains a 'psychological' novel in terms devised by Tagore himself, for it has the quality that Dipesh Chakrabarty (2000) describes as 'interiority', where external events, however dramatic on occasion, serve as the frame for the exploration of the characters' inner lives.

8   According to Sujit Mukherjee, this interest in psychology is not Tagore's individual achievement, but a reflection of the prevailing trends of his time: 'The tireless scrutiny of motives which Tagore turns upon the characters of his earlier novels . . . is as true of the spirit of the times as it is in accordance with the dictum announced by Tagore in his introduction to the novel *Chokher Bali* (1903)' (1964: 175). But though the figure of Binodini does not represent a 'modern' sensibility explicable through Western theory, her character also does not match the stereotypes of the nineteenth century Bengali woman created by Bankim, for Binodini is neither a 'prachina' who

CHOKHER BALI

worships her husband devotedly, nor a 'nabina' who neglects home and hearth in her pursuit of education and social sophistication, nor a coarse woman of the 'common' working class (Panja 2004: 214–18). Shormishtha Panja finds Bankim's stereotypes problematic, because 'the new woman is a male construct: we do not hear of the new woman from her own lips', and '[t]he new woman's desires, her sexuality are completely erased' (ibid.: 216). In contrast, Binodini 'is an intriguing amalgam of the various types of Bengali women that Chatterjee has put into exclusive compartments' (Panja 2004: 217). She asserts her needs and desires, flouting the image of the chaste 'bhadramahila'. 'Am I an inanimate object?', she cries. 'Am I not human? Am I not a woman?' (Tagore 2012: 69). In a letter to Mahendra she writes: 'I have no right to love or be loved. So, I play games to compensate for my lack of love' (ibid.: 238). As Dipesh Chakrabarty points out, the widow, denied voice and desire, represents the ultimate level of subalternity within the domestic sphere (2000: 66). Hence, in representing Binodini's claim to voice and identity, the text makes a strong statement about the need to evolve a new version of the modern subject. This subject is endowed with an interiority that anticipates the modernist stream-of-consciousness novel in the West, a feature even more noticeable in the narrative technique of the later novel *Ghare Baire*. Saranindranath Tagore argues that the Hegelian idea that '[a]ll historical change is . . . essentially dependent on the state' is replaced by an alternative historiography indicated by Rabindranath, namely, 'a history of the interior' (Saranindranath Tagore 2006: 17). Through their representations of the desiring widow, writers could inscribe the desire for freedom and self-expression into the very structure of the new Bengali subject (Chakrabarty 2000: 66). In the first part of the novel, Binodini is a transgressive figure, a widow who deliberately seduces a married man. But, in the second half of the text, her love for Bihari transforms her personality and she gradually turns to a life of austerity. She thus combines the dual stereotypes of the transgressive woman and the widow in love (Sogani 2002: 66).

9   Alongside this attempt to focus on the inner lives of the characters, the text also reveals Tagore's awareness of contemporary social issues. The novel presents a society in transition and a period of sweeping economic changes that would lead to the emergence of a new middle class in Bengal. Between 1875 and 1941, the former landowners, the bhadralok class, had begun moving from the countryside to the city in search of new professions such as medicine, engineering, law, education and civil service. By 1911, two-thirds of the urban population of Bengal lived in Kolkata and Howrah. *Chokher Bali* presents an impressionistic image of Kolkata as a city in search of a modern lifestyle. Mahendra trains for the medical profession, for instance, and Bihari dabbles in medicine and engineering, but for this emergent class, professional training is not a financial necessity. Mahendra's lifestyle is fairly affluent, and Bihari gives up college to start a hospital in his garden estate.

10   The social milieu depicted in this novel is full of contradictions, caught between tradition and modernity, Hindu orthodoxy and Brahmo liberalism. New and old systems of knowledge jostle for ascendancy here: Mahendra is a man of science, while his mother Rajalakshmi places her faith in the predictions of an astrologer. The society, though in flux, is still bound by old hierarchies of caste, class and community. The protagonists belong to a Hindu background, but Tagore's own Brahmo background is evident in many of the contextual details. Mahendra, for instance, marries

245

Asha without a dowry; this is more in keeping with Brahmo reformist practices than with Hindu custom. Yet, old attitudes persist; Binodini's lack of dowry determines the course of her life.

11   In this text, modernity also posits the need to 'modernize' gender roles within society. Through the figures of Asha, the child bride, and the three widows Binodini, Rajlakshmi and Annapurna, the text addresses debates about women's education, child marriage, gendered power relations within the family and the plight of widows. The novel is probably set between 1868, when Englishwomen were still deployed to teach female pupils, and 1883, when the university produced its first female graduate. Women would be taught primarily in Bengali, though basic English might also be included. Subjects of study would usually include mathematics, literature, the history of Bengal and needlework. In *Chokher Bali*, women's education is a domestic matter. Binodini's father ensures that she is taught by a 'mem', while Asha's education is left to the whims of her husband. Rajalakshmi is not highly educated, though she comes from a good family. The generation gap is highlighted in Rajalakshmi's ire at Mahendra's attempt to educate the illiterate Asha, though the latter's expertise does not go beyond the primer *Charupath*. In the nineteenth century, female education depended to a great extent on the presence of a male mentor, usually the husband. In *Chokher Bali*, though, Mahendra's efforts to educate Asha are merely a ploy to gain hours of intimacy with his bride. Here, Tagore does not glorify the husband's role in the wife's education; instead, the text casts an ironic light upon the entire enterprise. Yet, the text does not belittle the idea of women's education. When Asha is betrayed by her husband, she turns to self-education in an effort to develop her own personality.

12   Binodini's impact on the people around her also owes a great deal to her education. She can write sophisticated love letters in Bengali and leaves volumes of Bankim and Dinabandhu in Bihari's room. It is through their reading of Bankim's writings that Mahendra and Binodini develop their intimacy (Bhattacharyya 2004: 84). She knows English and can read the address on a letter in the railway station, though it is in Bengali that she has greater proficiency.

13   Debates about widow remarriage frame the narrative of Binodini's unrequited desire. There is evidence in the *Rigveda* that the practice of marrying the widow to her brother-in-law was prevalent in Aryan settlements around Punjab and Haryana. But by medieval times, the idea of wifely devotion or *pativratya* enjoined the widow's complete withdrawal from society, to lead a life of severe discipline and celibacy. The *Dharmashastras* decreed that the widow

> should give up adorning her hair, chewing betel-nut, wearing perfumes, flowers, ornaments and dyed clothes, taking food from a vessel of bronze, taking two meals a day, applying collyrium to her eyes; she should wear a white garment, should curb her senses and anger, . . . should be pure and of good conduct, should always worship God.
>
> (Kane 1974: 584)

From time to time, there had been attempts in different parts of India to improve the situation of widows, but it was only in the nineteenth century that the reformist movement made a concerted move to promote this cause. In Bengal, Ishwarchandra

CHOKHER BALI

Vidyasagar (1820–91) used scriptural examples in his essay 'The Marriage of Hindu Widows' (1855) to argue in favour of widow remarriage. His efforts played a major role in generating a new awareness about the plight of widows and the need to liberalize social attitudes towards them. The Widow Remarriage Act was passed in 1856. These changing attitudes are reflected in the literature in modern Indian languages in the second half of the nineteenth century. In Bengal, writers such as Bankimchandra, Tagore and Saratchandra Chatterjee wrote powerful novels on the subject of widowhood; women writers also addressed the theme, but often from alternative perspectives.

14   When Tagore wrote *Chokher Bali*, attitudes towards widows had become less straitlaced in progressive segments of the society. Binodini is expected to lead an austere life of self-denial, but is not compelled to lead an ascetic existence. Rajlakshmi recognizes her potential as a homemaker and companion and takes her to Kolkata to join her household. Bihari urges Mahendra to '[g]et the widow married; that would draw her poison' (Tagore 2012: 62). Yet, despite these changes, orthodox society still frowned upon the idea of widow remarriage. This is one of the reasons why Binodini rejects Bihari, for she wishes to protect him from the social stigma of having married a widow: 'I am a widow, a woman disgraced. I cannot permit you to be humiliated in the eyes of society' (ibid.: 355). Her renunciation is read by Rajul Sogani in quasi-moralistic terms: '*Chokher Bali* may be read as an allegory showing the victory of self-control over passion and spirit over instinct' (2002: 55). Sogani relates this to the political context of the time, citing Meenakshi Mukherjee's account of the valorization of suffering and martyrdom during the nationalist movement, to argue that the text reflects these contemporary attitudes (Mukherjee 1985: 106, cited in Sogani 2002: 55). Yet, this novel was written before Tagore became actively involved with the nationalist movement. More importantly, it is Binodini's desire, rather than her self-abnegation, that we remember at the end of the novel.

15   The idea of the desiring widow was not new to Bengali literature. Shortly after the publication of *Chokher Bali*, Tagore was accused of plagiarizing Panchkori Bandyopadhyay's novel *Uma* (1901) about a promiscuous widow named Binodini. In the Phalgun (February–March 1902) issue of the periodical *Sahitya*, Sureshchandra Samajpati alleges that the plot of *Chokher Bali*, as well as the name and character of Binodini, are exact imitations of Bandyopadhyay's novel (Samajpati 1902: 703, in Paul 1990: 4). Unlike the earlier text, though, Tagore's novel is neither sensational nor rigidly moralistic. Tagore was also familiar with Bankimchandra Chatterjee's *Bishabriksha* (1873) and *Krishnakanter Will* (1878), which are also tales of adulterous love. In *Chokher Bali*, he deliberately uses intertextuality as a device to draw attention to these literary connections. Bihari, for instance, challenges Mahendra about his growing attraction to Binodini, with an explicit reference to a Bankim novel: 'What's this! A second *Bishabriksha*, another tale of adulterous love!' (Tagore 2012: 62). But, Tagore consciously eschews Bankim's focus on plot and external event for the quality that Dipesh Chakrabarty calls 'interiority'. The difference between *Chokher Bali* and its literary precursors thus serves to underscore the modernity of Tagore's text.

16   This modernity is not identical with 'Western' traditions of sexual freedom. The idea of adulterous love in *Chokher Bali* may also be linked to the Vaishnavite celebration of love outside marriage, enshrined in the romance of Radha and Krishna (Sogani 2002: 67). In this mode of representation, conjugal love appears commonplace, lacking

the mystery and romantic yearning of forbidden love. Binodini is described as 'timeless and ageless, forever a Gopika, . . . With all her pangs of separation, . . . she had travelled through so many songs, so many rhythms, to arrive at the shores of the present time' (Tagore 2012: 340). Even the names Binodini and Bihari evoke the epithets 'Rai', 'Binodini' and 'Rasbihari', which are associated with Radha and Krishna, respectively. Tagore's modernity is thus of a different calibre; it draws upon an older Indian tradition of romance to interrogate the more recent tradition of conjugality and fidelity in nineteenth century Bengal. It is a modernity that cannot be severed from its rootedness in a specific cultural context.

17   Other widows in the novel testify to the variability of the position of widow, which depends on various factors such as economic status, access to property and wealth, and location. Wealth, for instance, is an empowering factor. Rajlakshmi, because she has a share in her husband's property, enjoys greater freedom than the married woman Asha. She exercises great control over her son and his household. Driven by her jealousy of Mahendra's infatuation with his bride, she is free to travel to her native place. At the end, she leaves a village to Bihari for his social work and gives two thousand rupees to Binodini. Annapurna is free to withdraw to Kashi when she chooses, and sets up a trust for poor people who have marriageable daughters. In rural areas, the social gaze is more pronounced, while in urban environments, the widow enjoys greater freedom (Sogani 2002: 64). This Binodini discovers to her cost when she moves back to her own village from Kolkata. In the city she can stay in Mahendra's apartment or visit Bihari's bachelor abode, but she is forced to leave her village home when Mahendra visits her there. Annapurna is the stereotypical virtuous and self-denying widow, devoted to her deity, and surrogate mother-figure for Mahendra, Asha and Bihari. 'She has completely obliterated herself and her desires' (Panja 2004: 221). Childless and widowed at eleven, she devotes herself to mothering all the young people. In the Kolkata house she is disempowered, a dependant, but once she moves away, she becomes the embodiment of her mythical namesake, the deity Annapurna who is a benign mother goddess full of tenderness and compassion. In this role, she exerts considerable influence upon the other characters, especially Asha, to whom she appears as 'the only living image of divinity in her life' (Tagore 2012: 314), and Binodini, who accompanies her to a life of asceticism at the end of the novel. In the concluding chapters, Annapurna plays a crucial role in resolving all the conflicts.

18   The two contrasting figures, Rajlakshmi and Annapurna, have been interpreted in Freudian terms as representing the radical split in the mother image as conjured up by men (Sogani 2002: 162). 'Whereas a good mother requires only a return to sexual pre-Oedipal innocence in order to gain her abiding love, the bad mother exacts the terrible price of castration and death' (Wulff 1984: 290–91). 'This pre-Oedipal fixation, reflected throughout Hindu culture can be traced in the exquisitely refined sublimation of spiritual discipline and abstract philosophy' (ibid.). Sogani's reading of Annapurna's character as 'the embodiment of such sublimation and discipline' seeks to locate the modernity of Tagore's narrative within the tradition of Western psychoanalysis. But the idealization of Annapurna in the text may also be interpreted in terms of the age-old institutionalization of motherhood in Indian tradition. In Bengal, as Jashodhara Bagchi points out, 'motherhood was all along a culturally privileged

CHOKHER BALI

concept . . . Bengali mothers proverbially stood for unstinting affection, manifested in an undying spirit of self- sacrifice for the family' (1990: WS-65).

19   The modernity of Tagore's representation of maternity in *Chokher Bali* lies not only in its ambivalence about the idea of motherhood, but also in its construction of the childless Binodini, whose yearning for maternity disrupts the polarization of 'good mother' and 'bad mother'. Binodini's latent maternal instinct comes to the fore when, in the scene where she visits Bihari at night and offers herself to him, after Bihari spurns her advances, she finds consolation in embracing Basant, Bihari's eight-year-old pupil. Binodini confounds the polarization of 'good' and 'bad' motherhood, offering us instead an alternative version of maternal desire.

20   Rajalakshmi is a different kettle of fish. She treats her son as a husband-substitute and feels threatened by his infatuation with Asha. Tagore mentions her envy of Asha as the root cause of Mahendra's involvement with Binodini, though Shormishtha Panja disagrees with this imputation (2004: 221–22). The representation of the darker side of mother-love in the figure of Rajalakshmi in *Chokher Bali* challenges the idealization of motherhood that had become central to the nationalist discourse in nineteenth-century Bengal. Even at twenty-two, Mahendra remains tied to his mother's apron strings: 'Like a baby kangaroo that lives in its mother's pouch even after birth, he had grown accustomed to the shelter of his mother's protective care' (Tagore 2012: 2). Later in the novel, Binodini accuses Rajalakshmi of being jealous of her daughter- in-law: 'Out of jealousy of your daughter-in-law, have you never wished to use this sorceress to beguile your son's mind? . . . I cast my spell, part knowingly, part unbeknownst to myself. You, too, laid your trap part deliberately, part unconsciously' (Tagore 2012: 222). Rajalakshmi is unable to defend herself against the charge. The text explodes the myth of motherhood to expose the hidden power politics that often underlie mother–son relationships. In *Pashchim Jatrir Diary* (*The Diary of a Westward Voyage*), Tagore says that there are 'two opposite shores to love. On one side there is the tyranny of liking, on the other the warm welcoming of love. These two types sometimes exist even in a mother's love. The one, in its attachment, seeks for self-satisfaction; this type of blind motherly love is evident in our country to a great extent' (1962: 101). Tagore argues that instead of allowing the child to grow, such mother-love overwhelms the child's senses. He adds that in our country, the expansion of the kingdom of mother-love has sapped our virility more effectively than the harsh handcuffs of foreign rule (ibid.). It is this negative aspect of maternal love that Rajalakshmi represents. In its unsparing portrayal of the devastating effects of possessive mother- love, *Chokher Bali* undercuts the dominant myth of motherhood to create a realist counterdiscourse. Here Tagore's creative practice also contradicts many of his own theoretical statements about mother hood in his prose writings. In 1889, for instance, he writes in the journal *Bharati*, 'It becomes natural for women to remain at home to serve the family, for the sake of their children; this is not male oppression, but a law of nature' (Bhattacharyya 2004: 31). In 'Prachin Sahitya' ('Ancient Literature'), Tagore detects in motherhood the union of beauty and blessedness: 'The position of the mother is a woman's primary position in our country; in our country, the birth of a child is a sacred, blessed thing'. He quotes Manu, the ancient lawgiver, to affirm that women, because they give birth to offspring, are destined to good fortune and worthy of devotion; they embody the light of the

household (Bhattacharyya 2004: 32). While Tagore's pronouncements here appear traditional and orthodox, his representation of the manipulative Rajalakshmi dismantles this glorification of motherhood.

21   By 1880, Tagore became aware of the decline of the joint family. *Chokher Bali* focuses on a small family with a single male head. The daughter-in-law, Asha, is expected to be subservient to Rajalakshmi, her mother-in-law. The dependents, Annapurna and Binodini, are short-term additions to this domestic setup. Although the joint family was on the wane and new ideas about companionate marriage were in the air, the transition was neither smooth nor simple. About conjugal marriage, Tagore observes in his essay 'Shakuntala: Its Inner Meaning' that this model, which works in a Western nuclear family, may create complications when transplanted into the Indian joint family with its web of relationships (1999: 249). The home is not a homogeneous space, but one that is 'inwardly fraught', as the tensions between the conjugal couple and the rest of the household reveal (Panja 2004: 224). The institution of marriage itself comes under scrutiny in *Chokher Bali*, where Mahendra's passion for Asha wanes very quickly after their marriage, even before he develops a relationship with Binodini. Yet, despite their estrangement at the personal level, the text demonstrates the survival of the formal marital bond between Asha and Mahendra. In the essay 'Samajbhed', written at around the same time as *Chokher Bali*, Tagore had pointed out that unlike Western societies, where marriage is a bond between individuals, Indian society regards marriage as a link between two families (Tagore 1961d). In *Chokher Bali*, the interventions of Rajlakshmi and Annapurna have much to do with the upheavals in the relationship between Mahendra and Asha. Asha's willingness to accept reconciliation with Mahendra at the end of the novel may be read, according to Sutapa Bhattacharyya, as Tagore's recognition that it would be likely for a woman in Asha's situation in nineteenth- century Bengal to give greater primacy to family duty than to her own individuality (2004: 45). Seen in this way, the ending, which strikes many readers as contrived, may be reinterpreted as Tagore's attempt at realism.

22   To appreciate this realism, it is necessary to locate the Mahendra–Asha relationship within the context of changing family dynamics in nineteenth-century Bengal. According to Tanika Sarkar, the Brahmo Marriage Act of 1873, the talk of introducing divorce in the 1880s and the Age of Consent Act of 1891 signified the Bengali babu's urge to introduce 'prem' (love) into the arranged marriage, seeking compensation and fulfilment in the private realm for the humiliation he faced from the British in the public domain (Sarkar 2001: 1–52). In *Chokher Bali*, it is Binodini who holds out the possibility of romance to Mahendra when his interest in Asha pales. Though order is ostensibly restored at the end of the novel and the estranged couple are reunited, the narrative leaves exposed the inadequacies and contradictions inherent in the patriarchal ideals of conjugal love and feminine virtue.

23   The complexity of Asha's character is also an aspect of the text's modern approach. Asha confounds the stereotype created by Bankimchandra Chatterjee, of the Anglicized Bengali woman who neglects her household duties in her pursuit of Westernized 'modernity'. She is innocent and inept, and her ignorance of domestic skills at first disarms Mahendra, but later annoys him, especially when he encounters Binodini's expertise in these areas. Although Asha is a Hindu wife, she is unable to accept Mahendra's

CHOKHER BALI

adulterous love for Binodini. She does not voice any protest, but she develops contempt for Mahendra from her inner sense of individual independence. No tradition or scriptural injunction keeps her devoted to her husband.

> She was unable to follow her mashi's advice, the dictates of the puranas, the discipline enjoined upon her by the scriptures; she could no longer worship this husband who had fallen from the pedestal of conjugal love. Today, she deconsecrated the lord of her heart, immersing him in the sea of shame that was Binodini.
>
> (Tagore 2012: 282)

This psychological transformation of a married Hindu woman marks the dawn of modernity (Bhattacharya and Bhattacharya 1991: 37). Though Asha forgives Mahendra in the end, she does so with a new sense of her own identity and her power to choose.

24   The figure of Bihari is crucial to our understanding of Tagore's treatment of modernity in this novel. According to Sogani, male protagonists like Bihari represent the individualism and the emerging national consciousness of educated Bengalis of the time (2002: 88). Bihari is an idealist; though educated, he does not pursue a profession but turns instead to social service, to work for the marginalized and the underprivileged. Although his disapproval of Mahendra's adulterous infatuation with Binodini suggests a conventional moralistic stance, his willingness to marry a widow later in the text is an index to his liberalism and his social conscience. In the tussle between reason and passion, Bihari struggles to uphold the principles of duty and moral uprightness. Yet, he fails to live up to his own ideals, first falling in love with Asha, married to another man, and then getting drawn, in spite of himself, to Binodini's allure. But it is precisely this fallibility, the ambivalence built into Bihari's character, that makes the representation psychologically complex, precluding a simplistic allegorical reading of the novel as the depiction of a battle between 'good' and 'evil', reason and passion, renunciation and desire.

25   Dipesh Chakrabarty regards the body as the site for this struggle between opposing tendencies in the text of *Chokher Bali*, pointing out that it remains an unresolved problem (2000: 74). Chakrabarty insists, though, that 'rup' or physical beauty is not an issue in *Chokher Bali*, but as Shormishtha Panja points out, both Mahendra and Bihari are acutely aware of Binodini's physical allure (Chakrabarty 2000: 71; Panja 2004: 219). Nowhere is this more evident than in the erotically charged scene where Mahendra discovers a flower-bedecked Binodini dreaming of Bihari: 'Through the open windows and doors, the moonlight streamed in, to fall upon the white bed. Weaving garlands of flowers plucked from the garden, Binodini had placed them in her hair, around her neck, and around her waist. Adorned with flowers, she lay on the moonlit bed like a vine laden with the weight of its blossoms' (Tagore 2012: 341). Here Binodini is both the object of Mahendra's gaze and the desiring subject who fantasizes about Bihari; her eroticized body becomes a signifier for this double desire. Elsewhere, Binodini's vicarious participation in Asha's conjugal life is conveyed textually through the figurative merging of the two women's physical charm: 'Nowadays, adorned by

LITERARY THEORY AND CRITICISM

her friend's hands, Asha would present herself to Mahendra, looking neat and tidy, well-dressed and perfumed. Part of her allure would be her own, part someone else's: in her attire, beauty and joyfulness, she seemed to have merged with her friend, like the two rivers Ganga and Yamuna' (ibid.: 80).

26   Having created a subversive figure like Binodini, though, Tagore seemed at a loss to find an appropriate resolution to her predicament. The original ending, first dropped and then restored in the 1941 edition of *Rabindra Rachanabali* with Tagore's approval, carries the narrative beyond the scene of forgiveness between Rajalakshmi and the estranged couple, Mahendra and Asha. The fact that Tagore changed the ending twice indicates his own dissatisfaction with the novel's denouement. Readers, too, are often dissatisfied with the ending of the novel. For instance, Buddhadeva Basu declares that the ending is weak and negligible: 'The denouement is nothing but a lifeless, patchwork job, and it seems hard to believe that this novel, created in "the factory of the mind", should end at this point' (1983: 190–91). In the literary supplement of the Bengali journal *Desh* (1991), writer Sunil Gangopadhyay complains that the male figures in *Chokher Bali* are like cardboard puppets manipulated by Binodini. In the end, he says, 'Tagore sticks the cardboard dolls back into their appointed niches in the wall, and smearing the fiery Binodini with ash, he banishes her to Benares . . . One feels reluctant to accept such a denouement as "the method of a new chapter in literature"' (1991: 138–39, in Bhattacharya 2002: 193).

27   Yet the ending may be read as a facet of Tagore's realism, for he could not imagine a happy ending for Binodini in the social context that to which she belonged. In *Heroines of Tagore*, Bimanbehari Majumdar lauds Tagore's realistic approach, linking Binodini's departure to Varanasi with the influence of Annapurna: 'From the sociological point of view it was necessary for Rabindranath to show how thousands of childless widows could reconcile themselves to their hard lot by a process of sublimation of sexual instinct' (1968: 216). Sogani argues that 'though the novel was written nearly half a century after the passing of the Widow Remarriage Act, yet Tagore could not conclude it in Binodini's marriage because of a moral interdiction against it, and not a social one' (2002: 55). The disruption triggered by Binodini's entry into the lives of Mahendra and Bihari allows of no neat resolution, when seen in relation to the social milieu within which their narrative is embedded. Binodini's difference, her gender, leaves a fracture at the heart of the idea of subjectivity.

Textual and rhetorical questions

Textual

1.   One of the key interpretations of the novel by Radha Chakrabarty is that the "psychological element is not identical with Western literary paradigms" and "Tagore's representation of Binodini's sexuality, for instance, does not replicate the Freudian paradigm." Binodini's "desire is fanned by the repressive social practices of nineteenth century Bengal, which do not match the Freudian narrative of the emergence of sexuality thorough the triangular relationship of father, mother and child." (paragraph 7) The writer further comments,

"Yet, though *Chokher Bali* cannot be read as a "psychoanalytical" novel in Freudian terms, it remains a "psychological" novel in terms devised by Tagore himself, for it has the quality that Dipesh Chakrabarty (2000) describes as "interiority", where external events, however dramatic on occasion, serve as the frame for the exploration of the characters' inner lives."

(paragraph 7)

Do you think that the "repressive social practices of the nineteenth century Bengal" (paragraph 7) is instrumental in shaping the desire and identity of Binodini? How is the shaping of Binodini's self a resistance of the existent social ideology (outside) and dislike of a family (inside)? Read the novel and analyse the essayist's interpretations.

2. Binodini's

"character . . . does not match the stereotypes of the nineteenth century Bengali woman created by Bankim, for Binodini is neither a "prachina" who worships her husband devotedly, nor a "nabina" who neglects home and hearth in her pursuit of education and social sophistication, nor a coarse woman of the "common" working class (Panja 2004: 214–18)."[2]

(paragraph 8)

Do the critics including Radha Chakrabarty suggest that Binodini is a complex rebel who enters an ideal house and disrupts it or "represents the ultimate level of subalternity within the domestic sphere (2000: 66)"? (paragraph 8). Discuss.

3. "Tagore's modernity is thus of a different calibre; it draws upon an older Indian tradition of romance to interrogate the more recent tradition of conjugality and fidelity in nineteenth century Bengal. It is a modernity that cannot be severed from its rootedness in a specific cultural context."

(paragraph 16)

What is the "older Indian tradition" the writer is referring to and how does the tradition shape the characters of Binodini and Mahendra? (paragraph 16). Discuss the idea of modernity in terms of maternity that the essayist presents?

4. Analyse the idea of mother and family that the essayist presents.

Rhetorical

1. Tagore's novel is adapted by Rituporno Ghosh. Watch the film after reading the novel and observe the scene selections by the director. What makes you uncomfortable about the crucial incidents from the novel that are discarded? What would you select to include from the incidents that are left out by Ghosh in his film? Write an essay on film adaptation after watching two versions of Jane Austin's *Emma*, one directed by Doug McGrath in his 1996 film *Emma* and the other directed byAmy Heckerling, *Clueless* made in 1995.

LITERARY THEORY AND CRITICISM

2. Among many terms used in literary criticism, some of the common terms are critical method, critical technique, critical approach, appreciation, evaluation, and explication which can be explored to understand the nuances of the terms. In the context of the essay written by Radha Chakrabarty the two other terms which can be discussed here, are "interpretation" and "analysis." The distinction can be understood in the following terms:[3] Interpretation is

> a process of getting at, revealing, or communicating a pre-existing meaning" and also as "a process of creating something new and personal to the interpreter as an extension of a pre-existing text.

> (1987, p. 24)

The analysis of a text involves:

> "relating of textual detail to its affect in a manner not normally compatible by ordinary reading".

> (1987, p. 28)

What is your opinion about the essay by Chakrabarty? Is it an interpretation or analysis of *Chokher Bali*, or an exclusive mode of criticism?

Discussion questions

1. The three women characters in Tagore's novels, Kusum in *Ghater Kotha* (*The Story of a River Stair*, 1884), Charu in *Nasta Nir* (*The Broken Nest*, 1901), and Binodini in *Chokher Bali* (*Eye-Sand*), 1903) belong to the time when rebel women and widows were shunned. Widow remarriage was one of the central issues of Indian society during the British rule. Kusum is very young and lives like a widow, Charu falls in love with her brother-in-law, and Binodini is a widow-rebel. Binodini is the only widow of the three women. They belong to a time of rigid patriarchal codes. The social reformer Ishwar Chandra Vidyasagar[4] had worked to change the ideology against widow marriage. "Woman as the object of *one* husband"[5] is one of the powerful age-old ideologies regarding women.

> A woman's salvation lay on the service of her husband, it followed that she lost her raison d'etre the moment her husband died (so that) widowhood came to be seen as the worst calamity that could ever befall a woman . . . because it practically invalidated her continued existence.
>
> (Sakuntala Narsimhan 1990 36, 40)[6]

Widowhood was (is) a reduced subject in social mobility which patriarchy needs as a form of control. Discourse Tagore's characters in the light of the ideology associated with the widow and women's condition in general (1000–1200 words).

2. There is the double bind related with the identity 'Widow;' There are both metonymic and metaphoric relations among identity markers like widow, Sati, Sati-devi, and *charitraheen*.[7] How are these terms of reference in a metonymic chain also used as metaphors? (500 words).

254

Inter-textual discussions

1. Radha in the iconic Hindi film *Mother India* (1957) is an ideal struggling widow who represents the idealism of woman as Mother India. Gayatri Spivak writes on Mahasweta Devi's *Stanadayani* (*Breast Giver*):

> Like the protagonist Jashoda, India is a mother-by-hire. All classes of people, the post-war rich, the ideologues, the indigenous bureaucracy, the diasporics, the people who are sworn to protect the new state, abuse and exploit her. If nothing is done to sustain her, nothing given back to her, and if scientific help comes too late, she will die of a consuming cancer. I suppose if one extended this parable the end of the story might come to "mean" something like this: the ideological construct "India" is too deeply informed by the goddess-infested reverse sexism of the Hindu majority. As long as there is this hegemonic cultural self-representation of India as goddess-mother (dissimulating the possibility of that this mother is a slave), she will collapse under the burden of the immense expectations that such a self-representation permits.[8]

Jashoda breastfeeds the children of a Jamindar household by being constantly pregnant and suffers from breast cancer. Jashoda as the "mother," the epitome of nationalismthe grand narrative – cuts across the idealism and myth of Bharat-mata (Mother India). Do you think Spivak questions and strikes at the core of nation as mother? Compare Radha and Jashoda (700 words).

Critical and creative thinking

1. In Bengali literature, Bankim Chandra Chattopadhyay's Rohini in *Krishanakanta's Will*, Rabindranath Tagore's Damini in *Chaturanga*, Sarat Chandra Chattopadhyay's Abhaya in *Srikanta*, and Kiranmayi in *Choritroheen* are some of the major characters who do not fit into the ideology of traditional Indian womanhood of that period. Who is your favourite woman character in the novels you have read from your literary tradition?
2. Tagore's "Sonar Tari" ("The Golden Boat")[9] is a poem of sadness and loneliness. Similarly, the speaker in "Deho" ("Body") by Kabita Sinha addresses the eternal gazer on a woman's body. Can you comprehend parallelisms between what is described in these poems and Binodini's life?
   Read the rest of the poem "Deho." It begins: "What do you want? Look, there she stands, the sorceress."
3. Read the poem "Widow" by Sylvia Plath and explain how a widow is described. It begins with an emphatic suggestive concept: "Widow. The word consumes itself."
4. *Deuki* (Nepal), *Matammas* (Tirupati, Andhra Pradesh), *Devdashis* (Odisha), *Nityasumangali* (Tamil Nadu), and *Nagarbadhu* (ancient Magadha dynastic times in India) were free from marriages. The freedom may be understood as bondage. What do you think?

Notes

1 Rabindranath Tagore, *Rabindra Rachanabali*, vol. 7, p. 347, in Biswas (2003: 728).
2 The citation in the essay refers to Prof. Shormishtha Panja.
3 See a comprehensive book on methods of criticism: Hawthorn, Jeremy (1988). *Unlocking the Text: Fundamental Issues in Literary Theory*. London: Edward Arnold (24, 28).
4 It is surprising to know that Sureshchandra Samajpati, grandson of Ishwarchandra Vidyasagar, attacked the novel *Chokher Bali*, "on the grounds of 'obscenity'" (52) in Sumanta Banerjee. (2011). "Rabindranath – A Liberal Humanist Fallen among Bigoted Bhadraloks" Source: *Economic and Political Weekly*, Vol. 46, No. 24 (June 11–17, 2011), 51–59.
5 Spivak, Gayatri Chakravorty (1999). *Critique of Postcolonial Reason. Towards a History of the Vanishing Present*. Cambridge: Harvard University Press (299).
6 Narsimhan, Sakuntala (1990). *Sati: Widow Burning in India*. Anchor Books: New York. (36, 40). Also see: Sandra M. Gilbert (2006). *Death's Door: Modern Dying and the Ways We Grieve*. W. W. Norton & Company: New York.
7 *Sati* used to be the widow who had to immolate herself on to her husband funeral fire. Hence, she is generally venerated as "*Devi*" or goddess. *Charitraheen* in Nepali, Bengali, Hindi, and in some other languages in South Asia means, "a wanton, fallen, characterless woman."
8 Spivak, Gayatri Chakravorty (1987). "A Literary Representation of the Subaltern: Mahasweta Devi's 'Stanadayini'" in *Subaltern Studies* Vol. V. Oxford University Press: Delhi.
9 For a translated version, see Alam Fakrul & Radha Chakravarty (2011). *The Essential Tagore*. Visva-Bharati: Shantiniketan (210).